PREEMPTION CHOICE

This book examines the theory, law, and reality of preemption choice. The Constitution's federalist structures protect states' sovereignty but also create a powerful federal government that can preempt and thereby displace the authority of state and local governments and courts to respond to a social challenge. Despite this preemptive power, Congress and agencies have seldom preempted state power. Instead, they typically have embraced concurrent, overlapping power. Recent legislative, agency, and court actions, however, reveal a newly aggressive use of federal preemption, sometimes even preempting more protective state law.

Preemption choice fundamentally involves issues of institutional choice and regulatory design: should federal actors displace or work in conjunction with other legal institutions? This book moves logically through each preemption choice step, ranging from underlying theory to constitutional history, to preemption doctrine, to assessment of when preemptive regimes make sense and when state regulation and common law should retain latitude for dynamism and innovation.

William W. Buzbee is a Professor of Law at Emory University School of Law and Director of the Emory Environmental and Natural Resources Law Program. He is a co-author of *Environmental Protection: Law and Policy*, fifth edition (2007). He has published widely on issues of regulatory federalism, environmental law, and administrative law, and three of his articles have appeared in collections of the ten best articles published in their year regarding environmental or land-use law. He has also testified before congressional committees regarding issues of federalism and environmental regulation. Prior to becoming an academic, he practiced public-interest and private-sector law in New York City.

Preemption Choice: The Theory, Law, and Reality of Federalism's Core Question

Edited by

WILLIAM W. BUZBEE

Emory University School of Law

CAMBRIDGE
UNIVERSITY PRESS

CAMBRIDGE UNIVERSITY PRESS
Cambridge, New York, Melbourne, Madrid, Cape Town,
Singapore, São Paulo, Delhi, Tokyo, Mexico City

Cambridge University Press
32 Avenue of the Americas, New York, NY 10013-2473, USA

www.cambridge.org
Information on this title: www.cambridge.org/9781107402324

First published 2009
First paperback edition 2011

A catalog record for this publication is available from the British Library

Library of Congress Cataloging in Publication data

Preemption choice : the theory, law, and reality of federalism's core question / edited by William
W. Buzbee.
   p. cm.
Includes bibliographical references and index.
ISBN 978-0-521-88805-9 (hardback)
   1. Exclusive and concurrent legislative powers – United States. I. Buzbee, William W., 1960–
II. Title. III. Series.

   KF4600.P73 2008
   342.73′041–dc22   2008042112

ISBN 978-0-521-88805-9 Hardback
ISBN 978-1-107-40232-4 Paperback

Contents

Contributors

William W. Buzbee is a Professor of Law and the Director of the Emory Environmental and Natural Resources Law Program. He has also been a Visiting Professor of Law at Columbia, Cornell, and Illinois Law Schools. He is a graduate of Amherst College and Columbia Law School, where he served as a Notes and Comments Editor for the *Columbia Law Review*. Before joining Emory's faculty, he clerked for federal judge José A. Cabranes and worked with the Natural Resources Defense Council and then for Patterson Belknap, Webb and Tyler in New York City. Professor Buzbee's scholarship tends to focus on environmental law, administrative law, and other public law topics, with his most recent publications focusing on regulatory federalism, urban sprawl and governance, citizen litigation, and regulatory design issues. His publications have appeared in *New York University Law Review, University of Pennsylvania Law Review, Michigan Law Review, Stanford Law Review* (co-authored), *Cornell Law Review* (co-authored), *Iowa Law Review, The Journal of Law and Politics*, and an array of other journals and edited volumes. Three of his articles have been named and republished as being among the ten best environmental or land-use law articles of that year. He is also a co-author of the fifth edition of Aspen's *Environmental Protection: Law and Policy*. Professor Buzbee is a founding Member Scholar of the Center for Progressive Reform, a Washington, D.C.-based regulatory think tank.

David E. Adelman is an Associate Professor and the Director of Law and Science Initiatives at the University of Arizona's James E. Rogers College of Law, where he has taught since the fall of 2001. Professor Adelman's research focuses on the many interfaces between law and science. His articles have addressed topics ranging from the implications of emerging genomics technologies for environmental regulation, to the parallels between legal and scientific judgment, to the influence of the rapid rise in patenting during the 1990s on biotechnology innovation. Prior to entering academia, he was an associate with Covington and Burling in Washington, D.C., where he litigated patent disputes and provided counsel on environmental regulatory matters, and a Senior Attorney with the Natural Resources Defense Council in its Nuclear and Public Health programs. Following his graduation from Stanford Law School, Professor Adelman clerked for the Honorable Samuel Conti of the U.S. District Court for the Northern District of California. He has been a member of the U.S. Department of Energy's Environmental Management Advisory Board and has served on two National Academy of Sciences committees.

William L. Andreen is the Edgar L. Clarkson Professor of Law at the University of Alabama School of Law and an Adjunct Professor of Law at The Australian National University College of Law. He is a graduate of the College of Wooster and Columbia University School of Law. Before joining the law faculty at the University of Alabama, Professor Andreen served as Assistant Regional Counsel for the U.S. Environmental Protection Agency, Region 4. In more recent years, he has served as an environmental advisor to the Tanzanian government, a Research Fellow at the Mekelle University Law School in Ethiopia, and a Fulbright Senior Specialist with the National Europe Centre at The Australian National University. His articles on environmental law have appeared in numerous journals. His 2004 *Alabama Law Review* article, "Water Quality Today: Has the Clean Water Act Been a Success?" and his 1989 *Indiana Law Journal* article, "In Pursuit of NEPA's Promise: The Role of Executive Oversight in the Implementation of Environmental Policy," were both chosen as among the top ten environmental and land-use law articles of those years and were republished in the *Land Use and Environment Law Review*.

Bradford R. Clark is the William Cranch Research Professor of Law at George Washington University Law School in Washington, D.C., where he teaches and writes in the areas of constitutional law, federalism, and federal courts. During the 2007–08 academic year, he was a Visiting Professor of Law at Harvard Law School. He has published numerous articles on constitutional federalism and the Supremacy Clause. Before entering teaching, Professor Clark served as a law clerk to Judge Robert H. Bork on the U.S. Court of Appeals for the D.C. Circuit and to Justice Antonin Scalia on the Supreme Court of the United States. In addition, Professor Clark worked as an Attorney Advisor in the Office of Legal Counsel in the U.S. Department of Justice, where he provided advice to the President, the Attorney General, and the heads of executive departments on a variety of legal and constitutional questions.

Kirsten H. Engel joined the James E. Rogers College of Law at the University of Arizona in 2005 with a broad background in environmental law and policy that spans academia and public-sector practice. Engel is widely published on various topics in her field, including environmental federalism and the potential for cooperative regional efforts to counteract the federal government's stance on global climate change, solid waste landfill regulation, and the deregulation of the electricity industry. Engel previously served as senior counsel for the Public Protection Bureau and acting chief of the Environmental Protection Division of the Massachusetts Office of the Attorney General. She also has worked as a staff attorney for the Sierra Club Legal Defense Fund as well as for the U.S. Environmental Protection Agency. She has held the positions of Associate Professor of Law at Tulane Law School and Visiting Associate Professor at Harvard and Vanderbilt Law Schools. She recently served as a member of Governor Janet Napolitano's Climate Change Advisory Group and sits on the board of directors of the Tulane Environmental Law Clinic.

William Funk, of Lewis and Clark Law School, is particularly well qualified to address his topic of agency claims of preemptive power. A professor of administrative and constitutional law and an author of numerous articles on administrative and constitutional law subjects, as well as of a leading casebook on administrative law, he has chaired the American Bar Association's (ABA) Administrative Law and Regulatory Practice Section and is currently co-chair of an ABA-wide task force addressing federal agency preemption of state tort and consumer protection law. Professor Funk's scholarship is informed by nearly ten years of practice in the federal government, including service as an Assistant General Counsel at the Department of Energy, Legislative Counsel for a committee of the House of Representatives, and an attorney for the Office of Legal Counsel in the Department of Justice.

Robert L. Glicksman is the Robert W. Wagstaff Professor of Law at the University of Kansas. A graduate of the Cornell Law School, Glicksman has taught and written about environmental and natural resources law for more than twenty-five years. He is a co-author of a leading environmental law casebook and a multivolume treatise on natural resources law, and his articles on federalism and environmental law have been published in journals that include the *University of Pennsylvania Law Review*, the *Wake Forest Law Review*, the *Washington University Journal of Urban and Contemporary Law*, and the *Environmental Law Reporter*. His work has been cited by the U.S. Supreme Court. He is also the co-author (with Sidney Shapiro) of the recent book, *Risk Regulation at Risk: Restoring a Pragmatic Approach* (Stanford University Press, 2003).

Thomas O. McGarity holds the W. James Kronzer Chair in Trial and Appellate Advocacy at the University of Texas School of Law. He has taught environmental law, administrative law, and torts at the University of Texas School of Law since 1980. In addition to a casebook on environmental law, he has written two books on federal regulation. *Reinventing Rationality* (1991) describes and critiques the implementation of regulatory analysis and regulatory review requirements that were put into place during the Carter and Reagan administrations. *Workers at Risk* (1993) (co-authored with Sidney Shapiro of Wake Forest) describes and critiques the implementation of the Occupational Safety and Health Act during its first twenty years. He has written dozens of law review articles and chapters on federal regulation, administrative law, and tort law. Professor McGarity has served on committees of the National Academy of Sciences and was a longtime consultant to the Administrative Conference of the United States and the Office of Technology Assessment. He has testified on numerous occasions before congressional committees. He has also delivered several endowed lectures, including the annual Order of the Coif lecture. In recent years, he has made several presentations on the topic of federal agency preemption of state common law claims. From 2001–07 Professor McGarity was the President of the Center for Progressive Reform, a nonprofit organization consisting of scholars who are committed to developing and sharing knowledge and information, with the ultimate aim of preserving the fundamental value of the life and health of human beings and the natural environment. He remains a Member Scholar and board member.

Nina Mendelson is a Professor of Law at the University of Michigan. Professor Mendelson is a summa cum laude graduate of Harvard University and a graduate of the Yale Law School, where she served on the *Yale Law Journal*. She served as a law clerk to Judges Pierre Leval (then of the Southern District of New York) and John M. Walker Jr. (of the Second Circuit) and has worked for the U.S. Senate and the U.S. Department of Justice. She currently serves as one of three American Special Legal

Advisors to the NAFTA Commission on Environmental Cooperation. Professor Mendelson's research on administrative law and preemption issues has been published by the nation's top law reviews, including the *Columbia Law Review*, the *New York University Law Review*, the *Cornell Law Review*, and the *Michigan Law Review*. She is also the author of "Some Legal Reforms to Increase Government Contractor Accountability," in Jody Freeman and Martha Minow, eds., *Outsourcing the U.S.* (Harvard University Press, forthcoming).

Trevor W. Morrison is a Professor of Law at Columbia Law School. Prior to 2008, he was an Associate Professor at Cornell Law School. He has also been a Visiting Professor of Law at New York University Law School. Professor Morrison teaches and writes about the federal courts and the structural dimensions of the Constitution. His scholarship has appeared in numerous outlets, including the *Cornell Law Review*, the *Columbia Law Review*, the *Michigan Law Review*, and the *Yale Law Journal*. Prior to entering academia, he clerked for Judge Betty Binns Fletcher of the U.S. Court of Appeals for the Ninth Circuit and for Supreme Court Justice Ruth Bader Ginsburg. He also served in the U.S. Department of Justice, first in the Office of the Solicitor General and later in the Office of Legal Counsel.

Robert A. Schapiro is Professor of Law at Emory University School of Law. Schapiro graduated from Yale Law School, where he was editor-in-chief of the *Yale Law Journal*. He served as a clerk for Judge Pierre N. Leval, then of the U.S. District Court for the Southern District of New York, and for Justice John Paul Stevens of the U.S. Supreme Court. Schapiro's research focuses on federalism, and his book manuscript, *Polyphonic Federalism: How a Federal System Protects Fundamental Rights*, is under contract with the University of Chicago Press. His publications include "Justice Stevens' Theory of Interactive Federalism," *Fordham Law Review* (2006); "Toward a Theory of Interactive Federalism," *Iowa Law Review* (2006); "Interjurisdictional Enforcement of Rights in a Post-Erie World," *William and Mary Law Review* (2005); "Unidimensional Federalism: Power and Perspective in Commerce Clause Adjudication," *Cornell Law Review* (2003, with William Buzbee); "Legislative Record Review," *Stanford Law Review* (2001, with William Buzbee); "Judicial Deference and Interpretive Coordinacy in State and Federal Constitutional Law," *Cornell Law Review* (2000); "Polyphonic Federalism: State Constitutions in the Federal Courts," *California Law Review* (1999); and "Identity and Interpretation in State Constitutional Law," *Virginia Law Review* (1998).

Christopher H. Schroeder is the Charles S. Murphy Professor of Law, Professor of Public Policy Studies, and Director of the Program in Public Law at Duke University. He also serves as counsel to the law firm O'Melveny and Myers. Schroeder served as deputy assistant attorney general in the Office of Legal Counsel, U.S. Department of Justice, and in 1996–7 was the acting assistant attorney general in charge of that office. Previously, he worked for the Senate Judiciary Committee, serving as its chief counsel in 1992–3. He is a member of the Center for Progressive Reform and sits on its board of directors. He is co-chair of the Separation of Powers and Federalism issue group for the American Constitution Society's Project on the Constitution in the 21st Century. Schroeder's scholarship includes work on constitutional law, democratic theory, and Congress. He is currently researching a book on presidential powers.

Robert R.M. Verchick holds the Gauthier–St. Martin Chair in Environmental Law at Loyola University, New Orleans. He is a graduate of Stanford University and of Harvard Law School and is a board member of the Center for Progressive Reform. An expert on environmental regulation and local government, Professor Verchick has represented local government interests in friend-of-the-court briefs before the U.S. Supreme Court and as a Major Group Delegate at the 2004 "Earth Summit" in Johannesburg, South Africa. His research on environmental law and constitutional law has appeared in (among other places) the *California Law Review*, the *Southern California Law Review*, and the *Harvard Environmental Law Review*. He is also the co-author of a book on feminist theory and the author of an upcoming book on Hurricane Katrina and environmental policy.

David C. Vladeck is a Professor of Law and Director of the Center on Regulation and Governance, O'Neill Institute, Georgetown University Law Center. Professor Vladeck teaches courses on federal courts, civil procedure, government processes, and civil litigation. Prior to joining the Georgetown faculty, Professor Vladeck served as an attorney with, and then was the director of, the Public Citizen Litigation Group, a nationally prominent public-interest law firm. Professor Vladeck has argued several cases before the U.S. Supreme Court and more than sixty cases in federal courts of appeals. A number of the cases Professor Vladeck handled involved preemption questions. Professor Vladeck's scholarship focuses on constitutional and regulatory issues, and he has written extensively on preemption. His recent writings include a 2008 article on FDA preemption in the *Cornell Law Review*; a 2007 article in the *Georgetown Law Journal*, "A Critical

Examination of the FDA's Efforts to Preempt Failure-to-Warn Claims," co-authored with David A. Kessler, M.D., who is dean and vice chancellor of the University of California San Francisco Medical School and formerly served as the Commissioner of the Food and Drug Administration; and a 2005 article in the *Pepperdine Law Review* entitled "Preemption and Regulatory Failure." Professor Vladeck also testifies frequently before Congress and testified on preemption in September 2007 before the Senate Judiciary Committee. Professor Vladeck is a founding Member Scholar of the Center for Progressive Reform and formerly served as a Public Member of the Administrative Conference of the United States.

Sandi Zellmer is the Hevelone Research Chair and Professor of Law at the University of Nebraska. She is also a co-director of the University's Water Resources Research Initiative, an interdisciplinary educational and research effort. She has been designated a Senior Specialist (Roster Candidate) by the J. William Fulbright Foreign Scholarship Board, and she is a Member Scholar of the Center for Progressive Reform as well as the Commission on Environmental Law of the World Conservation Union, a trustee of the Rocky Mountain Mineral Law Foundation, and an associate member of the Resilience Alliance, a multidisciplinary research group exploring the dynamics of complex adaptive systems. Zellmer has published numerous articles, book chapters, and commentary on biodiversity, constitutional law, water conservation and quality, and natural resources. Prior to teaching, she was an attorney for the U.S. Department of Justice Environment and Natural Resources Division, litigating resource management and regulatory issues for the National Park Service, National Forest Service, and other federal agencies.

Acknowledgments
William W. Buzbee

This book is the product of the shared efforts of numerous individuals and organizations. The idea for this book arose out of a number of papers first presented in discussion form at a November 2006 conference at Duke Law School, "Federalism in the Overlapping Territory." That conference was sponsored by the Duke Law School Program in Public Law, the Center for Progressive Reform, and the American Constitution Society. Key organizers and facilitators for that gathering were Professors Christopher Schroeder, Robert Glicksman, Robert Verchick, and Trevor Morrison. A February 2007 Thrower Symposium conference at Emory Law School, "The New Federalism: Plural Governance in a Decentered World," also involved several participants in this book who have further developed ideas presented at Emory. That gathering was sponsored by the family of Randolph Thrower, the *Emory Law Journal*, and the Emory Center for Federalism and Intersystemic Governance, with substantial faculty input by Professors Robert Ahdieh, Robert Schapiro, and William Buzbee. The book also involves chapters by scholars offering completely new work that was not shared at either conference.

I also thank my administrative assistant, Brenda Huffman, and Terry Gordon of the Emory Law School Library for their prompt and skillful assistance. Research assistants Annie Mackay, Daniel Adams, Chandani Patel, and Michael Eber provided assistance with this book and several related projects. I especially thank the remarkable scholars and staff associated with the Center for Progressive Reform (CPR), a regulatory think tank comprising experts in the fields of law, economics, philosophy, and science. Discussions of this book and strategies to strengthen it at several CPR meetings proved invaluable. The engaged, wise, and supportive people associated with Cambridge University Press, especially John Berger, copy editor Christine Dunn, and indexer Robert Swanson, immeasurably improved the book. Lastly, I personally thank my wife, Lisa E. Chang, and daughters, Tian and Seana Buzbee, for their support.

Introduction

William W. Buzbee

Debates over the federal government's preemption power rage in the courts, in Congress, before agencies, and in the world of scholarship. Much of this debate has been prompted by unusually aggressive assertions of preemption power by federal agencies starting about 2006, but several major legislative battles have also involved preemption choice. The Supreme Court has also been on a preemption roll, hearing an unusually large number of preemption cases.

Little debate is possible over the basic parameters of federal preemption power – under the U.S. Constitution's Supremacy Clause, federal law reigns supreme and hence preempts any conflicting law or law that federal legislation deems preempted. A few Supreme Court cases in the 1990s reasserted judicial scrutiny of federal assertions of legislative power, while others strengthened state claims of sovereign immunity and protection from federal meddling. Nevertheless, seldom will preemption debates turn on underlying constitutional questions of federal power.

Instead, preemption debates tend to concern three basic questions. The first is political: should the federal government act to preempt, and thereby displace or nullify, regulatory turf that might otherwise be shared with state or local law, be it statutory or common law in origin? The second is interpretive: has a federal act actually preempted the laws or legal activities of these other actors? A fairly vast literature focuses on the third facet of preemption debates, parsing the vagaries of the Supreme Court's doctrinal expositions regarding preemption. This scholarship is critical and invaluable, given the Supreme Court's increasingly frequent acceptance of cases involving preemption issues. The Court's sometimes befuddling disjuncture between stated doctrine and actually applied frameworks further explains the need for scholarship examining Supreme Court preemption doctrine. This book contains several chapters that further illuminate this body of ever-developing law.

This book, however, is unusual in its rich focus on the antecedent political and regulatory choice of whether to preempt. The Supreme Court's preemption cases follow often-heated political battles about preemption choice, typically arising in both legislative and regulatory settings. Political preemption choice thus involves legislators and federal agencies, as well as interpretations and policy goals manifested by state actors asserting their own views about retained regulatory power. And in cases where the antecedent political choice is unclear, or facts about the existence of a regulatory conflict are close, courts and sometimes agencies too must make preemption choices.

The question of preemption thus fundamentally involves a question of regulatory design and institutional choice. Should a social challenge be handled exclusively by federal law, perhaps by a single regulator? Or would that regulatory challenge be better addressed by leaving it to state and local law, be it statutory or common law, or allowing federal, state, and local regulation? Despite the often "state versus federal" nature of federalism and preemption discourse, the actual political preemption choice seldom requires preemption. Instead, regulatory schemes typically embrace overlapping, shared, and often-intertwined jurisdiction. Federal, state, and local governments all retain roles, as do courts at all three levels. Furthermore, both positive law (in the form of statutes and regulations) and common law turfs are typically preserved by federal law. Outright federal legislative preemption displacing state and local jurisdiction is a rarity, and explicit displacement of common law regimes is an almost nonexistent statutory choice if federal law does not create its own substitute compensatory regime.

Despite the prevalence of political embrace of federal-state overlap, courts and litigators, and partisans in legislative and regulatory venues, often argue for the elimination of this overlap. They oppose the inherently multilayered law that is the political norm. Perhaps surprisingly, despite the dominant political choice not to preempt, normative arguments in favor of preemption are far more developed than countervailing views justifying the prevalent nonpreemption choice. The arguments for preemption are most often rooted in a preference for less law and regulation, or at least more uniform, certain, and stable law, and frequently a linked goal of facilitating thriving markets and industry. Certainly pro-preemption arguments before legislatures, agencies, and courts are overwhelmingly articulated by industry. In contrast, those protected by regulation or advocating protection of the environment or a low-risk world tend to argue for the partial preemption of minimal federal protections, or floors. With federal floors, states retain latitude to enact non-conflicting positive law and litigants can continue to seek relief in court through common law regimes. State law merely has to be at least as protective as federal law.

This book looks at preemption choice from all perspectives but is especially valuable in filling a gap in the normative arguments regarding preemption. Virtually all chapters in this book contribute to the development of normative arguments against preemption by using theoretical, legal, and historical analysis to explore the logic behind the long dominant choice of retention of federal, state, local, and common law regulatory power. These normative arguments against preemption should be given greater weight, not only in legislative and regulatory settings but also when courts have to resolve tough statutory interpretation puzzles or need to assess whether some result of state law poses an insuperable conflict or obstacle to federal law. If a desire for uniformity and stability are the only values weighed on the scale, then preemption may too readily be found. Actual statutory texts usually do not favor preemption. Some laws do not command preemption but leave open the possibility of more particularized claims or conflicts requiring federal preemption. In those uncertain preemption settings, normative arguments for and against preemption are of great importance.

This book offers a diverse array of scholarly perspectives on preemption by many of this nation's foremost legal scholars of regulation and constitutional law. Their views and lenses vary, so distilling their arguments and insights is difficult. Nevertheless, they enrich preemption discourse by providing a more balanced perspective on preemption choice. No one disputes that certainty, uniformity, and stability are values worth consideration. Several chapters explore and enrich those common pro-preemption arguments. But those chapters, and most others, move on to develop far too neglected countervailing arguments and values. Some are rooted in durable strains of federalism theory, seeing retention of state domains and limited federal government as strong values evident in our Constitution's language and structure. Others look closely at the Constitution's structures and mandated procedures as requiring the formality of legislation before preemption should be found. Others explore the contrasting benefits and risks of a unitary federal response with benefits of allowing a multiplicity of regulatory actors, venues, and legal modalities. Histories of regulatory challenges and acts further illuminate the preemption choice issues, revealing how retention of diverse actors and parallel common law regimes can further public-regarding goals, while strong assertions of preemption can threaten to freeze the law or lead to neglect of changing discoveries about an underlying social ill. Contested assertions about the relative performance of federal and state actors are also reexamined. Other chapters develop arguments by analogy, drawing on other disciplines' insights about the retention of multiple versus single or homogenous institutional responses.

This book's chapters are offered at a level of legal rigor that will provide insights to lawyers, legal scholars, and law students, but it is also written to be accessible to other disciplines, especially students and scholars of government, political science, business and regulation, economics, and history. Students and scholars interested in regulation of industry, risk regulation, environmental policy, and law, will find most of this book of direct relevance. This book's subject lies at the heart of the federalism policy and debates, a subject of interest to a wide array of disciplines.

THE BOOK'S STRUCTURE AND CHAPTERS

This book is broken into four parts, each offering chapters developing the part's focus. The chapters obviously share a basic focus on preemption and necessarily address many of preemption's central debates, but are nevertheless distinct. The chapters are also all modest in length in order to facilitate readability.

Part I introduces readers to "Federalism Theory, History, and Preemption Variables." These three chapters introduce theoretical and historical underpinnings of preemption discourse, setting the stage for later chapters that tend to be more specific and applied in their focus. Professors Nina Mendelson and Robert Verchick start the book with a broadly encompassing chapter that begins by placing preemption in the context of federalism theories and discourse. Preemption choice, after all, is fundamentally a choice that implicates the heart of federalism debates over appropriate and necessary roles for federal and state governments. As they also discuss, preemption choice also implicates related theory about the benefits of centralized and decentralized responses to policy challenges. They then turn to an overview of how federalism themes and theories play out in legislative, regulatory, and judicial venues. They especially focus on interpretive questions and judicial preemption doctrine, providing an overview of issues and themes that later court-focused chapters develop in greater depth.

In Chapter 2, "From Dualism to Polyphony," Professor Robert Schapiro develops a language and analytical framework to think about the relative benefits of separate state and federal law and of legal regimes that allow the two to coexist and overlap. He does this in part by tracing U.S. constitutional law history. He reviews the formally abandoned but perhaps renascent "dual federalism" phase in doctrine that kept state and federal regulatory domains distinct. He then contrasts that era with today's dominant political choice of state and local regulatory overlap with federal law. Adopting and enriching from other scholarly and musical realms the concept of "polyphony," his chapter develops arguments for the benefits of polyphonic federalism, under which multiple legal actors' voices can blend. As he argues, multiple, interactive exercises of regulatory authority are both the dominant political choice and one that furthers values of plurality, dialogue, and redundancy. Rather than see preemption debates as about state versus federal turf, he suggests that the sounder and more necessary project is developing principles to manage this overlap, not seek to eliminate it.

Professor David Vladeck's Chapter 3, "Preemption and Regulatory Failure Risks," adopts a different perspective, melding narratives about product risks and related regulatory histories with a large body of scholarship exploring how and why regulation can fail to provide promised protections. Using these historical narratives and distillation of regulatory failure scholarship, he raises fundamental questions about the wisdom of precluding the coexistence of federal and state law, especially the ongoing existence of state common law regimes. These common law regimes, with their emphasis on proven harms and breaches of duties to sell a safe product, do not rely on overworked and sometimes uninterested regulators. Instead, the desire for compensation and private litigation incentives can reveal inadequacies of past regulatory acts. Common law actions can further the goals of federal regulatory regimes by creating incentives for reduced risk, even if common law litigation can sometimes prove embarrassing to federal agencies and upset stability and preclusion of liability favored by industry.

Part II turns away from the broader theoretical and historical perspective of Part I to two chapters exploring "The Layered Government Norm." Professor Trevor Morrison, in Chapter 4, explores "The State Attorney General and Preemption." One of the most distinctive legal changes over the past decade has been increasingly active and sometimes zealous investigations and litigation by state attorneys general. In many states, attorneys general are not appointed, but are elected. Acting to enforce state law, investigate violations of federal law, and sometimes act in *parens patriae* capacity to protect a state's citizens, state attorneys general have over the last decade often been more zealous in policing illegality than far larger federal agencies and prosecutors. Professor Morrison argues that due to state attorney generals' democratic accountability and their capacity to police illegality, preemption doctrine and legislative drafters should specially accommodate and protect their role.

In Chapter 5, "Federal Floors, Ceilings, and the Benefits of Federalism's Institutional Diversity," Professor William Buzbee provides both a historical and theoretical perspective on recent, unusual aggressive assertions of federal preemptive power by federal agencies and in legislation. Instead of the long-dominant choice of federal law serving as a "floor" that preempts only more lax state regulation and thereby preserves state positive and common law, recent actions seek to impose a federal "ceiling." A ceiling, however, actually works to displace regulatory schemes retaining multiple regulators and the different actors and modalities of common law litigation with a unitary federal choice. For a time, a unitary federal ceiling can benefit all with certainty, but it heightens pervasive risks of regulatory failure. The benefits of legal dynamism preserved with the institutional diversity of no preemption or a federal floor provide a sound counterweight to normative arguments for a single, displacing federal ceiling.

Part III focuses on "Judicial Treatment and Interpretive Choice." These four chapters turn away from political preemption choice to explore how judicial doctrine, mostly in Supreme Court decisions, addresses the preemption choice question. These chapters examine different facets of preemption doctrine, but in common find a frequent disjuncture between stated and applied doctrine. In particular, they all find that the Supreme Court's doctrine and normative frameworks tend to give short shrift to constitutional requirements and values. In addition, much recent preemption case law gives little attention to benefits of the diversity of legal voices typically preserved under our federalist forms of government. In short, a judicial conclusion in favor of preemption may too readily be found due to an imbalanced doctrinal perspective.

For example, in Chapter 6, "Supreme Court Preemption Doctrine," Professor Chris Schroeder provides a lucid window into the many strains and vacillations in the Supreme Court's preemption doctrine. His perspective is both historical and theoretical. He traces the fundamentals of preemption doctrine, illuminating the numerous different branches of preemption doctrine, among them analysis of congressional intent and of frameworks applied to determine whether the Court should find express or implied preemption. Despite the Supreme Court's often-stated "presumption against preemption," his analysis reveals the Court's erratic actual application of that claimed presumption. He provides close but concise analysis of the Supreme Court's most important preemption cases. He concludes by looking at recent and future controversies, warning against the risks of concentrating regulatory authority exclusively in a federal agency's hands.

Professor Sandi Zellmer, in Chapter 7, analyzes "When Congress Goes Unheard: Savings Clauses' Rocky Judicial Reception." Many regulatory statutes are not silent on the question of preemption but affirmatively state an intention to "save" state law, often in terms specifically allowing state law to provide greater protections than federal law. In some laws, these savings clauses are accompanied by other preemptive provisions. In addition, even with a savings clause, conflicts between federal and state law can arise. As Professor Zellmer illustrates, the Supreme Court has been erratic in the weight it gives to savings clauses in preemption cases. Despite the lack of provisions explicitly preempting state common law and the existence of savings clauses, the Court at times barely gives savings clauses any interpretive weight. The chapter identifies harms flowing from this erratic judicial treatment and suggests responsive statutory drafting strategies.

In Chapter 8, "Federal Preemption by Inaction," Professor Robert Glicksman addresses a counterintuitive wrinkle in preemption law and policy. Preemption arguments can arise in settings where federal inaction is claimed to preempt state regulation or common law. The risks of this unusual preemption twist are illustrated with close attention to debates over global climate change, where the federal government has been inactive, but state and local governments have begun to regulate. After reviewing relevant case law, state and local regulatory initiatives, and relevant strains in preemption doctrine, Professor Glicksman offers recommendations for Congress and for the courts. He does not rule out a role for preemption, but suggests it should be required or found only in rare circumstances.

Professor Bradford Clark, in Chapter 9, argues for a "Process-Based Preemption" doctrine. His analysis is rooted in constitutional text and structure, especially in close analysis of the Supremacy Clause. The Constitution creates a cumbersome process for creating any federal law that can be deemed "supreme" and therefore preemptive of state law. These procedural hurdles serve to preserve state law and are part of our constitutional system. Professor Clark therefore embraces as playing a "useful role in implementing the Constitution's political and procedural safeguards of federalism" both the oft-stated but sometimes neglected "presumption against preemption," and a clear statement requirement before an intent to preempt should be found. He further analyzes how such a presumption and clear statement requirement should influence agency assertions of preemptive power. He concludes that courts should not defer to such agency preemption claims absent clear statutory authorization. He closes by observing how enforcing such a process-based preemption doctrine would provide latitude for state law to be innovative in protecting public health, safety, and the environment.

Chapter 10 picks up on strains in the previous chapter, with Professor William Funk focusing on "Preemption by Federal Agency Action." Most preemption disputes today involve federal agencies in some way. Especially since 2005, numerous agencies have aggressively asserted power to preempt state regulatory and common law. Despite the prevalence of this preemption wrinkle, the Supreme Court has yet to articulate directly what kind of deference, if any, should be given to such agency claims of preemptive power. After reviewing different settings in which preemption claims can arise with agencies, Professor Funk offers both a distillation of relevant cases and a federal executive order. Of special importance, he provides close analysis of how statutes differ in the grants of authority to agencies. Some provide such authority clearly, while others do not, or provide both savings and preemption clauses. Like Professor Clark, but relying on close analysis of statutory law and recent regulatory actions, Professor Funk argues for a statutory clear statement authorizing agency assertions of preemptive power before it should be upheld by courts.

Part IV, "Preemption Tales from the Field," turns away from judicial treatment of preemption claims and related doctrine. The book's final three chapters provide analysis rooted in regulatory history, substantially influenced by underlying theory and past scholarship regarding effective regulation. Professor Thomas McGarity, in Chapter 11, observes a "Regulation–Common Law Feedback Loop in Non-Preemptive Regimes." This chapter provides a rich analysis of the strengths and weaknesses of the legal modalities of agency regulation and common law tort litigation. Whereas Professor Vladeck, in Chapter 3, analyzed regulatory failure risks and why tort regimes remained important, Professor McGarity argues for how both regulation and tort regimes are strengthened by their interactive learning, or what he calls their "feedback loop." Drawing on theory and recent high-visibility product risks initially poorly addressed through regulation, McGarity splits his chapter into two substantial sections: he first analyzes how agencies provide feedback and information used in courts, and then he turns to settings where information ferreted out in common law tort settings has led agencies to reexamine and revise earlier regulatory choices. Critical to this valuable feedback loop are the different incentives and distinct institutional strengths of each legal setting. He provides a succinct but detailed recounting of how industry and agencies initially failed to address risks of the nonstick coating chemical perfluorooctanic acid (PFOA) but then did so after discoveries elicited in civil tort litigation. Broad agency preemption of common law regimes could destroy the benefits of this mutual regulatory feedback.

In Chapter 12, "Delegated Federalism Versus Devolution: Some Insights from the History of Water Pollution Control," Professor William Andreen continues the focus on history. He responds to recent legal historical scholarship questioning the need for substantial federal environmental laws starting around 1970. Of most direct relevance to this book was federal assertion in

1972 of a preemptive regulatory floor that precluded more lax state water pollution protections. Professor Andreen's chapter provides a nuanced analysis of the Clean Water Act's delegated program structure. These provisions are a prime example of the prevailing political choice to enact laws utilizing overlapping and intertwined federal and state roles. He also reviews states' actual environmental performance, including many states' decision to preclude any more protections than provided by federal law. He then looks closely at historical data on water quality before and after the modern Clean Water Act was enacted, finding strong support for the traditional view that federal law quickly improved the quality of widely degraded rivers. By providing a federal floor, funding municipal treatment works, and allowing states to innovate and provide additional protections, water quality has improved from where it stood during the period of state primacy.

In Part IV's final chapter, Chapter 13, Professors David Adelman and Kirsten Engel examine the strength of what they call "Adaptive Environmental Federalism." This chapter weaves legal theory, history, and analogies to ecosystems, to suggest that static regulatory systems in the form of broadly preemptive federal regulation would undercut benefits of adaptive legal regimes and the legal dynamism that they can create. They suggest that the risk of dysfunctional preemption is especially high in the field of environmental law. They first dispute assumptions of static models of environmental federalism, explaining how environmental ills tend to be multilayered and multijurisdictional in cause and effect, complicating reliance on any single regulator. They also explain why legal schemes must allow for adjustment and tailoring to local and changing conditions. Dynamic environmental change requires legal regimes that are dynamic. Drawing on work in earlier chapters and other work by authors contributing to this book, Professors Adelman and Engel note a broad array of scholars developing an argument for dynamic, interactive, contextual, and polyphonic forms of federalism. Enriching this growing body of scholarship, they explore the science and benefits of "complex adaptive systems," using the concept both descriptively and normatively. As they show, adaptive systems can cope and flourish in settings that are complex and unpredictable, as are environmental challenges and legal institutions' responses to those challenges. They close by applying their framework to the challenge of climate change.

A brief concluding chapter draws together strains and arguments from the earlier chapters to derive a menu of "preemption choice variables." As is inevitable under our constitutional structure, preemption will at times be necessary and make sense. This book refines earlier scholarship and jurisprudence by identifying with greater precision when the choice to preempt is

William W. Buzbee

legally justified and appropriate. Most distinctively, this book's chapters collectively enrich federalism discourse by drawing on theory, history, and legal precedents to articulate normative rationales for the nonpreemptive regimes that remain the dominant political choice.

PART ONE

FEDERALISM THEORY, HISTORY, AND PREEMPTION VARIABLES

1   Preemption and Theories of Federalism

Robert R.M. Verchick and Nina Mendelson

INTRODUCTION

American government is an experiment in redundancy, with powers and duties shared among federal, state, and local decision makers. The arrangement is designed to divide power, maximize self-rule, and foster innovation, but it also can breed confusion. In the areas of public safety and environmental protection, state and federal leaders (to name the two most active players in these disputes) are often seen jockeying for the inside track, hoping to secure the resources or authority needed to promote their views of the public good or gain politically. To outside observers, the best outcomes are not obvious. For example, should the federal government be the exclusive regulator of automobile pollution, as it is of automotive fuel efficiency, or should (as U.S. Senators from California successfully argued in 1967) California also be allowed to set its own unique, more stringent standards? Should New Jersey be able to issue regulations requiring chemical plant managers to consider safer technology to reduce the risks of terrorism incidents, or should those requirements be imposed only if the U.S. Department of Homeland Security allows them?[1] Should state judges or juries be allowed to conclude, applying state tort law, that a pharmaceutical company has negligently failed to warn patients of drug side effects if the U.S. Food and Drug Administration has already approved the drug label? Deciding when federal law trumps state law can be a complicated process, involving the legislature, the judiciary, and even executive agencies. The guiding principles always include federalism.

Federalism is concerned with the distribution of power between the federal government and state governments. Most significantly, the Constitution gives

[1]   As this book was going to press, Congress expressly resolved this question by adopting a savings clause for state law on chemical plant security. Consolidated Appropriations Act, 2008, Pub. L. No. 110-161, § 534, 121 Stat. 1844, 2075 (2007) (to be codified at 6 U.S.C. § 121 note).

Congress the power to make laws in areas affecting interstate commerce, military defense, and civil rights. This delegation of powers contemplates some impingements on state autonomy. Meanwhile, the Tenth Amendment reserves powers to the states. With a federal government of limited powers, and states wielding plenary powers, realms of separate sovereignty and political accountability might seem to be the norm. Yet the modern understanding of the Constitution's provisions leaves generous room for state and federal overlap. Within these boundaries, however, Congress can use its lawmaking powers either to leave space for state authority or else to eclipse, or *preempt*, state power. The Constitution's Supremacy Clause makes clear that state law must yield to federal law as supreme. Preempting state law is not unfair, according to federalism theory, because political safeguards built within the legislative process (such as the fact that Senators are elected state by state) deter federal lawmakers from routinely bulldozing over the states' interests. This chapter focuses on Congress's preemption power and examines the most common legal and theoretical issues surrounding its use.

The two most important questions about preemption are related. The first is for the lawmaker: when, or in what way, should Congress act to preempt state laws in favor of federal ones? The second is for the judge: how do you know that state law has been preempted? In answering the first question, policy makers must consider the relative strengths of federal and state regulation. A more centralized federal approach promises uniformity, and with it fewer transaction costs associated with compliance, the containment of trans-boundary "spillover" effects, and economies of scale. A more decentralized, state-based approach is associated with greater government responsiveness and citizen participation, allowances for regional variability, and helpful experimentation among states.

As for the second question, sometimes Congress's intent to preempt state law is clear and plainly stated in a statute. But sometimes there is doubt. A statute may not declare preemption outright but may conflict with state law; or it may be so broad as to "occupy the field" of targeted regulation, leaving states with no power in the area. The courts have articulated a presumption, discussed in greater detail in the sections that follow, against reading a statute to preempt state law where Congress's intent is not clear. That somewhat inconsistently applied presumption is informed, in part, by concerns about not trenching on state authority or eclipsing state sovereignty "accidentally" without full consideration by a federal deliberative legislature. Besides examining the issues related to congressional decisions to preempt state law, this chapter will also examine the theoretical assumptions underlying judicial reluctance to read a statute as preempting state law.

PREEMPTION AND THE CONGRESS

Reading the Constitution, one might think it utterly clear, as some have argued,[2] that the federal government can freely preempt state governments from regulating the environment, pharmaceutical safety, employment relationships, or nearly any other subject that is within Congress's legislative authority. After all, the Constitution's Supremacy Clause states, "This Constitution, and the Laws of the United States which shall be made in Pursuance thereof . . . shall be the supreme Law of the Land; and the Judges in every State shall be bound thereby, any Thing in the Constitution or Laws of any State to the Contrary notwithstanding" (art. VI, cl. 2). Moreover, courts have long read the Commerce Clause, which authorizes Congress to regulate "Commerce . . . among the several States" (art. II, Sec. 8, cl. 3), as an independent prohibition of state laws that discriminate against or unduly burden interstate commerce.

In short, Congress could make policy for the nation, and its choices would be supreme notwithstanding contrary state government views. Assuming Congress is properly using its constitutional powers (such as the power to regulate commerce), the only constitutional obstacle might be the Tenth Amendment, which suggests that some powers "not delegated to the United States . . . are reserved to the States respectively, or to the people." But that amendment has been interpreted by the courts to restrain Congress from preempting state authority only narrowly – by, for example, "commandeering" state employees or resources to "enact or administer a federal regulatory program."[3] As we see it, the Tenth Amendment today presents no other obstacle to federal preemption even in traditionally "local" fields such as the protection of health and safety.

Despite Congress's broad preemptive power, many, if not most, areas of law are governed concurrently by federal and state governments. Lively debate continues in many settings about whether state regulatory authority should be forced to yield to federal power or whether Congress has actually acted to preempt state law and to what extent. The "presumption against preemption" applied by courts tends to moderate the extent to which states will be barred from regulating. Congress regularly legislates to share power or to preserve state authority.

Given an effective federal government with far-reaching power to regulate, why preserve state authority to regulate? Debates on whether to preempt state

---

[2] See Caleb Nelson, "Preemption," Virginia Law Review 66, no. 3 (2000): 225.
[3] See Printz v. United States, 521 U.S. 898, 933 (1997) (quoting New York v. United States, 505 U.S. 144, 157 [1992]).

law often draw on ideas of federalism – a general concern with the division of power between the federal and state governments and with maintaining core attributes of state sovereignty. A state's authority to devise its own laws is among these core aspects of state sovereignty.[4] As developed in a recent series of cases, another core aspect is preserving a state's sovereign immunity from private lawsuits seeking money damages, a protection emphasized by a now expansively interpreted Eleventh Amendment.[5]

Federalism advocates identify several benefits of preserving a state's sovereignty and autonomy to regulate. First, some argue that strong state authority, of which authority to regulate is a part, is important to the scheme of separation of powers developed by the Framers of the Constitution. Like the division of powers among the judicial, executive, and legislative branches of the federal government, maintaining significant state government power can help avoid the undue concentration of power in the federal government and preserve essential individual liberties.[6] Moreover, where a federal program depends on state and local implementation or cooperation, the involvement of states might prompt the federal government toward helpful moderation of its policies. For example, after Congress enacted the USA Patriot Act, many state and local governments objected, with some directing their officials not to participate in parts of the program.[7]

Second, if states possess robust authority to regulate, the policies chosen within a state will tend to be tailored to local concerns and to citizen preferences. For example, some western and southwestern states, where spicy Mexican candies are popular, monitor and regulate those candies for contamination with lead dust.[8] Although lead dust in these candies presents a significant safety threat, especially to children, the federal

---

[4] See Robert R. M. Verchick, "The Commerce Clause, Environmental Justice, and the Interstate Garbage Wars," Southern California Law Review 70, no. 5 (1997): 1239.

[5] Alden v. Maine, 527 U.S. 706 (1999); Coll. Sav. Bank v. Fla. Prepaid Postsecondary Educ. Expense Bd., 527 U.S. 666 (1999); Fla. Prepaid Postsecondary Educ. Expense Bd. v. Coll. Sav. Bank, 527 U.S. 627 (1999).

[6] See, e.g., Atascadero State Hospital v. Scanlon, 473 U.S. 234, 242 (1985) (the "'constitutionally mandated balance of power' between the States and the Federal Government was adopted by the Framers to ensure the protection of 'our fundamental liberties'").

[7] See Susan Schmidt, "PATRIOT Act Misunderstood, Senators Say; Complaints About Civil Liberties Go Beyond Legislation's Reach, Some Insist," Washington Post, October 22, 2003, A4 (noting "nearly 200 cities and three states have passed resolutions contending that the PATRIOT Act . . . tramples on civil liberties"); Ann Althouse, "The Vigor of Anti-Commandeering Doctrine in Times of Terror," Brooklyn Law Review 69, no. 4 (2004): 1253.

[8] E.g., Deborah Vanpelt, "State Fears Candies Pose Health Risk; Mexican suckers pulled from shelves," Tampa Tribune, December 9, 1994, 1 (describing efforts of Florida, California, Texas, and Arizona with respect to Mexican candies).

government failed for several years to give high priority to this regional issue.[9]

Third, preserving state regulatory authority may also benefit citizens by prompting greater engagement in government. Citizens are often presumed to be able to participate more directly in policy making at the state level. Greater state autonomy to regulate will mean more opportunities for citizens to participate in governance and seek responsive government. That may result in greater "civic virtue" in citizens by encouraging them to become better informed and more actively engaged in all levels of government.[10] Although it has been a benefit claimed for federalism, the goal of stimulating greater citizen engagement may logically lead to calls for concentrating power in localities, such as cities, rather than states.[11]

Fourth, preserving state authority to regulate can mean, in the words of Justice Louis Brandeis, that the states are able to function as "laborator[ies]" that can try "novel social and economic experiments" to solve society's problems. Other states and the federal government may learn from or adopt one state's innovative approach, ultimately benefiting the entire country.[12] To take this a step further, some scholars now argue that such regulatory innovation sets up a "competitive interaction" between the federal government and the states and among the states.[13] Professor Robert Schapiro develops this claim further in Chapter 2. Because citizens can compare the different responses of the federal and state governments to a particular problem, they may be better able to understand the range of options and hold government officials accountable for an inadequate response. That may in turn prompt regulators to be more thorough and more responsive to citizen preferences. For example, recent state and municipal efforts to reduce greenhouse gases

---

[9] In October 2006, the FDA finally issued guidance to industry indicating that if lead levels in candy likely to be eaten by small children exceeded the recommended level of 0.1 parts per million, the candy manufacturer could face enforcement action. See U.S. Food and Drug Administration, "Guidance for Industry: Lead in Candy Likely to be Consumed Frequently by Small Children," (October 2006) (available at http://www.fda.gov/OHRMS/DOCKETS/98fr/05d-0481-gdl0002.pdf).

[10] See, e.g., GREGORY V. ASHCROFT, 501 U.S. 452, 458 (1991).

[11] See Frank Cross, "The Folly of Federalism," CARDOZO LAW REVIEW 24, no. 1 (2002): 1.

[12] See NEW STATE ICE CO. V. LIEBMANN, 285 U.S. 262, 311 (1932) (Brandeis, J., dissenting) (describing states as "laborator[ies]").

[13] Kirsten Engel, "Harnessing the Benefits of Dynamic Federalism in Environmental Law," EMORY LAW JOURNAL 59, no. 1 (2006): 159; Roderick Hills, "Against Preemption; How Federalism Can Improve the National Legislative Process," NEW YORK UNIVERSITY LAW REVIEW 82, no. 1 (2007): 1; Robert Schapiro, POLYPHONIC FEDERALISM: HOW A FEDERAL SYSTEM PROTECTS FUNDAMENTAL RIGHTS (Chicago: University of Chicago Press, forthcoming); William W. Buzbee, "Asymmetrical Regulation: Risk, Preemption, and the Floor/Ceiling Distinction," NEW YORK UNIVERSITY LAW REVIEW 82, no. 6 (2007): 1547.

and address climate change have prompted a national dialogue questioning the extent of federal action on climate change. And federal action can also sidestep the pervasive risk of state failure to address a risk due to "free rider" temptations that could lead all states to delay in the hope that others will act.

Notwithstanding the federalism-related benefits of preserving state authority to regulate, there still may be reason to limit state control over a particular regulatory issue or to supplement it with federal regulation. A federal, rather than a state-focused, approach is more likely to effectively address problems that cross state lines. Consider a factory that dumps pollution in a rural Illinois river, making the river downstream, next to a populous Missouri town, unswimmable and undrinkable. The upstream state government may not have a strong incentive to take into account the harm to downstream, out-of-state residents – a "negative externality" from an in-state activity that may generate jobs and tax revenue. The federal government accordingly may select more appropriate water pollution standards. In addition, a uniform federal approach will minimize the risk that states will "race to the bottom, " competing with each other to loosen their environmental or other standards so as to attract new business.[14] Recent scholarship by Dean Richard Revesz argues that state regulators likely will select environmental standards that maximize citizen welfare overall rather than "racing to the bottom."[15] Other scholars, including Professor Kirsten Engel, disagree, persuasively arguing that politicians may have a strong incentive to be perceived as doing "everything possible" to attract a new business to the state, including relaxing environmental standards below an optimal level.[16] At a minimum, this scholarship raises important questions about whether state regulation may sometimes be affected by pathologies causing state regulators to choose less-than-optimal levels of environmental protection.

Finally, a national standard can give each citizen an assurance – even something of an entitlement – to a minimum level of safety, health, or environmental protection, no matter where he or she resides. A single federal approach, without separate state standard-setting, also has advantages for regulated entities. Those who must comply with regulation can face a

---

[14] Scott R. Saleska and Kirsten H. Engel, "'Facts Are Stubborn Things': An Empirical Reality Check in the Theoretical Debate over the Race-to-the-Bottom in State Environmental Standard-Setting," CORNELL JOURNAL OF LAW AND PUBLIC POLICY 8, no. 1 (1998): 55–62 (describing "race to the bottom" in environmental context, whereby relaxation of local standards leads to decline in locality's social welfare).

[15] E.g., Richard L. Revesz, "The Race to the Bottom and Federal Environmental Regulation: A Response to Critics," MINNESOTA LAW REVIEW 82, no. 2 (1997): 535.

[16] See Saleska and Engel, "Facts Are Stubborn Things," SUPRA n. 14, at 74–84.

regulatory regime that is more certain and uniform and thereby avoid multiple layers of regulation, which not only may be costly to comply with but also may be costly to figure out. This is one reason why regulated entities have frequently sought preemption. Pro-preemption arguments can have particular force when the regulatory requirement consists of a design requirement, such as specifying air-bag requirements for cars. Multiple design requirements could result in very high costs of compliance as manufacturers retool their assembly lines for different state requirements.

A unitary federal approach might also save resources, as only one government, the federal government, would invest its resources in developing regulatory standards. A fully encompassing federal regulation thus might benefit from economies of scale. Congress has sometimes completely preempted state regulatory requirements, as with the federal motor vehicle safety standards.

A very appealing approach is to capture benefits on both sides by creating a hybrid, power-sharing arrangement between the federal government and the states. For example, as in many environmental laws, Congress may specify that federal law serve as a "floor" of minimum protection but that states remain free to adopt standards that are more protective of health or the environment. That gives citizens a minimum level of protection but leaves states free to experiment or satisfy local calls for stricter protection. Even with federal environmental standards in place, some citizens may still face acute localized risks, called "hot spots" by environmentalists; preserving state authority to go beyond federal standards can allow an effective response to these local problems.[17] Alternatively, even if a particular consumer product does not violate federal standards, individuals injured by the product may still be free to go to state court and argue that under state tort law requiring, say, reasonable care, the manufacturer should be liable for product defects or failure to warn consumers. The continuing availability of tort claims is likely to prompt the manufacturer to address safety concerns that regulators have not yet anticipated.

In addition, as some have argued in the environmental setting, concurrent state and federal authority furthers the goal of precaution, by ensuring that the more stringent standards, whether national or local, take precedence. States

---

[17] See Zygmunt J. B. Plater et al., ENVIRONMENTAL LAW AND POLICY: NATURE, LAW, AND SOCIETY (New York: Aspen Publishers, 2004), 335 (discussing benefits of "savings" clauses in federal legislation); Robert R. M. Verchick, "Fair Distribution of Environmental Harms and Benefits," in A NEW PROGRESSIVE AGENDA FOR PUBLIC HEALTH AND THE ENVIRONMENT, ed. Christopher Schroeder and Rena Steinzor (Durham, NC: Carolina Press, 2004) (discussing distributional harms in environmental policy).

are generally barred from adopting environmental standards that are less protective than federal ones.

Finally, states implementing federal law under "delegated program" structures typically undertake significant responsibility to implement a federal program by, for example, developing their own individual requirements that will meet a federal program's goal or by issuing permits to individual companies or other entities that must comply with federal law. States thereby may retain greater flexibility to respond to local concerns – and to counterbalance federal authority – but within the framework of a federal program that seeks to address a particular issue at a national level.

Assuming that the states and the federal government do not require, say, disparate design standards, these sorts of power-sharing approaches can be advantageous and workable. They can help prevent "races to the bottom" and protect against federal inaction or other regulatory pathologies at both levels of government. However, they still may impose the burden on a particular company or entity of having to comply with more than one regulatory standard in a particular location.

Assuming the importance of federalism interests and a state's autonomy to regulate, how might those interests best be protected in a federal regime? One position is that the federal legislative process can adequately protect state autonomy. The Supreme Court has cited this "political safeguards" approach, for example, in declining to judicially enforce the Tenth Amendment, with the exception of the anti-commandeering requirement, as a constraint on federal power over state governments.

According to the "political safeguards" approach, Congress will select the appropriate balance between federal and state authority and will credit the need for state authority and autonomy.[18] First, state officials and organizations (such as associations of governors and attorneys general) frequently present their views through testimony to Congress or through informal means. Further, members of Congress are elected by district or by state, and so have an incentive to take state interests into account in considering legislative proposals. Moreover, Congress generally wants the cooperation and support of state governments in its programs and so will consistently consider state interests. Finally, because voters generally favor federalism values, members of Congress, responsive to electoral views, will also support state interests.

---

[18] E.g., Larry D. Kramer, "Putting the Politics Back into the Political Safeguards of Federalism," COLUMBIA LAW Review 100, no. 1 (2000); 215; Herbert Wechsler, "The Political Safeguards of Federalism: The Role of the States in the Composition and Selection of the National Government," COLUMBIA LAW REVIEW 54, no. 4 (1954): 543.

But not everyone accepts the "political safeguards" view. Some experts contend that because there is no guarantee that Congress will protect state interests, courts should help preserve state autonomy and authority by independently enforcing states' rights.[19] For example, as discussed earlier, judges have been willing to strike down federal statutes as violating the Tenth Amendment because they "commandeer" state resources for use in federal programs. Some also might characterize the judicial presumption against preemption, discussed in the next section, as a lesser form of independent judicial protection of state authority and autonomy.

PREEMPTION AND THE COURTS

Even once Congress has enacted a federal statute, with a full opportunity for states and state organizations to have their views heard, whether the statute preempts state law and to what extent may not be altogether clear. Congress may not foresee a relevant change, such as a change in technology or in state regulatory practice. For example, some have criticized the preemption language in the Employment Retirement Income Security Act (ERISA), which covers employee benefit plans; despite dramatic changes in the health care system – including an explosion of managed health care plans – the act has yet to be seriously updated.[20] Sometimes Congress will deliberately not answer a preemption question because its members cannot reach agreement. For example, in the fall of 2006, Congress debated whether states should be preempted from requiring any further federal chemical plant security measures beyond those required under federal law. Congress could not reach agreement at the time, and 2006 legislation requiring the setting of federal chemical plant requirements included no language either preempting state law or "saving" state law. And of course, sometimes statutory language is written in a way that is unintentionally vague or incomplete.

When faced with such a statute in the context of a dispute over whether state law is preempted, courts must interpret the statute to decide whether it preempts the state from regulating. As discussed in greater detail by Professor Schroeder in Chapter 6, a court may conclude that Congress has "expressly preempted" state law, usually through statutory language that specifies which laws are preempted. Courts also may infer (through "implied preemption"

---

[19] E.g., Frank B. Cross, "The Folly of Federalism," CARDOZO LAW REVIEW 24, no. 1 (2002): 1, 8–12; Marci A. Hamilton, "The Elusive Safeguards of Federalism," ANNALS OF AMERICAN ACADEMY OF POLITICAL AND SOCIAL SCIENCE 574 (March 2001): 94.

[20] E.g., Donald Bogan, "Protecting Patients' Rights Despite ERISA," TULANE LAW REVIEW 74, no. 3 (2000): 951.

analysis) preemptive intent when state law "conflicts" with the federal law. Sometimes conflict arises when compliance with both state and federal law is physically impossible. Other times a court will find conflict when a state law poses an obstacle to the full accomplishment of a federal goal ("obstacle preemption"). Finally, a court might conclude, as the Supreme Court has with immigration law, that Congress has "occupied the field" of a particular regulatory area. This form of preemption, called "field preemption," is based both on congressional intent and on whether the federal government has traditionally controlled regulation in the area.[21]

In determining whether Congress has preempted state law, modern courts have generally applied a presumption against preemption, especially in regulatory areas commonly left to the states. Courts have refused to find state law preempted unless a federal statute provides a "clear statement" that state law is to be preempted or other strong evidence that preemption is the "clear and manifest purpose" of Congress.[22]

How might the presumption be justified? A plausible response is that it is not justified at all, because Congress possesses the largely unfettered power to preempt state law freely. The correct judicial response to a statute that might preempt state law accordingly might be to apply no presumption. But sometimes courts need a "tiebreaker" to resolve whether an ambiguously worded statute actually does preempt state law. As a clear "default" rule used to break such ties, the presumption against preemption also provides Congress with greater certainty about how courts will interpret statutory language that does not clearly address preemption.[23]

Even though the use of some clearly stated tiebreaker by judges is useful, the question remains whether the judicial choice of the particular default rule – against preemption – is the right choice or an inappropriate "thumb on the scale." Congress frequently guards state interests. Perhaps, then, the presumption against preemption follows a reasonable assumption that unless Congress says otherwise, it does not intend to limit state regulation. However, congressional intent with respect to state law is not always clear. In the absence of legislative language that "saves" state law, perhaps courts should assume that Congress's main concern is the effectiveness of federal law, a priority that overrides state law with conflicting rules or values.

---

[21] See, e.g., HINES V. DAVIDOWITZ, 312 U.S. 52, 74 (1941) (finding Pennsylvania alien registration law preempted).

[22] See, e.g., RICE V. SANTA FE ELEVATOR CORP., 331 U.S. 218, 230 (1947), quoted in MEDTRONIC, INC. V. LOHR, 518 U.S. 470, 485 (1996).

[23] See Nina Mendelson, "Chevron and Preemption," MICHIGAN LAW REVIEW 102, no. 3 (2004): 737, 745–46.

If the presumption against preemption does not represent a judge's best guess at Congress's actual intent, how else might it be understood? By requiring a clear statement or some other strong evidence from Congress that it intends preemption, judges can reduce the chance of Congress thoughtlessly eclipsing state sovereignty. For example, if the statute specifically mentions state law preemption, it increases the chances that state law preemption will have received actual discussion in Congress. Thus, absent a clear statement or strong evidence, a presumption against preemption promotes legislative deliberation. Professor Bradford Clark, in Chapter 9, embraces this presumption, rooting his argument in the Constitution's language and structure.

In addition to a procedural bias in favor of more deliberation, a clear statement rule also imposes a substantive bias in favor of state autonomy. By raising the bar to establish preemption, the rule effectively protects a larger field of state authority. That may serve a judicial desire to minimize congressional tampering with the federal-state framework and, in the words of the Supreme Court, to avoid "serious intrusion into state sovereignty."[24] The effect is to give state autonomy and authority some additional protection in court beyond what states have been able to obtain in the political process. Although such an approach seems inconsistent with the "political safeguards" approach embraced by the Supreme Court in other settings, advocates of this approach stress the constitutional importance of the federal-state balance and argue that relaxing judicial constraints might put the federal fox in charge of the states' chicken coop. They argue that courts should more actively patrol the line between states and the federal government as part of reinforcing the constitutional structure and supporting the "tradition" of federalism.[25]

But applying a presumption against preemption also has significant downsides. For instance, insisting that courts always attempt to read statutes without clear preemptive language in the states' favor can force courts to adopt a more "federalist" interpretation of a statute even when that interpretation is not the best reading of the statute's language. Ours is a country of "laws, not men."[26] Too many deviations from statutory language by judges can undermine the integrity of the law. At its worst, the presumption against preemption could become a cloak for illegitimate judicial policy choices – enabling what Professors William Eskridge and Philip Frickey call "under-the-table constitutional lawmaking."[27]

---

[24] See MEDTRONIC, INC., v. LOHR, 518 U.S. 470, 488 (1996).
[25] See sources cited SUPRA n. 19.
[26] The phrase has been attributed to Livy. See Harold Bruff, "The Incompatibility Principle," ADMINISTRATIVE LAW REVIEW 59, no. 2 (2007): 225.
[27] William N. Eskridge and Philip P. Frickey, "Quasi-Constitutional Law: Clear Statement Rules as Constitutional Lawmaking," VANDERBILT LAW REVIEW 45, no. 3 (1992): 593, 635 (discussing clear statement rules).

Judges might simply be sneaking policy through the "back door," using the presumption against preemption to impose their own views of the correct balance of state and federal power. States can adequately protect the prerogative to regulate through their influence in Congress, and judges should be discouraged from displacing Congress by trying to minimize federal preemption of state law.[28]

On this view, the judiciary might leave the question of state law preemption wholly to the political process, applying no presumption at all. Some argue that the policy choices involved in preserving or preempting state authority to regulate are more appropriately made on a case-by-case basis by Congress, our most democratic institution and the one most accountable to voters. The argument is even stronger, given Congress's clear power under the Constitution's Supremacy Clause to preempt state law as part of exercising its other constitutional authorities.

In our view, preemption advocates make a persuasive claim – up to a point. Congress clearly has the prerogative to preempt state law and should not be forced to express that desire in any unusually specific or clear way as long as the ultimate meaning can be discerned. But where there is *significant* ambiguity, a rule favoring state authority is, it seems to us, appropriate. Such a clear *intent* rule would foster uniformity among courts and acknowledge the traditional interests in local control, while at the same time preserving for the Congress maximum latitude in expressing its desires. Professor Clark examines compromise positions like this more completely in Chapter 9.

SPECIAL CASES

Disagreements about preemption, in the courtroom and in the academy, tend to revolve around certain kinds of cases in which the merits of federal or state interests seem particularly strong. Such "special cases" often involve questions about which branch is asserting preemption, the nature of the laws being preempted, or both. Another notable case involves federal provisions designed to "save" a role for state decision making. We emphasize the special cases for three reasons. First, they test the endurance of preemption advocates and skeptics by asking just how far each will go in defending a theoretical position. Second, special cases sometimes point to weaknesses in a background rule, suggesting the need for fine-tuning or even exceptions. Finally, because these cases are drawn from current controversies in law and politics, they acquaint

[28] Id.

readers with the new frontiers of preemption analysis. Here is where the rubber meets the road.

Who Is Preempting?

Should preemption analysis change according to who is asserting preemption? Our analysis so far has assumed that Congress, explicitly or implicitly, commands the preemption. But as discussed in greater depth in Professor William Funk's accompanying Chapter 10, recently we have seen a trend in which state preemption is imposed not by Congress, but by executive agencies. In 2005, for instance, the Food and Drug Administration took the position that its labeling requirements for tuna preempted California's efforts to add any additional warnings on the product.[29] The California label would have warned consumers about the threat of mercury contamination; the FDA would have required no warning label. That same year, the U.S. Department of Transportation issued a proposed rule finding that its new "roof crush" standards for automobiles would preempt any additional requirements at the state level – including findings of liability under state tort law.[30] Sometimes, preemption is specifically authorized by Congress in the formative statute. Sometimes, as in the preceding examples, it is not. Agency-made regulation, if the agency is properly exercising the authority it received from Congress, can have the same preemptive effect as a federal statute.[31] And if compliance with both an agency regulation and state law is physically impossible, the agency regulation clearly prevails over the state law. Beyond this, courts and scholars disagree about how to interpret the bounds of underlying congressional authority. Must Congress expressly delegate to an agency the right to upend state law through regulatory act? Or may an agency infer such authority from less explicit or even ambiguous statutory language? If the latter, may agencies infer preemptive powers whenever convenient, or only as a "last resort" to accomplish federal goals?

---

[29] See U.S. Food and Drug Administration, "Letter to Bill Lockyer re a Suit Filed on June 21, 2004, PEOPLE OF THE STATE OF CALIFORNIA V. TRI-UNION SEAFOODS" (August 12, 2005) (available at www.cfsan.fda.gov/~dms/fl-ltr65.html).

[30] See National Highway Traffic and Safety Administration, Department of Transportation, "Proposed Rule: Federal Motor Vehicle Safety Standards; Roof Crush Resistance," FEDERAL REGISTER 70 (August 23, 2005): 49,223.

[31] See, e.g., LOUISIANA PUB. SERV. COMM'N V. FCC, 476 U.S. 355, 369 (1986). ("Pre-emption may result not only from action taken by Congress itself; a federal agency acting within the scope of its congressionally delegated authority may pre-empt state regulation."); FIDELITY FEDERAL SAVINGS AND LOAN ASSN. V. DE LA CUESTA, 458 U.S. 141, 153 (1982). ("Federal regulations have no less pre-emptive effect than federal statutes.")

A pro-preemption argument would assert that despite the agency twist, the federal actors should remain supreme. Federal agencies are enforcers of legislative command, and courts should interfere as little as possible with the federal enforcement of federal law. Moreover, as enforcers and implementers of federal statutes, agency officials have the closest understanding of how to achieve federal goals.[32] Agency officials are the first to know if the accomplishment of their delegated mission has been jammed by state "obstacles" or transformed into a functional "impossibility." In addition, although agencies are naturally focused on federal goals, they have incentives to consider state interests and federalism values. Top executive agency officials are appointed by and report to the President, and, even in relatively liberal administrations, the White House has guarded traditions of federalism. For instance, President Clinton's Executive Order 13,132[33] directs all federal agencies to be mindful of state powers when implementing federal law and specifically directs agencies (when possible) to favor interpretations that do not preempt state laws.[34] Should these safeguards fail, Congress always retains the power to correct agency overreaching by amending the authorizing statute. For example, in response to attempts by the Department of Homeland Security to preempt state security laws governing chemical facilities, Congress recently enacted a savings clause that preserves state law unless it actually conflicts with federal law.[35]

Preemption skeptics argue that regulatory preemption must be carefully contained. Agency officials are not directly accountable to voters, they warn, and agencies lack consistent White House supervision, whatever the executive orders say. Federal agencies are, by design, focused on federal needs and powers rather than state interests. As a practical matter, federal agencies are not set up to evaluate and protect state regulatory powers – and they rarely do.[36] By invoking obstacle preemption, a creative agency could preempt nearly any sort of state regulation simply by referencing a subordinate federal purpose that is somehow impeded by the state law.[37] Federal agencies are also sometimes subject to "capture" by big business and other powerful lobbies.

---

[32] Robert R. M. Verchick, "Toward Normative Rules for Agency Interpretation: Defining Jurisdiction under the Clean Water Act," ALABAMA LAW REVIEW 55, no. 3 (2004): 845.

[33] FEDERAL REGISTER 64 (1999): 43,255.

[34] But research suggests the directive is seldom followed. See Mendelson, SUPRA n. 23, at 783–4 (documenting remarkably low compliance by agencies with Executive Order 13,132).

[35] See SUPRA n. 1.

[36] See SUPRA. n. 34.

[37] See Nina Mendelson, "A Presumption against Agency Preemption," NORTHWESTERN UNIVERSITY LAW REVIEW 102, no. 2 (2008): 695.

All this makes an agency particularly ill-suited to weigh the interests of state and local interests in the course of accomplishing federal goals.

On this issue, we side with preemption skeptics. Agencies lack the expertise to evaluate the federal-state balance, and it is unclear how serious an incentive they face to fully consider state interests. Accordingly, absent clear evidence that Congress intended to grant such authority to agencies, general rulemaking delegation language should not be read to include the authority to preempt state law.

In 2007, the Supreme Court almost tested this argument in *Watters v. Wachovia Bank*.[38] In a 5-3 decision (Justice Thomas did not participate), the Court upheld a policy of the U.S. Comptroller of the Currency that shielded real estate lending by national banks from state consumer protection laws. The Comptroller's office had based its policy on the National Bank Act's general grant of authority to prescribe "restrictions and requirements" for real estate lenders.[39] The four appellate circuits examining the policy had found that although the statute did not preempt state consumer protection laws, the Comptroller's policy had; and because the statute granted the Comptroller broad powers, that agency-made preemption was just as valid as if it had been penned by Congress.[40] But in upholding the Comptroller's policy, the Supreme Court refused that gambit. Instead it found, perhaps implausibly, that the banking statute had preempted state consumer protection laws all along.[41] As a result, there was no need to decide whether a federal agency, on these or any other facts, has the independent power to preempt state law when Congress is mute.

Still, the case is instructive. For one thing, it shows the murky progression from legislative to agency-based preemption: it is not always easy to tell where one ends and the other begins. For another, *Wachovia Bank* reminds us that courts can interpret a set of facts in surprisingly different ways, bypassing (or, some might say, deliberately avoiding) questions or doctrines that at first seem relevant. Finally, *Wachovia Bank* teaches us to pay attention to the national or local features of the subject matter involved. In reaching its conclusion, the Court repeatedly emphasized the national significance of the interstate banking system, a network now more than one hundred years old and deeply embedded in the federal-state structure. Perhaps a different case, involving a less traditional federal role or a less pervasive statutory system, would come

[38] 127 S.Ct. 1559 (2007).
[39] Office of Comptroller of the Currency, "Notice: Preemption Determination and Order," FEDERAL REGISTER 68 (2003): 46,264.
[40] See WACHOVIA BANK, 127 S.Ct. at 1579 n. 16 (Stevens, J., dissenting) (citing cases).
[41] See id. at 1569.

out differently. We examine the importance of regulatory subject matter in the next subsection.

What Is Being Preempted?

Perhaps courts should adjust their standards for preemption according to what sort of state or federal regulation is at stake. Judges already do this in some ways, although not always clearly or consistently. As generally understood, the presumption against preemption requires courts to "start with the assumption that the historic police powers of the States were not to be superseded . . . unless that was the clear and manifest purpose of Congress."[42] The implication is that the presumption is most powerful where "the State's historic police powers" have been threatened.[43] In contrast, the presumption may have less force "when the State regulates in an area where there has been a history of significant federal presence."[44]

Where federal lawmakers cut too close to the bone, the Supreme Court has occasionally gone further, requiring not just clear *evidence* of preemptive intent (an approach we favor), but a clear *statement* of intent within the statute. Thus, in *Gregory v. Ashcroft*[45] the Supreme Court read a broad federal statute prohibiting age discrimination in employment not to cover state judges, leaving in place the state's constitutional requirement that state judges retire by age seventy. Writing for the majority, Justice Sandra Day O'Connor warned that the Court should not "upset the usual constitutional balance of federal and state powers" unless Congress made "its intention to do so unmistakably clear in the language of the statute."[46] Finding no clear statutory language intended to displace core state functions, the majority held that the age discrimination statute did not apply to state judges. In the environmental area, courts have rejected agency statutory interpretations that might "encroach upon a traditional state power."[47]

---

[42] Rice v. Santa Fe Elevator Corp., 331 U.S. 218, 230 (1947).

[43] Geier v. Am. Honda Motor Corp., 529 U.S. 861, 894 (2000) (Stevens, J., dissenting).

[44] United States v. Locke, 529 U.S. 89, 108 (2000). In addition, there is no presumption against preemption when a state intrudes on the sovereign prerogatives of the federal government by directly regulating the federal government or its agents. See generally Seth P. Waxman and Trevor W. Morrison, "What Kind of Immunity? Federal Officers, State Criminal Law, and the Supremacy Clause," Yale Law Journal 112, no. 8 (2003): 2195.

[45] 501 U.S. 452 (1991).

[46] Id. at 460–1 (quoting Atascadero State Hospital v. Scanion, 473 U.S. 234, 242 [1985]) (internal quotation marks omitted).

[47] See Solid Waste Agency of Northern Cook County v. U.S. Army Corps of Engineers, 531 U.S. 159, 172–3 (2001) (invalidating agency rule that asserted federal jurisdiction over certain intrastate waters under the federal Clean Water Act).

These practices have created a kind of "special case" analysis in which judges are reluctant to read federal laws to upset "historic" powers, "core" authority, or "traditional" balance. The rationale goes back to the debate about the Tenth Amendment and "political safeguards." Recall that, under today's understanding of the Constitution, the Tenth Amendment has been interpreted to protect state sovereignty in court in only limited ways, when federal law threatens to outright "commandeer" local executive or legislative resources. This understanding supplanted an earlier view, held a quarter century ago, that exclusively reserved to the states certain core powers, such as the authority to set labor standards for state employees.[48] That view was abandoned in the 1985 case *Garcia v. San Antonio Metropolitan Transit Authority*.[49] The effect was that state powers would now, for the most part, be protected by Congress through the political process, rather than through categorical judicial standards. However, the *Gregory* case adds a gloss to this rule by imposing a high burden to show congressional intent to interfere with core state functions before a court will read a federal statute to regulate those functions. As the Court in that case put it: "[I]nasmuch as this Court in *Garcia* has left primarily to the political process the protection of the States against intrusive exercises of Congress' Commerce Clause powers, we must be absolutely certain that Congress intended such an exercise."[50]

Suggesting that a state law most deserves protection from preemption when it implicates a "core power" is not without difficulties. For one, it is sometimes hard to determine when a core power is at stake and when it is not. Is a federal law banning guns near schools a law about crime or about the local educational environment? Are federal restrictions on wetlands development more properly seen as national environmental protections or intrusions on the local core power of land-use planning? In addition, what should one do when a core state power confronts a core federal power? *Wachovia Bank*, for instance, pitted Michigan's traditionally local interest in consumer protection against the federal government's traditionally national interest in banking. Was the Court correct in refusing to apply a presumption against preemption in *this* special case? New Jersey's effort to impose additional safety requirements on local chemical plants suggests a similar situation. There the state's traditionally local interest in public safety overlapped with the federal government's national interest in homeland security. For our part, we find arguments based on endemic powers very problematic. Sorting governmental interests is not like sorting checkers. Often particular regulatory interests cannot be assigned

[48] See National League of Cities v. Usery, 426 U.S. 833 (1976).
[49] 469 U.S. 528 (1985).
[50] GREGORY, 501 U.S. at 464.

to one side or the other; instead they are negotiated and shared. Modern theories of cooperative federalism and instrument choice emphasize this point. In addition, the categories used to define government objectives, like public safety or homeland security, are too easily manipulated by those aiming for a specific result.

Still, it is possible to imagine other special cases where the state powers subject to preemption seem unusually important or deserving of protection. In Chapter 4, for example, Professor Morrison would require a clear statement of intent before a federal law can be invoked to preempt "the core enforcement activities of an elected state attorney general."[51] This rule, in his view, would promote local self-governance, by deferring to local law-enforcement interests pursued by a popularly elected state law-enforcement official. It would promote national democratic accountability by forcing Congress to specifically consider and issue a statement about preemption in this area before its laws could be used to undermine such local law-enforcement efforts.

What Do "Savings Clauses" Save?

As we mentioned earlier, federal statutes concerned with public health or the environment often include a provision that preserves a state's right to regulate in an even more protective way. In the last decade, such provisions, called "savings clauses," have stirred controversy in the federal courts. As Professor Sandi Zellmer shows in Chapter 7, these clauses have received erratic treatment in the courts. Should savings clauses be interpreted broadly, as preemption skeptics argue? Or should they be read narrowly, as urged by advocates of national uniformity? The issue is ostensibly one of statutory interpretation. But because Congress can usually share or hoard its power as it sees fit, one's assessment often appears linked to views about federalism.

In *United States v. Locke*,[52] the Supreme Court unanimously held that the federal Oil Pollution Act of 1990, despite the existence of several savings clauses, preempted Washington State's ability to regulate oil tankers operating in state waters. The Court reasoned that because the savings clauses appeared in a section of the statute titled, "Oil Pollution Liability and Compensation," their otherwise broad language must be restricted to liability rules and could not be read to permit "substantive regulation of a vessel's primary conduct."[53]

---

[51] See Trevor W. Morrison, ch. 4, "The State Attorney General and Preemption." Morrison would include an exception for cases in which compliance with both the state and federal laws was physically impossible.

[52] 529 U.S. 89 (2000).

[53] Id. at 105.

As in the federal banking cases, the Court also emphasized the "federal" nature of the subject matter – in this case the "at-sea conduct of vessels" – declining to "give broad effect to savings clauses where doing so would upset the careful regulatory scheme established by federal law."[54]

Later in the same term, the Supreme Court narrowly construed another savings clause on a slightly different theory. In *Geier v. American Honda Motor Co.*,[55] the Court ruled 5-4 that a federal motor safety law preempted a state tort action alleging design defect for failure to include an air bag. Although the act expressly preempted "any safety standard" different from the federal standard, it included a savings clause stating that compliance with a federal standard "does not exempt any person from any liability under common law."[56] Nevertheless, the savings clause was insufficient to rescue the "no air bags" tort claim. The Court reasoned that the tort suit presented an obstacle that "conflicts" with the federal goal of preserving manufacturer flexibility to phase in air bags, thus creating a case for implied preemption.[57] The savings clause, the Court found, was not worded in a way to save state laws from implied preemption. Rather, the clause seemed targeted only at the *express* preemption contained in the "any safety standard" language.

The *Geier* opinion left many lawyers wondering what a savings clause is now able to save. The majority insisted that it had not changed any background preemption rules and suggested that savings clauses could negate obstacle preemption if properly worded, although it did not say how.[58] Justice Stevens, in dissent, accused the majority of unfurling a blanket rule that would always protect obstacle preemption from savings clauses.[59] He suggested the majority had dumped the traditional presumption against preemption in favor of the more immediate needs of the Department of Transportation.[60]

Can Congress, through a savings clause, deactivate implied preemption when state law poses obstacles to federal goals? Does such a functional barrier now conjure (as Justice Stevens decries) a sort of presumption *against* the presumption against preemption? The answer to the first question is presumably yes, because Congress in theory is free to create statutory goals flexible enough to tolerate state obstacles. Even so, *Geier* suggests this intent must be

---

[54] Id. at 106.
[55] 529 U.S. 861 (2000).
[56] 15 U.S.C. § 1397(k).
[57] GEIER, 529 U.S. at 871.
[58] Id. at 872.
[59] Id. at 900 n. 16 (Stevens, J., dissenting). ("The [majority] contends, in essence, that a savings clause cannot foreclose implied conflict pre-emption.")
[60] Id. at 888 (Stevens, J., dissenting).

stated very clearly. We may be approaching the point where "clear statements" are necessary both to invoke and to avoid preemption. The answer
to the second question is in the eye of the beholder. Although the presumption
against preemption is in no danger of abandonment, it does – in our view –
occasionally get misplaced.

CONCLUSION

As American federalism makes clear, redundancy is complicated. The push-
me-pull-you model of shared government offers big advantages, such as democratic responsiveness, innovation, and flexibility. But the costs are real, not
the least of which is the judicial effort necessary to keep all players within their
appropriate bounds. What makes this area of the law so fascinating is that, if
you study it long enough, it will inevitably pit your principles against a desired
outcome. States' rights look good to an environmentalist favoring stricter auto
pollution laws in California or safer standards at New Jersey chemical plants.
But states' rights arguments have also been used by courts to limit the protection of the nation's wetlands and immunize state agencies from environmental citizen suits. Conservatives have the same problem, sometimes
struggling, for instance, to show why federal gun restrictions may not be
foisted on the states but why federal marijuana restrictions may.[61] Although
not all of these cases involve preemption, they do involve the basic values at
stake in the preemption debate, namely a concern for local democracy and
state experimentation, on one side, and a desire for national uniformity and
efficiency on the other.

[61] See GONZALES V. RAICH, 545 U.S. 1 (2005) (upholding despite Commerce Clause challenge
     federal criminal ban on the manufacture, distribution, or possession of marijuana by intrastate
     growers and users of marijuana for medicinal reasons).

2 From Dualism to Polyphony

Robert A. Schapiro[*]

As this book makes clear, preemption is fundamentally a question of institutional choice: Should the federal government serve as the sole regulator in a particular area or should state and federal laws operate concurrently? Is the federal government alone the preferred institution to promulgate the law governing certain conduct, or does the combination of state and federal rules promise the best regulatory design? This basic question leads to two further inquiries: First, when should Congress or federal agencies choose unilateral or concurrent regulation, and second, how should courts discern this regulatory choice in specific situations? These questions are clearly intimately related. Understanding the background conceptions informing the initial regulatory choice will assist courts in interpreting the scope of federal law in the cases before them. The allocation of power among the states and the national government is the central issue of federalism, and a theory of federalism will shape the preemption decisions of regulators and courts.

This chapter seeks to illuminate the preemption question by situating it within a larger conception of federalism. An overall understanding of the relationship of federal and state authority will help to guide both federal regulators in deciding whether to preempt state law and courts in seeking to interpret the regulatory choice. First, I outline the historical evolution of the judicial understanding of federalism from the mid-nineteenth century to today. I discuss the judicial imposition of a theory of dual federalism, which

[*] Professor of Law and Associate Dean of Faculty, Emory University School of Law. E-mail: robert.schapiro@emory.edu. With respect to this project and many others relating to federalism, I have benefited from the insightful comments and warm collegiality of my fellow directors of Emory Law School's Center on Federalism and Intersystemic Governance, Robert B. Ahdieh and William W. Buzbee. Priya Bhoplay, Justin Critz, Michael Eber, and Andrew Fedder provided skilled research assistance. I am grateful for the help of Terry Gordon and Will Haines of the Emory University School of Law Library.

emphasized the need to divide the regulatory landscape between areas of exclusive federal control and exclusive state prerogative. Then I chart the decline of dual federalism after 1937.

This historical account sets the stage for the new, "polyphonic" conception of federalism that I offer. A polyphonic theory of federalism embraces the overlap and interaction of federal and state authority. Unlike older conceptions of "dual federalism," polyphonic federalism does not draw lines dividing state and federal areas of regulatory primacy. Rather, the key issue for regulators guided by polyphonic federalism is how to manage the concurrent exercise of state and federal power. I argue that as compared with dualism, polyphony offers a descriptively more accurate and normatively more appealing understanding of federalism. Because it does not attempt to divide targets of regulations into formalistic categories of "truly local" and "truly national," polyphonic federalism better accords with the social realities of the contemporary United States. Polyphonic federalism is normatively superior to dual federalism because it encourages regulators to harness the functional benefits of overlapping power, which I identify as plurality, dialogue, and redundancy.

After outlining polyphonic federalism, I describe the U.S. Supreme Court's recent return to dualist principles in several areas, including preemption. I show how over the last fifteen years, the Court has embraced concepts that it properly discarded in 1937. Relying on the polyphonic perspective, I point out the flaws in the Court's current framework and suggest a better approach, with a particular focus on preemption doctrine.

Applying the polyphonic understanding of federalism to preemption, this chapter makes two central claims: (1) a polyphonic understanding of federalism suggests that federal regulators should be wary of preempting state law; and (2) guided by the background principles of polyphonic federalism, courts should not grant federal regulations preemptive effect without clear evidence of federal regulatory intent.

DUAL FEDERALISM

Dual federalism constituted the dominant judicial conception of the relationship of the states and the national government until the New Deal Revolution of 1937. The key postulates of dual federalism are that the states and the federal government exercise exclusive control over nonoverlapping regions of authority, that these realms of exclusive control are defined by subject matter, and that the federal courts play an important and distinctive role in guarding the boundaries of the state and federal terrain. Firm borders demarcate spheres of state and federal control, and the courts monitor these boundaries.

Scholars debate whether federalism in the United States ever completely adhered to this model. As a practical matter, state and federal regulations sometimes overlapped. Such a situation arose in 1851 in *Cooley v. Board of Wardens*.[1] The case concerned a Pennsylvania law that required vessels entering or leaving the port of Philadelphia to hire a local pilot to guide them through the harbor. The state law clearly amounted to a regulation of interstate commerce, a power granted to Congress. If every state law touching on interstate commerce was invalid, then this regulation had to fall. The Court, however, sought to avoid the most drastic implications of dual federalism. To deal with this kind of situation, the Court propounded a distinction between commercial topics that required uniform regulation and those in which local variation was acceptable. As local pilotage represented a topic admitting of regional variation, state regulation was permissible.

The *Cooley* opinion, however, did not exert much influence in its own day.[2] More typical of the period were strong declarations of dual federalism, affirming the separateness of state and federal authority. Writing in 1858, Chief Justice Roger Taney described the system as follows: "The powers of the General Government, and of the State, although both exist and are exercised within the same territorial limits, are yet separate and distinct sovereignties, acting separately and independently of each other within their respective spheres."[3] Dual federalism clearly provided the general framework for federal-state relations until 1937.

Accounts of the pre-1937 era generally emphasize the limits on the authority of the federal government. The Supreme Court did narrowly construe the power in Congress in a variety of cases. The Court's embrace of dual federalism, however, also constricted the authority of the states. The Court enforced its conception of the proper spheres of state and federal law, and it invalidated incursions into the federal or into the state domains.

The Court employed a series of categorical distinctions in an effort to demarcate the boundary between state and federal authority. Thus, although Congress could regulate "commerce," it could not regulate "manufacture"; nor could Congress regulate activity with only an "indirect" rather than a

---

[1]   53 U.S. (12 How.) 299 (1851).
[2]   Paul Brest et al., Processes of Constitutional Decisionmaking (New York: Aspen, 4th ed. 2000), 162; Stephen Gardbaum, "New Deal Constitutionalism and the Unshackling of the States," University of Chicago Law Review 64, no. 2 (1997): 483, 508.
[3]   Ableman v. Booth, 62 U.S. (21 How.) 506, 516 (1859).

"direct" connection to commerce; nor could Congress regulate commerce if the legislation was designed to advance a social, rather than commercial, goal.

In *United States v. E.C. Knight*,[4] for example, the Supreme Court analyzed the constitutional scope of the Sherman Antitrust Act. The Court examined whether preventing the monopolization of sugar refining came within congressional power to regulate interstate commerce. The Court struck down the law, finding that sugar refining constituted manufacture not commerce, and thus did not fall within the scope of the Interstate Commerce Clause.[5] In *A.L.A. Schechter Poultry Corp. v. United States*,[6] the Court invalidated the National Industrial Recovery Act on the grounds that the activities it covered had at best an indirect effect on interstate commerce. *Carter v. Carter Coal Co.*[7] relied on a similar distinction between direct and indirect effects in striking down the Bituminous Coal Conservation Act. *Hammer v. Dagenhart*[8] concerned a federal statute prohibiting the interstate shipment of goods produced by child labor. Although the statutory prohibition fell on commerce, the Court concluded that the necessary effect of the law was to regulate child labor, which was a matter committed to the states, not to the national government.[9] Accordingly, the Court held that the legislation exceeded congressional power.[10] The Court emphasized the need to protect the prerogatives of the states by restricting federal power, even in areas of commercial regulation in which the Constitution appeared to grant authority to Congress. The Court explained, "The grant of authority over a purely federal matter was not intended to destroy the local power always existing and carefully reserved to the states in the Tenth Amendment to the Constitution."[11] In all of these cases, the Court relied on formalistic distinctions to draw lines between state and federal domains.

The Court also limited state authority in this period. Dual federalism sought to separate state power from federal power, and the Court struck down state laws that infringed on federal turf. The Court invoked the dormant Commerce Clause to invalidate state laws that regulated interstate commerce, and the Court also vigorously employed preemption doctrine to limit the overlap of state and federal regulation. With the expansion of the federal government and the integration of the national economy throughout the

[4] 156 U.S. 1 (1895).
[5] Ibid., 12.
[6] 295 U.S. 495 (1935).
[7] 298 U.S. 238 (1936).
[8] 247 U.S. 251 (1918).
[9] Ibid., 276.
[10] Ibid., 272.
[11] 247 U.S. at 274.

nineteenth and early twentieth centuries, a strict division between state and federal domains became difficult to maintain. As illustrated by *Cooley*, the Court struggled with the reality of overlapping jurisdiction. To further its project of separating state and federal power, the Court fashioned a theory of "latent exclusivity." Under this conception, states could regulate a variety of subjects, but only if Congress did not enact legislation in these areas. Once Congress did act, the Court held that congressional authority was exclusive. In effect, the Court developed an expansive doctrine of field preemption, broadly interpreting congressional action as prohibiting any state regulation, even if the state rules did not conflict with the federal.[12]

Stephen Gardbaum has identified *Southern Railway Co. v Reid*[13] as a key case in the development of the doctrine of latent exclusivity. *Southern Railway* concerned a North Carolina statute that regulated the rate practices of railroads in the state. In striking down this act, the Court used language that appeared to accept the potential exercise of concurrent state and federal power, while rejecting actual instances of overlap. In certain areas, either the states or the federal government could regulate. However, if the federal government did step in, then states lost all authority. The Court stated, "It is well settled that if the state and Congress have a concurrent power, that of the state is superseded when the power of Congress is exercised."[14] Even if an area could be regulated by the state or the federal government, state and federal power could not be exercised concurrently. The dual federalist framework could accept some ambiguity about where the line between state and federal authority stood, but a border was necessary. Congressional action provided the bright line that then formed a boundary dividing state from federal prerogatives.

THE DEMISE OF DUALISM

The New Deal programs that President Franklin Roosevelt proposed and Congress endorsed repudiated the axioms of dual federalism. In the midst of the Great Depression, with another world war brewing, the federal government sought to intervene throughout the economy and society to promote prosperity and security. The concatenation of local ills created a national problem that demanded a set of national solutions. The theory of dual federalism did not seem adequate to the task. In the election in the fall of 1936, the voters overwhelmingly supported Franklin Roosevelt and his policies.

[12] Ibid.
[13] 222 U.S. 424 (1912).
[14] Ibid., 436.

defibrillator short-circuited and failed. A wire in the device was too close to a component, causing an arc between them when the device fired.[2]

Joshua's doctors determined that the defibrillator's malfunction caused his death. Joshua may have been the first to die from a failure of a Guidant Prizm 2, but the company had known about the defect before this death. Guidant had received twenty-five reports of other failures of the device for exactly the same reason. By the time Joshua died, the device had been on the market for five years. Guidant had fixed the problem in 2002, three years before Joshua's death, but decided to sell its existing inventory first. After all, defibrillators are not cheap, costing $25,000 apiece. Thousands of these faulty defibrillators were sold after Guidant learned of the defect and had developed a new and safer device. Guidant also decided not to tell physicians or patients about the defect. Word of the defect might frighten patients into opting for potentially risky surgery to replace the device. And in Guidant's view, "reliability data" still showed the Prizm 2 to be "a highly reliable life-saving product."[3]

Shortly after his death, Joshua's doctors met with Guidant officials to discuss what the company planned to do to assist the twenty-four thousand patients who depended on the same device. Guidant offered to replace the devices that Joshua's doctors had implanted in their patients. But the company insisted that it would not inform other doctors, fearing that they too might want replacement devices. Guidant's efforts to keep the defect quiet did not succeed. The media disclosed that the short-circuiting problem had affected other Guidant defibrillators, and that Guidant had concealed the defect with those devices as well. Ultimately, three years after learning of the defect, after dozens of failures (including at least one other death and several heart attacks), and prodding from the Food and Drug Administration (FDA), Guidant decided to "recall" the Prizm 2 and several defibrillator models, affecting more than fifty thousand patients.[4]

---

[2] David C. Vladeck, "Preemption and Regulatory Failure," PEPPERDINE LAW REVIEW 33 (2005) 95–7; Thomas McGarity, THE PREEMPTION WAR (New Haven, CT: Yale University Press, 2008); Barry Meier, "Maker of Heart Device Kept Flaw from Doctors," NEW YORK TIMES, May 24, 2005, A1; Barry Meier, "Repeated Defect in Heart Device Exposes a History of Problems," NEW YORK TIMES, October 20, 2005, A1.

[3] McGarity, THE PREEMPTION WAR, 135.

[4] "Recalling" a medical device implanted into a patient's body presents its own complications. For many cardiac patients, the risk of additional surgery to explant a defective defibrillator, pacemaker, or heart valve outweighs the risk of retaining a defective product. See, e.g., Meier, "Maker of Heath Device Kept Flaw from Doctors." Many patients decide not to undergo replacement surgery but then endure the risk of life-threatening product failure. A young and otherwise healthy patient like Joshua would have likely opted for replacement surgery. See generally, Barry Meier, "Faulty Heart Devices Force Some Scary Decisions," NEW YORK TIMES, June 20, 2005, A1.

Tremendous democratic majorities were returned to Congress. The Democratic Party picked up 12 seats in the House of Representatives, bringing its total to 334, as opposed to 88 Republican members. In the Senate, the Democrats gained five seats, resulting in a total of seventy-six Democrats and sixteen Republicans, with four senators from minor parties.[15]

In 1937, in the midst of President Roosevelt's efforts to expand his control over the membership of the U.S. Supreme Court, the Court began to ratify this new approach to governance.[16] The Court never looked back, accepting a much broader conception of the realm of federal power. In cases such as *Wickard v. Filburn* and *United States v. Darby*, the Court expressed a new understanding of federalism. In *Darby*, the Court disavowed some of the tools it had previously used to separate state and federal spheres. The case arose out of a constitutional challenge to the Fair Labor Standards Act (FLSA). Those challenging the statute insisted that Congress had a social, not a commercial, purpose in enacting the FLSA. The Court rejected the premise of this argument, asserting, "The motive and purpose of a regulation of interstate commerce are matters for the legislative judgment upon the exercise of which the Constitution places no restriction and over which the courts are given no control."[17] The Court thus refused to review Congress's purpose in regulating commerce. The Court began to abandon the categories that it had erected in an effort to keep the state and federal spheres separate. The Court stopped deploying formal distinctions to fight against the concurrent exercise of state and federal power. Only the prohibitions contained in the Constitution, such as the Fifth Amendment, limited the federal commerce authority. As the Court explained in *Darby*, "[R]egulations of commerce which do not infringe some constitutional prohibition are within the plenary power conferred on Congress by the Commerce Clause."[18] The designation of an activity as within the police power of the states no longer disabled national regulation.

Wickard continued to dismantle the categories of dual federalism. *Wickard* concerned the constitutionality of the federal Agricultural Adjustment Act (AAA). The AAA limited farm production as a way to raise prices. Farmer Filburn exceeded his allotment and was subject to a penalty under the act. Filburn challenged the scheme, claiming that he was growing wheat for home consumption, and that Congress lacked authority to regulate homegrown

---

[15] By 1936, President Roosevelt had not had the opportunity to appoint any Justices to the U.S. Supreme Court.

[16] For a description of Roosevelt's "court packing" plan, see William E. Leuchtenburg, THE SUPREME COURT REBORN (New York: Oxford, 1995).

[17] UNITED STATES V. DARBY, 312 U.S. 100, 115 (1941).

[18] 312 U.S. at 115.

wheat not destined for the market. In rejecting Filburn's claim, the Court repudiated both the substantive and institutional components of dual federalism.

In *Wickard*, the Court disclaimed its prior invocation of formal limits on federal authority. Justice Jackson wrote, "[E]ven if appellee's activity be local and though it may not be regarded as commerce, it may still, whatever its nature, be reached by Congress if it exerts a substantial economic effect on interstate commerce and this irrespective of whether such effect is what might at some earlier time have been defined as 'direct' or 'indirect.'"[19] No longer would the Court use the categories of direct and indirect effects of commerce to separate state and federal authority.

The Court also transformed the institutional conception of federalism and its implementation. The Court disavowed a robust judicial role in enforcing limits on congressional power. In the Court's analysis, the constitutionality of the AAA turned on whether growing wheat for home consumption did have a substantial effect on interstate commerce. However, Justice Jackson explained that Congress must be the institution to evaluate that effect. The Court did not offer its own assessment of whether the home production of wheat had a substantial effect on interstate commerce. Instead, it deferred to the congressional resolution of that question. The Court stated: "This record leaves us in no doubt that Congress *may properly have considered* that wheat consumed on the farm where grown if wholly outside the scheme of regulation would have a substantial effect in defeating and obstructing its purpose to stimulate trade therein at increased prices."[20] The question for judicial review was not whether the activity substantially affected interstate commerce but whether Congress could rationally so conclude. The *Wickard* court eschewed an independent judicial evaluation of the factual predicate for the challenged legislation. The supporting factual circumstances were to be presumed, and any congressional conclusions would be accorded great deference.

Wickard and *Darby* illustrated how the decline of dual federalism unleashed national power. The end of dual federalism had important implications, as well, for the flip side of dual federalism, the limitations on the power of states under the doctrines of the dormant Commerce Clause and federal preemption. Justice Stone made this connection explicit in arguing that the Court should not use the preemption doctrine to avoid concurrent state and federal regulation. In *Hines v. Davidowitz*[21] he asserted that only

---

[19] WICKARD V. FILBURN, 317 U.S. 111, 125 (1942).
[20] Ibid., 128–9 (emphasis added).
[21] 312 U.S. 52 (1941).

clear congressional purpose to invalidate state law should justify a finding of
preemption:

> At a time when the exercise of the federal power is being rapidly expanded
> through Congressional action, it is difficult to overstate the importance of
> safeguarding against such diminution of state power by vague inferences as to
> what Congress might have intended if it had considered the matter or by
> reference to our own conceptions of a policy which Congress has not
> expressed and which is not plainly to be inferred from the legislation which
> it has enacted.[22]

These sentiments were uttered in dissent. The majority, however, adopted this
view in *Rice v. Santa Fe Elevator Corp.*,[23] which has become the classic
statement of the Court's reluctance to imply preemption. Speaking for the
Court, Justice Douglas wrote, "[W]e start with the assumption that the historic police powers of the States were not to be superseded by the Federal Act
unless that was the clear and manifest purpose of Congress."[24] Unlike the pre–
New Deal era, the touchstone was congressional intent. The Court did not
presume that federal intervention in an area automatically disempowered the
states. Concurrent state and federal regulation had become an accepted part
of the modern administrative state. Preemption doctrine no longer embodied
a default presumption against such overlap. The dormant Commerce Clause
doctrine followed a similar trajectory. The Court only struck down state laws
that discriminated against interstate commerce or unduly burdened interstate
commerce. Mere state regulation of interstate commerce no longer led to
invalidation.

The end of dual federalism thus had vital importance for the understanding
of the overall relationship of the states and the federal government. Federalism no longer meant the separation of state and federal spheres of authority.
Concurrent state and federal regulation became accepted. Further, the courts
no longer played a central role in managing the relationship of the states and
the federal government. The courts became much less active in patrolling the
bounds of federal power. Congress could reach any activity with a connection
to interstate commerce, and the Court generally deferred to Congress in
assessing that relationship. Similarly, given the background assumption of
concurrent regulation, the mere fact of federal legislation in a particular area
would not preempt state intervention. A holding of preemption depended on

---

[22] Ibid., 75 (Stone, J., dissenting); Gardbaum, "New Deal Constitutionalism," 537–8.
[23] 331 U.S. 218 (1947).
[24] Ibid., 230.

a congressional purpose to nullify state regulation in the area. A desire to preempt could not be inferred from the simple fact of concurrent regulation.

Since 1937, overlapping state and federal regulation has become the norm for many, if not most, subjects. Federal laws play important roles even in areas of traditional state primacy, such as family law,[25] education,[26] and crime.[27] Education represents the most salient example of the demise of dual federalism. The United States has a long tradition of local control of education. Yet education has become a national issue of surpassing political importance. The federal No Child Left Behind Act[28] (NCLB), which passed both houses of Congress with broad, bipartisan majorities,[29] instituted widespread federal regulation of local educational policies. NCLB requires states to establish proficiency goals for the performance of students. Yearly testing monitors the progress in achieving these benchmarks. Under the act, schools that fail to make adequate yearly progress toward the proficiency goals are subject to an escalating series of sanctions. For example, if schools fall below the standards for two consecutive years, students are allowed to choose a different school in the same district. After five years of failed performance, the school must surrender control to the state.[30] NCLB does not represent a federal takeover of education. State and local authorities retain the primary responsibility for running public schools. Under NCLB, public education in the United States involves the interaction of federal, state, and local governments.[31]

---

[25] Child Support Recovery Act of 1992, Pub. L. No. 102-521, 106 Stat. 3403 (codified as amended at 18 U.S.C. § 228 [1994]).

[26] No Child Left Behind Act, Pub. L. No. 107-10, 115 Stat. 1425 (2002) (codified in scattered sections of 20 U.S.C.).

[27] Michael A. Simons, "Prosecutorial Discretion and Prosecution Guidelines: A Case Study in Controlling Federalization," NEW YORK UNIVERSITY LAW REVIEW 75, no. 4 (2000): 893, 902–29; Sara Sun Beale, "Too Many and Yet Too Few: New Principles to Define the Proper Limits for Federal Criminal Jurisdiction," HASTINGS LAW JOURNAL 46, no. 4 (1995): 979, 993. ("The current increase in federal criminal jurisdiction is in fundamental tension with the values of decentralization promoted by federalism.")

[28] Pub. L. No. 107–10, 115 Stat. 1425 (2002) (codified at 20 U.S.C. §§ 6301–6578 [Supp. II 2002]).

[29] The vote on the final bill in the House of Representatives was 381–41. *See* Adam Clymer, "National Briefing: House Passes Education Bill," NEW YORK TIMES, December 14, 2001, A36. The vote in the Senate was 87-10. Diana Jean Schemo, "Senate Approves a Bill to Expand the Federal Role in Public Education," NEW YORK TIMES, December 19, 2001, A32.

[30] James E. Ryan, "The Perverse Incentives of the No Child Left Behind Act," NEW YORK UNIVERSITY LAW REVIEW 79, no. 3 (2004): 932, 942–3.

[31] James S. Liebman and Charles F. Sabel, "The Federal No Child Left Behind Act and the Post-Desegregation Civil Rights Agenda," NORTH CAROLINA LAW REVIEW 81, no. 4 (2003): 1703, 1723; James S. Liebman and Charles F. Sabel, "A Public Laboratory Dewey Barely Imagined: The Emerging Model of School Governance and Legal Reform," N.Y.U. REVIEW OF LAW AND SOCIAL CHANGE 28, no. 2 (2003): 183, 283–300.

By the same token, states have taken the lead in domains often associated with national regulation, including climate change, securities regulation, and the human rights aspects of trade policy. When he was New York's Attorney General, Eliot Spitzer took an active role in prosecuting types of corporate misconduct usually targeted by federal regulators.[32] His successor, Andrew Cuomo, followed a similar path. Cuomo pursued an aggressive program of investigating potential abuses in student loans, which are subject to a variety of federal regulations. Climate change and the regulation of low-emission vehicles have demonstrated a similar, productive interaction of state and federal rules.[33]

POLYPHONIC FEDERALISM

The decline of dual federalism created the need for a new conception of the relationship of the states and the federal government. "Polyphonic federalism" provides a useful framework for understanding the contemporary federal-state dynamic. From the polyphonic perspective, federalism consists of independent state and federal voices that interact together. Federalism does not require separating the world into areas of exclusive state and exclusive federal control. Rather, the key task of federalism is to manage the overlap of state and federal law.

I believe that the aural metaphor of polyphony is useful for several reasons. Spatial metaphors imply that state and federal regulatory domains must remain separate and distinct for federalism to function properly. Political scientists have debated whether a "layer cake" or a "marble cake" best reflects federalism. However, either of these spatial/gastronomic metaphors envisions state and federal regulation as inhabiting separate regions. It is difficult to imagine two things occupying the same space without combining into a new undifferentiated whole. The choice is layer cake, marble cake, or stew. The aural metaphor of polyphony presents an alternative in which state power and federal power exist in the same space but remain distinct voices of authority. Aurality allows concurrence and independence. In addition, polyphony emphasizes more than simple overlap. It is the interaction of the different voices that creates polyphony. Similarly, the interaction of state and federal

---

[32] Trevor Morrison's chapter in this volume (Chapter 4) discusses Spitzer's initiatives. Other sources include Robert B. Ahdieh, "Dialectical Regulation," CONNECTICUT LAW REVIEW 38, no. 5 (2006): 872–5; Judith Burns, "Mutual Funds under Fire," WALL STREET JOURNAL, September 10, 2003, C14; Jonathan Mathiesen, "Dr. Spitzlove or: How I Learned to Stop Worrying and Love 'Balkanization'," COLUMBIA BUSINESS REVIEW, no. 2 (2006): 311.

[33] Kirsten H. Engel, "Harnessing the Benefits of Dynamic Federalism in Environmental Law," EMORY LAW JOURNAL 56, no. 1 (2006): 159.

regulations allows federalism to realize its full potential. Concurrent state and federal jurisdiction can result not just in two sets of regulations but also in a regulatory regime superior to what could be achieved by the independent activity of either regulator. I will discuss examples in the following text, and later chapters detail more.

VALUES OF POLYPHONY

By promoting the interaction of state and federal law, the polyphonic approach produces a system of governance that is more innovative and resilient than the compartmentalized system of dual federalism.[34] In specific, polyphonic federalism advances the valuable characteristics of plurality, dialogue, and redundancy.[35] This list of values differs from the standard dualist account because the point is not to enumerate the potential benefits of dividing state and federal authority. Instead, polyphonic federalism seeks to harness the gains that flow from the overlapping exercise of power.

The plurality of federal and multiple state regulatory regimes produces a variety of different responses to a perceived threat, encouraging policy experimentation. People in different states can experiment with different legal solutions to common problems. Various possible formulas exist for addressing particular concerns. Federalism allows different states to try out different possibilities. The states and the federal government can operate as "laboratories,"[36] experimenting with divergent regulatory regimes. In some instances, the appropriate regulations may differ from region to region. No single best solution will dominate. In other areas, the states and the national government will converge on a single, preferred outcome.

Dialogue magnifies the value of plurality. Not only can each government try different responses to common problems, but also the different regulators can learn from each other. In their account of democratic experimentalism, Michael Dorf and Charles Sabel have emphasized the importance of bottom-up problem solving.[37] Regulators can learn from the best practices of other regulatory regimes. Kirsten Engel's theory of "dynamic federalism" conceives of a similar ongoing, dialectical process.[38] The interaction of state and federal

---

[34] The chapter in this book by David E. Adelman and Kirsten H. Engel (Chapter 13) discusses the advantage of federal-state interaction with specific attention to environmental regulation.

[35] Robert A. Schapiro, "Toward a Theory of Interactive Federalism," Iowa Law Review 91, no. 1 (2005): 243, 288–90.

[36] See New State Ice Co. v. Liebmann, 285 U.S. 262, 311 (1932) (Brandeis, J., dissenting).

[37] See Michael C. Dorf and Charles F. Sabel, "A Constitution of Democratic Experimentalism," Columbia Law Review 98, no. 2 (1998): 267.

[38] Engel, "Harnassing the Benefits of Dynamic Federalism."

regulators may produce a regulatory scheme superior to what either government would produce independently. Engel has demonstrated how the development of national low-emission vehicle standards built on such a productive
dialogue. The resulting regulatory scheme represented an advance on what
state or federal regulators had conceived.[39] Dialogue facilitates regulatory
innovation. The optimal regulatory regime develops and changes over time,
with constant interaction from a variety of forces, including information generated by other regulators.

Regulatory overlap facilitates redundancy as well. If one set of regulators
fails to address the problem, another set provides an alternative avenue for
relief. The failure of one government does not foreclose all possibility of
assistance. The different institutional positions of state and federal regulators
make redundancy especially powerful. Information and interest group dynamics may function differently at the state than at the national level. Each regulator may enjoy different strengths and weaknesses.[40] Federalism means that if
one channel of relief is blocked, citizens may pursue a different path. In this
way, the redundancy of polyphonic federalism responds to the complexity and
fallibility of regulatory regimes. It may be that in a specific context either the
federal government or a state government is ideally suited to address an issue.
However, in the second-best world of practical reality, other interest groups or
inertial forces may impede this optimal regulatory regime. Redundancy provides a second-best solution for dealing with problems.

PITFALLS OF POLYPHONY

Regulatory overlap has potential pitfalls. Concurrent regulation may undermine important principles of uniformity, finality, and accountability.[41] Sometimes great inefficiencies may result if diverse, potentially contradictory
regulations apply to a particular item. It may be prohibitively expensive for
the manufacturer of a hair dryer to comply with divergent warning requirements in every state. Even if the regulations are not actually incompatible,

---

[39] Ibid., 168–9.
[40] See Robert M. Cover, "The Uses of Jurisdictional Redundancy: Interest, Ideology, and Innovation," WILLIAM AND MARY LAW REVIEW 22, no. 4 (1981): 639, 656–7 (discussing the values of
redundancy); Robert M. Cover and Alexander Aleinikoff, "Dialectical Federalism: Habeas
Corpus and the Court," YALE LAW JOURNAL 86, no. 6 (1977) 1035, 1042–6 (discussing federalism as providing a redundant system for protecting rights); Martin Landau, "Federalism,
Redundancy and System Reliability," PUBLIUS 3, no. 2 (1973): 173, 188–9 (emphasizing role of
federalism in providing redundancy).
[41] Schapiro, "Toward a Theory of Interactive Federalism," 290–2.

the existence of multiple regulatory regimes imposes costs on firms who must ascertain and satisfy the rules of all the relevant polities. The existence of overlapping regulatory regimes also diminishes the certainty and finality of any particular regulatory outcome. Even within a particular state, a firm may be subject to state and federal restrictions. Clarifying and resolving any potential violation of one set of rules will not necessarily end compliance problems. Making peace with state regulators may not satisfy federal officials.

Accountability also may suffer in a polyphonic system. In limiting the authority of the national government, the U.S. Supreme Court has often emphasized the danger of blurring lines of responsibility. The Court hypothesizes that either federal commandeering of state government[42] or federal regulation of traditional state domains[43] undermines political accountability. Dissatisfied citizens might be confused about which level of government to blame. To the extent these accountability concerns are valid,[44] concurrent state and federal regulation might well pose the same kind of harm that the Court has recently sought to avoid in its Commerce Clause and anti-commandeering cases.

A federal system presents a different kind of concern that also could be understood as a threat to accountability. State regulation of interstate business may have differential effects in different states. A state's laws might impose burdens on out-of-state firms, while benefiting in-state consumers. Product safety rules, for example, might protect consumers in one state, while imposing costs on manufacturing processes that take place in other states. Depending on the structure of the market, firms might not be able to customize their price structure so as to force a state to internalize the costs of regulation.[45]

---

[42] New York v. United States, 505 U.S. 144, 168 (1992). ("[W]here the Federal Government compels States to regulate, the accountability of both state and federal officials is diminished.")

[43] United States v. Lopez, 514 U.S. 549, 576 (1995) (Kennedy, J., concurring) ("The theory that two governments accord more liberty than one requires for its realization two distinct and discernable lines of political accountability. . . ."); United States v. Morrison, 529 U.S. 598, 611 (2000) ("Were the Federal Government to take over the regulation of entire areas of traditional state concern, areas having nothing to do with the regulation of commercial activities, the boundaries between the spheres of federal and state authority would blur . . . " [quoting Lopez, 514 U.S. at 577 (Kennedy, J., concurring)]).

[44] Dean Edward Rubin has offered a powerful critique of this accountability argument. Edward Rubin, "The Myth of Accountability and the Anti-Administrative Impulse," Michigan Law Review 103, no. 8 (2005): 2073, 2083–91.

[45] Samuel Issacharoff and Catherine Sharkey, "Backdoor Federalization," UCLA Law Review 53, no. 6 (2006): 1353, 1386–9.

The project of federalism is to maximize the benefits, while minimizing the potential disadvantages of polyphony. Once federalism is understood in this way, an important institutional implication follows. The management of dynamic overlap is a task best performed by branches of government other than the courts. Legislators and administrators can make an assessment of the best interaction and negotiate toward the best resolution. Courts are good at drawing lines, at invoking categorical distinctions. However, as cases such as *Wickard* recognized, courts have much less ability to make fine-grained analyses of economic realities. As federalism analysis becomes more pragmatic and functional, the role for courts diminishes.

In sum, guided by the polyphonic approach, regulators should continue to embrace the productive possibilities of regulatory overlap. Concurrent regulation is not always desirable. Concerns for uniformity, finality, and accountability may require a unitary legal regime in some instances. However, regulators should be certain that these values outweigh the advantages of plurality, dialogue, and redundancy in particular situations. With an understanding of the value of concurrent regulation, courts should be hesitant to infer a purpose to preempt overlapping state regulation. Congress and administrative agencies have a greater capacity to weigh the benefits and harms of overlap. Moreover, courts certainly should not assume that regulators prefer a unitary federal regime. Courts must recognize and honor the regulatory embrace of interactive state and federal laws.

RETURN OF DUALISM

Recently, however, the U.S. Supreme Court has begun to veer back toward a dual federalist mind-set. In several areas, the Court has returned to the dual federalist project of constructing enclaves of exclusive federal and exclusive state control and then enlisting the judiciary in actively protecting the boundaries of the state and federal domains. This section outlines the return to dualism and employs the polyphonic perspective to highlight the flaws in this return to dualism and to suggest a better approach to preemption.

Since 1992, the Court has reached back into the past to impose restrictions on the federal government in three areas in particular. First, for the first time since 1937, the Court held that Congress had exceeded its authority under the Commerce Clause.[46] Second, overruling a recent decision, the Court held that the states enjoy a constitutional immunity from damages actions by

[46] United States v. Lopez, 514 U.S. 549 (1995).

private individuals, and that Congress cannot displace this immunity by stat-ute.[47] Third, in tension with another earlier case, the Court held that Con-gress cannot "commandeer" the legislative or administrative functions of state and local governments.[48]

In limiting the scope of federal power, the Court has sought to revive prior dualist classifications. In its cases interpreting the Interstate Commerce Clause, for instance, the Court has attempted to distinguish the "truly local" from the "truly national."[49] By invoking these categories, the Court seeks to reconstruct enclaves of exclusive state jurisdiction and exclu-sive federal jurisdiction. Unlike the true dual federalism of the pre-1937 period, the Court acknowledges broad areas of overlap. However, certain regions must remain free from intermingled state and federal regulation. In a further reversal of its post-1937 trajectory, the Court also contemplates a robust judicial role in constructing the boundaries of these exclusive domains. For the current Court, federalism has become once again a project of judicial line-drawing. The Court has abandoned the New Deal skepticism about (1) whether the truly local and the truly national remain meaningful categories and (2) whether, even if the truly local and the truly national retain some meaning, the courts are the institutions best suited to define the boundaries of the local and the national. In this project, the current Court rejects the lessons of the New Deal and the realities of contemporary society.

Dual federalism limited both state and federal power. Similarly, the Court's return to dualism has led it to strike down state and federal regulation. The Court's failure to accept the pervasiveness of concurrent state and federal regulation has led it to invalidate state action through an aggressive use of the dormant Commerce Clause and federal preemption. The Court has developed a broad understanding of the kind of state regulatory authority

---

[47] SEMINOLE TRIBE V. FLORIDA, 517 U.S. 44 (1996) (overruling PENNSYLVANIA V. UNION GAS Co., 491 U.S. 1 [1989]).

[48] NEW YORK V. UNITED STATES, 505 U.S. 144 (1992). The NEW YORK case is in tension with the GARCIA case, which appeared to contemplate a very limited role for the courts in enforcing federalism-based limitations on federal power. GARCIA V. SAN ANTONIO METRO. TRANSIT AUTH., 469 U.S. 528, 556 (1985). ("[T]he principal and basic limit on the federal . . . power is that inherent in all congressional action – the built-in restraints that our system provides through state participation in federal government action. The political process ensures that laws that unduly burden the States will not be promulgated.")

[49] UNITED STATES V. MORRISON, 529 U.S. 598, 617–18 (2000) ("The Constitution requires a distinction between what is truly national and what is truly local."); UNITED STATES V. LOPEZ, 514 U.S. 549, 567–8 (1995).

prohibited by the dormant Commerce Clause.[50] The Court's doctrine has occasioned widespread criticism. Both commentators[51] and justices[52] decry it as unprincipled and without foundation. As Jim Chen has noted, the term *quagmire* has become a commonplace in characterizing dormant Commerce Clause doctrine.[53] Maxwell Stearns recently captured the distinction of the dormant Commerce Clause as a much-maligned doctrine with a broad application:

> Despite these general criticisms of the doctrine, in the name of the dormant Commerce Clause, the Court has significantly limited the power of states to regulate across a wide range of subject areas, including train and truck safety, imports and exports of myriad goods and services, the conditions for the intake and outflow of solid and liquid waste, and insurance and corporate law.[54]

As in the pre-1937 period, dualism entails a broad dormant Commerce Clause, which diminishes the scope of state regulatory authority.

Although the Court seems to be in the midst of a struggle over preemption, current federal preemption doctrine at times manifests a similarly dualist spirit. The Court's growing commitment to creating a sphere of exclusive federal jurisdiction corresponds to a broad construction of the preemptive

---

[50] WEST LYNN CREAMERY, INC. V. HEALY, 512 U.S. 186 (1994) (holding state subsidy scheme unconstitutional); Richard H. Fallon Jr., "The 'Conservative' Paths of the Rehnquist Court's Federalism Decisions," UNIVERSITY OF CHICAGO LAW REVIEW 69, no. 2 (2002): 429, 460–1 (discussing the dormant Commerce Clause doctrine of the Rehnquist Court); Ernest A. Young, "Is the Sky Falling on the Federal Government? State Sovereign Immunity, the Section Five Power, and the Federal Balance," TEXAS LAW REVIEW 81, no. 6 (2003): 1551, 1591. ("Dormant Commerce Clause review has the effect of foreclosing or undermining a wide range of important state policies, such as responsible attempts at waste disposal, state safety regulation, and efforts to encourage important state industries" [footnotes omitted]).

[51] Julian N. Eule, "Laying the Dormant Commerce Clause to Rest," YALE LAW JOURNAL 91, no. 3 (1982): 425; Martin H. Redish and Shane V. Nugent, "The Dormant Commerce Clause and the Constitutional Balance of Federalism," DUKE LAW JOURNAL no. 4 (1987): 569.

[52] NEWFOUND/OWATONNA, INC. V. TOWN OF HARRISON, 520 U.S. 564, 595 (1997) (Scalia, J., dissenting, joined by Rehnquist, C. J., and Thomas and Ginsburg, J. J.) ("The Court's negative Commerce Clause jurisprudence has drifted far from its moorings."); ibid., 610 (Thomas, J., dissenting) (characterizing the Court's dormant Commerce Clause jurisprudence as "overbroad and unnecessary").

[53] See Jim Chen, "A Vision Softly Creeping: Congressional Acquiescence and the Dormant Commerce Clause," MINNESOTA LAW REVIEW 88, no. 6 (2004): 1764, 1792.

[54] See Maxwell L. Stearns, "A Beautiful Mend: A Game Theoretical Analysis of the Dormant Commerce Clause Doctrine," WILLIAM AND MARY LAW REVIEW 45, no. 1 (2003): 1, 10–11 (footnotes omitted).

reach of federal regulation. Cases such as *Geier v. American Honda Motor Company*[55] illustrate this approach. *Geier* concerned the ability of a state-law tort system to hold a manufacturer liable for an allegedly unsafe automobile. The specific question presented in *Geier* was whether federal automobile regulations preempted a state-law tort action that sought to impose liability based on the manufacturer's failure to equip an automobile with an air bag.[56] The federal statute at issue contained both an express preemption provision and a savings clause, which stated that "'compliance with a federal safety standard' does not exempt any person from any liability under common law."[57]

The Court held that neither the express preemption provision nor the savings clause applied. Falling back on "ordinary pre-emption principles," the Court concluded that the state tort suit was preempted because it "stood as an obstacle" to the accomplishment of a federal objective.[58] The Court showed no particular concern for accommodating the overlap of state and federal interest or power. *Geier* is just one of several recent decisions in which the Court has insisted on a wide sweep of federal preemptive authority.[59] As Caleb Nelson has demonstrated, the Court has developed a broad concept of conflict preemption under a theory of "obstacle preemption."[60] Under the

---

[55] 529 U.S. 861 (2000).
[56] Ibid., 864–5.
[57] Ibid., 868 (quoting 15 U.S.C. §1397(k)).
[58] Ibid., 881–2.
[59] Compare CIPOLLONE V. LIGGETT GROUP, INC., 505 U.S. 504, 517 (1992) (suggesting that implied preemption would not be found in statutes containing express preemption provisions), with FREIGHTLINER CORP. V. MYRICK, 514 U.S. 280, 288 (1995) (noting that an express preemption provision did not foreclose the finding of implied preemption), and GEIER, 529 U.S. at 869 (same). Other cases broadly construing preemption include RIEGEL V. MEDTRONIC, INC., 128 S. Ct. 999 (2008) (holding state tort suit preempted by federal regulation of medical devices); AM. INS. ASS'N V. GARAMENDI, 539 U.S. 396 (2003) (holding California statute requiring disclosure of information about Holocaust-era insurance policies preempted by foreign policy of the United States); LORILLARD TOBACCO CO. V. REILLY, 533 U.S. 525 (2001) (holding state statute regulating advertising of tobacco products preempted by federal law); CROSBY V. NAT'L FOREIGN TRADE COUNCIL, 530 U.S. 363 (2000) (holding state law restricting state transactions with companies doing business with Burma preempted by foreign policy of the United States); U.S. V. LOCKE, 529 U.S. 89 (2000) (holding state regulation of oil spills preempted by federal statute); GADE V. NAT'L SOLID WASTE MGMT. ASS'N, 505 U.S. 88 (1992) (holding state law regulating workers at hazardous waste sites preempted by federal law); Alison Cassady, TYING THE HANDS OF STATES: THE IMPACT OF FEDERAL PREEMPTION ON STATE PROBLEM-SOLVERS (National Association of State PIRGS, July 2004), 2 (asserting that "federal preemption has often tied the hands of state legislators and regulators eager to solve problems facing their constituents").
[60] Caleb Nelson, "Preemption," VIRGINIA LAW REVIEW 86, no. 2 (2000): 225, 228–9; Erwin Chemerinsky, CONSTITUTIONAL LAW: PRINCIPLES AND POLICIES § 5.2 (New York: Aspen, 3rd ed. 2006), 412–16 (discussing preemption of state laws that impede federal objectives).

obstacle preemption doctrine, a state law will be preempted if a court concludes that the state law will hinder the accomplishment of the purposes underlying the federal law. The Court has deployed this doctrine to strike down state regulations that it finds in tension with a federal statute, without regard to whether the state law actually conflicts with some textual provision of the federal enactment.[61] As evidenced by *Geier*, this approach narrows the scope of state authority in areas of concurrent state and federal regulation. The Court's broad invocation of obstacle preemption reflects its dualist outlook. When the federal government regulates in a particular area, the Court often presumes an exclusivist intent. The Court assumes that Congress would not contemplate concurrent regulatory efforts by the states. In some instances the Court accepts overlapping federal and state regulatory regimes. The *Bates* case provides a prominent recent example of this occasional acceptance of concurrent state and federal systems.[62] In *Bates*, the Court held that the federal regulation of pesticides did not preempt certain state-law tort claims. Despite cases like *Bates*, the trend toward greater preemption is disturbing.

Another example of the Court's dualist approach to preemption is *American Insurance Ass'n v. Garamendi*.[63] This case concerned efforts to assist beneficiaries in obtaining the proceeds of Holocaust-era policies sold to Jews in Europe. Insurance policies were common investment devices for Jews in the period before World War II. The value of such insurance policies owned by Jewish families has been estimated at figures ranging from \$17 billion to \$200 billion in today's currency.[64] The insurance companies erected onerous standards after World War II, making it difficult for beneficiaries to collect the proceeds. Eventually, the United States and Germany entered into an executive agreement to set up a claim resolution procedure. California sought to supplement this process by forcing insurance companies doing business in California to release more information about their Holocaust-era policies.

The insurance companies challenged the California statute, and in *Garamendi*, the U.S. Supreme Court invalidated the state law, holding it preempted. Normally, preemption cases involve finding a federal law that conflicts with state law. In this case, no such federal law existed. The executive agreement had the force of law, but it did not contain a provision preempting state remedies. Nevertheless, by a 5-4 vote, the Court held that the California law

---

[61] See BUCKMAN CO. V. PLAINTIFF'S LEGAL COMM., 531 U.S. 341 (2001); Daniel J. Meltzer, "The Supreme Court's Judicial Passivity," SUPREME COURT REVIEW (2002): 343, 366 (discussing BUCKMAN).

[62] 544 U.S. 531 (2005).

[63] 539 U.S. 396 (2003).

[64] See Michael J. Bazyler, HOLOCAUST JUSTICE: THE BATTLE FOR RESTITUTION IN AMERICA'S COURTS (New York: New York University Press, 2003), 110–11.

was invalid because it interfered with the national government's control of foreign relations.[65] Like *Geier*, *Garamendi* exemplifies the dualist approach to preemption. The California law did not conflict with the process established by the executive agreement. Nevertheless, the Court struck it down. The Court was determined to draw lines between state and federal domains, and the majority found that the insurance policy issue lay in an area committed exclusively to the federal government.

In cases such as *Geier* and *Garamendi*, the Court understands a choice of one regulatory path to be an implicit rejection of all others. This conception recapitulates the dualist project of separating state from federal spheres. If the Court instead assumed that Congress contemplated concurrent state efforts, then the preemption analysis would be quite different. The presumption of concurrence would decrease implied preemption of state laws that stand as an "obstacle" to the achievement of federal purposes. The polyphonic perspective emphasizes that obstacle preemption might actually undermine the statutory purpose. Eliminating complementary state schemes might contradict the regulatory goal of advancing health, safety, or other aims. Federal regulators may welcome and expect concurrent state efforts. A judicial presumption of federal exclusivity frustrates these assumptions. Given the pervasiveness of overlapping state and federal regulation, it is unreasonable for courts to assume a desire for preemptive federal regulation, in the absence of a clear expression of preemptive intent.

In the polyphonic conception, courts should apply a background presumption that state power and federal power can coexist.[66] In the absence of evidence to the contrary, courts should not strike down state laws because they operate in the same field as federal law. This presumption would apply in both the preemption and the dormant Commerce Clause settings. Both involve situations in which the courts must decide whether to permit state regulation in an area in which Congress could, but has not, clearly excluded the states. Courts should not be in the business of eliminating state regulatory plans in the name of creating uniform federal regulatory policy. The existence of multiple overlapping regimes of regulation represents one of the important consequences of federalism. Such concurrence promotes plurality, dialogue, and redundancy, values the legislature embraced in regulatory regimes preserving overlapping state and federal roles. The presumption of concurrence also would limit the scope of the Court's doctrine voiding nondiscriminatory state laws that impose an undue burden on commerce. The Court currently

---

[65] See GARAMENDI, 539 U.S. at 401.

[66] GEIER V. AM. HONDA MOTOR CO., 529 U.S. 861, 907 (2000) (Stevens, J., dissenting). ("Our presumption against pre-emption is rooted in the concept of federalism.")

applies a balancing test to such laws,[67] and the presumption in favor of concurrent regulation would serve as a factor weighing against invalidation. Such a presumption could be overcome by contrary evidence of an unusual need for uniformity.

The presumption of concurrence would leave large areas of preemption and dormant Commerce Clause doctrine unchanged. Congress could expressly preempt state law. States still could not discriminate against commerce from other states.[68] In the absence of congressional guidance, though, the presumption would lead the courts toward a greater acceptance of concurrent state regulation. The values of polyphonic federalism, then, correspond to deferential review when Congress clearly has decided to regulate an area. In conditions of less certainty, such as preemption and the dormant Commerce Clause, the courts would be more accommodating of state action.

CONCLUSION

Polyphonic federalism acknowledges the overlap of state and federal regulation. Rather than attempting to recreate a world of separate state and federal enclaves, the polyphonic perspective encourages policy makers and courts to realize the benefits that flow from concurrent regulation. The most common task facing regulators is not how to divide state and federal spheres of control but is how to manage the interaction of state and federal power so as to advance policy ends. The polyphonic perspective seeks to promote the benefits of concurrent regulation, while acknowledging the potential harms.

Recently, however, the Supreme Court has hearkened back to dual federalism. Its decisions limiting federal power and state power invoke the discarded assumptions of the dual federalist era. The Court cannot reverse the tide of concurrent regulation. However, the Court's decisions can impede the efforts of the federal government and the states to address important problems. The Court's preemption doctrine has had this unfortunate impact, as its decisions have interfered with the ability of states to promote health and safety. The Court's decisions do not reflect a necessary consequence of federalism. Rather, the Court's rulings reflect a discarded vision of federal-state relations. The acceptance of the polyphonic framework would allow the Court to focus on the important issues of federal-state interaction, rather than fighting a quixotic, rearguard action.

[67] PIKE v. BRUCE CHURCH, INC., 397 U.S. 137, 142 (1970); Laurence H. Tribe, AMERICAN CONSTITUTIONAL LAW, vol. 1, § 6–13 (New York: West, 3rd ed. 2000), 1100–2.
[68] Tribe, AMERICAN CONSTITUTIONAL LAW, § 6–6, 1059–68.

As discussed in the following chapters, the past seventy years have witnessed the benefits of interactive federal and state efforts. Polyphony has become the norm. It would be a grave mistake for courts to try to turn back the clock to dualism. Polyphonic federalism may present complex issues of design, but dual federalism imposes outmoded, simplistic understandings of federal-state relations.

3 Preemption and Regulatory Failure Risks

David C. Vladeck

INTRODUCTION

When the *Titanic* sailed on its maiden and final voyage on April 10, 1912, it carried 2,227 passengers and crew. Shortly after midnight on April 15, 1912, the *Titanic* hit an iceberg and sank in the frigid waters of the North Atlantic; 1,523 perished. The *Titanic* carried sixteen lifeboats with a capacity of 980 people – nearly 1,250 fewer spaces than needed. But the *Titanic* was in full compliance with then-current maritime safety regulations, which were set by the British Board of Trade. The Board of Trade's standard had been established in 1884. At that time, the largest vessel afloat was one-quarter of the size of the *Titanic*. The new generation of superliner – the *Titanic*, *Mauritania*, and *Lusitania* – carried far more passengers and crew than their predecessors. The Board of Trade knew this; it convened an advisory committee in 1911 to consider upgrading the lifeboat standard but took no action. A year later, tragedy stuck.[1]

Now fast-forward to March 2005. Joshua Oukrop, a college student, was on a spring-break trip to Moab, Utah, with his girlfriend. They went for a bike ride, but Joshua soon complained of fatigue, fell to the ground, and died of cardiac arrest. Why? Joshua had a common genetic disorder that causes erratic heartbeats that, if untreated, can trigger sudden cardiac arrest. But Joshua was able to lead a normal life because his doctors implanted a small, pocket-watch-sized, defibrillator into his chest. The defibrillator – a Guidant Prizm 2 – was programmed to deliver an electrical impulse to Joshua's heart when it went into arrest and jolt his heart back into a normal rhythm. But on that day in March, instead of delivering a life-saving charge to his heart, his

---

[1]   John P. Eaton and Charles A. Haas, Titanic: Destination Disaster The Legends and the Reality (New York: W.W. Norton, 1987), 113, 148; John Dudman, Great Disasters: The Sinking of the Titanic (New York: Bookwork Press 1988), 12–13, 20.

Often a page of history speaks volumes. The tragic deaths of Joshua Oukrop and the more than 1,500 that perished on the star-crossed *Titanic* offer a cautionary tale of the hazards of relying on regulatory standards alone to define an appropriate level of public safety. In both cases, regulatory bodies established and enforced standards designed to avoid the precise harm that befell Joshua and the *Titanic's* passengers. But in both cases, regulatory standards were not enough. There are sound reasons why regulatory and tort systems have historically operated together to place separate but reinforcing disciplines on the market. When functioning optimally, a regulatory system prevents harm, rewards innovation, and ensures that products on the market have a favorable risk-reward profile.

But all too often there are gaps that regulatory agencies cannot fill. In a perfect world, a regulatory agency would never lack the information, personnel, statutory power, technical expertise, or other resources needed to deal with emerging hazards. In the real world, however, agencies are often confronted with information gaps, bureaucratic inertia, intransigent companies, resource constraints, political interference, and other handicaps that limit the capacity of the agency to act in the public interest. Historically, tort litigation helped fill those gaps by forcing the disclosure of safety information that might otherwise be unavailable to regulatory agencies, deterring excessive risk taking, and providing compensation to those injured. But the safety net of tort litigation is under assault by aggressive, and often successful, assertions of federal preemption. That battle has been fought over Guidant's defibrillators. The company claimed blanket immunity from tort liability for its faulty defibrillators because, it asserted, all claims against it are preempted by federal law.

This chapter explores the intersection between the risk of regulatory failure and the tort system. It demonstrates the hazards of removing the tort system as a backstop to regulation. Cases involving medical devices, pharmaceuticals, and automobiles are used to illustrate these concerns. In each case, a preemption ruling would not only deprive the injured party of any compensation, but it would also seriously compromise the public health objectives that are embodied in the federal statute at issue, thereby diminishing the protection available to all Americans.

Before turning to the illustrations, it is useful to pause briefly to ask what causes regulatory failure. Why is tort law an important backstop to regulation? After all, federal agencies now regulate most of the products Americans use in their daily lives. Isn't that enough? The answer is "no." Students of regulation have identified three overarching structural limitations in the regulatory system that often lead to systemic regulatory failure. One problem is that agencies are often "captured" by the businesses they regulate. It is easy to see how this happens. Agency officials work closely with their counterparts in industry. They are all members of a small and discrete group of experts on a subject, so there is a natural interaction among them. Industry representatives also rotate in and out of the government through a "revolving door" that leads directly to the boardrooms and law offices of regulated industry. Over time, close relationships emerge, and the agency begins to see itself as much as an industry helpmate as a cop on the beat.[5]

This problem is especially acute in those agencies that regulate a single industry, like the National Highway Traffic Safety Administration (NHTSA), which regulates the automobile industry, or the Federal Railroad Administration (FRA), which regulates railroads. These agencies tend to form "partnerships" with the industries they regulate, which translates into decreased enforcement efforts and lenient regulation, often at the expense of public safety.[6]

A second recurring problem is that agencies are forced to depend on the industries they regulate for the information they need to regulate.[7] The asymmetry in information resources gives regulated industry an ability to manipulate the outcome of agency proceedings by withholding information, cherry-picking the information they provide to the agency, or manufacturing uncertainty by giving the agency incomplete, outdated, or inaccurate information. Generally, agencies have little ability to validate the information provided to them. Most agencies have limited information-gathering authority, most lack basic subpoena authority, and federal law circumscribes even the agencies' ability to secure information by surveying the industries they regulate.[8] There is little risk to companies that engage in game playing with agencies; sanctions are rarely if ever meted out to companies that fail to provide the agencies with complete and accurate information. But information drives the regulatory process, and, in this respect, it is industry, not the agency, that has the upper hand. That is not so in litigation. Court rules empower plaintiffs to engage in far-reaching discovery, permitting them to gain access to virtually any information that might be relevant to the plaintiff's claim. As a result, plaintiffs in litigation generally unearth information that was unavailable to the regulatory agency.[9]

---

[5] See, e.g., Stigler, "The Theory of Economic Regulation," BELL JOURNAL OF ECONOMICS AND MANAGEMENT SCIENCE 2, no. 3 (1981): 1–13; see generally, "Symposium on the Theory of Public Choice," VANDERBILT LAW REVIEW 74 (1988): 167.

[6] See, e.g., Perry Quirk, INDUSTRY INFLUENCE IN FEDERAL REGULATORY AGENCIES (Princeton, NJ: Princeton University Press, 1981).

[7] See Wendy Wagner, "When All Else Fails: Regulating Risky Products through Tort Litigation," GEORGETOWN UNIVERSITY LAW JOURNAL 95 (2007): 693.

[8] See Paperwork Reduction Act, 44 U.S.C. §§ 3501–3520.

[9] David C. Vladeck, "Defending Courts: A Brief Rejoinder to Professors Fried and Rosenberg," SETON HALL LAW REVIEW 31 (2001): 631.

The third and most pressing weakness of the regulatory process is chronic resource limitations. Agencies can only go as far as their resources will take them, but over the past decade or so, our regulatory agencies have suffered severe reductions in funding and in personnel while their regulatory responsibilities have increased.[10] NHTSA has fewer than seven hundred employees, yet it is responsible for regulating the automobile industry. The Occupational Safety and Health Administration (OSHA) is responsible for safeguarding our nation's workplaces, yet it has fewer than three thousand employees nationwide. And the FRA, which is charged with maintaining the safety of the 1.6 million rail cars operating over two hundred thousand miles of track, has fewer than four hundred inspectors.[11] These limitations have real-world consequences. With meager staffs, agency enforcement efforts are by necessity limited. Without adequate staffing, agencies cannot hope to promulgate needed regulations in a timely way, let alone keep regulations up-to-date. Many of the regulations on the books today are twenty or thirty years out-of-date, even though new technologies and other advances enable far more protective regulation. And agencies often take years, or even decades, to put new standards in place. Regulatory delay, or what experts call "ossification," led to the shortage of lifeboats on the *Titanic*. That problem remains a serious one today.

MEDICAL DEVICES AND JOSHUA OUKROP

Preemption cases involve more than dry and arcane questions of law. They almost invariably involve a story like Joshua Oukrop's – a tragic death or serious injury to someone caused by a product that failed them. The statute that is the centerpiece of litigation over Guidant's defibrillators – the Medical Device Amendment of 1976 (MDA) – was enacted in response to a series of highly publicized public health catastrophes caused by defective medical devices.[12] Most notorious was the Dalkon Shield. It was an intrauterine device introduced and widely marketed by the A. H. Robins Company without the

---

[10] See generally, Jerry Mashaw, "Reinventing Government and Regulatory Reform: Studies in the Neglect and Abuse of Administrative Law," UNIVERSITY OF PITTSBURGH LAW REVIEW 57 (1996): 405.

[11] McGarity, THE PREEMPTION WAR, 342–3.

[12] The term *medical device* includes an array of products, from cotton swabs to artificial heart valves. See MEDTRONIC, INC. v. LOHR, 518 U.S. 470, 476 (1996). Medical devices are categorized into three classes, based on the potential risk of harm posed. Class I devices, such as swabs, are subject only to general controls that provide a reasonable assurance of safety. Id. at 477. Class II devices, such as hearing aids, are subject to somewhat stricter controls, to ensure that they are both safe and effective for their intended use. Id. Class III devices are used to sustain human life or pose a serious risk to patients. Id. at 477–8.

FDA's prior approval. At the time, the FDA had limited authority over medical devices. In designing the device, Robins ignored its own experts, who urged that both ends of the device's "sheath" be sealed to prevent "wicking" of bacteria-laden fluids into the uterus. Robins touted the Dalkon Shield as a safe and effective alternative to birth control pills. Soon after it hit the market, however, women began contracting infections that caused death, infertility, or other serious injuries. Robins kept the device on the market for an additional year but finally stopped selling it in 1974. Robins refused to provide assistance to the 3.6 million women who still were using the Shield. More than two hundred thousand women sued Robins for their injuries; ultimately, the company, and then its successor, paid out nearly $3 billion in damages.[13]

To avoid a recurrence of this and similar tragedies, Congress enacted the MDA to create a comprehensive system of regulation of all medical devices. The MDA reserves the most rigorous regulation for what are called "Class III" devices – devices, such as defibrillators, pacemakers, and joint replacements, that sustain life or pose a serious risk to patients. As a general rule, before marketing a Class III device, a manufacturer must submit a premarket approval (PMA) application asking the FDA's permission to market the device for the specific uses identified in the application. There are two exceptions. First, any device manufactured prior to the passage of the MDA – a "grandfathered" device – is not subject to the PMA requirements. Second, a device manufactured after 1976 may bypass the PMA requirements if the manufacturer can show that it is "substantially equivalent" to a grandfathered device. Before granting a PMA, the FDA must find that there is a "reasonable assurance" that the device is safe and effective for its intended use.

There is an express preemption provision in the MDA. It provides that "no State . . . may establish or continue in effect with respect to a device intended for human use any requirement (1) which is different from, or in addition to, any requirement applicable under this chapter to the device, and (2) which relates to the safety or effectiveness of the device."[14] This language is important. Note that nothing in it says that Congress is acting to nullify existing state damages claims. There are federal statutes that do just that. But they do so in

---

[13] Morton Mintz, At Any Cost: Corporate Greed, Women, and the Dalkon Shield (New York: Pantheon Press, 1985); Richard B. Sobol, Bending the Law: The Story of the Dalkon Shield Bankruptcy (Chicago: University of Chicago Press, 1991).

[14] 21 U.S.C. § 360k(a).

unmistakable terms and generally provide a federal remedy in lieu of displaced state remedies.[15]

So the legal question in the Guidant case, and in every case involving medical devices, is what does the word *requirement* mean? There are two competing theories. First, the word *requirement* could be read to encompass only "positive" state law – that is, commands imposed by state statutes and regulations that carry the force of law. Under that interpretation, the MDA preemption provision would bar only state laws or regulations that imposed requirements different from, or in addition to, federal ones. State damages actions do not impose specific requirements, so they would not be preempted. The second theory is that the word *requirement* should be read more broadly to include state tort and damages law. A string of adverse jury awards might force a company to take action just as much as a state regulation directing it to do so, and that action might not be consistent with "requirements" imposed by the FDA.[16]

The Supreme Court had an opportunity to resolve that question in *Medtronic, Inc. v. Lohr*,[17] an action brought by a woman who nearly died when her pacemaker failed. Medtronic, the pacemaker's manufacturer, contended that the MDA entirely preempted her claims. But the Court rejected that argument. The pacemaker at issue in *Lohr* had not been specifically approved by the FDA; rather, it was allowed on the market because it was substantially similar to a class of pacemakers the FDA had previously approved. The Court said that the case would have been more difficult had the FDA specifically approved the pacemaker's design. But the Court did not reach that question.

---

[15] See, e.g., 42 U.S.C. §§ 2210 et seq. (Price-Anderson Act, which federalizes all claims for personal and property damage arising from significant accidents at civilian nuclear power plants); 42 U.S.C. §§ 300aa-1 et seq. (Vaccine Act, which federalizes all claims arising from personal injuries relating to the administration of vaccines); Air Transportation Safety and System Stabilization Act of 2001, Pub. L. No. 107-42, 115 Stat. 230 (2001) (9/11 Compensation Fund, which substitutes a federal remedy for tort claims 9/11 victims and their families could have asserted against the airlines whose planes were hijacked); 29 U.S.C. §§ 1001 et seq., (Employee Retirement Income Security Act of 1974, which federalizes disputes over employment related benefits).

[16] This argument is drawn from CIPOLLONE V. LIGGETT GROUP, INC., 505 U.S. 504, 548–9 (1992), which held that a preemption provision in the Public Health Cigarette Act of 1969, which preempted conflicting "requirement[s] or prohibition[s]," made no distinction between positive enactments and common law liability. Prior to CIPOLLONE, the Court had never held a federal statute or regulation preempted state law where doing so would leave the plaintiff without a remedy. More recently, the Court has signaled a shift back toward the pre-CIPOLLONE understanding. See, e.g., BATES V. DOW AGROSCIENCES, LLC, 544 U.S. 431 (2005) (holding that the word *requirement* in the federal pesticide statute does not reach common law tort claims).

[17] 518 U.S. 470 (1996).

The Court did divide, 5-4, on whether Ms. Lohr's defective manufacturing and failure-to-warn claims were preempted. The majority held that they were not. The dissenting justices, focusing on the word *requirement*, would have held that these claims were preempted because a jury award in Ms. Lohr's favor would impose "requirements" inconsistent with FDA regulations governing manufacturing practices and labeling requirements.

For years, lower federal and state courts were divided on whether the MDA preempts damage actions by individuals injured by devices specifically approved by the FDA. Typical of the decisions finding preemption is *Horn v. Thoratec Corp.*[18] Barbara Horn's husband Daniel suffered a heart attack, and his doctors determined that he needed a heart transplant. Although waiting for a donor heart, Daniel was placed on a device called the Heart-Mate, which "is a pump that assists the blood flow between the heart's ventricle and the aorta." Daniel began to bleed at the implant site. Doctors discovered that the device had become disconnected, causing an air embolus to travel to Daniel's brain, resulting in a fatal hemorrhage. Ms. Horn sued HeartMate's manufacturer, alleging that the HeartMate was defectively designed and manufactured, and that the company had failed to warn physicians and patients of the defect.

The court of appeals ruled 2-1 that Ms. Horn's claims were preempted. The majority found that FDA approval of HeartMate's PMA imposed "requirements" on the manufacturer, and that "Horn's general state law claims would impose substantive requirements on [the manufacturer] that would conflict with, or add to, the requirements imposed by the FDA involved in the design, manufacturing, fabrication and labeling of the HeartMate."[19] Other courts have reached similar conclusions and held that state law claims against manufacturers of devices subject to PMA approval by the FDA are preempted in their entirety.[20]

Many courts reached the opposite conclusion. To start with, these courts did not agree that obtaining a marketing license from the FDA – even through the rigorous PMA process – results in the imposition of federal requirements. After all, it is the manufacturer, not the FDA, who selects the design, manufacturing, fabrication, and labeling features that will satisfy the standards set forth in the MDA. The FDA's job is not to determine whether the device's design or performance is optimal or even whether the device is safer and more

---

[18] 376 F.3d 163 (3d Cir. 2004).

[19] Id. at 176.

[20] See, e.g., BROOKS V. HOWMEDICA, INC., 273 F.3d 785 (8th Cir. 2001); MARTIN V. MEDTRONIC, INC., 254 F.3d 575, 585 (5th Cir. 2001); MITCHELL V. COLLAGEN CORP., 126 F.3d 902, 922 (7th Cir. 1997).

effective than devices already on the market. So long as the statutory standards are met, the FDA must approve the device.

These courts also disagreed with the essential assumption made by the pro-preemption courts – namely, that a liability finding against the company "unquestionably would require" it to redesign its product.[21] That assumption confuses the imposition of a device-specific requirement that comes through positive state enactments (e.g., a wire must be two inches long) and the indirect effect of tort judgments.[22] An adverse jury ruling in *Horn* would not have *required* the device's manufacturer to do anything at all, other than to pay money damages. The manufacturer might decide to take measures to avoid a recurrence of the device's failure. But the manufacturer could also decide to do nothing, reasoning that the adverse ruling is simply an aberration or that the likelihood of recurrence is too remote to justify any change in the product's design, manufacturing, or labeling.

These courts also believed that removing the possibility of tort liability would undermine the public health values embodied in the MDA. As one court put it, under the companies' theory, "[o]nce a medical device manu-facturer obtains PMA approval; it would be insulated from liability even if it chose to conceal data from the FDA to maintain its approval."[23] The looming possibility of tort liability increases the likelihood that manufacturers will provide information to the FDA and the public in a timely fashion. As the Supreme Court has observed, tort law often informs regulatory decisions by "aid[ing] in the exposure of new dangers associated" with the product.[24]

The possibility of tort liability also strengthens the device manufacturers' incentive to comply with FDA requirements. As the Supreme Court recently said, tort litigation "emphasizes the importance of providing an incentive to manufacturers to use the utmost care in the business of distributing inherently dangerous items."[25] In the case of the Prizm 2, Guidant had an obligation to

---

[21] This was the conclusion of the majority in HORN, 376 F.3d at 176.

[22] Id. at 164 (Fuentes, dissenting).

[23] IN RE MEDTRONIC, INC., 465 F. Supp. 2d 886, 895 (D. Minn. 2006); see also IN RE GUIDANT CORP. IMPLANTABLE DEFIBRILLATORS PRODUCTS LIABILITY LITIGATION, 2007 U.S. Dist. LEXIS 42765, at [19] n.6 (D. Minn. June 12, 2007).

[24] BATES V. DOW AGROSCIENCES, LLC, 544 U.S. 431, 451 (2005). The Court added that state damages actions "may aid the exposure of new dangers associated" with the product and prompt the agency to "decide that revised labels are required in light of new information that has been brought to its attention." Id. at 451 (quoting FEREBEE V. CHEVRON CHEM. CO., 736 F.2d 1529, 1541–2 [D.C. Cir. 1984]); see also David A. Kessler and David C. Vladeck, "A Critical Examination of the FDA's Efforts to Preempt Failure-to-Warn Claims," GEORGE-TOWN LAW JOURNAL 96 (2008) 461, 491–5 (canvassing instances in which the FDA took regulatory action as a direct response to information revealed in state damages litigation).

[25] BATES V. DOW AGROSCIENCES, LLC, 544 U.S. 431, 450 (2005).

notify the FDA of the wiring defect in the device and to seek FDA approval before it modified the Prizm 2's design. But Guidant did not notify the FDA until the company filed its annual report nearly a year later, thereby preventing the FDA from warning physicians and patients or taking other action.[26] Nor did Guidant withdraw the Prizm 2, even though it knew its wiring was defective. Guidant kept selling the Prizm 2 until public pressure to pull the device became too intense. Without the risk of state damages litigation, device manufacturers will have only weak incentives to withdraw an outdated or risky device from the market, little incentive to make changes to improve the device's safety, and almost no incentive to warn physicians and patients of possible defects.[27]

Finally, in ruling against preemption, courts stressed the importance of preserving the compensatory role that tort litigation serves. The MDA was enacted to strengthen public protection in light of public health tragedies like that caused by the Dalkon Shield. Congress was well aware of the role that state damages litigation played in bringing the Dalkon Shield problem to the public's attention, forcing a recalcitrant company to take a dangerous product off the market, and compensating tens of thousands of women severely injured by the device through no fault of their own. As the Supreme Court recently concluded, had Congress intended "to deprive injured parties of a long available form of compensation, it surely would have expressed that intent more clearly."[28]

Nonetheless, the Supreme Court recently ruled in favor of medical device manufacturers in *Riegel v. Medtronic, Inc.*, a case involving a different medical device. The Court brushed aside the history of the MDA and questions of compensatory justice. Instead, the Court focused on the word *requirements* and found that, by choosing it, Congress had decided to cut off tort liability when it enacted the MDA. Justice Ginsburg was the lone dissenter. She argued that the Court's decision was contrary to Congress's purpose in enacting the MDA and would leave injured consumers without a remedy. The

---

[26] See, e.g., Meier, "Maker of Heath Device Kept Flaw from Doctors"; Jeff Swiatek, "Deposition Sheds Light on Guidant Defibrillator Case," INDIANAPOLIS STAR, February 22, 2006, C1.

[27] As the Court in the GUIDANT case put it: "[T]he Court is mindful of Guidant's arguments that allowing these claims to go forward will open the floodgates and unfairly stifle medical invention. The Court does not see such a harsh result. The FDA regulatory system and a state tort system can and should work together. Each serve[s] different, yet related, functions. A regulatory system ensures products on the market have a favorable risk-reward profile, and a tort system provides incentives to manufacturers to develop and maintain safe devices. In this way, private tort remedies strengthen federal standards." IN RE GUIDANT CORP. IMPLANTABLE DEFIBRILLATORS PRODUCTS LIABILITY LITIGATION, 2007 U.S. Dist. LEXIS 42765, at [35] (D. Minn. June 12, 2007).

[28] BATES V. DOW AGROSCIENCES, LLC, 544 U.S. 431, 449 (2005).

Court's decision did leave open one possible avenue of redress: suits are not barred if the manufacturer violated an FDA-imposed requirement.[29]

Shortly before the Court's ruling in *Riegel*, Guidant settled the cases brought by Joshua Oukrop's family and others injured by the Prizm 2. Medical device manufacturers are unlikely to settle cases in the future. *Riegel* gives them broad immunity from liability, no matter how egregious or knowing their misconduct. But *Riegel* is not the last word on medical device preemption. Efforts are already underway in Congress to set the decision aside, and the debate over the wisdom of preemption for medical devices continues.[30]

PRESCRIPTION DRUGS AND JAMIE GREGG

For most of its seventy-seven-year history, the FDA has regulated the drugs sold in the United States without interaction with the world of state-law damages litigation.[31] The federal drug safety laws do not explicitly preempt state damages actions for pharmaceutical products. No appellate court, before or after the advent of the FDA, has held that a state-law claim for a prescription drug is preempted by federal law. Congress has not acted to preempt or limit state damage actions despite the steady stream of failure-to-warn cases against pharmaceutical manufacturers by consumers injured by FDA-regulated drugs. But the FDA has historically stood on the sidelines in this litigation, seeing no tension between its regulatory responsibilities and the possibility of liability awards against drug companies.

The past few years have witnessed a complete turnabout in FDA policy. The agency now contends that failure-to-warn cases undermine its ability to protect the public health. It argues that a judicial determination that an FDA-approved label fails adequately to warn of risks may force manufacturers to add warnings that are not approved by the FDA. Even worse, the FDA says, adverse rulings could force manufacturers to add warnings that the FDA considered and rejected – thus placing manufacturers in the untenable position of having to violate federal law to avoid state damages judgments. For

---

[29] RIEGEL V. MEDTRONIC, INC., 128 S. Ct. 999 (2008).

[30] See Hearings on "Should FDA Drug and Medical Device Regulation Bar State Liability Claims?" before the H. Comm. on Oversight and Gov't Reform (May 14, 2008).

[31] The agency's modern history dates back to the enactment of the Food, Drug, and Cosmetic Act in 1938. John P. Swann, HISTORY OF THE FDA (Washington, DC: Food and Drug Administration, 2007). But the federal government's systematic regulation of pharmaceuticals began with the Federal Food and Drugs Act of 1906, when the agency was known as the Bureau of Chemistry.

these reasons, the FDA now maintains that federal law preempts many failure-to-warn claims based on product labeling approved by the FDA.[32]

No one knows whether Vioxx caused the heart attack that rendered Jamie Gregg, a thirty-two-year-old construction worker and father of three boys, an invalid. Before he collapsed from a heart attack, Jamie had been taking high doses of Vioxx for four years because of pain from a series of back surgeries. Doctors saved his life. But his brain had been deprived of oxygen for so long that he is now in a nursing home, unable to utter more than a few syllables or move his body.[33] Because of the lawsuits brought by people who believe that they or their loved ones were killed or injured by Vioxx, we now know a great deal about why the FDA approved Vioxx, why the agency allowed it to remain on the market even as the evidence mounted showing that it caused heart attacks and strokes, and the extent to which Merck, Vioxx's manufacturer, concealed information about Vioxx's risks from the FDA and the public.

A brief overview of the FDA's role in regulating drugs helps put in perspective the preemption battle now being waged in the courts over prescription drugs like Vioxx. Since the passage of the landmark 1938 Food, Drug, and Cosmetic Act (FDCA), the FDA must decide that a drug is safe and effective for its intended use before the drug may be marketed in the United States. To obtain FDA approval, a drug manufacturer must submit a "new drug application" (NDA). An NDA includes all information bearing on a drug's safety and efficacy, including the results of animal testing, pharmacological studies, and full reports of all of the clinical trials performed on human subjects.[34] New drugs that "address unmet medical needs" for "serious or life-threatening conditions" may receive accelerated or "fast track" consideration by the FDA. These drugs are subject to shorter review periods and approval may be based on less safety and efficacy information than other drugs.[35]

Drug labeling provides doctors information needed to make informed prescribing decisions. Because all drugs have adverse side effects, the labeling must address the drug's potential risks, contraindications, warnings, precautions, and adverse reactions. The manufacturer and the FDA discuss the content of these warnings in detail during the approval process, and the FDA approves the

---

[32] FDA, "Requirements on Content and Format of Labeling for Human Prescription Drug and Biological Products," FEDERAL REGISTER 71 (January 24, 2006): 3922 (codified at 21 C.F.R. pts. 201, 314, 601) ("2006 FDA Labeling Requirements").

[33] Alex Berenson et al., "Dangerous Data: Despite Warnings, Drug Giant Took Long Path to Vioxx Recall," NEW YORK TIMES, November 14, 2004, A1.

[34] 21 U.S.C. § 355(a)–(b) (2006).

[35] 21 U.S.C. § 356(a)(1) (2006); see also 21 C.F.R. § 314.500–.520; Government Accountability Office, "Drug Safety: Improvement Needed in FDA's Postmarket Decision-making and Oversight Process" (March 2006): 11 ("GAO Drug Safety Report").

precise final version of the drug's label.[36] The FDA's approval of a drug does not end the agency's oversight of the drug or its labeling. Prior to FDA approval, drugs are tested on relatively small populations of patients, for short periods of time that rarely exceed a year or two. Preapproval testing generally is incapable of detecting adverse effects that occur infrequently, have long latency periods, or affect subpopulations not included or adequately represented in the studies (e.g., the elderly, ethnic minorities, and pregnant women). FDA approval is not a warrant that the drug will not cause serious adverse effects even if properly used for its approved purposes.[37]

Because unanticipated adverse effects often emerge with approved drugs, there are procedures that regulate modifications to drug labeling. Generally, labeling changes proposed by the manufacturers require prior FDA approval. There are exceptions, however. Most importantly, "labeling must be revised to include a warning about a clinically significant hazard as soon as there is reasonable evidence of a causal association with a drug; a causal relationship need not have been definitively established." The manufacturer must promptly inform the FDA of the change and submit a Supplemental NDA that the FDA then reviews after the fact. But this "safety valve" option allows manufacturers to provide physicians, health care professionals, and patients with up-to-date information without the having to secure the FDA's advance approval. The FDA has long made it clear that its labeling rules are no obstacle to manufacturers providing warnings to doctors and patients through labeling, advertising, or "Dear Doctor" letters without prior FDA clearance as soon as the manufacturer discovers risks that are not clearly stated on the label.[38]

Until 2002, the agency took the position that its regulatory responsibilities could coexist with state failure-to-warn litigation. Since then, however, the agency has argued that failure-to-warn litigation risks "erod[ing] and

---

[36] 21 U.S.C. § 355(d) (2006). The FDA labeling regulations are extensive and include specific requirements on the format and content of drug labels. See 21 C.F.R. §§ 201.56, 201.57, 201.80. In 2006, the FDA promulgated new regulations intended to streamline labeling and make it easier for health care providers to access key information. The new rules add a number of features, including a "highlights" section of the label that provides ready access to the most commonly sought information about the drug, a new format for labeling, and new requirements to make hazard and adverse reaction information more accessible. 2006 FDA Labeling Requirements, SUPRA, n. 24.

[37] See Institute of Medicine, "The Future of Drug Safety: Promoting and Protecting the Health of the Public" (Washington, D.C.: National Academies Press, 2006), 36.

[38] 21 C.F.R. § 314.70(b) (2006) (FDA must approve any "major" labeling change in advance); see also id. (defining what changes are deemed "major"); see also 21 C.F.R. §§ 201.57(c)(6), 201.80(e) (2006) (authorizing labeling changes without prior FDA approval); FDA, "Labeling and Prescription Drug Advertising Content and Format for Labeling for Human Prescription Drugs," FEDERAL REGISTER 44 (June 26, 1979): 37,434–47 (manufacturers have an obligation to promptly inform physicians and patients of risks not clearly stated on the label).

disrupt[ing] the careful and truthful representations of the benefits and risks that prescribers need to make appropriate judgments about drug use. Exaggeration of risk could discourage appropriate use of a beneficial drug." The agency now urges courts to dismiss these cases at the threshold.[39]

In the Vioxx litigation, preemption was Merck's key defense. But courts rejected Merck's argument, and the information that has been disclosed as a result of that litigation sheds considerable light on the conduct of both the FDA and Merck. Vioxx belongs to a class of drugs known as "COX-2 inhibitors." These drugs were developed as a new generation of pain relievers for patients with arthritis and rheumatism, equally effective as painkillers like ibuprofen in blocking pain but with less risk of gastrointestinal bleeding. Recognizing that these drugs might mark a significant therapeutic advance, the FDA accelerated approval, with Vioxx's approval coming in 1999.[40] Merck trumpeted Vioxx's approval with its "biggest, fastest, and best launch ever."[41] In 2000, just its second year on the market, Vioxx was the number one direct-to-consumer advertised drug – $160 million for consumer ads, more than was spent that year to advertise Budweiser or Pepsi – and retail sales quadrupled even though Vioxx cost an average of two to three dollars a pill, while the older generation anti-inflammatory drugs cost just a few pennies each. An estimated 105 million prescriptions were written for Vioxx in the United States between May 20, 1999 and September 30, 2004, involving twenty million patients. At the height of its sales Vioxx brought in more than $2.5 billion for Merck.[42]

Integral to Merck's marketing strategy was the ability to advertise that Vioxx presented less of a risk of gastrointestinal bleeding than comparable pain medications. But when the FDA approved Vioxx, the agency required Vioxx's label to contain the standard warning about gastrointestinal bleeding. Merck then sponsored additional studies to prove that Vioxx posed less of a risk of gastrointestinal bleeding. The major study – the Vioxx Gastrointestinal Outcomes Research (VIGOR) study – compared Vioxx to another pain medication, naproxen, over an eighteen-month period. The study concluded that Vioxx did reduce the bleeding risk. It also showed Vioxx patients suffering a four- to five-fold increase in heart attacks and strokes over the patients taking naproxen. Merck shared the

[39] 2006 FDA Labeling Requirements, 3935.
[40] See generally, Barry Meier et al., "Medicine Fueled by Marketing Intensified Trouble for Pain Pills," NEW YORK TIMES, December 19, 2004, A1; Alex Berenson et al., "Dangerous Data: Despite Warnings, Drug Giant Took Long Path to Vioxx Recall," NEW YORK TIMES, November 14, 2004; "GAO Drug Safety Report," 11.
[41] Robert Langreth, "FDA Approval of Vioxx Allows Merck to Compete with New Arthritis Drugs," WALL STREET JOURNAL, May 24, 1999, B1.
[42] National Institute for Health Care Management, "Prescription Drugs and Mass Media Advertising, 2000," (2001): 5.

results with the FDA and argued that the differential in cardiovascular risk was not attributable to an increased risk from Vioxx but was instead due to naproxen's ability to suppress heart disease.[43] Merck touted these results in press releases and public statements saying that the study found "NO DIFFERENCE in the incidence of cardiovascular events" between Vioxx, a placebo, and other pain-killers.[44] The FDA permitted Merck to remove the gastrointestinal bleeding warning from Vioxx's label, giving it a big edge over competing products.

But the FDA did not share Merck's optimism about Vioxx's cardiovascular risk. An FDA advisory committee recommended in early 2001 that a prominent warning be placed on Vioxx alerting physicians and patients to the risks of heart attack and stroke. These warnings signal a high degree of risk. Merck vigorously opposed this proposal. After nearly a year and a half of negotiations, the FDA and Merck reached a compromise: Merck would place a warning on Vioxx that persons with a history of heart disease should use Vioxx with caution; but no prominent warning, which would have undercut Merck's marketing campaign, would be required.[45] Merck continue to test Vioxx to see whether it could treat certain forms of cancer. Vioxx and a placebo were given to otherwise healthy pain patients who were genetically susceptible to polyp formation. After eight-een months, scientists ordered the study terminated because the Vioxx patients

[43] The VIGOR data was also published in the New England Journal of Medicine. See Claire Bombardier et al., "Comparison of Upper Gastrointestinal Toxicity of Rofecoxib and Naproxen in Patients with Rheumatoid Arthritis," New England Journal of Medicine 343, no. 21 (November 23, 2000): 1520. The Journal later published an "Expression of Concern" detailing certain inaccuracies in the data and raising concerns about the conclusions of the original paper. See Gregory D. Curfman et al., "Expression of Concern," New England Journal of Medicine 353, no. 26 (December 29, 2005): 2813. The Journal published responses from the original authors. See Correspondence, "Response to Expression of Concern Regarding VIGOR Study," New England Journal of Medicine 354, no. 11 (March 16, 2006): 1196.

[44] McGarity, The Preemption War, 10; see also Gina Kolata, "Good Pill, Bad Pill: Science Makes it Hard to Decipher," New York Times, December 22, 2004, C1; Anna Wilde Mathews and Barbara Martinez, "Warning Signs: E-Mails Suggest Merck Knew Vioxx's Dangers at Early Stage," Wall Street Journal, November 1, 2004, A1.

[45] The FDA has no statutory authority to compel a manufacturer to change a label of a drug once the drug has been approved. The FDA can threaten to bring proceedings to withdraw the drug's approval, or to have a court declare the product misbranded, but these are resource-intensive, time-consuming processes that the agency rarely employs. The FDA's inability to force a labeling change to Vioxx is the most recent, and perhaps most widely publicized, example of this problem. Dr. Sandra Kweder, Deputy Director of the FDA's Office of New Drugs, said in Senate testimony that it took over a year to negotiate a labeling change for Vioxx. "They rejected many of our proposals." "We don't have the authority to tell a company, 'This is how your label has to look.'" Instead, Dr. Kweder said, "We have to negotiate with the company the specific language of how things should be worded, the placement, those kinds of things, after talking to them." FDA Drug Approval Process: Up to the Challenge? Before the S. Comm. on Health, Edu-cation, Labor and Pensions, 109th Cong. 23 (March 1, 2005). See also Gardiner Harris, "FDA Official Admits 'Lapses' on Vioxx," New York Times, March 2, 2005, A1.

were experiencing a far higher incidence of cardiovascular problems than the placebo group. Two weeks later, Merck pulled Vioxx from the market. One FDA scientist has estimated that Vioxx may have caused more than twenty-five excess heart attacks and strokes.[46]

Not surprisingly, thousands of lawsuits were filed against Merck. Nearly six thousand federal cases were consolidated for pretrial proceedings in the U.S. District Court for the Eastern District of Louisiana. Merck moved to dismiss the cases against it on preemption grounds. The court summarized Merck's arguments as follows: "Merck contends that a finding of implied preemption is appropriate because the federal regulatory scheme devised for regulating prescription drugs cannot function properly if juries applying state law are allowed to 'force' drug manufacturers to add information to prescription drug labels beyond language that the FDA has approved."[47] As the court observed, Merck did not claim that Congress decided to nullify state law. The FDCA is silent on the question of preemption. For that reason, Merck argued that the court should find "implied" preemption because application of state law against Merck would threaten the FDA's ability to achieve its goals, a position the FDA now shares. The FDA argued that cases like Jamie Gregg's challenge the FDA's determination that the drug's labeling was adequate. Labeling decisions require the agency to engage in a complex balancing of interests. Warnings that overstate or exaggerate risks are no more help to physicians and patients than warnings that downplay risks. Striking the right balance takes expertise and judgment. For these reasons, the FDA claims, the final say over drug labeling must be left to the manufacturer and the FDA and should not be subject to second-guessing by courts.[48]

---

[46] Memorandum from David J. Graham, MD, MPH, Associate Director for Science, Office of Drug Safety to Paul Seligman, MD, MPH, Acting Director, Office of Drug Safety, "Risk of Acute Myocardial Infarction and Sudden Death in Patients Treated with COX-2 Selective and Non-Selective NSAIDs" (September 30, 2004).

[47] In re Vioxx Prods. Liab. Litig., 2007 U.S. Dist. LEXIS 48367 [*8] (E.D. La. 2007).

[48] Merck and other companies have argued that the FDA's views on preemption are entitled to deference from the courts. Some courts have agreed, citing the Supreme Court's decision in Chevron, U.S.A. v. Natural Resources Defense Council, Inc., 467 U.S. 837 (1984). See, e.g., Colacicco v. Apotex, Inc., 432 F. Supp. 2d 514 (E.D. Pa. 2006), Appeal Filed, No. 06-3107 (3d Cir.); In Re Bextra and Celebrex Mktg. Sales Practices and Prod. Liab. Litig., 2006 WL 2374742 (N.D. Cal. August 16, 2006). Others have not, including the court handling the Vioxx cases. In Re Vioxx Prods. Liab. Litig., 2007 U.S. Dist. LEXIS 48367 [*8] (E.D. La. 2007). There are a number of reasons why courts have refused to defer to the FDA, including (1) Congress did not delegate to the FDA the authority to decide the preemption question, see Gonzales v. Oregon, 126 S. Ct. 904, 915 (2006); (2) the FDA did not develop its new position through notice and comment rule making or other formal means, which makes deference inappropriate, see United States v. Mead Corp., 533 U.S. 218, 226–7 (2001); and (3) the FDA's new position on preemption conflicts with its long-standing contrary position, which undercuts the agency's deference claim. See Mead, 533 U.S. at 228.

The plaintiffs' lawyers had several responses to that argument. First, the arguments favoring preemption understate the ability of drug manufacturers to change labeling unilaterally to respond to newly discovered risks or to seek labeling changes from the FDA. Labeling decisions are not set in stone. Because adverse effects of drugs often do not become apparent until the drug is on the market, drug labels are constantly being updated. Drug manufacturers have significant authority – and a responsibility – to modify labeling when unforeseen hazards emerge and may do so without securing the FDA's prior approval. Merck had ample authority to warn physicians and patients about the serious risks of heart attacks and strokes far more quickly than it did.[49]

Second, arguments favoring preemption are based on an unrealistic assessment of the agency's practical ability, once it has approved a drug, to detect unforeseen adverse effects and to take prompt and effective remedial action. There are eleven thousand FDA-regulated drugs on the market (including both prescription and over-the-counter drugs); with nearly one hundred more approved each year. The reality is that the FDA does not have the resources to perform the Herculean task of monitoring comprehensively the performance of every drug on the market. Both the National Academies of Science's Institute of Medicine and the Government Accountability Office have recently issued reports critical of the agency's ability to keep unsafe drugs off the market and to respond effectively to unforeseen hazards with newly approved drugs.[50] These reports undermine the FDA's claim that it can single-handedly monitor the safety of every drug on the market.

Third, a preemption finding would deprive both the FDA and the public of vital information about the drug. Prior to a drug's approval, drug companies are required to provide the FDA with all data – positive and negative – relating to the drug's safety and efficacy, chemical formulation, proposed manufacturing, and patent protection. Companies are under no duty to provide the agency with records of internal discussions or evaluations by company physicians and scientists. Postapproval, the FDA's information-gathering power is more limited. Companies must provide to the FDA records "relating to clinical experience" and adverse reactions and must also permit the FDA to review business records during the course of a factory inspection. Companies have no obligation to give the FDA their evaluations of the drug's performance in the market, let alone their assessment (memos, e-mails, and so forth)

---

[49] 21 C.F.R. § 314.70(b) (2006) (FDA must approve any "major" labeling change in advance); see also id. (defining changes that are deemed "major").

[50] See IOM Report, Supra at 157; "GAO Drug Safety Report," Supra at 10–11.

of the drug's safety profile. Although the FDA has substantial information-gathering power, its authority is by no means comprehensive.[51]

The information-gathering tools lawyers have in litigation are, by any measure, more extensive than the FDA's. The FDCA does not give the FDA the most important tool trial lawyers have – the right to subpoena potentially relevant information from any source.[52] A few examples drawn from the litigation over Vioxx show the informational advantage in litigation. For instance, litigation uncovered internal company memos and e-mails not provided to the FDA that showed that Merck was acutely aware of Vioxx's heart-attack risk long before Merck alerted the FDA about the risk. One memo warned that a study of Vioxx, conducted to show that it decreased the risk of gastrointestinal problems, should be limited to patients also taking aspirin; otherwise there would be a "substantial chance that significantly higher rates" of cardiovascular disease would show up in the Vioxx group. An internal e-mail similarly warned that if Vioxx patients did not receive aspirin, "you will get more thrombotic events and kill [the] drug." In response, a senior company doctor agreed that "the possibility of increased CV [cardiovascular] events is of great concern," and she recommended that potential subjects with high risk of cardiovascular problems be kept out of the study so cardiovascular problems "would not be evident." Evidence uncovered in litigation also revealed that in 2000 Merck scientists were considering combining Vioxx with other agents to reduce the risk of heart attacks and strokes.[53] The FDA was aware of none of this when it acceded to Merck's demand that no black-box warning would go on Vioxx's label.

The federal district court supervising the Vioxx cases recently rejected Merck's preemption defense. That court does not have the last word. Merck

---

[51] See 21 U.S.C. §§ 355(b)(1)(A)-(F) (contents of a new drug application); 21 U.S.C. §§ 355(k), 374 (postapproval requirements).

[52] COMPARE Fed. R. Civ. P. 26–7, 45, *with* 21 U.S.C. §§ 355(k), 374. Any party to civil litigation in federal court may compel any person to provide testimony under oath or furnish records relevant to, or reasonably calculated to lead to the discovery of any information relevant to, any issue in the case. State discovery rules generally are equally permissive. The FDA's information-gathering power is more limited. The FDA's authority does not reach evaluations and analyses performed by companies on their drugs, let alone to company e-mails and internal deliberations over possible safety hazards. See also Wagner, "When All Else Fails," SUPRA n. 7; Vladeck, "Defending Courts," SUPRA n. 9.

[53] McGarity, THE PREEMPTION WAR, 17; Anna W. Mathews and Barbara Martinez, "Warning Signs: E-Mails Suggest Merck Knew Vioxx's Dangers at Early Stage"; Heather Won Tesoriero, "Attorneys Question Disclosure by Merck of Vioxx-Study Deaths," WALL STREET JOURNAL, September 28, 2005, D4 (reporting that litigation uncovered Merck-sponsored studies finding a high death rate among Alzheimer's patients taking Vioxx as compared to placebo group). These Vioxx examples echo prior FDA experience. Wagner, "When All Else Fails," at 707 n. 73 and 711 nn. 79–82 (and authorities cited therein).

will appeal the ruling through the federal appellate courts. And other drug preemption cases are working their way up to the U.S. Supreme Court. Recently the Supreme Court of Vermont rejected a drug company's preemption claim, and the company has asked the U.S. Supreme Court to grant review. The Court asked the Solicitor General of the United States to weigh in. It may be that the U.S. Supreme Court will soon tell us whether Jamie Gregg's case against Merck may proceed, or whether the FDA's approval of Vioxx's label forecloses Jamie's right to sue. In the meantime, however, the litigation continues to uncover information about Vioxx that was never provided to the FDA.[54]

DEFECTIVE VEHICLES AND MAJOR BARRY MUTH

Every year, more than ten thousand people die in rollover crashes and another twenty-four thousand are seriously injured. Although rollovers constitute just 3 percent of all passenger vehicle crashes, they account for one-third of all fatalities in passenger vehicles and more than 60 percent of all deaths in sport utility vehicles (SUVs).[55] The NHTSA was established by Congress in 1966 to set safety standards that are "practicable" and "meet the need for motor vehicle safety." When Congress wrote the Federal Motor Vehicle Safety Act (Safety Act) – the legislation creating NHTSA – it addressed how NHTSA standards would affect state law. The act first provides that no state may "establish or . . . continue in effect . . . any safety standard applicable to the same aspect of performance" that is not "identical" to the federal standard. Congress was careful to add a "savings clause" that provides that "[c]ompliance with" a NHTSA standard does "not exempt a person from any liability at common law."[56]

One of NHTSA's first standards was for roof strength. The standard, issued in 1971, requires that the "roof over the front seat area" be strong enough to withstand a force equal to 1.5 times the unloaded weight of the vehicle (measured by forcing a steel plate against the roof, simulating contact with the ground in a rollover crash), and that the roof must prevent the plate from moving more than five inches. The standard does not apply to vehicles

---

[54] IN RE VIOXX PRODS. LIAB. LITIG., 2007 U.S. Dist. LEXIS 48367 [*8] (E.D. La. 2007) (Vioxx preemption ruling); LEVINE V. WYETH, 2006 VT 107, PET. FOR CERT. FILED SUB. NOM. WYETH V. LEVINE, No. 06-1249 March 14, 2007), 127 S. Ct. 2451 (2007) (inviting Solicitor General to file a brief expressing the views of the United States).

[55] "Federal Motor Vehicle Safety Standards; Roof Crush Resistance, Notice of Proposed Rulemaking," FEDERAL REGISTER 70 (August 23, 2005), 49,223, 49,226–7 ("NHTSA Roof Crush Proposal").

[56] 49 U.S.C. §§ 30103(b)(1) and (e).

weighing in excess of six thousand pounds, thereby exempting light trucks, vans, and buses. NHTSA has not upgraded the standard despite the introduction and popularity of SUVs, such as the Ford Explorer, which have a high center of gravity and are thus rollover prone.[57] Nor, despite its promises, has NHTSA ever issued a rollover standard, which would better regulate the performance of vehicles in real-world accidents.

Survivors of rollover crashes often face severe brain and spinal cord injuries. Consider one example: Major Barry Muth was serving in the Army in Saudi Arabia when a rollover crash changed his life forever. He and a colleague, Major Julius Wineglass, were driving in a Ford Crown Victoria near Riyadh, when Wineglass, who was driving, lost control of the vehicle and ran it into a three-foot-high barrier. Apparently the left front wheel of the vehicle climbed the side of the barrier, causing the vehicle to flip and land on its roof. Both men were wearing seatbelts. Wineglass suffered only minor injuries. On Muth's side of the vehicle, however, the roof crush was so severe that he sustained serious spinal damage, leaving him a quadriplegic with only limited use of his arms and hands.[58]

Muth and his family sued Ford, alleging that the Crown Victoria did not provide adequate rollover/roof crush protection. At trial, Muth's expert testified that the vehicle's roof had collapsed twelve to fifteen inches on the passenger side, and that increasing the thickness of the steel in several parts of the roof structure would have reduced roof collapse to two to three inches. Ford did not dispute that a stronger roof would be feasible. Rather, it contended that the cause of serious injuries in rollover crashes was not roof strength, but the fact that even a seat-belted passenger will drop five inches in a rollover, which is more than the normal three-to-four inches of clearance between the head and the roof. After hearing the evidence, the jury sided with Muth, finding Ford's design of the roof of the Crown Victoria was defective. The jury concluded that if the roof had buckled only a few inches rather than a foot or more, Muth would not likely have been seriously injured. The jury awarded Muth and his family nine million dollars in damages. Ford appealed, but the court of appeals rejected Ford's arguments.

So, then, why is there an issue of preemption? In the *Muth* case, Ford did not even contend that state law was preempted by NHTSA's roof-strength standard. That will soon change. NHTSA is in the process of finalizing a new roof-strength standard that would require the roofs of new vehicles to be able to withstand a force equal to 2.5 times the unloaded weight of the

[57] "NHTSA Roof Crush Proposal," 49,225–6.
[58] MUTH V. FORD MOTOR CO., 461 F.3d 557 (5th Cir. 2006).

vehicle and maintain enough headroom to accommodate a midsize male occupant. NHTSA acknowledges that 70 percent of the vehicles on the road today meet or exceed that standard, and that the revised standard will save only fifty-five of the more than ten thousand lives lost annually to rollover crashes. Nonetheless, NHTSA takes the position that its new standard, once issued, will preempt all challenges to roof strength based on state law, extinguishing claims like that brought by Barry Muth and his family.[59]

What authority, one might ask, does NHTSA have to make this determination? After all, the Safety Act says that compliance with a NHTSA standard does "not exempt a person from any liability at common law." Another provision of the act makes it clear that NHTSA standards are minimum standards that manufacturers may exceed. If that were not the case, then auto manufacturers like Volvo, BMW, and Subaru could not make vehicle roofs that far exceed NHTSA's roof strength standard. The answer lies in the Supreme Court's controversial decision in *Geier v. American Honda Co.*[60] In that case, the Court had to decide whether NHTSA's "occupant protection" (passive restraint) standard preempted state law. The standard, first adopted in 1967, initially required manufacturers to install lap and shoulder belts, but NHTSA soon found that many occupants did not bother fastening their belts. Consumer groups urged NHTSA to require a new technology – air bags – that operated automatically.[61]

NHTSA revised the standard in 1971 to require either air bags or automatic seatbelts for front seat occupants by 1975. The auto industry objected. Henry Ford and Ford President Lee Iacocca met secretly with President Nixon to urge that the standard be scrapped. After the meeting, Nixon called Secretary of Transportation John Volpe and told him to rescind the rule, which he did. NHTSA then adopted industry's proposal that it mandate the use of "ignition interlock" devices that prevented the car from starting until front-seat occupants had buckled up. The public hated the hard-to-use interlock devices, and Congress soon amended the Safety Act to forbid their use.

It was not until the Carter administration that NHTSA revived the passive-restraint standard. In 1977 the agency gave the industry until model year 1982 to install air bags or automatic belts. But the Reagan administration rescinded the standard in 1981. Insurance companies and consumer groups sued NHTSA, challenging the validity of the rescission. In *Motor Vehicle*

---

[59] "NHTSA Roof Crush Proposal," 49,245–6.

[60] 529 U.S. 861 (2000).

[61] The history of this standard, summarized in the text, is drawn from extended discussions in Geier, 529 U.S. at 875–84, and id. at 891–2, 903–4 (Stevens, J., dissenting), and in McGarity, The Preemption War, 100–7.

Manufacturers Association v. State Farm Insurance Co.,[62] the Supreme Court agreed, finding that NHTSA had arbitrarily bowed to industry pressure in rescinding the standard. Having no choice, NHTSA issued a new standard that required manufacturers, over a lengthy phase-in period, to install either air bags or nondetachable belts, although the standard reflected a slight preference for air bags.

NHTSA's new standard was criticized for further delaying the widespread introduction of air bags. By this point, the evidence demonstrated that air bags were easy to install, affordable, and far more protective than automatic belts. As a result of NHTSA's gradual phase-in, however, many new cars were not equipped with air bags, leading to needless injuries and deaths. One such case involved a young woman, Alexis Geier, who was seriously injured when her 1987 Honda, equipped with just a shoulder harness and lap belt, crashed into a tree. She sued, claiming that cars lacking air bags were defectively designed. But the Court held, 5-4, that her claim was preempted because NHTSA's standard gave manufacturers a choice of installing air bags or nondetachable belts. The Court's opinion is complicated, but it deserves some attention.

The Court first rejected Honda's argument that Geier's claim was expressly preempted under the Safety Act because the act's preemption provision applied only to positive state standards that were not identical to the federal standard. The Court also noted that the act's "savings clause" preserved Geier's claim. Nonetheless, the Court found the claim preempted because permitting a tort claim to go forward would conflict with NHTSA's decision to provide for a gradual phase-in of air-bags to "lower costs, overcome technical safety problems, encourage technological development, and win widespread consumer acceptance."[63] In their dissent, four Justices argued that federal regulatory objectives "would not be frustrated one whit by allowing state courts to determine whether in 1987 the lifesaving advantage of air bags had become sufficiently obvious that their omission might constitute a design defect in some new cars."[64] The dissenters' point was borne out by the fact that NHTSA later estimated that as many as sixty-three thousand more lives could have been saved had all manufacturers installed air bags at the outset.[65]

Geier has effectively ended litigation challenging the absence of air bags in passenger vehicles. But *Geier's* basic message – that in implied preemption cases the courts should defer to agency claims that state law damage actions

[62] 463 U.S. 29 (1983).
[63] GEIER, 529 U.S. at 867–71, 875.
[64] GEIER, 529 U.S. at 903–4 (Stevens, J., dissenting).
[65] Jack Keelber, "Passive Restraints: A Deadly Mistake," ATLANTA JOURNAL AND CONSTITUTION, August 16, 1991, S1.

might impede the fulfillment of federal objectives – has not been lost on NHTSA. It now argues that its new roof-strength standard should broadly preempt state law claims. There is reason for concern over NHTSA's new preemption theory. To begin with, there are questions about NHTSA's capacity to regulate the massive automobile industry without the backstop of state damages law. NHTSA faces formidable challenges in doing battle with the industry because it is so profoundly outmatched. NHTSA is one "David" facing many "Goliaths." NHTSA is a tiny agency, with only a skeletal staff (625 employees), with limited information-gathering authority and no demonstrated ability to act quickly in the face of emerging safety hazards.[66] It took the Ford Explorer debacle to prompt NHTSA to revise its roof-strength standard. Congress had to step in to require NHTSA to force manufacturers to install tire-pressure warning gauges.[67] NHTSA's fuel safety standard is at least thirty-five years out of date, even though fuel-fed fires are a leading cause of fatalities in vehicle crashes.[68]

NHTSA also has a track record of giving ground to placate the powerful automobile industry. Consider air bags. The *Geier* majority accepts at face value the agency's assertion that a gradual phase-in of air bags was important to develop "widespread public acceptance" of the device and cites *State Farm* in setting out the history of air-bag regulation. But the majority says nothing about the Court's *ruling* in *State Farm* – namely, that NHTSA had improperly succumbed to industry pressure to delay the introduction of air bags. The *State Farm* Court famously observed that "[f]or nearly a decade, the automobile industry has waged the regulatory equivalent of war against the airbag," and the Court faulted NHSTA for capitulating to industry rather than fighting to serve the public interest.[69]

NHTSA has bowed to industry pressure on other occasions as well. Career NHSTA employees claim that the preemption language inserted into the roof-strength standard was written by political employees at the behest of the auto industry.[70] Given how little the standard will accomplish in terms of reducing deaths and injuries from rollover crashes, some auto-safety groups claim that

---

[66] See Vladeck, "Defending Courts," at 638–9; see also Department of Transportation Fiscal Year 2008 Budget Request, 70 (NHTSA staffing authorization).

[67] See PUBLIC CITIZEN V. MINETA, 340 F.3d 39 (2d Cir. 2003) (noting that Congress mandated tire-pressure warning gauges be installed in passenger vehicles and overturning NHTSA rule because it wrongly adopted the approach preferred by industry).

[68] Barry Meier, "Officials Did Little, Despite Report Saying U.S. Wasn't Cutting Fatal Car Fires," NEW YORK TIMES, November 21, 1992, A7.

[69] 463 U.S. at 49.

[70] Myron Levin and Alan Miller, "Industries Get Quiet Protection from Lawsuits," LOS ANGELES TIMES, February 19, 2006, A1.

the new standard's major purpose is to provide a liability shield to industry, not enhanced protection to consumers.[71] There is a powerful argument that the most effective discipline on the automobile industry has not been NHTSA but has been state damage actions, which have forced the industry to develop roofs far stronger, and fuel systems far safer, than NHTSA's outdated standards. This concern is reflected in the Safety Act. The "savings clause" stands as a clear signal that Congress intended to preserve the corrective justice function of state damage claims. Only time will tell, however, whether NHTSA's broad preemption theory carries the day in court.

CONCLUSION

As these examples illustrate, the risk of the preemption doctrine is that, unless preemption is carefully limited to situations in which state and federal law cannot coexist, the abolition of state damage actions will do more harm than good. All too often, federal agencies are underfunded, understaffed, information-deprived, and politically constrained so they cannot, on their own, fulfill the functions assigned to them by Congress. State damages actions provide an important backstop to the regulatory process. They compensate injured parties, deter excessive risk-taking, shine a spotlight on defective products, and uncover safety information that is not otherwise available to the public or regulatory authorities.

This chapter focused on extreme examples of regulatory failure, where an agency lacks the resources or political will do to its job effectively, or where an agency is "captured" or unduly influenced by the industry it is charged with regulating. But even when the regulatory process works well, preemption comes at a high cost. Consider again the plight of Major Barry Muth. If NHTSA's preemption argument succeeds, then cases like his will be dismissed. Automakers will escape responsibility for such injuries. Automakers are likely to avoid government sanction as well because NHTSA does not penalize companies for the kind of design flaws Ford made. Under this approach, incentives for companies to design safer cars, and to make modifications when design defects become apparent, are far weaker. Barry Muth's case illustrates the limitations of the regulatory system to force companies to act in the public interest.

[71] "Roof Crush: Safety Advocates Discuss Adequacy of Roof Strength Standard, Seek Upgrade," BNA PRODUCT SAFETY LIABILITY REPORTER 35 (July 30, 2007): 695.

PART TWO

THE LAYERED
GOVERNMENT
NORM

4   The State Attorney General and Preemption

Trevor W. Morrison

According to the National Association of Attorneys General (NAAG), "the rise of preemption of state laws and regulations by federal administrative agencies, rather than directly by Congress" is "[p]erhaps the most significant development in federal preemption in the last several decades."[1] This kind of preemption is typically found in an agency ruling or regulation declaring certain state laws or activities preempted, even though the underlying statute is silent on the issue. That NAAG would view "agency preemption" as particularly worrisome is hardly surprising: the main casualties are often state attorneys general, whose broad investigative and enforcement powers under state consumer protection, health, environmental, and other state laws are displaced by the agency's action.

This chapter examines the implications of agency preemption for state attorneys general, and vice versa. Its principal intended audience is not so much the courts as Congress and the federal agencies; its prescriptions are less about judicial doctrine (though there are implications along those lines) than about choices the legislature and agencies could make to better accommodate the important functions of state attorneys general. Congress, I suggest, should directly address whether any or all of the work of state attorneys general should be preempted by any particular enactment it passes and should include provisions making clear the extent of its intent to preempt. In the absence of clear statutory language addressing the question, I argue that agencies should be reluctant to promulgate regulations preempting the investigative or enforcement authority of state attorneys general. Unlike the Supreme Court's current "presumption against preemption," the approach I advocate does not focus on the particular subject matter of the state or federal law in question. Instead, it focuses on the identity of the actor enforcing the state law. Given the electoral

---

[1]   National Association of Attorneys General Preemption Working Group, THE LAW OF PRE-EMPTION (Washington, D.C., 2004), 19.

accountability of most state attorneys general and their long-standing mandates to enforce state laws in pursuit of the public interest, I suggest that unelected federal agencies should be particularly reluctant, absent a clear statutory mandate, to displace the work of state attorneys general. Instead, federal law should preempt the work of state attorneys general only by express statutory language.

To get to those prescriptions, Part I first provides a brief overview of the federalism-related values that bear most directly on state attorneys general. Part II then introduces the state attorney general, emphasizing that most states' versions of this office are directly elected and that they typically wield broad authority not only to litigate in the public interest but also to monitor compliance with both state and federal law. As Part III describes, however, the courts' current preemption doctrine takes no special account of state attorneys general. In addition, judicial preemption doctrine is sufficiently malleable and unpredictable that it can be difficult to know when, and why, the actions of state attorneys general will be preempted. Although it is certainly possible that the courts could improve their doctrine in this area, a more direct approach would be for Congress and federal agencies themselves to take account of the state attorney general. Part IV proposes that they do just that. Finally, Part V identifies and responds to a potential objection.

FEDERALISM AND DEMOCRATIC ACCOUNTABILITY

In Chapter 1 of this volume, Professors Mendelson and Verchick explore the theoretical underpinnings of, and connections between, preemption and federalism. Building on that discussion, I want to highlight here four points that will help situate state attorneys general within the framework of federalism.

First, although there are a variety of accounts of federalism, its core characteristics include the following: (1) the powers of the federal government are limited but supreme within their compass; (2) the residual powers of the states are broad and plenary; and (3) the areas in which the Constitution grants the federal government exclusive authority are few, while the areas subject to concurrent and overlapping federal and state regulation are many. This last point is critical. The Constitution tends not to create exclusive federal and state zones but to tolerate overlapping federal and state regulation.[2]

---

[2]   UNITED STATES V. LOCKE, 529 U.S. 89, 109 (2000). ("It is fundamental in our federal structure that States have vast residual powers. Those powers, unless constrained or displaced by the existence of federal authority or by proper federal enactments, are often exercised in concurrence with those of the National Government."); Caleb Nelson, "Preemption," VIRGINIA LAW REVIEW 86, no. 2 (2000): 225. ("The powers of the federal government and the powers of the state overlap enormously. Although the Constitution makes a few of the federal government's powers exclusive, the states retain concurrent authority over most of the areas in which the federal government can act.")

Ordinarily, then, the fact that the federal government is competent to act in a particular area does not by itself preclude state involvement in that area. To be sure, there are exceptions to this principle. Some domains, like foreign affairs, the Constitution commits to exclusive federal control.[3] But in the main, the Constitution creates overlapping and even interacting zones of federal and state governance.

Second, federalism is often presented in instrumental terms.[4] That is, federalism is depicted not as an end in itself but as a means of achieving other important goals. Many of the modern Supreme Court's statements about federalism take this form. In *Gregory v. Ashcroft*, for example, Justice O'Connor's majority opinion identified a number of ends to which the Court considers federalism a useful means:

> This federalist structure of joint sovereigns preserves to the people numerous advantages. It assures a decentralized government that will be more sensitive to the diverse needs of a heterogeneous society; it increases opportunity for citizen involvement in democratic processes; it allows for more innovation and experimentation in government; and it makes government more responsive by putting the States in competition for a mobile citizenry.[5]

Third, as the passage from *Gregory* reveals, democratic accountability is often identified as one of federalism's key payoffs.[6] The idea here is that "[t]he greater accessibility and smaller scale of local [and state] government allows individuals to participate actively in governmental decision-making. This participation, in turn, provides myriad benefits, [including that it] fosters accountability among elected representatives."[7] This is really a

---

[3] AMERICAN INS. ASS'N V. GARAMENDI, 539 U.S. 396, 413 (2003) (discussing "the Constitution's allocation of the foreign relations power to the National Government.") Immigration is arguably another such area, although recent scholarship suggests that state and local governments may legitimately have more of a role in this area than is commonly thought. See Clare Huntington, "The Constitutional Dimension of Immigration Federalism," VANDERBILT LAW REVIEW (forthcoming 2008); Cristina M. Rodríguez, "The Significance of the Local in Immigration Regulation," MICHIGAN LAW REVIEW 106, no. 4 (2008): 567; Peter H. Schuck, "Taking Immigration Federalism Seriously," UNIVERSITY OF CHICAGO LEGAL FORUM (2007): 57. In part, these pieces build on earlier work by Peter Spiro. See, e.g., Peter J. Spiro, "The States and Immigration in an Era of Demi-Sovereignties," VIRGINIA JOURNAL OF INTERNATIONAL LAW 35, no. 1 (1994): 121.

[4] Michael C. Dorf, "Instrumental and Non-Instrumental Federalism," RUTGERS LAW JOURNAL 28, no. 4 (1997): 825.

[5] GREGORY V. ASHCROFT, 501 U.S. 452, 458 (1991).

[6] Dorf, "Instrumental and Non-Instrumental Federalism," 828.

[7] Deborah Jones Merritt, "The Guarantee Clause and State Autonomy: Federalism for a Third Century," COLUMBIA LAW REVIEW 88, no. 1 (1988): 1, 7.

point about decentralization: by allowing states substantial room to govern, federalism brings citizens into closer proximity with their government than would be the case in a purely national system. That closer proximity puts at least some citizens in a better position to monitor and influence government, which in turn makes government more accountable to its constituents. Although this theoretical idea will not always be perfectly realized in practice, the point here is that our federalist system is structured to pursue it.[8]

Fourth and finally, because federalism's default position is one of overlapping federal and state governance, the federal government's decision to regulate in a particular area does not necessarily entail giving up the benefits associated with decentralized state power. Congress may decide that a particular issue within its jurisdiction demands uniform national treatment, in which case it may decide to displace state authority. But its decision to act in that area need not entail displacing the states. The exercise of national power does not necessarily undermine decentralized democratic accountability.

THE STATE ATTORNEY GENERAL

Having reprised the features of federalism that are most pertinent here, I now turn to the state attorney general. There are two key points here: (1) the vast majority of state attorneys general are democratically elected, and (2) most are invested with robust investigative and enforcement powers under a broad range of state (and sometimes federal) laws.

Democratic Accountability. Unlike the federal government, the vast majority of state governments feature executive branches that are formally divided, with executive power apportioned among different executive actors not subject to direct gubernatorial control.[9] In nearly every state, one of those executive actors is the state attorney general. Indeed, the attorney

---

[8]   As Roderick Hills puts it, this decentralizing structure is "the American version of 'subsidiarity,' the principle that power ought to be decentralized to the lowest practicable tier of social organization, public or private." Roderick M. Hills Jr., "Is Federalism Good for Localism? The Localist Case for Federal Regimes," JOURNAL OF LAW AND POLITICS 21 (Spring/Summer 2005): 190.

[9]   William P. Marshall, "Break Up the Presidency? Governors, State Attorneys General, and Lessons from the Divided Executive," YALE LAW JOURNAL 115, no. 9 (2006): 2446; Patrick C. McGinley, "Separation of Powers, State Constitutions and the Attorney General: Who Represents the State?" WEST VIRGINIA LAW REVIEW 99, no. 4 (1997): 721.

general is popularly elected in forty-three states.[10] Thus, the overwhelming majority of state attorneys general are electorally accountable to the citizens of their states.

This feature resonates strongly with federalism's concern for democratic accountability. As noted in the preceding text, part of the virtue of decentralized government is that it increases the responsiveness of government to localized priorities. State attorneys general are in a position to deliver that responsiveness or pay the penalty on election day. Any individual attorney general may or may not do a good job of pursuing the voting public's policy priorities. But as a matter of institutional design, state-by-state election of state attorneys general makes them well situated to deliver at least some of federalism's benefits of decentralization.

Powers. The powers and duties of the state attorney general have "dramatically expanded" over time, and they also vary somewhat from state to state.[11] Generally speaking, though, most attorneys general have long had the authority and duty to enforce the laws of the state in the public interest.[12] "The state exists to 'promote the health, safety . . . and welfare of the people,'"[13] and the state attorney general plays a central role in the pursuit of those ends. Typically, the state attorney general is given "wide discretion in making the determination as to the public interest" and is further empowered to "exercise all such authority as the public interest requires."[14] Thus, although the precise subject matter of the laws has changed (and multiplied) over time, the state attorney general has long had the power and responsibility to assess the public interest and to enforce state law in accordance with that assessment.

[10] Lynne M. Ross, ed., STATE ATTORNEYS GENERAL: POWERS AND RESPONSIBILITIES (Washington, DC: Bureau of National Affairs, 1990) (hereinafter "Ross, POWERS AND RESPONSIBILITIES"), 15. In five of the remaining seven states (Alaska, Hawaii, New Hampshire, New Jersey, and Wyoming), the attorney general is appointed by the governor, ibid., though in three of those (Hawaii, New Hampshire, and New Jersey), the governor may not remove the attorney general at will. Marshall, "Break Up the Presidency?" 2448 n. 3. The attorney general is selected by secret ballot of the state legislature in Maine and by the Supreme Court in Tennessee. Ross, POWERS AND RESPONSIBILITIES, 15. For the balance of this chapter, my references to the state attorney general assume that the office is subject to direct democratic election. In the small number of states where that is not the case, the prescriptions of this chapter may apply with less force.

[11] Ross, POWERS AND RESPONSIBILITIES, 11.

[12] Ibid., 13; Jason Lynch, "Federalism, Separation of Powers, and the Role of State Attorneys General in Multistate Litigation," COLUMBIA LAW REVIEW 101, no. 8 (2001): 1998.

[13] Richard P. Ieyoub and Theodore Eisenberg, "State Attorney General Actions, the Tobacco Litigation, and the Doctrine of PARENS PATRIAE," TULANE LAW REVIEW 74, nos. 5–6 (2000): 1863.

[14] FLORIDA EX REL SHEVIN V. EXXON CORP., 526 F.2d 266, 268–69 (5th Cir. 1976).

Two specific dimensions of the state attorney general's powers bear high-lighting here. The first is the power to investigate regulated entities' level of compliance with relevant state – and, in some cases, federal – law. Perhaps the most important form of investigative authority in this context is known as visitorial power. In many states, the attorney general is authorized to engage in "[v]isitation," which "is the act of a superior or superintending officer, who visits a corporation to examine into its manner of conducting business."[5] Typically, "[v]isitors of corporations have power to keep them within the legitimate sphere of their operations, and to correct all abuses of authority, and to nullify all irregular proceedings."[6] State attorneys general are com-monly granted this power over corporations and other entities doing business in the state. In New York, for example, the attorney general is empowered to investigate instances of "persistent fraud or illegality in the carrying on, con-ducting or transaction of business" in the state, and to "issue subpoenas . . . [,] take proof[,] and make a determination of the relevant facts" in connection with such investigations.[7]

In addition, some states authorize the attorney general to enlist the subject-specific visitorial authority of other executive-branch officials. Michigan law, for example, provides that its attorney general may initiate a proceeding with the commissioner of insurance and financial services to determine whether an entity covered by state banking or related laws is complying with them.[8] The commissioner, in turn, can investigate the complaint, refer the matter to the appropriate federal regulatory authority if it targets a state-chartered subsidiary of a national bank, and take further action if the matter is not "adequately pursued" by the federal agency.[9]

In sum, state attorneys general exercising their visitorial and related inves-tigative powers are in a position to ascertain whether regulated entities within their jurisdictions are complying with relevant state and federal laws, respond to consumer and other public complaints, and root out unlawful conduct that

---

[5] GUTHRIE V. HARKNESS, 199 U.S. 148, 158 (1905).

[6] Ibid., 157–8.

[7] McKinney's Exec. Law § 63(12). As discussed later in this chapter, a divided panel of the U.S. Court of Appeals for the Second Circuit recently concluded that federal banking laws preempt this provision as applied to national banks, even when the investigation is focused on a bank's compliance with state laws that are themselves not preempted by federal law. See CLEARING HOUSE ASS'N V. CUOMO, 510 F. 3d 105 (2d Cir. 2007). That decision exemplifies the problem to which this chapter is addressed.

[8] Mich. Comp. Laws Ann. § 445.1663(1). The Supreme Court has concluded that this and related provisions of Michigan law are preempted by the National Bank Act. See WATTERS v. WACHOVIA BANK, N.A., 127 S. Ct. 1559 (2007). That decision is also reflective of the problem to which this chapter is addressed.

[9] Ibid., § 445.1663(2).

might otherwise go undetected. The mere fact that a regulated entity is subject to the attorney general's visitorial power undoubtedly creates a powerful incentive to comply with the law. Where that fails, the visitorial power can be used to generate the information needed to decide whether, when, and how to enforce the law. As discussed in the following text, some of that enforcement may come from the attorney general him- or herself. But as the Michigan example shows, state investigations can also yield information that is turned over to the responsible federal agency for possible enforcement at that level. In this way, state investigation can aid federal enforcement and perhaps even spur federal agencies into action and out of the stasis to which they sometimes fall prey.[20]

Enforcement can also happen at the state level, the principal responsibility for which usually resides with the state attorney general. Whether under state statutory or common law, attorneys general typically possess broad authority to sue in the public interest. As to the former, states such as California have statutes empowering the attorney general to prosecute suits for injunctive relief and civil penalties against "[a]ny person who engages, has engaged, or proposes to engage" in "any unlawful, unfair or fraudulent business act or practice [or] unfair, deceptive, untrue or misleading advertising."[21] As to the latter, states such as Louisiana recognize the attorney general's power to act in a *parens patriae* capacity by initiating nuisance, fraud, and other actions to protect the public.[22] In these and other respects, the state attorney general's investigative authority is complemented by broad power to enforce state law in the public interest.

The picture that emerges here is of the state attorney general as a democratically accountable officer charged with safeguarding the public and, to that end, invested with broad-ranging authority to monitor compliance with state (and sometimes federal) laws and to initiate enforcement actions when necessary. This combination of accountability and authority makes the attorney general a particularly important state institution. Although there certainly are occasions when federal law needs to displace this institution in order to advance some overarching regulatory goal, such displacement carries substantial costs. Given those costs, it is sensible to pause before construing any particular federal law to preempt the work of the state attorney general.

[20] For more on the phenomenon of federal regulatory failure, see Chapters 3 and 11 of this volume by Professors Vladeck and McGarity, respectively.

[21] Cal. Bus. and Prof. Code §§ 17200-17205. These same provisions of California law also allow private individuals to sue, provided they have "suffered injury in fact and ha[ve] lost money or property as a result of" the complained of activity. Ibid. § 17204. Actions by the attorney general need not establish that anyone has suffered such harm.

[22] See generally, Ieyoub and Eisenberg, "State Attorney General Actions."

STATE ATTORNEYS GENERAL UNDER CURRENT
PREEMPTION DOCTRINE

Although there are both democratic and basic law-enforcement reasons to be reluctant about preempting state attorneys general, a number of recent cases have done so quite readily.

Consider, for example, *OCC v. Spitzer*.[23] The case involved a regulation promulgated by the federal Office of the Comptroller of the Currency (OCC) construing the National Bank Act to grant the OCC "exclusive visitorial authority with respect to the content and conduct of activities authorized for national banks under Federal law."[24] Under that construction, the OCC deems state attorneys general to be prohibited from enforcing against national banks not only state laws targeting banking in particular, but also state laws of general application forbidding such things as racial discrimination. The OCC does not deny the applicability of state antidiscrimination laws to national banks' lending and other practices. Instead, it takes the position that the OCC has exclusive authority to investigate national banks and to prosecute enforcement actions to compel their compliance with both federal and state law. The National Bank Act contains no such provision; the OCC's regulation is thus an example of agency preemption. The district court in *OCC v. Spitzer* agreed with the OCC on this point, broadly concluding that the agency has "exclusive authority to investigate national banks and prosecute enforcement actions to compel their compliance with state and federal laws regulating the conduct of federally authorized banking activities."[25] A divided panel of the U.S. Court of Appeals for the Second Circuit recently affirmed that decision.[26]

OCC v. Spitzer may or may not be rightly decided under current preemption doctrine; there are plausible claims on both sides of the case. But to the

---

[23] 396 F. Supp. 2d 383 (S.D.N.Y. 2005), Aff'd Sub Nom. Clearing House Ass'n v. Cuomo, 510 F. 3d 105 (2d Cir. 2007).

[24] 12 C.F.R. 7.4000(a)(3); see also 12 C.F.R. 7.4000(b)(2) (providing that the National Bank Act's "court of justice" exception "pertains to the powers inherent in the judiciary and does not grant state or other governmental authorities any right to inspect, superintend, direct, regulate or compel compliance by a national bank with respect to any law, regarding the content or conduct of activities authorized for national banks under Federal laws").

[25] OCC v. Spitzer, 396 F. Supp. 2d at 385. For summaries of some other recent episodes in agency preemption, see Myron Levin and Alan C. Miller, "Industries Get Quiet Protection from Lawsuits," Los Angeles Times, February 19, 2006, A1; Caroline E. Mayer, "Rules Would Limit Lawsuits: U.S. Agencies Seek to Preempt States," Washington Post, February 16, 2006, D01.

[26] See Clearing House Ass'n v. Cuomo, 510 F. 3d 105 (2d Cir. 2007).

extent the doctrine at least arguably permits results such as this, it makes preempting the work of state attorneys general quite easy. To see how this is so, it is helpful to review the main features of preemption doctrine as it currently exists.[27]

Preemption doctrine is designed to implement the Constitution's instruction, in the Supremacy Clause, that when state and federal law are incompatible, federal law trumps.[28] Although the doctrine is not always consistently applied, its basic contours are reasonably clear. Preemption may be either express or implied. The former is straightforward: "[W]ithin constitutional limits Congress may pre-empt state authority by so stating in express terms."[29] The latter is more varied and may be subdivided into field and conflict preemption: "[A] federal statute implicitly overrides state law either when the scope of a statute indicates that Congress intended federal law to occupy a field exclusively, . . . or when state law is in actual conflict with federal law."[30] The category of implied conflict preemption may be divided one step further, into cases "where it is 'impossible for a private party to comply with both state and federal requirements'" and cases "where state law 'stands as an obstacle to the accomplishment and execution of the full purposes and objectives of Congress.'"[31] This last subcategory, sometimes called *obstacle preemption*, is where many agency preemption cases may be found.

As the Supreme Court has repeatedly made clear, preemption is ultimately a matter of congressional intent and purpose.[32] Yet the interpretive methods employed in these cases are often based in constitutional or other substantive norms not contained in the statute and not directly contemplated by Congress. Perhaps the most significant is the "presumption against preemption." This interpretive rule directs courts to "start with the assumption that the historic police powers of the States were not to be superseded . . . unless that

---

[27] The doctrine is described in greater detail by Professor Schroeder in Chapter 6 of this volume.

[28] See U.S. Const. art. VI, cl. 2. ("This Constitution, and the Laws of the United States which shall be made in Pursuance thereof; and all Treaties made, or which shall be made, under the Authority of the United States, shall be the supreme Law of the Land; and the Judges in every State shall be bound thereby, any Thing in the Constitution or Laws of any State to the Contrary notwithstanding.")

[29] Pac. Gas and Elec. Co. v. State Energy Res. Conservation and Dev. Comm'n, 461 U.S. 190, 203 (1983).

[30] Freightliner Corp. v. Myrick, 514 U.S. 280, 287 (1995).

[31] Ibid. (quoting English v. General Elec. Co., 496 U.S. 72, 78–79 [1990], and Hines v. Davidowitz, 312 U.S. 52, 67 [1941]).

[32] See, e.g., Medtronic, Inc. v. Lohr, 518 U.S. 470, 485 (1996). ("'[T]he purpose of Congress is the ultimate touchstone' in every pre-emption case.") (quoting Retail Clerks Int'l Ass'n v. Schermerhorn, 375 U.S. 96, 103 [1963]).

was the clear and manifest purpose of Congress."[33] The presumption does not apply in all cases; it applies only where preemption would displace some aspect of "the States' historic police powers."[34] It is inapplicable, therefore, "when the State regulates in an area where there has been a history of significant federal presence."[35]

Quite clearly, the presumption against preemption is "rooted in the concept of federalism"[36] – specifically, the idea that the Constitution contemplates an ongoing role for the states in areas traditionally regulated by them, and that the courts ought to interpret federal laws with a presumption in favor of preserving that role. In that respect, it is similar to certain clear statement rules developed in cases like *Gregory v. Ashcroft*. In *Gregory*, the Court considered whether a federal statute banning age discrimination in employment applied to state judges despite a state constitutional requirement that they retire by age seventy. The case came to the Court only a few years after it had decided, in *Garcia v. San Antonio Metropolitan Transit Authority*,[37] that any constitutionally based norm against congressional encroachment on core state governmental functions was not susceptible to direct judicial enforcement. For the *Gregory* Court, that lack of direct judicial enforcement provided a basis for adopting a federalism-favoring rule of statutory construction: "[I]nasmuch as this Court in *Garcia* has left primarily to the political process the protection of the States against intrusive exercises of Congress' Commerce Clause powers, we must be absolutely certain that Congress intended such an exercise."[38] To that end, the Court announced that it would not construe federal statutes to "upset the usual constitutional balance of federal and state powers" unless Congress has made "its intention to do so unmistakably clear in the language of the statute."[39] Finding no clear statement that the age discrimination statute was intended to apply to core state functions, the Court held it did not apply to state judges.

The larger idea behind clear statement rules of this sort is that federal regulation in areas of core state concern has the potential to upset the federal-state balance even where federal law just creates a regulatory overlay. Although it

---

[33] RICE V. SANTA FE ELEVATOR CORP., 331 U.S. 218, 230 (1947).

[34] GEIER V. AM. HONDA MOTOR CORP., 529 U.S. 861, 894 (2000) (Stevens, J., dissenting).

[35] UNITED STATES V. LOCKE, 529 U.S. 89, 108 (2000). In addition, there is no presumption against preemption when a state intrudes on the sovereign prerogatives of the federal government by directly regulating the federal government or its agents. See generally Seth P. Waxman and Trevor W. Morrison, "What Kind of Immunity? Federal Officers, State Criminal Law, and the Supremacy Clause," YALE LAW JOURNAL 112, no. 8 (2003): 2195.

[36] GEIER, 529 U.S. at 907 (Stevens, J., dissenting).

[37] 469 U.S. 528 (1985).

[38] 501 U.S. at 464.

[39] Ibid., 460.

may be within Congress's power to effect such changes, the Court has declared that it will not deem Congress to have intended such a result absent a clear statutory statement to that effect.[40] Viewed in this light, clear statement rules of this sort share a certain kinship with the presumption against preemption.[41] Both implement federalism norms by directing courts to interpret statutes so as to favor the preservation of certain state powers, roles, and prerogatives.[42]

But there is a problem with both the presumption against preemption and federalism-enforcing clear statement rules, at least as they are currently formulated. They are all structured around substantive triggers that require courts to identify and attach great consequence to the "historic" functions of the states. Yet in *Garcia*, the Court rejected a closely related enterprise as "unsound in principle and unworkable in practice."[43] There, the question was whether the Constitution contains a judicially enforceable limit on Congress's authority to regulate states in the performance of traditional state government functions. In rejecting its earlier attempt in *National League of Cities v. Usery*[44] to enforce such a limit, the Court concluded, first, that as a practical matter it "ha[d] made little headway in defining the scope" of traditional government functions.[45] Second, the Court stressed a "more fundamental problem" with the undertaking: even assuming courts could separate the traditional from the modern, there is no reason to think the federal system should favor the former over the latter.[46] States should be free to innovate

---

[40] See WILL V. MICHIGAN DEPT. OF STATE POLICE, 491 U.S. 58, 65 (1989) ("[I]f Congress intends to alter the 'usual constitutional balance between the States and the Federal Government,' it must make its intention to do so 'unmistakably clear in the language of the statute.'") (quoting ATASCADERO STATE HOSPITAL V. SCANLON, 473 U.S. 234, 242 [1985]).

[41] See GREGORY, 501 U.S. at 461 (referring to the presumption against preemption in the course of defending its clear statement rule).

[42] There are important differences between the presumption against preemption and federalism-protecting clear statement rules. Put simply, the former can be overcome with something less than a clear statutory statement. A true clear statement requirement is really a rule of specific drafting: the requirement can be satisfied only by express language in the text of the statute. See Ernest A. Young, "The Rehnquist Court's Two Federalisms," TEXAS LAW REVIEW 83, no. 1 (2004): 1, 23 n. 90. The presumption against preemption may be better described as an interpretive "standard that simply urges courts to err on the side of state autonomy while still considering all potentially relevant sources of statutory meaning." Ibid. This is a significant difference. "If GREGORY's 'plain statement' rule were applied to preemption, . . . entire bodies of preemption doctrine might be called into question." Ibid.

[43] 469 U.S. 528, 546–7 (1985).

[44] 426 U.S. 833 (1976).

[45] GARCIA, 469 U.S. at 539.

[46] See ibid., 545–6. ("The essence of our federal system is that within the realm of authority left open to them under the Constitution, the States must be equally free to engage in any activity that their citizens choose for the common weal, no matter how unorthodox or unnecessary anyone else – including the judiciary – deems state involvement to be.")

within the boundaries of their regulatory authority, and the Constitution should not be construed to hinder such innovation. Thus, the Court abandoned the project of directly enforcing any constitutional limit on the federal government's power to regulate the states, other than the limits entailed in the enumeration of federal power.

The presumption against preemption and the *Gregory* clear statement rule both invite courts to resume essentially the same kind of analysis abandoned in *Garcia*, though now in service of rebuttable presumptions about statutory meaning.[47] Yet if the Court was right in *Garcia* that this sort of analysis is neither feasible nor desirable in the context of direct constitutional enforcement, there is a strong argument that the same should be true for these rules of (constitutionally informed) statutory interpretation.[48]

Moreover, the problems with the presumption against preemption and the *Gregory* clear statement rule are even more acute when applied to cases implicating state attorneys general. Not only is it impractical to expect courts to be able to determine whether particular issues fall within a zone of "core" or "historic" state concern, but also this approach encourages courts to focus on the subject matter of the laws at issue rather than the institutions involved in the implementation of those laws. This indifference to institutions renders preemption doctrine insensitive to the close connection between the state attorney general and core federalism values such as democratic accountability. By not taking account of that connection, current preemption doctrine does not adequately weigh the federalism-related costs of displacing the work of the state attorney general. The point here is not that federal law should avoid preempting state attorneys general at all costs. Rather, the point is that the decision whether to preempt should take more direct account of this key state institution. The next section shows how Congress and federal agencies can do precisely that.

TOWARD CONGRESSIONAL AND AGENCY SOLICITUDE FOR STATE ATTORNEYS GENERAL

It may be an uphill challenge to persuade the courts to become more sensitive to preemption's particular impact on state attorneys general. But Congress

---

[47] Justice Blackmun criticized the Court's decision in GREGORY on this very ground. See GREGORY, 501 U.S. at 477 (Blackmun, J., dissenting) (criticizing the Court's adoption of a clear statement rule as "directly contraven[ing] our decision in GARCIA").

[48] The formal distinction between constitutional and statutory interpretation seems insufficient to support the divergence between GARCIA and GREGORY. After all, "[a]ny theory of statutory interpretation is at base a theory about constitutional law." Jerry Mashaw, "As if Republican Interpretation," YALE LAW JOURNAL 97, no. 8 (1988): 1685–6.

and the administrative state need not wait for the courts to act. Instead, they can and should adopt an approach that takes special account of the state attorney general and that refrains from preempting its work absent a specific legislative choice to do so. The prescription here contains two straightforward steps. First, when passing a statute that carries the potential of preempting state law to any degree, Congress should devote special attention to whether any or all of the work of state attorneys general (disaggregating, possibly, the attorney general's investigative and litigating functions) should be preempted and should include a provision making clear the extent of its intent to preempt. Second, in the absence of such clear statutory language, federal agencies should indulge a strong presumption against preempting state attorneys general by regulation. Both of these suggestions flow from the same underlying view: federal law should preempt the core investigative and enforcement work of state attorneys general only by express statutory language.

The argument in favor of this approach tracks the federalism-related values discussed earlier. Most importantly, it protects the values of democratic accountability and self-governance – values that, as discussed in previously, are core virtues of federalism itself. The connection to those values in this context is plain. When a state attorney general decides to enforce (or investigate compliance with) a particular state law in a particular context, that decision has a double claim to democratic legitimacy: it reflects the democratically accountable state legislature's decision to enact such a law and to make it enforceable by the attorney general, and it also reflects the democratically accountable attorney general's decision to enforce the law. Federal agencies, in contrast, have a much more attenuated claim to democratic legitimacy. They are not directly elected, and as a practical matter they usually are not subject to close oversight by the President. Thus, to the extent federalism is a means to the ends of democratic accountability and citizen control of government, those ends seem best pursued by shielding state attorneys general from agency preemption.

At the same time, the approach I advocate here leaves Congress entirely free to displace state attorneys general to the extent it deems appropriate. My approach simply encourages Congress to address the state attorney general head-on and to enact express statutory language specifying whether, and to what extent, it intends to preempt the work of the state attorney general.

This approach ensures that the decision to preempt is made via a process structured to take account of the interests of the states. According to the familiar "political safeguards of federalism" thesis, the system of state representation in Congress makes the federal legislative process the principal constitutional means of protecting federalism.[49] But that system is not engaged unless Congress turns its attention to the particular issue at hand. This same thinking underlies the judiciary's use of the federalism-enhancing clear statement rules discussed in Part III. The point of those rules is to help clarify that the democratically accountable federal legislature – not merely a court or administrative agency – did intend to regulate in a way that implicates the federalism norm in question. As the Court has described, "in traditionally sensitive areas, such as legislation affecting the federal balance, the requirement of clear statement assures that the legislature has in fact faced, and intended to bring into issue, the critical matters involved in the judicial decision."[50] In that sense, clear statement rules express a strong preference between two kinds of potential interpretive errors. By requiring a clear statement before construing a statute to implicate the federalism norm in question, courts express a preference for erring on the side of the states rather than against them. The same is true for the particular approach I am urging here, which would require Congress to adopt a practice of specifying the extent to which it intends to preempt the investigative, enforcement, and other core powers of state attorneys general.

Not only does the approach advocated here maximize the democratic accountability of decisions to oust state attorneys general, but it also recognizes the enormous potential value of state attorneys general to the enforcement of both state and federal law. Especially given the ever-present pressure on federal agency budgets, state attorneys general can be invaluable yet cheap (from the perspective of the federal fisc) partners in the law-enforcement effort. As discussed in the preceding text, the exercise of visitorial power by state attorneys general can help federal agencies learn more about the extent to which relevant federal laws and regulations are being followed. Regardless of whether the agency will then deem formal enforcement proceedings to be in order, the key point is that state attorneys general can help the agency make that decision on the basis of better information. That sort of assistance should not be rendered unavailable except by the intentional and express decision of Congress.

The calculus is much different if Congress enacts express language specifying its intent to preempt state attorneys general. Instead of an unelected agency

---

[49] See generally, Herbert Wechsler, "The Political Safeguards of Federalism," COLUMBIA LAW REVIEW 54, no. 4 (1954): 543.

[50] GREGORY, 501 U.S. at 464; see EEOC v. ARABIAN AM. OIL CO., 499 U.S. 244, 262 (1991) (Marshall, J., dissenting). ("Clear-statement rules operate less to reveal actual congressional intent that to shield important values from an insufficiently strong legislative intent to displace them.")

displacing the work of an elected state official, the most democratically account-able branch of the federal government will have determined that the costs of allowing state attorneys general to continue working in the area outweigh the benefits, decided therefore to preempt that work, and memorialized that deci-sion in clear terms. At that point, the federal government will have delivered democratic accountability as best it can. Preemption properly follows.

I would note one potential alternative here. Because the decision whether to preempt in any particular context requires access to information that Con-gress might not have had at the time it legislated, it may be appropriate for Congress to delegate preemption authority to the relevant regulatory agency. It is not my aim here to delve into all the elements of such delegations; Professor Funk addresses them in greater detail in Chapter 10. Rather, I want only to note that a Congress wanting to delegate preemption authority to the agency can still be attentive to the special role of state attorneys general by clearly specifying whether the agency's preemption power extends to state attorneys general.

AN OBJECTION: THE EXTRATERRITORIALITY PROBLEM

Having laid out the case for special congressional and agency solicitude for the state attorney general, I now identify and respond to a potential objec-tion to the argument as I have presented it. One might argue that, far from delivering on the values of democratic accountability as I have suggested, state attorneys general are often *un*democratic and *un*accountable in impor-tant ways. The concern here is with extraterritoriality. If, for example, the attorney general in New York successfully sues a manufacturer based in California over defects in its products sold in New York, the effects of a large civil fine or other costly remedy may be borne in part by the workers in the manufacturer's California plant (if it must lay off employees) or even by the general citizenry of California (if the layoffs lead to an economic downturn).[51]

Some scholars maintain that extraterritoriality of this sort undermines any attempt to resist preemption on grounds of democracy or self-governance:

---

[51] See Samuel Issacharoff and Catherine M. Sharkey, "Backdoor Federalization," UCLA LAW REVIEW 53, no. 6 (2006): 1353, 1386 (noting the "specter of spillover effects, whereby a state uses its liability regime to benefit in-state residents with larger compensation payments, or exports the costs of its regulation to out-of-state manufacturers and product consumers in the rest of the nation").

If the state juries in, say, Creek County, Oklahoma, routinely impose enormous liability on out-of-state automobile corporations simply to enrich local plaintiffs and the local bar, then this is a burden on the self-governing capacity of states where those automobile manufacturers have their primary places of operations. In effect, Oklahoma is regulating and taxing the businesses of Michigan without considering the desires of the persons most affected – those dependent on Michigan's tax base and sources of employment. Why is not such taxation and regulation without representation an attack on "civic republican values"?[52]

Proponents of this view also stress that even Justice Brandeis, the champion of the much-invoked "laboratory" model of federalism, endorsed state creativity and experimentation only to the extent that it would not harm the rest of the country.[53] Where the efforts of one state do spill over into another, the argument goes, neither the laboratory model nor the democratic accountability norm applies.

I disagree. Consider again the hypothetical case brought by the New York attorney general against the California company. Assuming *arguendo* the existence of extraterritorial effects, it does not follow that New York and California are identically situated in this case. As discussed in Part I, the structure of our federalist system contemplates overlapping federal and state regulation. The default presumption is in favor of state regulatory authority. In the New York and California hypothetical, preempting the New York lawsuit would mean departing from that default presumption by denying New York its regulatory authority. In contrast, *not* preempting the lawsuit would not mean the same thing for California. Even if the New York attorney general's suit would have the extraterritorial effects we have assumed, that would not deprive California of its formal regulatory authority. California's ability to achieve all the regulatory outcomes it seeks for its people might be compromised by the economic downturn, but that is not the same as preempting its regulatory authority. Federalism and preemption must be principally concerned with the latter, not the former, because otherwise the extraterritoriality issue would swallow the Constitution's default rule in favor of state regulation.

To put the same point slightly differently, every act of state governance inevitably has at least some extraterritorial effects. Even laws that apply only

---

[52] Roderick M. Hills, "Against Preemption: How Federalism Can Improve the National Legislative Process," NEW YORK UNIVERSITY LAW REVIEW 82, no. 1 (2006): 1, 5–6. Others have made the same basic point. See, e.g., Issacharoff and Sharkey, "Backdoor Federalization," 1387–8.

[53] NEW STATE ICE CO. V. LIEBERMAN, 285 U.S. 262, 311 (1932) (Brandeis, J., dissenting). ("It is one of the happy incidents of the federal system that a single courageous state may, if its citizens choose, serve as a laboratory; and try novel social and economic experiments without risk to the rest of the country") (emphasis added).

to entirely in-state entities and populations will inevitably affect that state's comparative position vis-à-vis other states by making it a more or less attractive place to live, work, and do business. Yet this observation does not grind federalism to a halt. Instead, we generally accept that the exercise of any one state's regulatory authority can have effects in other states. The mere possibility of such effects should not change the default presumption in favor of state regulation and against preemption. In the context of the hypothetical raised here, the risk that the New York attorney general's actions might have some adverse consequences in California should not by itself lead us to abandon our presumption in favor of preserving the attorney general's authority.

There are limits, of course. First, the Constitution imposes constraints via the "dormant Commerce Clause." The Supreme Court's doctrine in that area provides that states may not regulate in a manner that unduly discriminates against out-of-state actors[54] or that controls conduct beyond the state's borders.[55] Dormant Commerce Clause doctrine, then, addresses the extraterritoriality issue by establishing boundaries beyond which no state attorney general may venture.

In addition to those constitutional limits, Congress can intervene and preempt state attorneys general in a particular field if it concludes that their presence has generated too many extraterritorial costs. Nothing I have said here is intended to deny Congress's authority to intervene in that way. My point, rather, is simply that in light of the state attorney general's democratic pedigree and potential value as an investigator and law enforcer, Congress should specify when it intends to preempt the work of the state attorney general, or, at the least, when it intends to authorize agencies to do so.

CONCLUSION

The state attorney general is a significant institution in state government, combining direct democratic accountability with expansive powers to act in the public interest. Too often, the judicial doctrine of preemption accords no special consideration to this important institution. As this chapter has shown, however, Congress and federal agencies can and should overcome that judicial neglect. Put simply, greater solicitude for the state attorney general should become part of the legislative and administrative preemption calculus.

[54] See, e.g., BROWN-FORMAN DISTILLERS CORP. v. NEW YORK STATE LIQUOR AUTH., 476 U.S. 573 (1986).

[55] See, e.g., EDGAR v. MITE CORP., 457 U.S. 624 (1982).

5 Federal Floors, Ceilings, and the Benefits of Federalism's Institutional Diversity

William W. Buzbee*

INTRODUCTION

Federal regulatory schemes commonly utilize cooperative federalism structures and involve standard setting or other federal actions that serve as a regulatory "floor." Such floors preempt and thereby preclude any more lax regulatory choices by state or local governments. With such floors, state and local governments, and common law schemes as well, all can impose either more stringent regulatory requirements or common law incentives to create less risk. With the partial preemption of regulatory floors, targets of regulation often confront multiple lawmakers and overlapping regulatory obligations. Another sort of federally preclusive action, so-called ceiling preemption, is also possible but has been far less common. Regulatory ceilings involve federal actions or standard setting that preclude additional, more protective regulatory choices by other levels of government and sometimes can preclude common law liabilities. But these two sorts of preemptive actions reflect more than just choices about the levels of protection provided by regulation. When one works through the logic of federal actions and the implications of the Supremacy Clause, so-called ceilings actually constitute a unitary federal choice precluding other actors' ongoing interaction and revisiting of earlier regulatory choices. Regulatory floors, in contrast, provide an array of regulatory benefits lost with the far more completely preclusive "ceiling preemption."[1]

* I thank research assistants Annie Mackay, Daniel Adams, Chandani Patel, Meg Harmsen, and Michael Eber, all of whom assisted with this essay or related research and publications.
[1] I explore this floor/ceiling distinction in two recent works. See William W. Buzbee, "Asymmetrical Regulation: Risk, Preemption, and the Floor/Ceiling Distinction," NEW YORK UNIVERSITY LAW REVIEW 82, no. 6 (December 2007): 1547; William W. Buzbee, "Interaction's Promise: Preemption Policy Shifts, Risk Regulation, and Experimentalism's Lessons," EMORY LAW JOURNAL 57, no. 1 (2007): 145. This chapter draws and builds on those works, although the "Asymmetrical Regulation" article is a substantially longer work.

This is not to claim that ceilings or more fully preemptive federal actions do not have their place. Such preemptive standards are consistent with a persistent strain in Supreme Court jurisprudence that values distinctly delineated federal and state terrains akin to that long-embraced under the "dual federalism" doctrine. Under conflict preemption doctrine rooted in the Supremacy Clause, it is also necessarily the case that where federal legal requirements in application come into direct conflict with state or local law, federal law prevails. In some limited settings, a distinct, final, single answer about legal obligations will make sense.

In statutory and regulatory regimes, however, Congress and agencies have for many years overwhelmingly manifested a preference for regulatory overlap and interaction, harnessing the strengths of state and federal institutional actors and forcing the two to interact. Common law regimes, and the incentives they create for ongoing assessment and improvement by sources of risk, have also typically been preserved under savings clauses. State and local governments, as well as common law regimes, have thus typically retained latitude under federal risk regulation to surpass the stringency of federal regulation or provide additional protections through different strategies.

Fully preemptive federal standards, especially in their recently asserted form of ceilings operating as a unitary federal choice, pose an array of institutional risks. Some of these risks are readily apparent, although others are less obvious. All are illuminated by applying recent scholarship regarding regulatory federalism, especially analyses of other forms of preclusive regulatory action, as well as recent work on "regulatory experimentalism." This chapter explains how, in the risk regulation setting, the messy clashing and interaction of real-world multilayered regulatory federalism utilized with federal floors creates incentives and markets for pragmatic improvement and innovation that will seldom exist with federal regulatory ceilings.

Due to an array of recent regulatory and legislative developments, analysis of the distinct implications of federal floors and ceilings is far more than a merely academic exercise. Most significantly, legislative and regulatory debate over climate change legislation has explicitly confronted the floor/ceiling choice, with previously resistant industry tentatively indicating support for climate change legislation dealing with greenhouse gases (GHGs), provided federal law would preclude disparate or additional state and local regulation. Similarly, both in legislative and regulatory settings, the chemical industry has been pushing for federal law to preclude additional state and local regulation of risks posed by chemical facilities. In addition, during 2006 and 2007, numerous agencies proposed or asserted that regulatory actions preclude additional state, local, or even common law actions. In short, many of the most fundamental risk-regulation debates now center on the floor versus ceiling preemption choice. This chapter provides analysis of this choice.

FLOORS AND CEILINGS: TWO DISTINCTIVE CHOICES

After briefly reviewing the ongoing judicial flirtation with the largely abandoned "dualist" federalism perspective, and then describing the far more common political choice of multilayered legal regimes where federal law sets only a regulatory law floor, this part turns to the recent unusual embrace of federal regulatory ceilings. In an array of recent regulatory and legislative actions and proposals, federal agencies and legislators have embraced ceiling preemption. Such ceilings function as a unitary federal choice resulting in complete displacement of other regulatory actors. All institutional diversity is lost.

Despite congressional embrace of regulatory schemes utilizing multiple levels of regulators, judicial doctrine and much scholarly commentary continue to express a normative preference for more clean delineation of federal and state powers.[2] The "dual federalism" phase in judicial federalism doctrine constituted an extreme form of this preference for neatly divided authority. As Professor Schapiro traces in Chapter 2, "dual federalism" constitutional doctrine imposed, as a matter of constitutional law, a clean line between what was federal and what was state. The occupation by one in an area meant the exclusion of the other. That phase in constitutional doctrine has passed, but a judicial preference for such clean delineation of federal and state roles reemerges periodically in judicial doctrine, sometimes changing outcomes by tipping the interpretive scale.[3] For example, as discussed by Professor Schroeder in Chapter 6, in three of the Supreme Court's most recent major federalism decisions, Court divisions largely turned on disputed claims regarding whether the subject of regulation involved primarily federal or state turf.[4]

[2] See, e.g., U.S. v. Morrison, 529 U.S. 598, 617–18 (2000) (explaining that the Constitution "requires a distinction" between what is regulated nationally or locally); Printz v. U.S., 521 U.S. 898 (1997). For two articles discussing this frequent judicial interpretive preference in federalism cases, see William W. Buzbee and Robert A. Schapiro, "Legislative Record Review," Stanford Law Review 54, no. 1 (2001): 87; Robert A. Schapiro and William W. Buzbee, "Unidimensional Federalism: Power and Perspective in Commerce Clause Adjudication," Cornell Law Review 88, no. 5 (2003): 1199.

[3] See Edward S. Corwin, "The Passing of Dual Federalism," Virginia Law Review 36, no. 1 (1950): 1, 17; Robert A. Schapiro, "Justice Stevens' Theory of Interactive Federalism," Fordham Law Review 74, no. 4 (2006): 2133; Paul Wolfson, "Preemption and Federalism: The Missing Link," Hastings Constitutional Law Quarterly 16, no. 1 (1988): 69, 91–2. For an example of the vestiges of dual federalism, see Solid Waste Agency of No. Cook Co. v. U.S. Army Corps of Engineers, 531 U.S. 158 (2001).

[4] Gonzales v. Oregon, 546 U.S. 243 (2006); Gonzales v. Raich, 545 U.S. 1 (2005); Rapanos v. U.S., 126 S. Ct. 2208 (2006).

In the modern political realm and the contemporary administrative state, however, dual federalism approaches are a rarity. Instead, Congress has repeatedly chosen to create regulatory schemes that call on a role for federal, state, and sometimes even local governments.[5] These multilayered regulatory schemes, often identified as cooperative federalism structures or delegated program federalism, typically involve enactment of a federal statute that regulates a risk or addresses a social ill or need. Such cooperative federalism schemes are especially prevalent in the environmental law field.[6] Such laws do not, however, depend solely on federal actors for their implementation and enforcement. Through an array of statutorily created incentives or choices, state and local actors will often assume critically important regulatory duties. They are constrained, however. They cannot adopt more lax requirements, but they are typically explicitly allowed to set more protective regulatory requirements. Seldom does any actor completely surrender its involvement.

Federal regulatory schemes also often countenance the ongoing independent existence of state and local regulation and potential common law liabilities pertaining to the same subject as federal law. State tort and nuisance common law is the most typical and significant retained area of independent authority that, in impact, involves state common law overlap with federal law. As discussed by Professor Zellmer in Chapter 7, through "savings clauses" Congress often expressly states its intent to preserve such state roles.[7] In short, under floor preemption, the federal government through legislation or regulatory action sets minimum required levels of protective stringency. Such floors leave room for more protective state and local regulation or incentives created through common law regimes. Floor standards typically seek state and local involvement under cooperative federalism strategies. The result both under delegated program schemes and federal bodies of regulation "saving" state law is federal law that calls on and retains a role for all three layers of government.

[5] See William W. Buzbee, "Contextual Environmental Federalism," NEW YORK UNIVERSITY ENVIRONMENTAL LAW JOURNAL 14, no. 1 (2005): 108 (discussing federal and state interaction under multilayered federal regimes); Robert A. Schapiro, "Toward a Theory of Interactive Federalism," IOWA LAW REVIEW 91, no. 1 (2005): 243 (emphasizing benefits of interaction among courts and other regulatory actors rather than more common desire to keep regulatory roles separate).

[6] See e.g., Endangered Species Act of 1973 16 U.S.C. § 1531(c)(2) (2000); Clean Water Act, 33 U.S.C. § 1251(b)(2000); Clean Air Act 42 U.S.C. § 7402(a)(2000). See also Jonathan H. Adler, "Judicial Federalism and the Future of Environmental Regulation," IOWA LAW REVIEW 90, no. 2 (2005): 377, 384–7 and n. 35 (discussing cooperative federalism schemes); Buzbee, CONTEXTUAL ENVIRONMENTAL FEDERALISM, SUPRA n. 5.

[7] See e.g., Clean Water Act (2005) (citing Clean Water Act, 33 U.S.C. § 1370 [2000]); Toxic Substances Control Act, 158 U.S.C. § 2617 (a)(1)(2000); Resource Conservation and Recovery Act, 42 U.S.C. § 6929 (2000); Federal Insecticide, Fungicide and Rodenticide Act, 7 U.S.C. § 136v(a)(2000).

THE NEW EMBRACE OF CEILING PREEMPTION

Despite this long-existing choice in federal law to retain roles for state, local, and common law regimes, industry has periodically responded to the costs of disparate states' regulation with calls for preemptive federal law. Seldom, however, has industry succeeded in obtaining more than the benefit of federal law that will act to preempt direct legal conflicts. Occasionally, industry has secured the uncommon benefit of "complete preemption," where federal law takes over a field and often provides its own substitute compensatory regime. Industry has also at times secured strongly preemptive federal law when federal law or regulation requires either particular product designs or substantial production investment benefiting from economies of scale. This is most notably true in motor vehicle pollution regulation under the Clean Air Act. Federal emission limitations are set, and states are precluded from imposing additional standards of their own. Only a special break allowing for California innovations, on which other states can piggyback, makes this less than a completely preemptive federal area of law. As mentioned in the preceding section, however, far more common are federal laws that set floors, allow greater state or local stringency, and preserve common law regimes and the protections and compensation they can afford.

Strongly preclusive federal standards acting as a ceiling have recently emerged as a favored option in an array of federal risk legislation or regulation. These actions propose or purport to preempt not only state regulatory law but sometimes also common law. Perhaps of greatest importance, GHG climate change proposals are actively being debated in Congress. Industry's support is apparently conditioned on, if not motivated by desire for, a federal legislative fix preempting any state or local regulation of activities emitting such gases. As stated by Shell Oil's president, "We cannot deal with 50 different policies . . . we need a national approach to greenhouse gases."[8] Numerous state and local

---

[8] Steven Mufson and Juliet Eilperin, "Energy Firms Come to Terms with Climate Change," WASHINGTON POST, November 25, 2006, A1. Numerous states and cities in legislation have started to regulate GHGs, and common law suits have been filed as well. See Kristen H. Engel and Scott R. Saleska, "Subglobal Regulation of the Global Commons: The Case of Climate Change," ECOLOGY LAW QUARTERLY 32, no. 2 (2005): 183; Kristen H. Engel, "Harnessing the Benefits of Dynamic Federalism in Environmental Law," EMORY LAW JOURNAL 56, no. 1 (2006): 159 (exploring the same developments and theory but linking them to larger benefits of retaining latitude for dynamic interaction at different levels of government). As discussed by Professor Glicksman in Chapter 8, recent debates concern whether any states should have authority to regulate motor vehicle GHG emissions, or if that should be exclusively federal domain. See Alex Kaplun, "Climate: Rep. Dingell Defends Plan to Limit State GHG Authority, E&E News PM" (June 7, 2007) (reviewing motor vehicle emission preemption debate and reporting auto industry concern with "50 different standards").

initiatives regulating GHG emissions follow federal reluctance to address the causes of climate change.[9]

Recently, the Department of Homeland Security (DHS) issued a proposed regulation that initially appeared intended to supplant state and local ability to regulate risks associated with chemical plants.[10] Until now such risks were subject to regulation by all levels of government. The underlying law contains no provision granting power to preempt, which has led critics in the press and regulatory process to complain that DHS was overreaching and violating the law.[11] In its Interim Final Rule, DHS disavowed intent to engage in "field" preemption that would displace state, local, or common law related to chemical plant security, instead asserting its power to declare situations of "conflict" preemption.[12] Subsequent skirmishing in legislative settings led to insertion during 2007 of alternative competing legislative language trying either to uphold or preclude such preemptive power.[13] Since the spring of 2006, often with the explicit support of industry, numerous agencies have asserted such preemptive impact of regulations involving product safety and pharmaceutical approvals, claiming power to supplant state and local regulation, and common law liabilities as well.[14]

---

[9] See MASSACHUSETTS V. EPA, 127 S. Ct. 1438 (2007), where the Court rejected U.S. EPA's claimed lack of statutory authority and also found EPA's justifications for not acting, assuming it did have statutory authority, to lack adequate legal and factual justification.

[10] See Department of Homeland Security, Notice of Proposed Chemical Facility Anti-Terrorism Standards, 71 FEDERAL REGISTER 78276-01 (December 28, 2006).

[11] See Editorial, "Chemical Insecurity," NEW YORK TIMES, January 23, 2007, A18.

[12] See Interim Final Rule, Chemical Facility Anti-Terrorism Standards, 72 FEDERAL REGISTER 17688 (April 9, 2007). Despite the FEDERAL REGISTER discussion disavowing anything other than an intent to preserve the possibility of conflict preemption, the actual regulation still contains references to state or local laws, regulations, or actions that not only "conflict" with federal requirements but that "hinder, pose an obstacle to or frustrate the purposes of this Part." Id.

[13] As of the drafting of this chapter, the fate of these competing provisions was unresolved. Compare Stephen Labaton, "Congress Poised to Vote for Higher Minimum Wage," NEW YORK TIMES, May 24, 2007, with Linda Roeder, "House-Passed Homeland Security Bill Includes Chemical Security State Preemption," Chem. Reg. Rep. (BNA), 31, no. 26 (June 20, 2007) and Jeffrey H. Birnbaum, "Chemical Makers and Trial Lawyers Square Off Over Iraq Spending Bill," WASHINGTON POST, April 10, 2007, A15.

[14] For a recent thorough survey of these many actions, see Eric Lipton and Gardiner Harris, "In Turnaround, Industries Seek U.S. Regulations," NEW YORK TIMES, September 16, 2007, A1; Catherine Sharkey, "Preemption by Preamble: Federal Administrative Agencies and the Federalization of Tort Law," DEPAUL LAW REVIEW 56, no. 2 (2007): 227; Stephen Labaton, "Silent Tort Reform" Is Overriding States' Powers, NEW YORK TIMES, March 10, 2006, C5 (finding that "the 'silent tort reform' movement . . . has quietly and quickly been gaining ground"). See also Buzbee, ASYMMETRICAL REGULATION, SUPRA n. 1 at 1570–75 (discussing broad preemption power claims by the Consumer Products Safety Commission, the Food and Drug Administration, the National Highway Traffic Safety Administration, and the Department of Homeland Security).

These new, aggressive forms of unitary federal choice ceiling preemption are quite distinct from the far more typical floor preemption. With regulatory floors, the federal government sets a minimum required level of stringent protection, and states, local governments, and common law regimes can lead to even more protective results. Ceilings, however, act as a unitary federal choice. As discussed in the following section, a unitary federal standard and its accompanying loss of institutional diversity undercuts many of the chief virtues of federalist forms of government.

DISTINGUISHING THE IMPLICATIONS
OF FLOORS AND CEILINGS

The particular risks of unitary federal choice ceiling preemption are apparent when analyzed through the lens of literature on regulatory federalism and other potentially preclusive federal regulatory acts, as well as literature on regulatory failure risks and benefits of regulatory structures fostering innovation. This section briefly summarizes these bodies of work, and then links their insights to critique the distinct implications of regulatory floors and ceilings.

Two bodies of scholarship from recent decades critique federal actions that preclude contrary state choices. One concerns the "race-to-the-bottom rationale" for federal standard setting, especially in the environmental law arena. The other focuses on the "regulatory compliance" defense to tort claims, often in the setting of products approved or licensed by federal regulators. Implicit in both areas of analysis is a critique of elements of the floor versus ceiling choice.

Congress has long-explained federal environmental standard setting as justified by concerns about interjurisdictional competition among states for business. Under this rationale for federal regulation, states will compete for business and ultimately, following a downward competition to create an attractive regulatory environment for industry, adopt suboptimal levels of environmental protection. Environmental cleanliness is sacrificed for more immediate and tangible benefits of jobs and taxes, even if each jurisdiction in an island setting would choose to preserve the environment. During the 1990s, a counterargument emerged. Dean Richard Revesz challenged the adequacy of such a rationale, seeing its ultimate logic as weighing against retention of any federalist structures.[15] States, he argued, will necessarily

---

[15] See e.g., Richard L. Revesz, "The Race to the Bottom and Federal Environmental Regulation: A Response to Critics," Minnesota Law Review 82, no. 1 (1997): 535; Richard L. Revesz, "Rehabilitating Interstate Competition: Rethinking the 'Race-to-the-Bottom' Rationale for Federal Environmental Regulation," New York University Law Review 67, no. 6 (1992): 1210.

compete for businesses and their associated benefits. No state or local government has the same array of assets and needs. When the federal government takes an area of potential state bargaining off of the table, some states will need to utilize a less-appealing menu of regulatory bargaining chips. The net result will be harms to states that would prefer environmental sacrifice to other choices. The only way to eliminate such regulatory competition and sacrifice, he argued, is to eliminate the federalist structures that create inter-jurisdictional competition. He thus derives an argument against preclusive federal standard setting, seeing it as an argument against federalism itself.

The regulatory compliance defense literature, in contrast, analyzes the proposition that federal approvals of products should immunize manufacturers from liability under state law for injuries caused by such products. Advocates of such a defense argue that some federal approvals really constitute a finding that a product is optimal, not just acceptable, and hence should either logically or necessarily under the Constitution preempt contrary conclusions under state law.[16] In addition, tort reform advocates believe that taking cases away from courts and juries would lead to a more thriving industry, especially in areas like pharmaceutical production.[17] Champions of the regulatory compliance defense thus embrace and argue for a greater preclusive impact of federal regulatory actions.

Both lines of argument have come under attack. Numerous scholars powerfully challenged Revesz's arguments with empirical and theoretical arguments.[18] Similarly, prominent scholars identified harms that would flow from the embrace of a regulatory compliance defense. At heart, both debates are about the wisdom of federal actions precluding contrary or additional actions under state regulation and common law. The whole recent race-to-the-bottom debate is about federal standards that serve as floors and preclude more lax state standards. These two bodies of scholarship shed considerable light on the floor/ceiling distinction.

First, critics of the race-to-the-bottom rationale for federal regulation are actually discussing what is a partially preemptive action at most. Greater laxity is precluded, but actual federal standards, especially in federal environmental laws, give states the option to be more protective. Hence, some states are denied their preferred choice, while others preferring environmental cleanliness obtain

---

[16] Lars Noah, "Rewarding Regulatory Compliance: The Pursuit of Symmetry in Products Liability," GEORGETOWN LAW JOURNAL 88, no. 7 (2000): 2152–3.

[17] Peter Huber, "Safety and the Second Best: The Hazards of Public Risk Management in the Courts, COLUMBIA LAW REVIEW 85, no. 2 (1985): 316–17.

[18] Kristen H. Engel, "State Environmental Standard-Setting: Is There a Race and Is It 'To the Bottom,' " HASTINGS LAW JOURNAL 48 no. 2 (1997): 271.

their desired outcome from protective federal law or their own more stringent enactments. Furthermore, with cooperative federalism structures that involve states in implementing and tailoring federal requirements to state and local environments, a possibility of diverse regulatory approaches remains. Revesz bemoans the loss of regulatory diversity matching each jurisdiction's particular attributes, but federal floors at most limit the diversity that laxity might offer. More stringent regulation remains a choice, plus in tailoring regulatory requirements under delegated programs and in making "best available" technology determinations, state and local actors confront ongoing incentives for innovation and regulatory interaction. Incentives created by potential liability under state common law create an additional area of potential legal diversity.

Similarly, two major counterarguments exist against the regulatory compliance defense. One is historical and statutory: few, if any, areas of federal approvals include statutory language embracing such a regulatory compliance defense. Instead, such laws often have savings clauses, language limiting the reach of federal approvals, and often no mention whatsoever of common law claims. Such laws also seldom contain any compensation scheme for victims of product harms. The second argument is rooted more in an embrace of regulatory diversity. As further explored by Professors Vladeck in Chapter 3 and McGarity in Chapter 11, state law, especially tort law, can prompt reexamination of regulatory choices and products that otherwise might escape any legal scrutiny after initial approvals. Producers selling an outdated product and regulators who may be captured, lazy, or overworked can be jolted into action by the tort system. Industry may prefer the tort immunity that would accompany a regulatory compliance defense, but the absence of such a defense leaves latitude for states, local governments, and common law regimes to explore the adequacy and safety of products or other activities creating risk. In effect, the current liability norm functions as a floor, making federal approvals the minimally required hurdle for many products but leaving latitude for other legal regimes to conclude that a less risky product or conduct was possible.

A related body of recent scholarship more generally critiques the world of regulation, identifies common forms of regulatory failure, and advocates more flexible and experimental modes of regulation. Any regulatory design choice needs to take into account and adjust for numerous regulatory failure risks.[19] Among those

---

[19] One cannot assume that a policy goal, once defined, will translate into successful action. Policy makers must consider institutional settings and stakeholders' incentives. See William W. Buzbee, "Urban Sprawl, Federalism, and the Problem of Institutional Complexity," FORDHAM LAW REVIEW 68, no. 1 (1999) 57, 59–61; William W. Buzbee, "Sprawl's Dynamics: A Comparative Institutional Analysis Critique," WAKE FOREST LAW REVIEW 35, no. 3 (2000): 509, 516–18.

common risks are regulatory inertia,[20] capture,[21] poor initial choice or error,[22] outdated choices, and inadequate funding of administrative agencies. Creation of effective regulatory schemes must further anticipate status quo bias,[23] which can make any initial choice sticky, as well as risk-adverse regulators.[24] These recent calls for a different, more innovative mode of regulation go by several names, most prominently "democratic experimentalism," but are also captured by labels such as "rolling rule regimes" and Professor Sabel's concept that in business and

[20]   The mere possibility that another regulatory actor, such as a state attorney general, may act and reveal missed wrongdoing can serve to counter inertial tendencies of other government actors. See Robert B. Ahdieh, "Dialectical Regulation," CONNECTICUT LAW REVIEW 38, no. 5 (2006): 863 (discussing the role of state attorney generals in prompting federal regulatory action). Professor Morrison, in Chapter 4, reviews the role of state attorneys general and develops arguments for why preemption of their role should require explicit statutory language.

[21]   In its strong form, George Stigler claimed that regulation is typically actually for the benefit of the ostensibly regulated target. See George Stigler, "The Theory of Economic Regulation," BELL JOURNAL OF ECONOMICS AND MANAGEMENT SCIENCE 2, no. 1 (1971): 3. More usual "capture" theory arises out of concerns with the revolving door between industry and regulators or regulators who, over time, become too cozy with the industry they are supposed to monitor. Much of so-called capture behavior can arise out of agencies' dependence on information that industry provides. See Richard B. Stewart, "The Reformation of Administrative Law," HARVARD LAW REVIEW 88, no. 8 (1975): 1669, 1684–7.

[22]   Regulatory actors may commit a regulatory error by choosing imprudently, leading either to overly zealous or inefficient action or an action that itself causes unnecessary harms. See Richard B. Stewart, "Preclusion of Tort Liability: Limiting the Dual Track System," GEORGETOWN LAW JOURNAL 88, no. 7 (2004): 2167 (arguing in favor of a regulatory compliance defense).

[23]   See J. B. Ruhl and James Salzman, "Mozart and the Red Queen: The Problem of Regulatory Accretion in the Administrative State," GEORGETOWN LAW JOURNAL 91, no. 4 (2003): 757, 818 (asserting that '[o]ver time, the accretion of rules will present more regulatory decision nodes, which will add to the path dependence of present regulatory positions, and will therefore limit the options for new rules"); Clayton P. Gillete, "Lock-in Effects in Law and Norms," BOSTON UNIVERSITY LAW REVIEW 78, no. 3 (1998) 813, 817 (finding that administrative law is subject to "lock-in" and "path dependence" because "regulations provide signals of acceptable behavior and promise rewards to those who conform . . . [and thus] threaten[] evolutionary processes that might return still greater rewards"). See generally, Donald T. Hornstein, "Complexity Theory, Adaptation, and Administrative Law," DUKE LAW JOURNAL 54, no. 4 (2005): 913, 926–8 (arguing that the Impossibility Theorem may be used to explain why administrative law is "extremely sensitive to initial conditions, a phenomenon related to path dependence"). See also Jeffrey J. Rachlinski, "The Psychology of Global Climate Change," UNIVERSITY OF ILLINOIS LAW REVIEW, no. 1 (2000): 299, 307–8 (discussing industry investment and link to status quo bias).

[24]   See William W. Buzbee, "Remembering Repose: Voluntary Contamination Cleanup Approvals, Incentives, and the Costs of Interminable Liability," MINNESOTA LAW REVIEW 80, no. 1 (1995): 35, 90–3 (discussing legal, business, and psychiatric insights regarding risk aversion in analysis of agency reluctance to create a mechanism to review and approve voluntary contamination cleanups). In addition, agencies face a modestly increased burden when changing approaches. They must confront the old approach, admit that a change is proposed, and explain it adequately so the change is not adjudged to be arbitrary and capricious. See Kevin M. Stack, "The Constitutional Foundations of Chenery," YALE LAW REVIEW 116, no. 5 (2007): 952. This will make any change more risky than maintenance of the status quo.

politics, there should be "learning by monitoring" (LBM).[25] This work has two main components, both of which illuminate risks of a regulatory ceiling.

The first is that many areas of regulation are characterized by volatility and diversity, with concomitant changing states of knowledge. Advocates of experimentalism and related forms of regulation claim that rigid forms of regulation are ill-suited to accomplish their designated tasks. Federal standard setting is generally vilified as too rigid[26] and the process of generating federal standards as being dysfunctional unless the law contains provisions empowering citizens to provoke or force action.[27] The second component of experimentalist work and regulation builds off of insights drawn from study of industrial production, especially at Toyota plants.[28] Rather than a top-level bureaucrat choosing in a final way how a car should be produced, "learning by monitoring" should occur that will improve both the production process and resulting product.[29] Under learning by monitoring, the production process is monitored, with best practices "benchmarked," and then production adjustments adopted. Information is pooled, so

[25] For a sampling of such scholarship see, e.g., Michael C. Dorf and Charles F. Sabel, "A Constitution of Democratic Experimentalism," COLUMBIA LAW REVIEW 98, no. 2 (1998): 267, 287; Jody Freeman, "Collaborative Governance in the Administrative State," UCLA LAW REVIEW 45, no. 1 (1997): 1; Bradley C. Karkkainen, "New Governance in Legal Thought and in the World: Some Splitting as Antidote to Overzealous Lumping," MINNESOTA LAW REVIEW 89, no. 2 (2004): 471; Bradley C. Karkkainen, "Environmental Lawyering in the Age of Collaboration," WISCONSIN LAW REVIEW 2002, no. 2 (2002): 555, 567–71; James S. Liebman and Charles F. Sabel, "A Public Laboratory Dewey Barely Imagined: The Emerging Model of School Governance and Legal Reform," NEW YORK UNIVERSITY REVIEW OF LAW AND SOCIAL CHANGE 28, no. 2 (2002): 183, 189–90; Orly Lobel, "The Renew Deal: The Fall of Regulation and the Rise of Governance in Contemporary Legal Thought," MINNESOTA LAW REVIEW 89, no. 2 (2004): 342, 396, 461; Eric W. Orts, "Reflexive Environmental Law," NORTHWESTERN UNIVERSITY LAW REVIEW 80, no. 4 (1995): 1227; Charles Sabel et al., "Beyond Backyard Environmentalism," in BEYOND BACKYARD ENVIRONMENTALISM, ed. Joshua Cohen and Joel Rogers, (Boston: Beacon Press, 2000), 3, 6–7, 13–15; Charles F. Sabel and William H. Simon, "Destabilization Rights: How Public Law Litigation Succeeds," HARVARD LAW REVIEW 117, no. 4 (2004): 1015, 1082–94; Susan Sturm, "Second Generation Employment Discrimination: A Structural Approach," COLUMBIA LAW REVIEW 101, no. 3 (2001): 458, 479–89. For an earlier work exploring similar issues, see Ian Ayres and John Braithwaite, RESPONSIVE REGULATION: TRANSCENDING THE DEREGULATION DEBATE (New York: Oxford University Press, 1992).

[26] Dorf and Sabel, "Constitution of Democratic Experimentalism," SUPRA n. 25, at 278, 370, 437, 443n587; Lobel, "Renew Deal," SUPRA n. 25.

[27] Agencies frequently miss statutory deadlines, while altogether neglecting tasks that are not subject to statutory mandates. See Alden F. Abbott, "The Case Against Federal Statutory and Judicial Deadlines: A Cost-Benefit Appraisal," ADMINISTRATIVE LAW REVIEW 39, no. 2 (1987): 171, 176–9; Bradley C. Karkkainen, "Information-Forcing Environmental Regulation," FLORIDA STATE UNIVERSITY LAW REVIEW 33, no. 3 (2006): 861, 897; Sidney A. Shapiro and Robert L. Glicksman, "Congress, the Supreme Court, and the Quiet Revolution in Administrative Law," DUKE LAW JOURNAL 1988, no. 5 (1988): 819, 839.

[28] See Dorf and Sabel, "Constitution of Democratic Experimentalism," SUPRA n. 25, at 292–310.

[29] Id.

others engaged in the same task can adopt this new "benchmarked" best-produc-tion method. Recent works observe analogous political and regulatory actions and argue that this mode of pragmatic adjustment can and should be more widely adopted in the world of government and law.[30] This literature argues that for effective regulatory choices, one needs to have a diversity of actors and institu-tions, providing them room for experimentation, sharing, and learning.[31]

Much of this work focuses on provision of government services, such as education, child welfare, prisons, welfare, and social safety net programs.[32] Its analysis of safety and risk regulation is a bit sketchier; it criticizes federal standard setting and many status quo arrangements yet lauds laws such as the Clean Air Act (CAA) and its cooperative federalism structures in place since 1972.[33] Experimentalist literature both advocates and chronicles these innovations, with experimentalist regimes already replacing some more tradi-tional arrangements under our federalist form of government.

Much as reexamination of race-to-the-bottom and regulatory compliance scholarship reveals substantial risks in the setting of a single preclusive standard, unitary federal choice ceiling preemption risks are apparent when examined in light of the insights of experimentalist literature, as well as long-established scholarship about regulatory failures.[34] Handing all regulatory power to one actor is the antithesis of the diversity of actors called for in the experimentalist literature. With complete displacement, especially if common law venues are preempted, no actor or institution has any room or incentive to criticize and seek change outside the federal regulatory venue. Change will come only if the preempting federal actor, be it an administrative agency or the legislature, decides to change its previous decision.[35] The more standard floor preemption,

---

[30] Id.

[31] Id. at 314.

[32] See Dorf and Sabel, "Constitution of Democratic Experimentalism," SUPRA n. 25, at 329, 346; see, e.g., Sabel and Simon, "Destabilization Rights," SUPRA n. 25, at 1019.

[33] Dorf and Sabel, "Constitution of Democratic Experimentalism," SUPRA n. 25, at 345–54, 433–4; see also id. at 352, 358, 376, 433 (discussing other Clean Air Act provisions).

[34] See, e.g., William W. Buzbee, "Regulatory Underkill in an Era of Anti-Environmental Major-ities," in ALTERNATIVE GROUNDS: DEFENDING THE ENVIRONMENT IN AN UNWELCOME JUDICIAL CLIMATE, ed. Michael Allan Wolf (Washington, DC: Environmental Law Institute, 2005), 141 (discussing numerous ways regulatory goals can be subject to underkill strategies and dynamics, leading to substantial disparity between legal goals and implemented reality); Daniel A. Farber, "Taking Slippage Seriously: Noncompliance and Creative Compliance in Environmental Law," HARVARD ENVIRONMENTAL LAW REVIEW 23, no. 2 (1999): 297 (dis-cussing "slippage" at each level of environmental implementation, rendering law less rigid and burdensome than indicated by statutory and regulatory edicts).

[35] Legislation seldom requires or rewards agency reexamination and assessment of past action, and agencies seldom find reexamination in their own interest. See Thomas O. McGarity, "Some Thoughts on 'Deossifying' the Rulemaking Process," DUKE LAW JOURNAL 41, no. 6 (1992): 1385.

in contrast, displaces some state choices but retains a diversity of actors and creates incentives for innovation. More stringent regulation remains an option. Furthermore, common law regimes' different incentives and informational modalities mean that actors other than regulators can question the efficacy and adequacy of an earlier regulatory choice. In the common law setting, injured plaintiffs and their attorneys have financial incentives to dig for evidence of unduly risky products or action. Furthermore, the latitude provided by civil litigation discovery allows litigants to probe the adequacy of a decision based not on an agency record at the time of a regulatory action but based on all information relevant to assessment of the reasonableness of an action or perhaps a product's risks. Subsequent innovations or belatedly revealed risks thus can be uncovered through common law litigation.

The experimentalist literature also illuminates the floor/ceiling choice in part by what it does not resolve. This scholarship often seems implicitly to assume that in the governance setting all interested parties will have the wherewithal and incentives to participate, give voice, and monitor these "rolling rules." Markets will, it is claimed, exist and reward regulatory learning by monitoring. In the settings of the government service provision, this expectation is not far-fetched, given the presence of large institutional players in a context where, as in business settings, analogous measures of efficiency and accomplishment are possible.

Most recent embraces of ceiling preemption, however, arise in the risk-regulation area. Product risks, climate changes harms, and chemical facility risks, for example, have been settings where proponents of unitary federal choice ceiling preemption have been most active. Quite clearly, industry wants the certainty provided by ceiling preemption.[36] If regulations or legislation are unlikely to change, and common law liabilities are no longer a risk, those creating risk face a far less threatening regulatory environment.[37] Risk regulation presents challenges quite distinct from provision of government services. Risk regulation is characterized by strong clashing groups – often industry versus consumers, unions, or environmental groups. Difficult regulatory choices are often at the

---

[36] For a variant on this argument, see Alan Schwartz, "Statutory Interpretation, Capture, and Tort Law: The Regulatory Compliance Defense," AMERICAN LAW AND ECONOMICS REVIEW 2, no. 1 (2000): 1 (discussing inefficiencies associated with disparate state standards and questioning presumption that Congress would want additional state regulation and common law). See, e.g., Stigler, "Theory of Economic Regulation," SUPRA n. 21 (arguing that regulation tends to be actually for the benefit of those ostensibly regulated).

[37] The room for change facilitated by multilayered regulatory structures is arguably in tension with "rule of law" values that stress clear mandates, legal stability, and distinct lines of accountability. See, e.g., Antonin Scalia, "The Rule of Law as the Law of Rules," UNIVERSITY OF CHICAGO LAW REVIEW 56, no. 4 (1989): 1175.

bounds of science.[38] Great disparities in resources exist, with industry facing tremendous costs but having resources and cost-avoidance incentives to remain players.[39] Organized not-for-profits can offer expertise and serve as a counterweight to industry or sometimes misguided government actors but are dwarfed in power, money, and personnel. Citizens, especially in more local settings, tend to have no resources, face conflicts such as jobs and children, and have little or no time to participate in ongoing regulatory revisions.

In this sort of polycentric setting of risk regulation, with clashing interests and disparate resources, regulatory failure risks are perhaps at their highest. The government response is often not to act at all; act and duck and not revisit old choices;[40] or succumb to industry pressure. Industry will invest in the initial regulatory choice and lobby against change.[41] Citizens will be outgunned, and even issue-based not-for-profits will often lack the resources to stick with the ongoing process of adjustment.

[38] E.g., setting standards for emissions of pollutants from particular industries based on an assessment of what can be accomplished with "best available technology" requires huge amounts of time, money, and technological knowledge. See, e.g., Wendy Wagner, "The Triumph of Technology-Based Standards," ILLINOIS LAW REVIEW 2000, no. 1, 83, 94–5 (noting the considerable demands of standard setting but arguing it is comparatively less demanding than other seemingly more ideal forms of regulation).

[39] Well-funded industries and motivated not-for-profits will stand ready to litigate after lengthy rule making. See Bruce A. Ackerman and Richard B. Stewart, "Reforming Environmental Law," STANFORD LAW REVIEW 37, no. 5 (1985): 1333 (bemoaning conflicts and the resulting rigid regulation of modern environmental regulation and suggesting alternative, more context-sensitive modes); Howard Latin, "Ideal Versus Real Regulatory Efficiency: Implementation of Uniform Standards and 'Fine Tuning' Regulatory Reform," STANFORD LAW REVIEW 37, no. 5 (1985): 1267 (developing contrary arguments in support of current schemes and criticizing Ackerman and Stewart's arguments, and seeing regulatory conflict as reason not to utilize more "fine-tuned" forms of regulation).

[40] See, e.g., McGarity, "Some Thoughts on 'Deossifying' the Rulemaking Process," SUPRA n. 35, at 1436 (noting that "[g]iven all of the barriers to writing a rule in the first place, few agencies are anxious to revisit the process in light of changed conditions or new information"); Cary Coglianese, "Empirical Analysis and Administrative Law," UNIVERSITY OF ILLINOIS LAW REVIEW no. 4 (2002): 1111, 1126 (stating that "[i]n some cases, agencies have allegedly retreated altogether from efforts to establish new regulations"); Jerry L. Mashaw and David L. Harfst, THE STRUGGLE FOR AUTO SAFETY (1990) (arguing that the U.S. National Highway Traffic Safety Administration stopped revisiting its regulations after 1976). See also Leslie Kux, "Looking Back at Existing Rules: Agency Perspectives on Analysis Requirements," ADMINISTRATIVE LAW REVIEW 48, no. 3 (1996): 375, 378 (analyzing the administration's objection to certain bills proposing lookback provisions).

[41] See, e.g., MOTOR VEHICLE MFRS. ASS'N v. STATE FARM MUT. AUTO. INS. CO., 463 U.S. 29 (1983) (reviewing industry opposition to imposition of additional safety features in cars); Dorf and Sabel, "Constitution of Democratic Experimentalism," SUPRA n. 25, at 357–64 (reviewing the history of STATE FARM as evidence of need for less oppositional forms of regulatory process). See also Keith Bradsher, HIGH AND MIGHTY, SUVS: THE WORLD'S MOST DANGEROUS VEHICLES AND HOW THEY GOT THAT WAY (New York: Public Affairs, 2002), 31–4 (reviewing American Motors' resistence to addressing stability and rollovers in Jeeps).

In ways not yet addressed and distinguished in regulatory experimentalism scholarship, the overall institutional arrangements of regulatory floors provide a surely imperfect but potentially effective antidote to regulatory failure. Federal standards acting as regulatory floors are somewhat rigid, in ways bemoaned by experimentalists. The multilayered nature of such regulatory floor schemes, however, actually ends up creating a realistic setting where interaction and innovation can occur. Floor preemption regimes provide a second-best solution that looks a great deal like what experimentalists advocate. With floor preemption, which sets a minimum level of stringency and retains common law regimes, a diversity of regulatory choices remain an option, although lax state regulation is ruled out.[42] Jurisdictions wanting to be the low-risk, clean environment state can go further, as sometimes seen in states such as California, Minnesota, and Oregon. In addition, states are typically left room or obligated to tailor implementation to local settings. Furthermore, broad citizen suit provisions with attorney's fee rights create a market for citizens and not-for-profits to challenge illegal private or government actions. With cooperative federalism structures that usually accompany floor preemption and room left for diverse and more stringent regulation, numerous levels of regulatory action are venues for innovation.[43] Multiple actors remain regulatory players.

In addition, if regulators set a standard and never go back, the possibility of common law claims, which are typically preserved under floor preemption savings clauses, creates a setting where actors not in the clashing regulation world can be entrepreneurs.[44] Plaintiffs and lawyers can engage in discovery,

---

[42] In contrast to federal unitary choice preemption and sometimes unrealistic experimentalist aspirations, floor preemption can work by promoting reexamination and virtually precluding stasis despite human and institutional flaws such as inertia, selfishness, short-sightedness, and lack of willpower. See, e.g., Matthew D. McCubbins et al., "Structure and Process, Politics and Policy: Administrative Arrangements and the Political Control of Agencies," VIRGINIA LAW REVIEW 75, no. 2, (1989): 431, 440 (arguing that to steer agencies to desired outcomes, legislatures can either write "into the law precisely what the agency is to achieve and how it is to do so" or "constrain an agency's policies . . . by enfranchising the constituents of each political actor"); Matthew D. McCubbins and Thomas Schwartz, "Congressional Oversight Overlooked: Police Patrols Versus Fire Alarms," AMERICAN JOURNAL POLITICAL SCIENCE 28 (1984): 165–6 (developing theory that participation and ligation rights serve as "fire alarms" that will alert legislators if laws are not being implemented).

[43] The possibility of federal "overfiling" or rejection of permit choices, or citizen suits or Administrative Procedure Act (APA) challenges if a permit violates the law, means that authority is pervasively monitored and checked. See, e.g., ALASKA DEP'T OF ENVTL. CONSERVATION v. EPA, 540 U.S. 461 (2004) (affirming U.S. EPA power to object to lax state permit issued in violation of Best Available Control Technology requirement).

[44] Retaining common law regimes – with their different array of actors and incentives – is particularly likely to create incentives for reexamination of regulatory choices. It is the different incentives and institutional structures of common law regimes that create a possible means to overcome a major weakness in "experimentalist" regimes, namely, the ordinary lack of incentives for regulators to engage in reflection, reexamination of past actions, admissions of error, and unsettling of the status quo.

motivated by monetary incentives or a desire for justice. They can and often do show that a federal standard still leads to harm and perhaps is not strict enough.[45] Such incentives and discoveries are many, especially in connection with risks posed by tobacco,[46] C8 or PFOA used in Teflon,[47] and certain heart stents. California's federally preserved right to impose more stringent air pollution requirement on motor vehicles similarly reveals possible improvements over the presumptive national, federal standards.[48]

At first blush, any preemption thus appears contrary to "experimentalist" advocates' goal of ongoing monitoring and revision. However, the form of multilayered federalism retained by floor preemption, with its preservation of state roles and usual saving of common law regimes, actually creates a more realistic sort of interactive tension than one finds in sometimes idealized descriptions of experimentalist regulation. In these settings of risk regulation and other poorly addressed risks, one finds a real-world setting characterized by clashing interests and a somewhat messy set of institutions, where no one controls the agenda and choice in a final way. Most critically, floor preemption's

[45] Professor Robert Rabin argues that despite the flaws in tort liability regimes, they serve a valuable role in eliciting information about product risks that might otherwise be overlooked. Robert Rabin, "Reassessing Regulatory Compliance," GEORGETOWN LAW JOURNAL 88, no. 7 (2004): 2049. As Professor McGarity discusses in Chapter 11, tort litigation can serve as a sort of "feedback loop," eliciting information that leads to reexamination of past federal regulatory actions. For a work advocating latitude for tort claims for harms caused by pesticides and tracing regulatory and common law regimes and institutions' review of risks, as well as the relative strengths of such regimes and institutions, see Alexandra B. Klass, "Pesticides, Children's Health Policy, and Common Law Tort Claims," MINNESOTA JOURNAL LAW SCIENCES AND TECHNOLOGY 7, no. 1, (2005): 89. For works also discussing feedback interactions, but with more of an emphasis on tort claims and industry learning, see Joseph Frueh, "Pesticides, Preemption, and the Reform of Tort Protection," YALE JOURNAL ON REGULATION 23, no. 2 (2006): 229, 308 (discussing how tort litigation provides feedback to manufacturers); David A. Hyman and Charles Silver, "The Poor State of Health Care Quality in the U.S.: Is Malpractice Liability Part of the Problem or Part of the Solution?" CORNELL LAW REVIEW 90, no. 4 (2005): 893, 919–23 (describing the wave of malpractice lawsuits and negative publicity surrounding anesthesia that prompted changes to ASA monitoring guidelines and standards); Mary L. Lyndon, "Tort Law and Technology," YALE JOURNAL ON REGULATION 12, no. 1 (1995): 137, 163–5 (arguing that the issue is not whether tort law or agency law provides the best response to risks posed by technologies but how tort law and agencies can work together to address those risks); Richard Merrill and Jeffrey Francer, "Organizing Federal Food Safety Regulation," SETON HALL LAW REVIEW 21, no. 1 (2000): 61, 64 (noting that tort law provides feedback, albeit incomplete, to the food industry).

[46] See David Kessler, A QUESTION OF INTENT (New York: Public Affairs, 2001), 250–60 (reviewing history of FDA efforts to regulate tobacco products); Catherine T. Struve, "The FDA and the Tort System: Postmarketing Surveillance, Compensation, and the Role of Litigation," YALE JOURNAL OF HEALTH POLICY LAW 5, no. 1 (2005): 587, 591 n. 12.

[47] See Chapter 13.

[48] For discussion of these provisions and the regulatory dynamics they create, see Anne E. Carlson, "Federalism, Preemption, and Greenhouse Gas Emissions," UNIVERSITY OF CALIFORNIA, AT DAVIS LAW REVIEW 37, no. 1 (2003): 281.

retention of multiple institutions and the different modalities and incentives of common law litigation mean that one need not rely on hyperinvolved citizens and selfless bureaucrats to prompt regulatory reexamination and adjustment. The possibility of common law liabilities, something usually retained with floor preemption and its savings clauses, creates ongoing private incentives to challenge the status quo. Preserved common law regimes are thus particularly valuable antidotes to complacency and ineffective regulation.

In contrast, with its reliance on a single federal actor who must get the regulatory response right on the first try, unitary federal choice ceiling preemption's weaknesses are revealed by experimentalism's underlying regulatory critique. This conclusion is consistent with the strain in race-to-the-bottom and regulatory compliance defense scholarship that is wary of any overly preclusive, rigid forms of federal regulatory action.

THE COUNTERARGUMENTS FOR CEILINGS

The counterarguments for ceilings largely track those made by advocates of the regulatory compliance defense. The regulatory uncertainty created by multilayered regulatory regimes and the possibility of common law liability will impose burdens on industry and reduce economies of scale. Compliance will often require state-by-state analysis and assessment of changing tort law liability standards. These arguments against use of regulatory floors are at their strongest when federal requirements are akin to design standards or where economies of scale are lost with multilayered law. Such settings will arise and at times justify a more completely preemptive federal action, perhaps even a unitary federal choice ceiling. Such regulatory choices, however, must be adopted with due regard for the risks and dysfunctions that may result.

In the hot-button regulatory debates of recent years, few regulatory ceilings appear justified. In settings of dynamism and uncertainty, especially where problems are caused by diverse sources at different scales, and manifested in different ways, a single federal answer displacing all other regulatory approaches and institutions is particularly risky.[49] Climate-change legislation

---

[49] Effective regulation and preemption choice require attention to the many dimensions of risk creation and the conditions necessary for an effective regulatory response. See William W. Buzbee, "Recognizing the Regulatory Commons: A Theory of Regulatory Gaps," IOWA LAW REVIEW 89, no. 1 (2003): 7–36 (discussing scholarly inattention to the "regulatory commons" problem, the many dimensions relevant to regulatory action, and the reasons regulatory gaps may result where a regulatory opportunity is shared among potential regulators, such as in settings of social ills such as urban sprawl, climate change, or overfishing). For recent application of this concept in an in-depth examination of overfishing ills, see Hope M. Babcock, "Grotius, Ocean Fish Ranching, and the Public Trust Doctrine: Ride 'Em Charlie Tuna," STANFORD ENVIRONMENTAL LAW JOURNAL 26, no. 1 (2007): 3, 4–6, 68–71.

limiting GHG emissions will emerge at a time of scientific uncertainty, technological innovation, and harms arising from diverse sources and activities that seldom match the reach of any particular jurisdiction. Barely regulated sources of risk, namely carbon dioxide and other GHGs, will become pervasively regulated. With such change and volatility, a rigid ceiling would be highly risky. Similarly, the location-specific risks of chemical facilities seem poorly suited to any one-size-fits-all federal set of requirements. If regulatory tailoring in light of localized knowledge and risks can be effective, a preemptive federal regulation could be disastrous and dysfunctional. Product approvals are similarly seldom appropriate for the freezing of the law that comes with regulatory ceilings, but they may at times make sense if a federal approval really is explicitly meant to set optimal requirements. Even then, however, the risk of outdated approvals remains considerable. Furthermore, close parsing of underlying law to find statutory justification is necessary.

CONCLUSION

Preemption, with its inherent displacement of state or local actors' roles, is necessarily in tension with forms of law and regulation that embrace interaction and legal revision by a diversity of actors at different scales. The partial preemption of regulatory floors is different in implications than preemption in the form of a ceiling that functions as a unitary federal choice. Such ceilings can completely displace other actors, undercutting the possibility of innovation and revision in response to diverse and changing settings. Regulatory floors, in contrast, retain the possibility of several layers of legal actors and maintain incentives for innovation and adjustment.

PART THREE

JUDICIAL TREATMENT AND INTERPRETIVE CHOICE

6   Supreme Court Preemption Doctrine

Christopher H. Schroeder*

In the United States, law and policy always function within layers of government authority – federal, state, and local. This book primarily examines the choices policy makers, legislatures, or agencies face in allocating and coordinating responsibility among these layers; choices that will always be constrained by any limits placed on them by the U.S. Constitution, as interpreted by the Supreme Court. This chapter explores the doctrine that the Supreme Court has elaborated to address one set of those constraints, namely the doctrine of preemption.

Preemption doctrine rests on Article VI of the Constitution, which provides that the laws and treaties of the United States "shall be the supreme law of the land . . . anything in the Constitution or Laws of any State to the contrary notwithstanding." When is a state or local law "contrary" to the laws or treaties of the United States? The doctrine of preemption seeks to answer that question, in all the various contexts in which it may arise. Although major elements of the doctrine have been clearly delineated by the Supreme Court, the outcomes of specific clashes between federal and state law prove to be far from certain. The beginning sections of this chapter examine the stated doctrine and some of its difficulties. The chapter concludes by discussing four topics that are currently matters of considerable controversy: (1) when do broad federal statutes preempt the abilities of the states and localities to address unanticipated, new environmental, health and safety concerns? (2) when do federal statutes preempt state damages actions? (3) what role do federal agencies play in defining the boundaries of the preemptive effects of statutes? and (4) what are the implications of the "regulatory vacuum" that can result from concentrating too much authority at the federal level?

* Charles S. Murphy Professor of Law and Professor of Public Policy Studies, Director of the Program in Public Law at Duke University.

PREEMPTION'S TOUCHSTONE: CONGRESSIONAL INTENT

So long as Congress is acting within its enumerated powers, such as the Commerce Clause, Congress also has the authority under the Supremacy Clause to push aside state law. The question of when a state law has been pushed aside – and therefore cannot be enforced – thus always turns on a seemingly simple question: in enacting the federal law, did Congress intend to preclude state law or laws from also operating? In the Court's words, preemption "is basically [a question] of congressional intent. Did Congress, in enacting the Federal Statute, intend to . . . set aside the laws of a State?"¹ Although Congress clearly can preempt state law, federal law can also be "supreme" without state law being contrary to it, *if* the federal authority decides that it wants to permit state laws to continue to operate notwithstanding the federal law.² So the crucial question is how to interpret the content of the federal law, and that depends on congressional intent.

Suppose Congress enacts a law establishing when avocados are mature enough to be marketed.³ The State of California also has standards for the marketability of avocados. California's standards relate to different criteria than the federal standards, and some avocados meeting the federal standards also meet the California standards, but some do not. Is California's statute preempted by the federal law? Consider two different purposes that Congress might have had in mind in enacting the federal law on avocado marketing. It might have intended to grant an unqualified federal right to growers to market federally compliant avocados. In that case, California could not enforce its ban on avocados that fail to meet its different standards because if it did that, growers who had a federal right to market their produce could not do so. However, Congress might have only intended to establish minimum standards, perhaps to protect consumers rather than necessarily to confer a right on growers. In that case the different California standard does not conflict with the purpose of the federal law, and the state can enforce it. Answering the question whether the federal avocado law preempts the California law requires gaining an understanding of what Congress intended when it enacted the federal law. This often proves difficult to do.

¹ BARNETT BANK OF MARION COUNTY. N.A. v. NELSON, 517 U.S. 25, 30 (1996).
² The only exception arises when state and federal laws are impossible to satisfy simultaneously. It would violate an individual's due process protections to create a situation in which his or her only choice was to decide which law to violate. Literal impossibility cases are quite rare. See discussion in the following text, at nn. 41–2.
³ The avocado illustrations are loosely based on FLORIDA LIME AND AVOCADO GROWERS, INC. v. PAUL, 373 U.S. 132 (1963).

Sometimes Congress addresses the question of its preemptive intentions head-on through language it includes in the statute. Two different kinds of statutory provisions can explicitly address preemption. To indicate what state laws it wants to preempt, the statute can include an *express preemption* provision. In the federal avocado law, for instance, if Congress's intention was to create a federal right to market, it might include a provision stating that "no state may enforce a marketing standard different from the federal standard." In the environmental, health, and safety areas, Congress sometimes wants to create a system of uniform, national standards; express preemption provisions are a means of ensuring this result.[4] Congress can also indicate what state laws it does not want to preempt, by including a *savings clause* in the statute. Congress could indicate its intention to create a set of minimum standards for avocados, for instance, by placing in the statute a section that says, "nothing in this statute shall prohibit a state from establishing additional conditions for avocados to be marketed." Many federal environmental and safety statutes contain savings clauses that permit states to have tougher pollution control standards than required by the federal law.[5] A common type of savings clause in health or safety statutes is one that preserves state law tort remedies. Because regulatory statutes only rarely provide for compensation for the injured, Congress often intends to leave those state remedies in place.[6]

Statutes can contain both preemption provisions and saving clauses, sometimes more than one of each. The Clean Air Act (CAA), for instance, contains a savings clause allowing more protective ambient air quality standards,[7] a savings clause preserving common law and other state remedies,[8] and a preemption clause precluding states from requiring any emissions standards for automobiles and other moving sources that differs from the federal standard.[9]

---

[4] See, e.g., the Clean Air Act preemption clause, quoted in n. 9 below.

[5] E.g., the CAA stipulates that "nothing in this Act shall preclude or deny the right of any State or political subdivision thereof to adopt or enforce [any pollution standard] . . . except that . . . such State or political subdivision may not adopt or enforce any . . . standard . . . which is less stringent than the [federal] standard. . . ." 42 U.S.C. § 7416.

[6] E.g., the National Traffic and Motor Vehicle Safety Act provides that "[c]ompliance with any Federal motor vehicle safety standard issued under this subchapter does not exempt any person from any liability under common law." 49 U.S.C. §30103(e).

[7] See n. 5.

[8] 42 U.S.C. §7604(e).

[9] 42 U.S.C. §7543(a). The motor vehicle preemption clause illustrates how detailed these can be: "No State or political subdivision thereof shall adopt or attempt to enforce any standard relating to the control of emissions from new motor vehicles or new motor vehicle engines subject to this part. No State shall require certification, inspection, or any other approval relating to the control of emissions from any new motor vehicle or new motor vehicle engine as condition precedent to the initial retail sale, titling (if any), or registration of such motor vehicle, motor vehicle engine, or equipment."

EXPRESS PREEMPTION

Determining the preemptive effect of a federal statute is often made easier by
the inclusion of express preemption or saving clauses. Even when such clauses
are included, however, controversies arise over how the clauses are to be
interpreted. This is because it is difficult for Congress to anticipate and decide
in advance how every possible state law that impacts an area of regulation
reached by a federal statute ought to be addressed. For instance, Congress
enacted the Medical Device Amendments (MDAs) to the Food, Drug and
Cosmetic Act (FDCA) in 1976[10] to establish for the first time a federal regulatory authority over medical devices – everything from tongue depressors to
artificial heart valves to defibrillators. These amendments included a provision stating that "no State or political subdivision of a State may establish or
continue in effect with respect to a device intended for human use any
requirement – (1) which is different from, or in addition to, any requirement
applicable under this chapter to the device, and (2) which relates to the safety
or effectiveness of the device or to any other matter included in a requirement
applicable to the device under this chapter."[11] Clearly, Congress wanted to
make sure that some state requirements that differ from those established by
the Food and Drug Administration (FDA) pursuant to the MDA could not be
enforced, so that manufacturers of such devices would face a single uniform
set of requirements. Nonetheless, it took the Supreme Court to settle whether
this preemption provision covered state tort claims, because it was debatable
whether "any requirement" was limited to statutory requirements and requirements established by state regulation, or whether it also included obligations
created by state rules of tort liability.[12]

Thus, even when Congress enacts an express preemption provision, disputes can arise as to its meaning. The courts are called on to interpret the
statute by ascertaining Congress's intentions. Express preemption cases therefore do not so much constitute a completely separate class of cases but rather a
subset of a larger group of cases in which the courts are asked to ascertain
Congress's preemptive intentions.

In dealing with this particular group of cases, the Supreme Court frequently articulates one particular principle or canon of statutory interpretation. This is the "presumption against preemption," which is designed to
implement respect for federalism values. The presumption against

[10] Pub. L. 94-295 (1976).
[11] 21 U.S.C. §360k(a).
[12] RIEGEL V. MEDTRONIC, 128 S. Ct. 999 (2008), MEDTRONIC V. LOHR, 518 U.S. 470 (1996).

preemption begins with "the starting presumption that Congress does not intend to preempt state law."[13] Sometimes the Supreme Court also notes that the presumption is especially strong when the state law at issue amounts to an exercise of the states' traditional powers to protect the public health, safety, and morals: "[B]ecause the States are independent sovereigns in our federal system, we have long presumed that Congress does not cavalierly pre-empt state-law causes of action. In all pre-emption cases, and particularly in those in which Congress has legislated in a field which the States have traditionally occupied, we 'start with the assumption that the historic police powers of the States were not to be superseded by the Federal Act unless that was the clear and manifest purposes of Congress.' "[14] Thus, "where the text of a preemption clause is open to more than one reading, courts ordinarily 'accept the reading that disfavors preemption.' " [15]

The presumption against preemption instructs the courts to give federal statutes a "narrow reading"[16] in order to avoid interpretations that would override state law and to look for a "clear" statement that Congress means to preempt state law.[17] Beyond this boilerplate, what the presumption against preemption actually requires in practice is frequently a matter of disagreement among the justices. In 1992, for instance, the Court decided that state common law tort suits based on failure of cigarette manufacturers to warn of the health consequences of smoking amounted to state efforts to impose "requirements . . . based on smoking and health" and were therefore preempted by a provision of the 1969 Public Health Cigarette Smoking Act of 1969 prohibiting such state requirements.[18] Three justices dissented on the ground that the presumption against preemption required "unambiguous evidence of congressional intent necessary to displace state common-law damage claims."[19] The dissenters thought that "requirements" should be read to be limited to regulatory standards established by legislation or agency regulation, and that the congressional record lacked any evidence that

[13] NEW YORK STATE CONF. OF BLUE CROSS AND BLUE SHIELD PLANS V. TRAVELERS INS. CO., 514 U.S. 645, 654 (1995).

[14] MEDTRONIC, INC. V. LOHR, 518 U.S. 470, 485 (1996), quoting HILLSBOROUGH COUNTY V. AUTOMATED MEDICAL LABORATORIES, INC. 471 U.S. 707, 7156 (1985) and RICE V. SANTA FE ELEVATOR CORP., 331 U.S. 218, 230 (1947).

[15] Ginsbug, J., dissenting in RIEGEL V. MEDTRONIC, INC., 128 S. Ct. 999, 1014 (2008) (quoting BATES V. DOW ARGOSCIENCES, LLC, 544 U.S. 431, 449 [2005]).

[16] CIPOLLONE V. LIGGETT GROUP, 505 U.S. 504, 516 (1992).

[17] "Congress . . . should manifest its intention clearly. . . . The exercise or federal supremacy is not lightly to be presumed." NEW YORK STATE DEPARTMENT OF SOCIAL SERVICES V. DUBLINO, 413 U.S. 405, 413 (1973).

[18] CIPOLLONE V. LIGGEST GROUP, INC., 505 U.S. 504 (1992).

[19] Id. at 530 (Justices Blackmun, Kennedy, and Souter, concurring in part and dissenting in part).

Congress meant to block common law damages lawsuits brought against tobacco manufacturers.

Although express preemption and savings clauses are quite common, there are also many occasions when a court faces a preemption challenge to state law in which no such clause is applicable. In such cases, the court must decide whether the Congress has preempted state law by implication. It is to these situations that we next turn. Before leaving express preemption, however, it is useful to reiterate that here, as in the implied preemption cases to which we are about to turn, the touchstone question is one of congressional intent. So long as Congress stays within the ambit of its own enumerated powers, such as its authority to regulate interstate commerce, Congress's ultimate authority to preempt state law through express statutory provisions is clear. "It is well established that within constitutional limits Congress may pre-empt state authority by so stating in express terms."[20]

IMPLIED PREEMPTION

Return to the federal avocado law. An express preemption clause could make clear that Congress had enacted a regulatory ceiling, blocking stricter state laws, while a savings clause could make clear that Congress had enacted a regulatory floor, thus permitting additional state requirements. Let's assume, however, that the statute contains neither type of clause. Without such legislative guidance, such a statute can plausibly be read as either a floor or a ceiling. Because there is no express statutory language one way or the other, the issue now is whether the statute preempts state law by implication. Once again, the answer to this question depends on what Congress intended. How is a judge to decide? The Court has identified some general considerations to guide that determination.

In *Gade v. National Solid Waste Management Ass'n*, the Court summarized the entire landscape of its preemption doctrine, including both express preemption and the various types of implied preemption:

> Pre-emption may be either express or implied, and is compelled whether Congress' command is explicitly stated in the statute's language or implicitly contained in its structure and purpose. Absent explicit pre-emptive language, we have recognized at least two types of implied pre-emption: field pre-emption, where the scheme of federal regulation is so pervasive as to make reasonable the inference that Congress left no room for the States to

---

[20] Pacific Gas and Electric Co. v. State Energy Resources Conservation and Dev. Comm'n, 461 U.S. 190, 203 (1983).

supplement it, and conflict pre-emption, where compliance with both federal and state regulation is a physical impossibility, or where state law stands as an obstacle to the accomplishment and execution of the full purposes and objectives of Congress.[21]

The *Gade* quotation, which drew on earlier decisions and has been subsequently referred to on a number of occasions by the Supreme Court, supplies a taxonomy of the ways that a statute lacking express preemption language might nonetheless be found to have preempted state laws. This can happen if Congress has enacted legislation that "occupies a field," leaving no room for state regulation on the subject even if the specific state law does not directly conflict with any specific federal provision. It can happen if complying with both federal and state laws amounts to a "physical impossibility." Finally, it can happen if state law stands as an obstacle to achieving the full purposes and objectives of Congress. These last two situations – physical impossibility preemption and obstacle preemption – are considered subtypes of "conflict" preemption.

Ubiquitous as this classification scheme has become in judicial discussions of preemption, both courts and commentators have questioned its value. The Supreme Court has acknowledged that it has been unable to keep the categories "rigidly distinct," and that "field pre-emption may be understood as a species of conflict pre-emption."[22] Professor Tribe has concluded that "labels like 'conflict' and 'field' preemption rarely offer much real help in the inherently difficult task that lies at the heart of preemption analysis – the task of determining statutory meaning."[23] Still, they are categories the Supreme Court continues to employ, so it is best first to understand how the Court has used them and then to examine some of the recurring controversies that arise under them.

FIELD PREEMPTION

The Court finds implied field preemption when it concludes that Congress has intended federal law to be the exclusive law in a certain area of regulation.

---

[21] 505 U.S. 88, 98 (1992).
[22] ENGLISH v. GENERAL ELEC. CO., 496 U.S. 72, 79n15 (1990).
[23] Laurence H. Tribe, AMERICAN CONSTITUTIONAL LAW (Minneapolis, MN: Foundation Press, 3rd ed., 2000), 1, 1204. See also, Caleb Nelson, "Preemption," VIRGINIA LAW REVIEW 86 (2000): 225, 262: "Once we recognize that all preemption cases are about contradiction between state and federal law, we should begin to question the usefulness of dividing them into the separate analytical categories of 'express' preemption, 'field' preemption, and 'conflict' preemption."

As a consequence, state laws within that area are overridden even though they do not directly conflict with any specific federal regulation within that field. "When the Federal Government completely occupies a given field or an identifiable portion of it . . . the test of pre-emption is whether 'the matter on which the State asserts the right to act is in any way regulated by the Federal Act' "[24] and not whether the state regulation conflicts with a specific federal requirement. In these cases, a critical question can often be how the "field" that has been preempted is to be defined.

An early illustration is provided by *Rice v. Santa Fe Elevator Corporation.*[25] In 1931, Congress enacted the U.S. Warehouse Act, regulating the operation of grain elevators, an activity traditionally regulated by the states. The act gave the Secretary of Agriculture authority to license and regulate grain elevators, including the authority to revoke a license if an operator charged excessive or discriminatory rates, but it did not give the secretary authority to set rates directly. In a challenge brought by grain elevator operators against the Illinois Warehouse Commission claiming the commission was requiring it to charge discriminatory rates, the Supreme Court ruled that the federal law had pre-empted the Illinois rate-setting authority. As the Court summarized the contentions of the opposing parties, respondents "argued . . . that [the federal law] should be construed to mean that the subjects which the Secretary's authority touches may not be regulated in any way by any state agency, though the scope of federal regulation is not as broad as the regulatory scheme of the State and even though there is or may be no necessary conflict between what the state agency and the federal agency do. On the other hand, petitioners argue that since the area taken over by the federal government is limited, the rest may be occupied by the States; that state regulation should not give way unless there is a precise coincidence of regulation or an irreconcilable conflict between the two."[26]

After examining the legislative history of the federal act, the Court concluded that Congress's intent in enacting the 1931 law was to eliminate dual state and federal regulation of any warehouse that chose to obtain with a federal license. It concluded that "a licensee under the federal Act can do business 'without regard to State acts'; that the matters regulated by the

---

[24] SILKWOOD V. KERR-McGEE CORP., 464 U.S. 238, 260 (1984), quoting PACIFIC GAS AND ELECTRIC CO. V. STATE ENERGY RESOURCES CONSERVATION AND DEV. COMM'N, 461 U.S. 190, 213 (1983).

[25] 331 U.S. 218 (1947).

[26] Id. at 229. The opinion of the Court addresses a number of other regulatory issues besides rates where Illinois regulation might be seen to be complementary to rather than in conflict with specific regulatory choices made by the federal statute. See id., 229–33.

Federal Act cannot be regulated by the States; that on those matters a federal licensee (so far as his interstate or foreign commerce activities are concerned) is subject to regulation by one agency and by one agency alone."[27]

Rice is an example of the Court finding field preemption in light of its view that the "scheme of federal regulation [was] so pervasive as to make reasonable the inference that Congress left no room for the States to supplement it."[28] This turns out to be just a different version of the same floor versus ceiling issue raised by the avocado act. In an early field preemption case, Justice Holmes captured the ceiling versus floor idea: "When Congress has taken the particular subject-matter in hand, coincidence is as ineffective as opposition, and a state law is not to be declared a help because it attempts to go farther than Congress has seen fit to go."[29]

The similarity between these two issues means that it should be no surprise that deciding whether field preemption has occurred requires the same search for congressional intent as does deciding whether a federal standard operates as a regulatory ceiling or floor. In *Rice* and elsewhere, one factor the Court examines is whether the statute was meant to be "pervasive." If it was, this then suggests that Congress intended to occupy the field, apparently based on the belief that the more comprehensive Congress's regulatory enactment is, the less likely it is that Congress intended to leave holes in its regulations to be filled in by the states. "Pervasiveness" is a difficult concept to pin down with specificity, however, and in any event the ultimate resolution of the question turns on what Congress intended in this specific case, not as a matter of generalities. So in "pervasiveness" cases the Court continues to examine the legislative history of the particular federal statute that has been put at issue. In *Rice*, for instance, the Court found evidence that Congress had become dissatisfied with the pre-1931 system whereby both state and federal regulatory authority governed grain elevators, and that it wanted to eliminate the dual system in the specific case of grain elevators.

Pacific Gas and Electric Co. v. State Energy Resources Conservation and Development Comm'n[30] also shows that defining the field that has been occupied by federal legislation demands a close reading of the legislative history and intent. There, the Court determined that the Atomic Energy Act (AEA) gave the Atomic Energy Commission "exclusive jurisdiction to license the

---

[27] Id. at 234.
[28] Id. at 230.
[29] Charleston and W. Carolina R. Co. v. Varnville Furniture Co., 237 U.S. 597, 604 (1915) (Holmes, J.).
[30] 461 U.S. 190 (1983).

transfer, delivery, receipt, acquisition, possession and use of nuclear materials. . . . Upon these subjects, no role was left for the states."[31] Thus, the AEA occupied the field of safety and radiological concerns related to the use of nuclear fuels. The petitioners in the case had argued, however, that the AEA had occupied a broader field of regulation, namely the entire range of regulation governing whether or not a nuclear reactor could be built. The Supreme Court disagreed, finding that Congress had left certain aspects of public utility regulation in the hands of the states, such as the regulation of utility rates and the determination of whether new power generating facilities were needed. This dual arrangement gave states some room to regulate in ways that might affect the ability of public utilities to build nuclear reactors, even though the federal government had occupied the field of safety and radiological concerns surrounding those facilities. So there was field preemption as to safety and radiological issues but no field preemption of regulation of electric utilities generally, conclusions that the Supreme Court reached by delving into the congressional findings and discussions surrounding the Atomic Energy Act. Unlike the situation in *Rice*, these sources revealed no general dissatisfaction with state regulation of electric utilities across the board but only a desire to retain complete federal control over the radiological issues raised by the civilian use of nuclear power.

Field preemption has also been found when "the federal statutes touch a field in which the federal interest is so dominant that the federal system must be assumed to preclude enforcement of state laws on the same subject."[32] Such fields are ones in which the federal government has historically taken the lead, such as matters relating to foreign affairs. These areas of historical federal presence are the inverse of those where state police powers have historically been primary. Field preemption in such areas of primary federal authority similarly amounts to the inverse of the "presumption against preemption" that operates in areas where state regulation has historically been dominant. Here, the Court is using the criterion of dominant federal interest much as it has used the criterion of regulatory pervasiveness, as an indicator of whether or not the Congress intended to occupy the field.

Hines v. Davidowitz involved a Pennsylvania statute requiring aliens to register with the state, carry a state-issued identification card, and pay a small registration fee. A year after the Pennsylvania legislature passed its statute, Congress enacted a law requiring alien registration, but it did not require

---

[31] Id. at 207.
[32] PENNSYLVANIA V. NELSON, 350 U.S. 497, 503 (1956).

aliens to carry an identification card. Congress could have included a provision preempting state registration requirements, but it did not do so. An alien, furthermore, could comply with both statutes. Nonetheless, the Court found the Pennsylvania law was preempted by the federal legislation. Congress's power over foreign policy, the Court reasoned, is supreme, and the treatment of citizens of other countries is often a vital concern in the relations between two countries. "One of the most important and delicate of all international relationships, recognized immemorially as a responsibility of government, has to do with the protection of the just rights of a country's own nationals when those nationals are in another country. Experience has shown that international controversies of the gravest moment, sometimes even leading to war, may arise from real or imagined wrongs to another's subjects inflicted, or permitted, by a government."[33]

Accordingly, it was important that state laws not interfere with whatever Congress had decided with respect to the treatment of aliens. The Court concluded that Congress had meant to occupy the field of alien registration requirements, despite Congress not having said so in the statute – all the while acknowledging that determining the scope of the field preemption principle was a difficult task:

> There is not–and from the very nature of the problem there cannot be–any rigid formula or rule which can be used as a universal pattern to determine the meaning and purpose of every act of Congress. This Court, in considering the validity of state laws in the light of treaties or federal laws touching the same subject, has made use of the following expressions: conflicting; contrary to; occupying the field; repugnance; difference; irreconcilability; inconsistency; violation; curtailment; and interference. But none of these expressions provides an infallible constitutional test or an exclusive constitutional yardstick. In the final analysis, there can be no one crystal clear distinctly marked formula. *Our primary function is to determine whether, under the circumstances of this particular case, Pennsylvania's law stands as an obstacle to the accomplishment and execution of the full purposes and objectives of Congress.* And in that determination, it is of importance that this legislation is in a field which affects international relations, the one aspect of our government that from the first has been most generally conceded imperatively to demand broad national authority.[34]

Later cases illustrate the difficulty of applying the idea of field preemption to the diverse array of laws states have enacted that affect aliens. In *Takahashi v.*

---

[33] HINES v. DAVIDOWITZ, 312 U.S. 52, 63–4 (1941).
[34] Id. at 67–8 (emphasis added).

Fish and Game Comm'n, the Supreme Court held that a state law denying commercial fishing licenses to aliens who were not eligible for citizenship was preempted.[35] Later, in *De Canas v. Bica*, a state law prohibiting undocumented aliens from employment that would adversely affect resident workers was found not to be preempted. In *De Canas*, the Supreme Court found Congress had intended to permit state regulation of the employment of undocumented aliens, "to the extent consistent with federal law."[36]

Preemption based on the preeminence of the federal government in foreign affairs operates outside of the context of immigration as well. In *Crosby v. National Foreign Trade Council*,[37] the Supreme Court addressed a Massachusetts law preventing the expenditure of public funds to buy goods or services from companies that did business with Myanmar (formerly Burma). The law was a reaction to widespread human rights abuses in that country. In a unanimous opinion, the Supreme Court held that the state doing-business restriction was preempted by the federal sanctions that Congress had enacted against Myanmar. The Massachusetts sanctions reflected a decision by the state that Massachusetts did not wish to spend its citizens' tax monies by paying companies that were supporting the Myanmar government through their involvement in that country's economy – something that would seem squarely within its traditional, discretionary authority. The sanctions could have been viewed as supplementary to the federal sanctions. As Holmes said, however, "[w]hen Congress has taken the particular subject-matter in hand . . . a state law is not to be declared a help because it attempts to go farther than Congress has seen fit to go."[38] Here, the Supreme Court judged that Congress had taken the subject to Myanmar sanctions "in hand," to the preclusion of state law.

The Supreme Court decided that the federal legislation intended to keep sanctions against Myanmar within a certain range, notwithstanding the absence of any language expressly preempting supplementary state sanctions, and that this range did not permit supplementation by states. For that reason, the Massachusetts doing-business ban was preempted. Quoting *Hines*, the *Crosby* Court reasoned that "when the question is whether a Federal act overrides a state law, the entire scheme of the statute must of course be considered and that which needs must be implied is of no less force than that which is expressed. If the purpose of the act cannot otherwise be accomplished–if its operation within its chosen field else must be frustrated and

[35]   334 U.S. 410 (1948).
[36]   424 U.S. 351, 361 (1976).
[37]   530 U.S. 363 (2000).
[38]   See text at n. 29.

its provisions be refused their natural effect–the state law must yield to the regulation of Congress within the sphere of its delegated power."[39] The absence of an express preemption provision was not dispositive, moreover, because "a failure to provide for preemption expressly may reflect nothing more than the settled character of implied preemption doctrine that courts will dependably apply, and in any event, the existence of conflict cognizable under the Supremacy Clause does not depend on express congressional recognition that federal and state law may conflict."[40]

CONFLICT PREEMPTION

Outside of areas of field preemption that have already been recognized in past decisions, the Supreme Court in recent years has shown reluctance to find additional federal statutes to have engaged in field preemption.[41] In contrast, the Supreme Court continues to decide in numerous cases that "conflict" preemption exists. As already noted, the Supreme Court treats conflict preemption cases as divided into "physical impossibility" and "obstacle" types. The second of these proves much more consequential than the first.

Physical impossibility cases are restricted to situations in which it would be literally impossible for someone to comply with both statutes. Suppose, for instance, a federal law required all colleges to report address changes for all their foreign students whenever the colleges learned of such changes. If a state law prohibited colleges from disclosing certain information about their students, including home addresses, it would be physically impossible to comply with both at once. Physical impossibility cases present the clearest instances of implied preemption, for it seems quite impossible that Congress would enact a law requiring persons to perform some activity with the intention that a state law could effectively prohibit that which the Congress chose to require. The Supreme Court interprets the physical impossibility component of conflicts preemption just this narrowly, applying it only where state and federal law impose irreconcilable duties.[42] When, however, one sovereign merely permits what the other forbids, no physical impossibility exists because an individual can comply with both laws by refraining from the conduct. There are very few actual case law examples of physical impossibility.

---

[39] Id. at 373.

[40] Id. at 387–8.

[41] See Camps v. Newfound/Owatonna, Inc., v. Town of Harrison, 520 U.S. 564, 617 (1997) (Thomas, J., dissenting). ("[O]ur recent cases have frequently rejected field pre-emption in the absence of statutory language expressly requiring it.")

[42] See Geier v. American Honda Motor Co., 529 U.S. 861, 867 (2000) (describing a case of impossibility as "a case in which state law penalizes what federal law requires").

In contrast to the physical impossibility type of conflict preemption, statutes can be found to pose "obstacles" to federal statutes much more easily. For example, state statutes that forbid what a federal law permits (or condition it in ways not provided for by the federal law), which would not present a case of physical impossibility preemption, are quite capable of running afoul of the Supreme Court's implied preemption analysis by being found to be an "obstacle" to fully achieving the purposes and objectives of the federal statute. Unlike physical impossibility preemption, obstacle preemption is doing box office business these days.

As an example of a state law that is preempted because its "stand[s] as an obstacle to the accomplishment and execution of the full purposes or objectives of Congress,"[43] consider the air-bag litigation in the District of Columbia. In 1984, the Department of Transportation issued a regulation requiring auto makers to equip some but not all of their 1987 vehicles with passive restraints, which could be satisfied by installing air bags. When Alexis drove her 1987 Honda Accord into a tree, causing her serious injury, she sued Honda, alleging a design defect based on Honda's failure to equip her car with an air bag. The Supreme Court determined that enabling a gradual phase-in of air bags was one of the purposes of the 1984 regulation, and that the common law tort suit against Honda would create an obstacle to achieving that objective. A verdict in Alexis's favor would have created "a rule of state tort law imposing . . . [a] duty [that] by its terms would have required manufacturers of all similar cars to install airbags rather than other passive restraint systems, such as automatic belts or passive interiors. . . . [This duty] would have stood as an obstacle to the gradual passive restraint phase-in that the federal regulation deliberately imposed."[44]

Four justices dissented in *Geier*. They saw the purposes of the 1984 regulation quite differently. The record indicated that the Secretary of Transportation responsible for the regulation wished to encourage the introduction of air bags into American automobiles.[45] To the dissent, the objectives of the Safety Act and the specific air-bag regulation "would not be frustrated one whit by allowing state courts to determine whether in 1987 the lifesaving advantages of airbags had become sufficiently obvious that their omission might constitute a design defect in some new cars."[46] The dissent and the

---

[43] HINES V. DAVIDOWITZ, 312 U.S. at 67.

[44] GEIER V. AMERICAN HONDA MOTOR CO., 529 U.S. 861, 881 (2000); id. (damages liability "would have presented an obstacle to the variety and mix of devices that the federal regulation sought.").

[45] Id. at 801 (Stevens, J., dissenting) ("Although the standard did not require airbags in all cars, it is clear that the Secretary did intend to encourage wider use of airbags.").

[46] Id. at 888 (Stevens, J., dissenting).

majority ended up disagreeing over whether the gradual phase-in was, in effect, a ceiling on how fast manufacturers could be required to install air bags or a floor that could be accelerated by supplemental state laws.

Pacific Gas and Electric Co. v. State Energy Resources Conservation and Development Comm'n,[47] which we have already encountered for its holding with respect to field preemption, turned on a similarly nuanced reading of the objectives of a federal statute. Even though the Supreme Court determined that the Atomic Energy Act did not occupy the field of electric utility regulation, there was "little doubt that a primary purpose of the Atomic Energy Act was, and continues to be, the promotion of nuclear power."[48] The California state regulation at issue in the case arguably stood as an obstacle to that objective because it imposed a moratorium on the certification of new nuclear reactors in the state until its Energy Commission determined that a means for permanent disposal of the long-term radioactive waste from reactors had been "demonstrated." At the time, no one contended that such long-term disposal technology had been demonstrated, so the result of the California state requirement was to prevent any California utility from building a new reactor. The utility company "strongly contended" – and did so quite plausibly – that the California moratorium frustrated the promotion of nuclear power, concededly a primary objective of the federal statute.

The Supreme Court, however, read the federal objective in a more refined manner. It judged that the act did not embody a federal policy to pursue nuclear power "at all costs."[49] States retained regulatory authority over economic questions of whether nuclear as opposed to other forms of electrical generation ought to be used, and the absence of safe long-term storage created economic uncertainty as to what operating a reactor would cost. "Therefore, while the argument of petitioners and the United States has considerable force, the legal reality remains that Congress has left sufficient authority in the states to allow the development of nuclear power to be slowed or even stopped for economic reasons."[50]

The standard formulation of the obstacles test for preemption would suggest that a state law should be preempted if it stands as an obstacle to the full achievement of federal purposes. *Pacific Gas and Electric,* however, is exemplary in comprehending that while Congress surely has objectives for statutes when it enacts them, it may well not want those objectives pursued "at all costs." One suspects that Congress seldom enacts statutes with the idea that a

[47] 461 U.S. 190 (1983).
[48] 461 U.S. at 221.
[49] Id. at 200.
[50] Id. at 222–3.

single objective ought to be pursued at all costs. To the contrary, the unremitting pursuit of any single objective may impact other objectives that Congress also wishes to pursue, requiring some accommodation or trade-off. Then, too, most legislation embodies compromises; it is frequently the case that the winning coalition includes members who are willing to support the pursuit of an objective but only up to a point. These possibilities cast some doubt on whether it really is appropriate to find that state laws are preempted on the basis that they stand in the way of the full pursuit of a federal objective. When the issue is overriding state laws, why doesn't the same federalism-based instinct that animates the presumption against preemption operate to insist on a high degree of confidence that Congress sees state law as an impermissible obstacle to greater fulfillment of federal objectives before obstacle preemption is found?[51]

Pacific Gas and Electric is exemplary, but it is also unusual. The health and safety area, in particular, is one in which proper regard for the role of state and local government in matters of their citizens' health and safety ought to produce more deference to state laws.[52] Often it does not. It is at least plausible, is it not, that the federal policy of enabling manufacturers to phase in the installation of air bags recognized in *Geier* was not meant to be pursued "at all costs"? Even if you accepted the majority's interpretation of the federal objectives, and even if state damages awards would accelerate the phase-in,[53] it might still be the case

[51] See, e.g., Caleb Nelson, n. 23, at 281: "The mere fact that Congress enacts a statute to serve certain purposes does not automatically imply that Congress wants to displace all state law that gets in the way of those purposes. To draw this inference, one would need additional information about the particular statute in question. It follows that a general doctrine of "obstacle preemption" will displace more state law than its own rationale warrants: In the name of "congressional intent," it will read federal statutes to imply preemption clauses that the enacting Congress might well have rejected."

[52] Another recent case in the which the Supreme Court did show more solicitude toward traditional state roles is GONZALES V. OREGON, 546 U.S. 243 (2006). GONZALES arose after Oregon enacted its Death with Dignity Act, establishing a regulated procedure for physicians to provide lethal medicines to terminally ill patients. In 2001, Attorney General Ashcroft issued an interpretive rule stating that a physician's providing medicines whose distribution was tightly regulated under the federal Controlled Substances Act (CSA) would violate the CSA – and likely be a federal felony – because assisting suicides was not a legitimate medical practice. If this was a proper interpretation of the CSA, it would have preempted the Oregon state law. (Compare GONZALES V. RAICH, 545 U.S. 1(2005), holding that the CSA's prohibition on the distribution or possession of marijuana preempted California's state law authorizing the medicinal use of marijuana.) The Supreme Court, however, citing cases like MEDTRONIC for the proposition that the Constitution allows the states "great latitude under their police powers to legislate as to the protection of the lives, limbs, health, comfort and quiet of all persons," ruled that the CSA did not place the determination of legitimate medical practices in the attorney general's hands but left it in state hands, where it has traditionally and historically been. In a 6-3 decision, it upheld the Oregon law.

[53] The dissent disputed that a damages award would have that effect. See 529 U.S. at 901-902 (Stevens, J., dissenting).

that it was more consistent with congressional intent to permit injured individuals their full range of common law remedies. Providing redress for tortious injury falls squarely within the category of the state's historical police powers, which the Supreme Court often says warrant special solicitude.

In writing about obstacle preemption, nonetheless, the Supreme Court at times seems to take just the opposite tack, showing solicitude not for federalism values but instead for a very aggressive pursuit of federal purposes. It continues regularly to repeat the doctrine that "[i]n the absence of explicit statutory language signaling an intent to pre-empt, we infer such intent where . . . the state law stands as an obstacle to the accomplishment and execution of congressional objectives"[54] and to maintain that federal statutes "reveal a *clear*, but implicit, pre-emptive intent" when state laws "stan[d] as an obstacle to the accomplishment and execution of the *full* purposes and objectives of Congress."[55]

FUTURE CONTROVERSIES

Over the years, federal statutory law has become increasingly dense and complex, a trend that shows no signs of abating. As advocates for and opponents of new environmental, health, and safety initiatives continue to press their positions at all levels of government, the diversity of political opinion throughout the country will continue to produce new clashes between state, local, and federal policies. When the clashes involve state and federal laws, it will be up to the federal courts to employ preemption doctrines to assess when local or statute laws are "contrary" to federal ones.

As a result, we should anticipate seeing increasing volumes of both express and implied preemption cases. Although it is not uncommon for Congress to anticipate the question of how state law ought to interact with new federal legislation, and then to write express preemption or savings clauses, Congress seldom addresses all the contexts in which state local and federal laws will bump up against one another. Courts will continue to struggle over the meaning of express preemption clauses when those clauses use terms that do not clearly reveal their reach. One particularly vexing problem arises when an older federal statute containing an express preemption clause confronts regulatory issues that were unanticipated at the time of the federal enactment. When Congress enacted the 1975 Energy Policy and Conservation Act (EPCA), for example, it established federal Corporate Average Fuel

---

[54] E.g., Northwest Cent. Pipeline v. State Corp. Comm'n of Kansas, 489 U.S. 493, 509 (1989).

[55] Barnett Bank, 517 U.S. at 31 (quoting Hines v. Davidowitz, 312 U.S. 52, 67 [1941]) (emphasis added).

Economy (CAFE) standards,[56] while at the same time providing that no state could "adopt or enforce a law or regulation relating to fuel economy standards or average fuel economy standards."[57] As states increasingly take the initiative to innovate programs to reduce greenhouse gases (GHGs), a trend analyzed by Professor Glicksman in Chapter 8, the meaning of this express preemption provision has become a central battleground in legal challenges to those programs. The contention is that when states enact measures to reduce the greenhouse gas contribution of automobiles, they are writing laws or regulations "relating to" fuel economy standards, because improving fuel economy is the chief means of reducing carbon dioxide emissions from the internal combustion engine. All sides concede, though, that there was no mention of GHGs or concern for climate change when Congress enacted the EPCA, a piece of legislation driven entirely by the Organization of the Petroleum Exporting Countries (OPEC) energy crisis of the early 1970s and the consequent desire of American lawmakers to reduce American dependence on foreign oil. Arguments over the application of EPCA's preemption clause will turn on two opposing claims about the implied intention of an enacting Congress who quite obviously lacked any specific intention with respect to state GHG regulatory programs. In support of state latitude to regulate in this area, courts might see such efforts as consistent with EPCA. After all, why a federal law whose principal objective is to improve fuel economy should have the effect of blocking state efforts to lower GHG emissions is something of a mystery, because improving fuel economy further is an excellent way to reduce those gases. The best argument for preemption rests on legislative desire to provide manufacturers with the benefits of regulatory stability as well as the economies of scale created when manufacturers can design vehicles to comply with a uniform national standard rather than a number of different federal and state standards.

To date, supporters of state-level GHG initiatives have won several preliminary victories on this issue. A Vermont district court has decided that the EPCA preemption clause did not prevent Vermont from adopting California's approach to reducing GHG emissions from automobiles.[58] In a second suit, a California federal district also has upheld California's GHG standards, although on a different legal theory than the Vermont court.[59] The courts of appeals, and eventually the Supreme Court, will have to resolve the issue.

---

[56] Pub. L. No. 94-163, § 301 (current version codified as 49 U.S.C. §§ 32901-19).

[57] 49 U.S.C. § 32919(a).

[58] GREEN MOUNTAIN CHRYSLER PLYMOUTH DODGE JEEP v. CROMBIE, 508 F.Supp.2d 295 (D.Vt., 2007).

[59] This lawsuit challenged California's Pavley Amendment, which requires "maximum feasible and cost-effective reduction" of GHGs beginning in model year 2009. CENTRAL VALLEY CHRYSLER-JEEP, INC. v. GOLDSTENE, 529 F. Supp. 2d 1151 (E.D. Ca. 2007).

As state and local governments undertake further efforts to reduce their contribution to the problems of global warming, the preemption clauses of older statutes like EPCA – written at a time when Congress had no particular intention toward state and local GHG policy at all – will be ongoing sources of litigation. Ironically, the CAA's preemption provisions can also get in the way of state measures that it seems unlikely Congress meant to prevent, simply because the provisions were written broadly at a time when particular state air-pollution initiatives were unanticipated and hence not planned for in the legislation. *Engine Manufacturers Ass'n v. South Coast Air Quality Management District*[60] illustrates the problem.

In *Engine Manufacturers*, the South Coast Air Quality Management District had written rules requiring owners of vehicle fleets, such as garbage collection companies, utility companies, and schools, to purchase certain percentages of alternative-fuel vehicles, low-emissions vehicles, or zero-emissions vehicles as these vehicles became "commercially available." Designed to help the Los Angeles air basin ameliorate its persistent local air quality problems, these Fleet Rules ran into the CAA's express preemption of "any" state or local "standard relating to the control of emissions from new motor vehicles."[61] Because the fleet purchasing requirements were tied to levels of emissions in the purchased vehicles, the Engine Manufacturers Association argued that they were preempted. The Supreme Court agreed.

When Congress wrote the auto-emissions preemption clause into law in 1970, it did so because auto manufacturers persuasively argued that asking manufacturers to comply with multiple, differing state standards would perhaps be impossible and certainly would raise the price of automobiles substantially. The preemption clause ensured that manufacturers would only have to meet a single national emissions standard.[62] The Fleet Rules written by the district did not require manufacturers to produce vehicles meeting its emissions

---

[60] 541 U.S. 246 (2004).

[61] 42. U.S.C. § 7543(a).

[62] The CAA actually authorizes two mandatory standards – the federal standard and the California standard. By the time the 1970 CAA was written, California already had established emissions standards for automobiles sold in California, prompted by auto-related smog problems that were the worst in the nation at the time. Congress recognized California's claim to retain the authority to write standards best suited to its local needs by providing an exemption for their standards. 42 U.S.C. § 7543. The exemption is not automatic. In order to receive it, California must submit its standards to EPA for review; EPA can refuse to grant the exemption on limited grounds. In ENGINE MANUFACTURERS, California had not applied for an exemption for the district's Fleet Rules. As a result of an amendment to the CAA in 1977, other states than California can elect to adopt California's standards. This explains why Vermont was able to adopt the GHG reduction strategy that was at issue in the CROMBIE litigation, see n. 58.

requirements, so it is difficult to see how they posed a threat to this fundamental purpose of the preemption provision. Instead, the Fleet Rules created a ready market for extremely low-emissions vehicles that would have provided incentives for manufacturers to develop compliant vehicles, as each would know they could lose market share to competitors if the competitor produced compliant vehicles that the fleet owners would then be under an obligation to purchase. That kind of market incentive, however, seems entirely consistent with both the purpose behind the preemption provision and the broader purposes of the CAA of improving and maintaining air quality throughout the country. Nonetheless, by an 8-1 vote, the Supreme Court held that the broadly written preemption clause meant the Fleet Rules could not be enforced.

Clashes over whether federal laws block state law tort or damages actions are another sort of conflict that will be ongoing. Oftentimes these will be express preemption cases, as in *Cipollone*,[63] *Medtronic*,[64] and *Riegel*.[65] Implied preemption cases can also raise the issue, however. The statute at issue in *Geier*,[66] for instance, contained an express preemption provision, but the Supreme Court concluded that its prohibition of "any safety standard" that differs from the federal standard was best given "a narrow reading that excludes common-law actions."[67] This conclusion did not save the state damages claim from being preempted by the statute, however, because as we have seen, the Supreme Court went on to apply implied preemption doctrine, reasoning that the possibility of tort damages based on the claim that the absence of an air bag amounted to a design defect would interfere with accomplishing the objectives of the federal safety statute.[68]

Because *Cipollone* found a statute's prohibition on differing state "requirements" to preempt some state tort claims, litigants have asserted the preemptive effect of similar language in other statutes, or have argued that alternative formulations, such as "standards" (see, e.g., *Geier*), ought to be similarly interpreted. The Supreme Court's decisions in these cases have often been closely divided, and there are several recent decisions that may signal that the Supreme Court is "trying to put the *Cipollone* genie back in the bottle" by taking a more charitable stance toward common law actions.[69] In *Bates v.*

[63] 505 U.S. 504, 516 (1992).
[64] 518 U.S. 470, 485 (1996).
[65] 128 S. Ct. 999, 1014 (2008).
[66] See n. 44.
[67] 529 U.S. at 868.
[68] See text at nn. 43–6.
[69] David C. Vladeck, "Preemption and Regulatory Failure," PEPPERDINE LAW REVIEW 33 (2005): 95, 100.

Dow Agrosciences,[70] for instance, the Supreme Court was asked to interpret the Federal Insecticide, Fungicide and Rodenticide Act's (FIFRA) provision that a "state shall not impose or continue in effect any requirements for labeling or packaging in addition to or different from those required by [FIFRA]"[71] to preclude design defect or breach of express-warranty claims. The Supreme Court declined this invitation. It ruled that even if an adverse verdict in a defective design case might prompt a manufacturer to change its pesticide label or packaging, such suits did not impose "requirements." "A requirement is a rule that must be obeyed; an event, such as a jury verdict, that merely motivates an optional decision is not a requirement. The proper inquiry calls for an examination of the elements of the common-law duty at issue, not for speculation as to whether a jury verdict will prompt the manufacturer to change its label."[72]

Oftentimes, preemption decisions by the Supreme Court regarding state damages claims simply spawn follow-on litigation, as litigants and lower courts test competing interpretations of what the Supreme Court decided or test its implications for other statutes and other types of common law claims. After *Medtronic* held that the state law claims involved there had not been preempted by the MDA,[73] preemption claims under the MDA have scarcely abated at all. One reason for the confusion is the split nature of the *Medtronic* decision. Although there was a clear majority for certain basic propositions, a concurrence by Justice Breyer seemed to intimate that he saw more preemption of state damages claims than the four-person plurality did, and some courts have seized on that to interpret *Medtronic* more narrowly than have other courts.[74] The Supreme Court's most recent MDA decision – ironically involving another Medtronic device – held that the MDA did preempt state law tort claims against devices that had undergone full premarket evaluation and approval at the FDA.[75]

The post-*Medtronic* MDA litigation, beyond illustrating the ongoing ferment regarding the preemption of state damages actions, also exposes another highly controversial feature of current preemption litigation. This is the phenomenon of "preemption by preamble." In recent years a number of federal agencies have issued statements, often in the preambles of rules or regulations

---

[70] 544 U.S. 431 (2005).
[71] 7 U.S.C. § 136v(b).
[72] 544 U.S. at 443.
[73] See text at nn. 11–13.
[74] See generally, Vladeck, n. 69, for an excellent analysis of MEDTRONIC's holding and of the question of preemption of state damages claims more broadly.
[75] RIEGEL v. MEDTRONIC, 128 S. Ct. 999 (2008). RIEGEL involved a faulty balloon catheter used in angioplasty surgery.

published in the *Federal Register*, announcing the agency's interpretation of the scope of the preemption provision in a statute administered by the agency. These recent statements, all issued by agencies of the George W. Bush administration, all come down in favor of broad preemption of state damages actions, oftentimes reversing positions taken by prior administrations regarding the scope of preemption. In recent years, the FDA, the Consumer Product Safety Commission, and the National Highway Traffic Safety Administration have all issued such preemption statements.[76]

Agency pronouncements regarding the preemptive effect of their regulations are not new. An executive order issued by President Clinton and still in effect instructs that a federal regulation should "specif[y] in clear language the preemptive effect, if any, to be given to the regulation."[77] Nonetheless, these recent agency statements represent a shift from prior agency practice, in at least two ways. First, as David Vladeck notes, federal agencies "ha[ve] historically resisted becoming enmeshed in private products liability litigation."[78] Although the United States is often asked by the Supreme Court to state its views in preemption cases, these preamble statements amount to the agencies reaching out to inject their views into litigation without court invitation. In this regard, it is important to note that the FDA's preamble statement was issued after the FDA had filed a number of amicus briefs in FDA-related tort litigation urging the Supreme Court to adopt the view it eventually stated formally by preamble.[79] This is the second shift: the view being expressed in favor of broad preemptive reach of particular federal statutes represents a switch of legal position from prior positions of the United States with respect to the same statutory provisions. With respect to the MDA, for instance, the U.S. amicus filing in *Riegel* acknowledged that the administration's current position was directly contrary to the position of the United States in a similar case nine years prior. Under the Bush administration's new view, FDA premarket approval for Medtronic's balloon catheter established a federal requirement that preempted state damages actions.[80] The FDA's activism

---

[76] For these statements and a review of the phenomenon, see Catherine M. Sharkey, "Preemption by Preamble: Federal Agencies and the Federalization of Tort Reform," DePaul Law Review 56 (2007): 227.

[77] Executive Order No. 12,988, 61 Federal Register 4731 (February 7, 1996), at § 3(b)(1)(B).

[78] Vladeck, n. 69, at 122.

[79] Id. at 122, n. 216 (describing amicus brief efforts of the FDA during the tenure of Dan Troy as chief counsel to the FDA).

[80] See Brief of the United States as Amicus Curiae in Riegel v. Medtronic, No. 06-179, at 16-17 (noting the government's switch of position compared to the position taken in Smith Industries Medical Systems, Inc. v. Kernats, cert. denied, 522 U.S. 1044 [1998]).

and its change of legal position amount to "a complete transformation" under the Bush administration.[81]

The role of federal agencies in determining the scope of federal preemption presents some complex questions. One involves the extent to which the *Chevron* doctrine applies. Under *Chevron*, any reasonable construction of a statute made by an agency is supposed to carry the day, so long as the Congress has not "spoken to the precise question at issue."[82] It is not clear whether the Supreme Court considers the question of preemption to be one to which *Chevron* deference applies.[83] The issue was briefed in a 2007 case involving the National Bank Act, but the Supreme Court's decision did not reach the issue.[84]

In 1963, Judge Henry Friendly focused on the problems created by poorly written statutes, whose defects are beyond the competence of courts to correct, in the law review article "The Gap in Lawmaking – Judges Who Can't and Legislators Who Won't."[85] The most perverse consequences of allocating too much authority to the federal government through doctrines governing congressional and agency preemption creates a similar problem of "states who can't and federal authorities who won't." Suppose, for instance, that before *Medtronic* (a 5-4 decision) the FDA had published a forceful statement in a regulatory preamble announcing that its superintendence of such medical devices preempted state law. If that pronouncement had received *Chevron* deference, the Court might well have preempted state law. The result would have left the individual injured by the device without a legal remedy and the state without the power to enact supplementary safety regulations to protect their citizens. FDA's authority to require manufacturers to recall, replace, or refund defective devices would be the sole enforcement mechanism of a regulatory regime entirely concentrated within a single, overworked and heavily criticized federal agency.[86]

---

[81] Vladeck, n. 69, at 122.

[82] CHEVRON V. NATURAL RESOURCES DEFENSE COUNCIL, 467 U.S. 837 (1984).

[83] For a discussion of the question, see Nina Mendelson, "Chevron and Preemption," MICHIGAN LAW REVIEW 102 (2004): 737 (concluding CHEVRON deference ought not to apply).

[84] WACHOVIA BANK V. WATTERS, 127 S.Ct. 1559 (2007). Justice Stevens, joined by Chief Justice Roberts and Justice Scalia, would have reached the issue to decide that in order for an agency to have the authority to announce the preemptive effect of a regulation – as opposed to issuing a regulation that a court subsequently determines has preemptive effect – such authority must be clearly given by Congress. Even then, "when an agency purports to decide the scope of federal preemption, a healthy respect for state sovereignty calls for something less than CHEVRON deference." Id. at 1584 (Stevens, J., dissenting).

[85] 63 COLUMBIA LAW REVIEW 787 (1963).

[86] The Medtronic hypothetical is taken from Sharkey, n. 76.

The concentration of regulatory authority entirely in a federal agency's hands can have very deleterious consequences. The ossification of federal rule making makes federal agencies very slow-moving beasts. They are reluctant to revise standards or programs in light of new knowledge and changed circumstances due to the cumbersome, labor-intensive nature of the enterprise, fraught as it is with the hazards of hard-look judicial review. None of the federal agencies that have issued statements of preemption in regulatory preambles, for instance, has been an active rule maker in recent years, preferring instead to engage in negotiations with the regulated community to persuade "voluntary" recalls or modifications of products or drug labels. In comparison, states and localities are relatively more nimble. "States are often pioneers in consumer protection," for example, "providing the impetus for new or improved federal regulation."[87] If attacks grounded in preemption are successful in stifling the initiatives states are taking with respect to GHGs and global warming, while Congress and the Environmental Protection Agency (EPA) remain stalemated and silent, global warming will become a poster child for the perverse effects of states who can't and federal authorities who won't.[88]

Additional concerns arise when federal preemption results in eliminating any prospect for compensatory damages for injured persons, which is a very real possibility because so few federal regulatory schemes provide for compensation for injuries. Even when civil remedies are incorporated into federal schemes, they can be inadequate. Such is the case with the Employment Retirement Income Security Act (ERISA), which includes a broad preemption of all state law, statutory and court-made, "related to" a benefit plan. Even though ERISA includes a mechanism for enforcing plan contracts against providers, the narrow interpretation that mechanism has been given has, in Justice Ginsburg's estimation, created a "regulatory vacuum": "[V]irtually all state remedies are preempted but very few federal substitutes are provided."[89]

These, then, are four problem areas – the risk that broad federal statutes will preempt the ability of states to address new environmental, health, and safety concerns; the preemption of state damages actions; the ability of federal

[87] Statement of the Honorable Thomas H. Moore, Consumer Product Safety Commissioner, U.S. Consumer Product Safety Commission, Statement of the Honorable Thomas H. Moore on the Final Rule and Preamble for the Flammability (Open-Flame) of Mattress Sets (February 16, 2006), http://www.cpsc.gov/cpscpub/prerel/prhtml06/06091.html.

[88] For more discussion of the advantages of overlapping authorities in the environment, health, and safety area, see Christopher H. Schroeder, "Federalism's Values in Programs to Protect the Environment," in STRATEGIES FOR ENVIRONMENTAL SUCCESS, ed. Michael Allan Wolf (Washington, D.C.: Environmental Law Institute, 2005), 247.

[89] AETNA HEALTH INC. V. DAVILA, 542 U.S. 200, 222 (2004) (Ginsburg, J., concurring).

agencies to mark the boundaries of the preemptive effects of statutes and regulations; and, in the worst case, the "regulatory vacuum" that can result from concentrating too much authority at the federal level. Looking forward, these problem areas will be continuing battlegrounds over preemption doctrine and policy.

CONCLUSION

Grounded in the Supremacy Clause, the question of preemption necessarily arises in our system, in which federal regulatory authority under its enumerated powers and state police power regulatory authority overlap to cover many of the same activities. The Supremacy Clause makes the federal government the final arbiter of the question. Because the ultimate issue in preemption cases is so fundamental and important, the doctrines the Supreme Court has developed to resolve preemption controversies have been and will continue to be the subjects of controversy. The doctrine has grown into a multipart universe consisting of express and implied preemption, the latter encompassing both field preemption and conflict preemption, which is further divided into physical impossibility and obstacle preemption.

Complicated in many ways, preemption doctrine could never be entirely eliminated. It could, however, be profoundly influenced not only by changes at the judicial level but also by changes in politics and policy. Preemption is a field of constitutional law in which policy and law are inextricably intertwined. Because the touchstone of preemption analysis is congressional intent, Congress can specify in the statutes it enacts how decision-making authority should be allocated between the two levels of government. Interpretive controversies will undoubtedly remain; but to the extent Congress can first form a judgment and then articulate it in statutory language, the question is entirely within its competence to decide.

The role of federal agencies in setting preemption policy is less well defined, but one thing is clear: the aggressive pro-preemption positions being taken currently by federal agencies – changes from the earlier stance of most federal agencies – could be reversed by an administration that thought greater deference to state law was appropriate. Here, too, policy and law legitimately intersect, because the law of preemption is importantly influenced by the policy preferences of the administration in office.

7 When Congress Goes Unheard: Savings Clauses' Rocky Judicial Reception

Sandi Zellmer

INTRODUCTION

As shown in other chapters of this book, the preemption doctrine has been applied inconsistently by the courts, and, in many cases, the results have failed to promote either federal-state comity or institutional competence. Preemption is particularly troublesome when Congress has included a savings clause in the federal statute at issue.

Many, if not most, federal public health and environmental statutes include broadly crafted savings clauses intended to leave ample room for state law to provide increased protection beyond the federal regulatory floor. Recent Supreme Court cases reveal a pattern of hostility toward savings clauses in cases involving state regulatory programs. In contrast, although the Court's reception of savings clauses for common law tort claims has been unpredictable, by and large tort claims have been treated more favorably. The inclusion of generously worded savings clauses governing state tort claims may explain these results in some contexts, but the text of most savings clauses is so similar that, as the Supreme Court has noted, not even the "most dedicated hair-splitter" could distinguish them.[1] Instead, the Court apparently views positive enactments and formal regulatory programs issued by state legislatures and state agencies as a greater threat to the implementation of federal programs and the accomplishment of federal goals than tort claims. As discussed in the following section, recent cases suggest that a critical distinction may be drawn between regulatory requirements and the inducements created by common law liabilities, but close parsing of modestly different statutory language may also explain the results, as may some justices' predilection against multilayered regulatory burdens.

---

[1] BATES v. DOW AGROSCIENCES LLC, 544 U.S. 431, 446n21 (2005).

Congress has, in some instances, muddied the waters by including both preemption clauses and savings clauses. Dueling clauses pose a difficult interpretive conundrum for courts. Both savings clauses and preemption clauses serve to demarcate the boundaries of federal and state law, but, unlike preemption clauses, savings clauses strike the balance in favor of states and state law remedies. In many Supreme Court cases, however, their combined effect has been to weaken state police powers and, in turn, diminish the protection of health, safety, and environmental quality by leaving gaping holes in the regulatory framework. Although this phenomenon is less pronounced in the tort context, there are some cases where savings clauses have been effectively neutralized by preemption clauses, leaving victims without any remedy, federal or state, for their injuries.

The chapter seeks to identify preemption patterns and principles from the Supreme Court's case law on statutory savings clauses. It begins with an assessment of the need for savings clauses in federal legislation. It then turns to the Supreme Court's treatment of savings clauses when victims seek tort remedies for harm caused by federally regulated activities. Next, it assesses the Court's treatment of savings clauses when state governments seek to impose more stringent regulatory requirements than imposed by the federal floor. A comparison of case law in five areas – pollution, workplace safety, nuclear energy, medical devices and drugs, and pesticide use – indicates a willingness to provide some redress to injured persons but, at the same time, a strong leaning against the imposition of protective state regulations above the federal regulatory floor. In the latter set of cases, it is hard to avoid the conclusion that judicial outcomes appear to be driven by a results-oriented, antiregulatory sentiment rather than by statutory language or overarching congressional goals. The results in the regulatory cases have often fallen short of protecting people and their environment and have frustrated or even eviscerated legislative objectives as well as federalism ideals.

If savings clauses were given appropriate weight in the regulatory context, as they generally are in the common law context, dangerous regulatory gaps would be less likely. Meanwhile, a pattern of cooperative federalism would be more likely to emerge, as state and federal entities would be motivated and empowered to capitalize on each of their institutional strengths and to craft coordinated regulatory solutions. No magic language can ensure that courts or agencies will not find state law preempted, but careful drafting may promote more rational, equitable results. The chapter concludes with suggestions for crafting a statutory savings clause that may be more likely to be given broad effect by the courts.

THE NEED FOR SAVINGS CLAUSES

Advocates and scholars alike place a heavy emphasis on federal law for protecting public health and the environment, for good reason. The federal government is often in the best position to remedy national problems such as air and water pollution, hazardous workplace conditions, and the manufacture and sale of dangerous chemicals and drugs. It possesses greater resources, expertise, and data-collection capabilities than any single state. In addition, federal law can provide uniform, forward-looking solutions to widespread problems.

Before the explosion of federal public health and environmental requirements in the 1970s, state and local authorities exercised their police powers through regulations and common law theories to combat the multifarious problems of an increasingly industrialized society. Federal and state courts alike accepted the doctrines of nuisance, trespass, and strict liability as appropriate means to address the effects of harmful industrial activities. The Supreme Court routinely applied a presumption against preemption to tort claims for harm from pollution and other activities affecting public health and welfare, even in heavily regulated areas where the federal interest was deemed most compelling.[2] Unless regulated entities could rebut this presumption by showing a clear manifestation of congressional intent to preempt state remedies, courts could allow compensation for harm.

Statutory savings clauses reflect the congressional desire to preserve the presumption against preemption and, more generally, state authority and state remedies. Where Congress includes a savings clause, it recognizes the need either to fill a regulatory void or to enhance protection for affected communities through complementary federal and state authorities. The preemption of state law in these areas inevitably causes a regulatory vacuum, where the states are prevented from regulating broad spheres of harmful activity even though federal regulation is lacking or, in some cases, completely absent. As a result, both states and their residents are worse off than before the passage of federal law.

SAVING STATE COMMON LAW

Most federal public health and environmental statutes neither explicitly preclude nor independently authorize private recovery of compensatory damages for personal injury or property damage. Although some federal statutes

---

[2] GEIER V. AMERICAN HONDA MOTOR CO., 529 U.S. 861, 894 (2005) (Stevens, J., dissenting).

authorize citizens' suits as a supplemental enforcement scheme, they only allow injunctions and the assessment of civil penalties payable to the federal treasury, not to the private plaintiff.[3] As a result, individuals seeking compensation for harm caused by a federally regulated activity are limited to whatever relief is provided by state law. Even where federal law addresses the harmful activity through prescriptive regulations and prohibitions, state common law serves as an important gap-filler by providing for compensatory and punitive damages.[4]

With some exceptions, the Supreme Court has generally accepted supplemental state-law remedies as consistent with congressional objectives to protect health and welfare. Although the pattern is not wholly consistent, at least some common law tort claims for water and air pollution, pesticide use, workplace injuries, defective medical devices, and radiation poisoning from nuclear plants have been allowed to proceed. Conversely, tort claims have often been displaced where the relevant statute lacks a savings clause or includes both a savings clause and a preemption clause.

POLLUTION

Air and water pollution is governed by a cooperative federalism framework intended not only to respect states' historic police powers to protect public health and safety within their borders but also to authorize uniform federal standards that transcend state lines. State tort law remedies for harm caused by pollutants have long coexisted with federal and state regulatory programs and have proven to be an important part of the cooperative federalism formula. Most recently, dozens of states and cities, increasingly frustrated with the federal government's failure to curb greenhouse gas (GHG) emissions through regulatory means, have brought common law nuisance claims against power plants and automobile manufacturers in hopes of combating climate change.[5] These claims can only be successful if they are saved from preemption.

---

[3] See 7 U.S.C. §§ 136–136y (providing no private right of action for harms caused by pesticides); 33 U.S.C. § 1365 (providing no right to compensatory damages under the Clean Water Act); 42 U.S.C. § 300j-8 (providing no right to compensatory damages under the Safe Drinking Water Act); 42 U.S.C. § 7604 (providing no right to compensatory damages under the CAA); 42 U.S.C. § 9607 (providing no right to compensatory damages for injuries due to releases of hazardous substances).

[4] Alexandra B. Klass, "Common Law and Federalism in the Age of the Regulatory State," IOWA LAW REVIEW 92, no. 2 (2007): 545, 567–8.

[5] CONNECTICUT V. AM. ELEC. POWER CO., 406 F. Supp. 2d 265, 274 (S.D.N.Y. 2005); CALIFORNIA V. GENERAL MOTORS, Complaint, No. 3:06-cv-05755-MJJ (N.D. Cal. September 20, 2006).

State and local governments have long grappled with pollution problems through smoke-abatement ordinances and the like, and air-pollution prevention falls squarely within states' traditional police powers of protecting their citizens' health. The Clean Air Act (CAA) expressly states congressional intent that "air pollution prevention ... and air pollution control at its source is the primary responsibility of States and local governments."[6] It comes as no surprise that, perhaps more than any other federal statute, the CAA is peppered with savings clauses.[7] Power plants and automobile manufacturers have asserted that claims to remedy GHG emissions are preempted, but precedent generally cuts the other way – tort claims for recovery for harms caused by air pollutants have been considered supplemental to the other applicable statutory and administrative requirements of the CAA.[8] The Supreme Court has not yet had occasion to address the preemptive effect of the CAA in this context, but it has reconciled common law tort claims with the Clean Water Act, which has a similar legislative background and contains a similar savings clause.

Some of the earliest preemption battles over pollution involved the Clean Water Act, aimed at restoring and maintaining the chemical, biological, and physical integrity of the nation's waterways. As one means of accomplishing this goal, Congress included several savings clauses to preserve statutory and common law claims and to preserve states' ability to impose more protective pollution control requirements and to establish and enforce rights to allocate and use water resources.[9]

In the early days after enactment, it appeared that these savings clauses preserved both federal and state common law claims for harm caused by water pollution. The door was slammed shut on the use of federal common law as a remedy for interstate pollution, however, in *Illinois v. Milwaukee*.[10] The state of Illinois asserted a federal common law nuisance claim against Wisconsin cities for dumping untreated sewage into Lake Michigan. The lower courts agreed that federal common law required the defendants to treat their sewage more stringently than compelled by the Clean Water Act, emphasizing the expansive nature of the savings clause: "[n]othing in this section shall restrict

---

[6] 42 U.S.C. § 7401(a)(3); TRAIN V. NATURAL RES. DEF. COUNCIL, INC., 421 U.S. 60, 64 (1975).

[7] 42 U.S.C. §§ 7604(e), 7412(d)(7), 7416.

[8] HER MAJESTY THE QUEEN V. CITY OF DETROIT, 874 F.2d 332, 344 (6th Cir.1989); NORTH CAROLINA EX REL COOPER V. TENNESSEE VALLEY AUTHORITY, 439 F.Supp.2d 486 (W.D.N.C. 2006); IN RE Methyl Tertiary Butyl Ether Products Liability Litigation, 341 F.Supp.2d 386 (S.D.N.Y 2004). GUTIERREZ V. MOBIL OIL CORP., 798 F.Supp. 1280 (W.D. Tex. 1992); U.S. V. ATLANTIC-RICHFIELD CO., 478 F.Supp. 1215 (D. Mont.1979).

[9] 33 U.S.C. §§ 1251(g), 1365(e), 1370.

[10] MILWAUKEE V. ILLINOIS (Milwaukee II), 451 U.S. 304 (1981).

any right which any person ... may have under any statute or common law to seek enforcement of any effluent standard or limitation or to seek any other relief."[11] The Supreme Court reversed. Despite the explicit savings clause, the Court believed that interstate pollution must be addressed by federal regulatory standards only, not federal common law. The decision failed to give weight to either the plain language of the savings clause, which makes no distinction between federal and state rights but preserves any common law right, or to congressional intent to preserve all types of supplemental remedies to ensure accomplishment of statutory goals.[12] Rather than giving full effect to the statutory language, the Court articulated a myopic view that, in a case involving one state against polluters in another state, a presumption in favor of displacement of federal common law was consistent with the long-standing presumption against displacement of state common law. Certainly, the foreclosure of federal common law to rectify harms caused by federally regulated activities makes the preservation of state common law all the more important. Subsequently, in *International Paper v. Ouellette*, the Supreme Court confirmed that state common law was still a viable avenue for redressing interstate water pollution.[13] Once again, however, it read the savings clause narrowly in concluding that only the law of the source state, not the affected state, would be applied. The Court believed that this limitation was necessary to ensure that the regulatory decisions of the source state were respected, thereby ensuring that economically beneficial activities in one state would be impervious to unpredictable complaints by other, often competing, states.

Preemption has also been asserted to shield polluters from liability for oil spills in interstate waters. In response to the 1989 wreck of the *Exxon Valdez* off the coast of Alaska, Congress adopted the Oil Pollution Act of 1990 (OPA), which integrated a mélange of provisions governing tanker vessels by imposing federal design requirements and penalties for spills.[14] Various bills related to oil spills had been considered prior to passage of the OPA, but preemption had been a major sticking point. In the end, Congress preserved the states' ability to respond to oil spills through two savings clauses. The first is concerned with cleanup: "Nothing in this Act ... shall ... be construed ... as preempting the authority of any State ... from imposing any additional

[11] MILWAUKEE V. ILLINOIS, 599 F.2d 151, 155, 163 (7th Cir. 1979) (citing 33 U.S.C. § 1365(e)), rev'd, 451 U.S. 304 (1981).

[12] Robert L. Glicksman, "Federal Preemption and Private Legal Remedies for Pollution," UNIVERSITY OF PENNSYLVANIA LAW REVIEW 134, no. 1 (1985): 121, 179.

[13] INTERNATIONAL PAPER CO. V. OUELLETTE, 479 U.S. 481 (1987).

[14] 33 U.S.C. §§ 2701–61. In particular, the OPA amended the Comprehensive Emergency Response, Compensation and Liability Act (CERCLA), 42 U.S.C. § 9607, and the Clean Water Act, 33 U.S.C. § 1321.

liability or requirements ... with respect to the discharge of oil ... or any removal activities in connection with such a discharge. ..."[5] The second relates to liability and penalties: "Nothing in this Act ... shall in any way affect, or be construed to affect, the authority of the United States or any State ... to impose additional liability or additional requirements; or to impose, or to determine the amount of, any fine or penalty ... for any violation of law; relating to the discharge, or substantial threat of a discharge, of oil."[6]

As for Exxon, after months of trial, a jury awarded billions of dollars in compensatory and punitive damages under Alaska law to fishermen and landowners injured by the oil spill. Because the OPA does not apply retroactively, Exxon invoked the Clean Water Act in an attempt to preempt common law punitive damages awards. The Ninth Circuit Court of Appeals rejected Exxon's contention. The court gave weight to the Clean Water Act's savings clause and reasoned that the absence of a federal private right of action could more reasonably be construed as leaving private claims intact than as implicitly destroying them.[7]

The wreck of the *Exxon Valdez* motivated coastal states all the way from Alaska to Florida to enact oil spill legislation. Some of these statutes impose preventative measures while others impose liability on the vessel owner and operator for cleanup costs and other damages. The Supreme Court has not yet addressed the interplay of common law liability and the OPA, but it has had occasion to address the OPA's preemptive effect on a state's preventative regulatory requirements, as described later in this chapter.[8]

WORKPLACE SAFETY

One of the few areas where savings clauses are consistently given full effect involves tort claims arising from workplace hazards. In response to a veritable epidemic of industrial injuries and deaths, Congress passed the Occupational Safety and Health Act of 1970 in order to provide "safe and healthful working conditions."[9] To accomplish this goal, Congress authorized the secretary of labor, acting through the Occupational Safety and Health Administration (OSHA), to promulgate health and safety standards for workplaces.

Like most federal health and welfare statutes, the act is designed to prevent injuries rather than to compensate victims for harm. Accordingly,

---

[5] 33 U.S.C. § 2718(a).
[6] 33 U.S.C. § 2718(c).
[7] In re Exxon, 270 F.3d 1215, 1231 (9th Cir. 2001), aff'd in part, 128 S. Ct. 2605 (2008).
[8] See infra nn. 61–3 and accompanying text.
[9] 29 U.S.C. § 651(b).

Congress explicitly saved common law and statutory rights to ensure redress: "Nothing ... shall be construed ... to enlarge or diminish or affect in any other manner the common law or statutory rights, duties, or liabilities of employers and employees under any law with respect to injuries, diseases, or death of employees arising out of, or in the course of, employment."[20] In light of the savings clause and Congress's broad remedial purpose, courts have generally found that tort claims arising out of workplace injuries are not preempted by OSHA. One court, in allowing tort claims by workers injured by welding fumes, observed that "no other enactment contains a savings clause more broad," plainly evidencing Congress's intent to leave common law liabilities "absolutely unchanged."[21] Other courts have been equally willing to construe OSHA's savings clause broadly to preserve state tort claims.[22] Like the OPA, however, state regulatory programs governing occupational safety have been treated far less favorably.[23]

NUCLEAR ENERGY

In a case that gained notoriety from the movie *Silkwood*, Karen Silkwood's estate sought recovery for injuries caused by exposure to plutonium while working at Kerr-McGee's federally licensed nuclear plant.[24] Kerr-McGee argued that state-authorized awards of punitive damages should be preempted because they would punish and deter conduct related to radiation hazards, an area within the exclusive domain of the Atomic Energy Act. The Supreme Court rejected this argument, in an opinion that gives weight to the statutory language as well as the overarching congressional intent regarding nuclear safety.

Congress gave the relationship between federal and state law close attention in the debates preceding passage of the Atomic Energy Act. It ultimately adopted a pervasive federal regulatory scheme to ensure the safe operation of nuclear plants. Accordingly, the act preempted state safety laws but explicitly preserved other state regulatory authorities in two separate savings clauses.[25] Although neither of these clauses applied directly to common law claims, subsequent statutory amendments in the Price-Anderson Act more

---

[20] 29 U.S.C. § 653(b)(4).
[21] IN RE Welding Fume Products Liability Litigation, 364 F.Supp.2d 669, 687–8 (N.D.Ohio 2005).
[22] See LINDSEY V. CATERPILLAR, INC., 480 F.3d 202 (3rd Cir. 2007); PEDRAZA V. SHELL OIL CO., 942 F.2d 48 (1st Cir.), cert. denied, 502 U.S. 1082 (1991); BARRIENTOS V. UT-BATTELLE, LLC, 284 F.Supp.2d 908 (S.D. Ohio 2003).
[23] See INFRA nn. 59–60 and accompanying text.
[24] SILKWOOD V. KERR-McGEE CORP., 464 U.S. 238 (1984).
[25] See INFRA nn. 53–5 and accompanying text.

clearly evidenced the intent not to displace state tort law by placing a cap on liability for nuclear meltdowns.[26]

Although noting that none of these provisions offered a definitive resolution to Kerr McGee's preemption challenge, the Supreme Court looked to them nonetheless as evidence of congressional intent to preserve state tort remedies, including Silkwood's punitive damage award. Not only was there no "irreconcilable conflict" between the federal and state requirements, but the Court also concluded that preemption of common law remedies would be especially inappropriate given that no federal remedies existed for persons injured by radiation exposure.[27] In the years following the *Silkwood* opinion, the Court reaffirmed its holding by allowing workers compensation claims and claims for retaliation and intentional infliction of emotional distress against nuclear power plants, demonstrating that state remedies have a viable role to play, even in heavily regulated areas such as nuclear power.[28] As described later in this chapter, certain state regulatory programs related to nuclear power have also survived preemption challenges, bucking the otherwise applicable trend toward preemption of state regulation.[29]

MEDICAL DEVICES, DRUGS, AND CIGARETTES

State common law remedies for harms caused by drugs and medical devices such as pacemakers have been the subject of fierce preemption battles. Savings clauses have played a role in nearly every dispute. In one case, the absence of a savings clause left the Supreme Court free to deny a remedy for wrongful death caused by one of the most addictive and dangerous products on the market – cigarettes. Tobacco use, according to the Court, "poses perhaps the single most significant threat to public health in the United States."[30] Yet the Court's 1992 decision in *Cipollone v. Liggett Group* shielded tobacco companies from failure-to-warn claims brought by smokers and their families.[31] Cipollone, whose mother died of lung cancer, alleged that the tobacco companies failed to provide adequate warnings about the risks of smoking, expressly warranted that their products were not dangerous to consumers' health, and conspired to conceal medical evidence about smoking

---

[26] Pub.L. No. 85-256, 71 Stat. 576 (1957).

[27] 464 U.S. at 251, 256.

[28] ENGLISH V. GENERAL ELECTRIC, 496 U.S. 72 (1990); GOODYEAR ATOMIC CORP. V. MILLER, 486 U.S. 174 (1988).

[29] See INFRA nn. 52–6 and accompanying text.

[30] LORILLARD TOBACCO CO. V. REILLY, 533 U.S. 525, 570 (2001) (citing FDA v. BROWN and WILLIAMSON TOBACCO CORP., 529 U.S. 120, 161 [2000]).

[31] 505 U.S. 504 (1992).

risks. The companies' defense turned on the Public Health Cigarette Smoking Act, which was intended to both warn the public of the hazards of smoking and to protect economic interests of tobacco companies by imposing uniform cigarette labeling and advertising requirements.[32] The act provided that, other than statements or labeling required by the act, "[n]o requirement or prohibition based on smoking and health shall be imposed under State law with respect to the advertising or promotion of any cigarettes."[33] The Court construed "requirement or prohibition" as "easily" encompassing tort actions because "regulation can be as effectively exerted through an award of damages as through some form of preventive relief."[34]

The Court's conclusion that the act expressly preempted all claims related to omissions or inclusions in cigarette advertising represents a marked departure from *Silkwood*. A key distinction was that, unlike the Atomic Energy Act and most other federal health and welfare statutes, the Cigarette Smoking Act included no savings clause. Absent a savings clause, it was easier for the *Cipollone* Court to infer that Congress was indifferent about leaving injured plaintiffs with no remedy. Although a few courts recognized this distinction, a trend quickly emerged in the lower courts to construe *Cipollone* as requiring an expansive reading of preemption clauses, regardless of the presence of a savings clause in the statute under consideration.[35]

Just a few years after *Cipollone*, the Supreme Court took a more nuanced approach to the Medical Device Act (MDA), a statute with both a savings clause and a preemption clause.[36] *Medtronic Inc. v. Lohr* involved a negligence action against the manufacturer of a pacemaker that had failed. Like the Cigarette Smoking Act, the MDA specified that "no State . . . may establish . . . *any requirement* which is different from, or in addition to, any requirement . . . which relates to the safety or effectiveness of the device."[37] The Court reasoned that the word *requirement*, as used in the MDA, entailed the imposition of a specific, positive duty on the manufacturer and therefore did not preempt common law claims. It acknowledged that *Cipollone* had held that the Cigarette Smoking Act's preemption of state "requirements" included tort claims but found that act distinguishable because it preempted only a limited

---

[32] Cigarette Labeling and Advertising Act of 1965 § 2, as amended in Public Health Cigarette Smoking Act of 1969, Pub. L. No. 91-222, 84 Stat. 87 (1970) (codified in 15 U.S.C. § 1334 [2000]).

[33] 15 U.S.C. § 1334.

[34] 505 U.S. at 521.

[35] Betsy J. Grey, "Make Congress Speak Clearly: Federal Preemption of State Tort Remedies," BOSTON UNIVERSITY LAW REVIEW 77, no. 3 (1997): 559, 564, 582.

[36] MEDTRONIC, INC. v. LOHR, 518 U.S. 470 (1996).

[37] 21 U.S.C. § 360k(a) (emphasis added).

set of state requirements – those related to advertising or promotion. In contrast, according to the Court, a sweeping interpretation of the phrase "any requirement" as used in the MDA "would require far greater interference with state legal remedies, producing a serious intrusion into state sovereignty while simultaneously wiping out the possibility of remedy for . . . injuries."[38]

The MDA was distinct from the Cigarette Smoking Act in another important way – it included a savings clause for liabilities related to devices recalled for posing unreasonable risks of harm.[39] Although this clause was not strictly applicable to the pacemaker at issue in *Medtronic*, the Court of Appeals viewed it as evidence of congressional intent to preserve common law remedies.[40] The Supreme Court agreed that, "[t]o the extent that Congress was concerned about protecting the industry, . . . any such concern was far outweighed by concerns about the primary issue motivating . . . enactment: the safety of those who use medical devices."[41] Yet it completely ignored the savings clause, which would have lent strong support to this conclusion.

PESTICIDES

Congress attempted to respect the states' historic role in controlling the application and use of pesticides, herbicides, and other agricultural products when it passed the Federal Insecticide, Fungicide, and Rodenticide Act of 1972 (FIFRA).[42] As in the MDA, Congress carved out spheres of federal and state authority by including both preemption and savings clauses. To ensure nationwide uniformity, the statute creates a centralized regulatory framework by giving the Environmental Protection Agency (EPA) exclusive power over registration, labeling, and packaging requirements. Its preemption clause provides that states "shall not impose or continue in effect any requirements for labeling or packaging in addition to or different from those required under [FIFRA]."[43] Meanwhile, FIFRA's savings clause authorizes any state to impose additional restrictions on the sale or use of pesticides within the state

---

[38] MEDTRONIC, 518 U.S. at 487. In 2008, the Court in RIEGEL V. MEDTRONIC, 128 S. Ct. 999, reviewed another MDA case to decide whether to preempt tort claims for injuries sustained when an FDA-approved balloon catheter ruptured. In a decision focused on the MDA's strong express preemption language and rigorous premarketing regulatory approvals and postapproval industry disclosure obligations for such medical devices, it found that regulatory approvals constituted "requirements" and therefore preempted "duties" the Court characterized as imposed by state common law.

[39] 21 U.S.C. § 360h(d).

[40] 56 F.3d 1335, 1342 (11th Cir. 1995).

[41] 518 U.S. at 502–3.

[42] 7 U.S.C. §§ 136–136y.

[43] 7 U.S.C. § 136v(b).

in recognition of regional and local factors such as climate, geographic variation, population density, and water supply.[44]

In a 1991 case, *Wisconsin Public Intervenor v. Mortier*, the Supreme Court construed the savings clause expansively to afford room for local governments, as political subdivisions of states, to restrict or prohibit aerial spraying to protect the health of their citizens.[45] Despite this precedent and FIFRA's explicit savings clause, after *Cipollone* was handed down, almost all federal courts and many state courts held that tort claims related to pesticides were preempted.[46] The Supreme Court reversed this trend in *Bates v. Dow Agrosciences* in 2005 by allowing claims for crop damages allegedly caused by defective design and manufacture of herbicides, breach of express warranty, and violation of the Texas Deceptive Trade Practices Act. According to the Court, the term *requirements*, as used in FIFRA's preemption clause, reaches positive enactments as well as other compulsory forms of law but does not preclude jury verdicts simply because they might motivate an optional decision to revise a label. As in *Medtronic*, the Court distinguished the much-broader language of the preemption clause at issue in *Cipollone*, prohibiting any state "requirement or prohibition ... with respect to the advertising or promotion of any cigarettes," from FIFRA's preemption clause, prohibiting only labeling or packaging requirements *"in addition to or different from"* federal requirements.[47] As for the plaintiff's fraud and failure-to-warn claims, the Court held that they would be preempted if they imposed an additional or different labeling or packaging obligation than FIFRA.

The *Bates* Court gave appropriate weight to the statutory savings clause, in large part because the long-standing history of state regulation and common law remedies weighed in favor of construing the clause broadly. It explained:

> The long history of tort litigation against manufacturers of poisonous substances adds force to the basic presumption against pre-emption. If Congress had intended to deprive injured parties of a long available form of compensation, it surely would have expressed that intent more clearly. Moreover, this history emphasizes the importance of providing an incentive to manufacturers to use the utmost care in the business of distributing inherently dangerous items.[48]

---

[44] 7 U.S.C. § 136v(a), (c)(1).
[45] 501 U.S. 597, 607–8 (1991).
[46] Alexandra B. Klass, "Bees, Trees, Preemption and Nuisance: A New Path to Resolving Pesticide Land Use Disputes," Ecology Law Quarterly 32, no. 4 (2005): 763, 783.
[47] Bates v. Dow Agrosciences LLC, 544 U.S. 431, 447 (2005) (emphasis in original) (citing 15 U.S.C. § 1334(b); Cipollone, 505 U.S. at 515).
[48] Ibid., 449 (citing Silkwood, 464 U.S. at 251).

Unlike *Cipollone*, where the statute prescribed certain "immutable" warning statements, Congress intended pesticide labels to evolve over time as more information comes to light about the pesticide's efficacy and effects. The Court was persuaded that tort remedies would aid, rather than obstruct, the functioning of FIFRA and the accomplishment of congressional goals. This rationale extends well beyond FIFRA. Common law tort claims can serve as a catalyst for regulatory evolution and for eventual improvement, not just for pesticide use but also for a broad range of federally regulated activities. In Chapter 11, Professor McGarity discusses such "feedback loops" and provides several regulatory histories.

HARMONIZING COMMON LAW REMEDIES
WITH SAVINGS CLAUSES

As in *Bates*, in most circumstances federal regulatory requirements and state common law can be easily harmonized. Savings clauses reflect congressional recognition that preserving common law remedies strengthens the overall stability of the law, both by drawing on the unique attributes of different levels and branches of government and by providing justice to injured individuals. Even where statutes include both savings and preemption clauses, courts can give savings clauses appropriate weight by staying true to the long-standing presumption against preemption.

Statutes that include both preemption and savings clauses, such as FIFRA and the MDA, create a conundrum for courts attempting to give proper weight to both. No doubt, the inclusion of a savings clause weighs against a global finding of express preemption. But when it comes to implied preemption, the Supreme Court's approach to dueling statutory provisions has, in some cases, treated the savings clause not only as nondispositive but also as nonexistent. Absent a strong backdrop of historic state involvement in areas such as agricultural products and harmful medical devices, the Court has been quick to conclude that, read together, preemption and savings clauses merely reflect a "neutral policy" toward preemption.[49] A determination that preemption and savings clauses neutralize each other leaves the courts free to look outside the statutory text and to place weight on probusiness sentiments and on federal agency conclusions – even informal, litigation-driven conclusions – that tort actions pose an obstacle to the accomplishment of federal objectives.[50] The result has been to displace any state law that occupies

[49] GEIER V. AMERICAN HONDA MOTOR CO., 529 U.S. 861, 870–1 (2000).
[50] Ibid., 883; see INFRA Chapter 10, "Preemption by Federal Agency Action."

the same sphere of influence as the federal law in question, whether or not the "offending" state law conflicts with the federal requirement or objective. This outcome is just as detrimental for injured parties as in *Cipollone*, where the statute in question included no savings clause at all. *Cipollone* can perhaps be rationalized (if not justified) by the long history of federal presence in tobacco marketing and sales and by Congress's apparent intent to occupy the entire field through a pervasive federal regulatory scheme. The inclusion of both a savings clause and a preemption clause in other areas, however, should not be construed the same way.

SAVING STATE REGULATORY POWER

State regulatory regimes have been far more vulnerable to preemption inva-lidation than common law claims, despite the presence of statutory savings clauses. In recent years, state regulations have been struck down almost with-out exception whenever those regulations would impose greater economic burdens on industry than established by the federal regulatory floor. The recent trend has prompted some scholars to equate the modern-day preemp-tion doctrine with the Lochner era of the early 1900s in which the Court employed an array of tools to strike down progressive economic and social regulation.[51] As the states have become more aggressive in filling gaps left by lax federal regulatory schemes and federal enforcement failures, for-profit corporations, developers, and other antiregulatory forces have become equally aggressive in wielding preemption as an obstacle to the implementation of protective state laws related to the environment and other aspects of public health and welfare.

NUCLEAR POWER

A high watermark of modern regulatory savings clause jurisprudence was a 1983 case involving a state's moratorium on the construction of nuclear power plants. In *Pacific Gas and Electric v. State Energy Resources Commission*, the Supreme Court found that, although Congress had provided the federal Nuclear Regulatory Commission absolute power to regulate the safety of nuclear power, the states retained their traditional authority over reliability, cost, and other economic concerns related to electricity.[52] At issue was a California statute that conditioned the construction of nuclear power plants

---

[51] Paul Wolfson, "Preemption and Federalism: The Missing Link," HASTINGS CONSTITUTIONAL LAW QUARTERLY 16, no. 1 (1988): 69 (citing LOCHNER V. NEW YORK, 198 U.S. 45 [1905]).

[52] PACIFIC GAS AND ELEC. CO. V. STATE ENERGY RESOURCES COMM., 461 U.S. 190, 205 (1983).

on a finding that adequate means of disposal would be available for nuclear waste. The Court recognized that, although nuclear energy and nuclear waste were areas extensively regulated by the federal government, Congress intended to leave sufficient authority to allow states to slow or even stop the development of nuclear power for economic reasons.

Two savings clauses played a role in the resolution of the case. The first, found in § 274(k), was narrowly drawn to apply only to the particular topic addressed in that section, that is, certain federal-state agreements: "Nothing in this section shall be construed to affect the authority of any State or local agency to regulate activities for purposes other than protection against radiation hazards."[53] The Court was willing to consider it for guidance nonetheless. It recognized that "Congress, by permitting regulation 'for purposes other than protection against radiation hazards' underscored the distinction . . . between the spheres of activity left respectively to the federal government and the states."[54] It then turned to the more generally applicable savings clause of § 271: "Nothing in this chapter shall be construed to affect the authority or regulations of any Federal, State or local agency with respect to the generation, sale, or transmission of electric power produced through the use of nuclear facilities licensed by the Commission."[55] The Court concluded that this provision removed any doubt that questions of rate making and the public need for additional electric plants were to remain in state hands. It then engaged in an unusual foray into the legislative history of the California statute to find a nonsafety rationale for the moratorium. An *Assembly Report* provided the sought-after economic justification that "without a permanent means of disposal, the nuclear waste problem could . . . lead[] to unpredictably high [electricity] costs."

The Court also expressed alarm that a dangerous gap would be left in the regulatory framework if states were stripped of all power over the construction of new plants:

> While the NRC does evaluate the dangers of generating nuclear power, it does not balance those dangers against the risks, costs, and benefits of other choices available to the State. . . . It is almost inconceivable that Congress would have left a regulatory vacuum; the only reasonable inference is that Congress intended the states to continue to make these judgments.[56]

More than twenty years after the *Pacific Gas* decision, the United States has yet to provide a permanent nuclear waste repository, while spent fuel rods

[53] 42 U.S.C. § 2021(k).
[54] 461 U.S. at 210.
[55] 42 U.S.C. § 2018.
[56] 461 U.S. at 208.

from the nation's reactors continue to accumulate. The potential consequences of improper storage and disposal cry out for a federal solution, but so long as none is forthcoming, states such as California have struggled to fill, or at least alleviate, the regulatory gap by limiting nuclear reactor construction or expansion and by restricting the transportation and disposal of nuclear waste. Other than construction moratoria, states have been rebuked at nearly every turn in the lower courts, which have invalidated state statutes notwithstanding the Supreme Court's instruction against congressional occupation of the field of nuclear energy.[57] By construing *Pacific Gas* narrowly, however, the trend is consistent with contemporary Supreme Court cases, which have viewed state regulatory programs far less favorably in the years following *Pacific Gas*.

WORKPLACE SAFETY

Preemption challenges to state regulatory programs began to gain more traction in the early 1990s. In some cases, state regulations have been struck down despite strongly worded savings clauses such as those found in the Occupational Safety and Health Act. Along with the explicit savings clause for common law remedies, Congress also specified that states are free to "assert jurisdiction under State law over any occupational safety or health issue with respect to which no [OSHA] standard is in effect."[58] States are authorized to assume responsibility for the development and the enforcement of occupational safety and health standards, but such plans may be approved only if the secretary certifies that the state standards are "at least as effective" as federal standards, and that the state will dedicate sufficient resources to administration and enforcement. Although many states simply adopt the OSHA regulations as their own, several have adopted more stringent requirements than provided by the federal floor on a range of subjects ranging from fire codes to criminal-enforcement schemes.

In *Gade v. National Solid Wastes Management Ass'n*, a trade association sued to prevent Illinois from enforcing state laws providing for the licensure of workers at hazardous waste sites.[59] Both the association and OSHA argued that OSHA's standards for the training of workers who handle hazardous wastes preempted Illinois law. Emphasizing its desire to avoid subjecting

---

[57] See, e.g., SKULL VALLEY BAND OF GOSHUTE INDIANS v. NIELSON, 376 F.3d 1223 (10th Cir. 2004), cert. denied, 546 U.S. 1060 (2005); U.S. v. KENTUCKY, 252 F.3d 816 (6th Cir. 2001); U.S. v. MANNING, 434 F.Supp.2d 988, 1006 (E.D. Wash. 2006); ABRAHAM v. HODGES, 255 F.Supp.2d 539 (D.S.C. 2002).

[58] 29 U.S.C. § 667(a).

[59] 505 U.S. 88 (1992).

employers to duplicative regulation, the Supreme Court agreed that the act preempted any nonapproved state regulation of an occupational issue for which a federal standard had been adopted. Its opinion contracted the scope of the statutory savings clause by presupposing "a background pre-emption of all state occupational safety and health standards whenever a federal standard governing the same issue is in effect."[60] The Court noted, however, that state laws of general applicability, such as traffic safety laws and fire codes, would not be preempted because they regulate workers as members of the general public and not strictly as workers; in short, such generally applicable requirements would not be considered "occupational" standards. In the wake of *Gade*, states are precluded from issuing regulations that directly concern worker safety if any related federal standard exists, even when the state regulations advance congressional objectives by setting more protective standards than required by the federal regulatory floor and even when enforcement of the state requirement would not preclude or otherwise conflict with enforcement of the federal standard. In effect, the *Gade* Court allowed OSHA's standards to occupy the entire field of licensure and training even though Congress evidenced its intent, through the statutory savings clause, not to do so.

POLLUTION

Like OSHA, the OPA has been given broad preemptive effect in the regulatory context. As is typical of other environmental statutes, the OPA envisions a role for state regulators and includes an explicit savings clause for protective state requirements. When it comes to regulating vessel safety, however, the notion of cooperative federalism is illusory at best. In *U.S. v. Locke*, the Supreme Court displaced Washington's requirements for navigation watch procedures, training requirements for crew members, and maritime casualty reporting.[61] The Ports and Waterways Safety Act, as amended by the OPA, authorizes the federal government to regulate the design, construction, operation, and staffing of tanker vessels but retains the states' authority to impose requirements "relating to the discharge, or substantial threat of a discharge, of oil," and to regulate matters reflective of local peculiarities of their ports and waterways.[62] Regardless, the Court held that the OPA preempted Washington's requirements. It explained away the OPA's savings clause by finding that its placement in Title I limited its scope to oil pollution liability and compensation, while vessel manning requirements are contained in Title II,

---

[60] Ibid., 100.
[61] 529 U.S. 89 (2000).
[62] 33 U.S.C. § 2718(c); 33 U.S.C. § 2702(a).

which includes no savings clause. According to the Court, giving broad effect to the savings clause would "disrupt national uniformity" and "upset the careful regulatory scheme established by federal law."[63] Ironically, the Court concluded that a restrictive reading of the savings clause best respected a federal-state balance. The Court also explained away the presumption against preemption of traditional police powers of the states, finding it inapplicable when the state regulates activities marked by a history of substantial federal presence, such as maritime law.

State regulatory programs governing other types of pollution have fared poorly as well. A recent addition to the Court's cases preempting state regulatory authority invalidated an attempt to control air pollution from vehicles. As in the OPA, Congress embraced a cooperative federalism model in the CAA to preserve the authority of the states to make policy decisions within their borders while authorizing EPA to establish national ambient air-quality standards and certain emission limitations. A key feature of this approach is the ability of states to adopt their own state implementation plans to meet national air-quality standards by controlling source-by-source emissions in a fashion that balances the state's own economic and environmental concerns.[64] Statutory savings clauses explicitly retain states' latitude to implement air-quality requirements for factories, power plants, and other stationary sources.[65] The act includes a savings clause applicable to motor vehicles as well, but the Supreme Court has given this provision short shrift, while expansively reading a preemptive provision limiting state standard setting.

This occurred in *Engine Manufacturers Association v. South Coast Air Quality Management District*, where the Court, at the behest of a trade association representing manufacturers of diesel engines, invalidated a local regulation requiring local fleet operators to purchase or lease only vehicles that met stringent emission standards.[66] The regulation was adopted by California's South Coast Air Quality District, which had become one of the most polluted regions in the United States due in large part to excessive vehicle traffic. The manufacturers relied on a preemption clause found in § 209(a) to challenge the regulation: "No State or any political subdivision thereof shall adopt or attempt to enforce any standard relating to the control of emissions from new motor vehicles or new motor vehicle engines subject to this part."[67] To offset this provision, § 209(d) incorporates a savings clause that

---

[63] 529 U.S. at 105–6.
[64] 42 U.S.C. § 7410(k).
[65] See n. 7 and accompanying text.
[66] 541 U.S. 246 (2004).
[67] 42 U.S.C. § 7543(a).

explicitly allows states "otherwise to control, regulate, or restrict the use, operation, or movement" of vehicles.[68] Through § 209, Congress acted to prevent states from imposing production mandates that would cause "undue economic strain on the industry" by forcing vehicle manufacturers to produce engines with state-specific characteristics as a condition of sale.[69]

According to the Supreme Court, the South Coast District's regulation was a "standard" within the preemption provision of § 209(a). Rather than looking closely at the statute, the Court invoked *Merriam-Webster's Dictionary*, which defines *standard* as that which "is established by authority, custom, or general consent, as a model or example; criterion; test." This generic definition freed to Court to find that "a standard is a standard even when not enforced through manufacturer-directed regulation" and to ignore the savings clause that would seemingly preserve a local requirement that certain types of vehicles be used within the district.[70]

In dissent, Justice Souter criticized the majority's unduly broad construction of the term *standard* as violating the plain meaning of § 209(a). As Justice Souter also noted, the majority ignored the presumption against preemption that "the historic police powers of the States were not to be superseded by the Federal Act unless that was the clear and manifest purpose of Congress."[71] Section 209 may not be a "model of clarity," as Justice Souter correctly noted, but tiebreakers in interpreting statutes that are "unsystematic, redundant, and fuzzy about drawing lines" must cut in favor of sustaining more protective state and local rules. Local rules that motivate, but do not compel, manufacturers to develop and market vehicles that meet stringent emission controls are consistent both with congressional intent regarding motor vehicles and the overall purposes of the statute, "which sought to rectify states' unwillingness or inability to address air pollution problems, not to restrict their efforts."[72]

Although the South Coast experience demonstrates that air pollution is both a local and a national problem and that solutions are necessary at both levels, it might seem counterintuitive to say that local governments can play an important role in addressing global issues such as climate change. However, both common law remedies and state and local regulatory programs have proven necessary to begin to fill the regulatory gap left by the federal failure to take a meaningful stance on GHG emissions. Acting alone, local air-quality initiatives

---

[68] 42 U.S.C. § 7543(d).
[69] 541 U.S at 261 (Souter, J., dissenting).
[70] Ibid., 252–3.
[71] Ibid., 260 (citing MEDTRONIC, INC. V. LOHR, 518 U.S. 470, 485 [1996]).
[72] Albert C. Lin, "Erosive Interpretation of Environmental Law in the Supreme Court's 2003–04 Term," HOUSTON LAW REVIEW 42, no. 3 (2005): 565, 584–5.

may have very little impact on overall emission reductions, but they may trigger action at the national level. As Professors Engel and Adelman explain, environmental law is replete with examples where state and local initiatives successfully motivated a comprehensive federal regulatory response on topics ranging from acid rain to mercury emissions.[73] As for preemption, there is reason to believe that state and local restrictions on emissions from stationary sources, such as power plants, would be less vulnerable than restrictions on mobile sources, given the historic state and local presence in regulating stationary sources and the absence of the countervailing federal interest in transportation efficiencies and nationwide vehicle-manufacturing standards.

MEDICAL DEVICES AND DRUGS

An anomaly in the Supreme Court's recent preemption jurisprudence can be seen in a case involving the individual's ability to seek the assistance of a doctor in making deeply personal medical choices. The Court has demonstrated a greater willingness to respect state regulatory choices in this area in part because Congress has been exceptionally careful to include a strongly worded savings clause and in part because of the historic backdrop of state authority regarding medical practice.

A doctor's ability to use lethal drugs to assist terminally ill patients with suicide has long been the subject of heated debate. Congress has provided no federal resolution, and states have taken vastly different approaches to fill the void. Dr. Jack Kevorkian was prosecuted and jailed under Michigan law for injecting lethal drugs at the behest of a patient dying of Lou Gehrig's disease. In contrast, an Oregon law specifically allows physician-assisted suicide through a statute that authorizes licensed physicians of terminally ill patients to administer lethal drugs but only after counseling about palliative alternatives and ensuring that patients are competent to make life-ending decisions.

The Oregon law provoked a preemption challenge by the U.S. attorney general under the Controlled Substances Act. The act's savings clause cautions against displacement of state regulation by stating that, absent a direct conflict, none of the act's provisions should be construed as indicating an intent "to occupy the field ... to the exclusion of any State law on the same subject matter which would otherwise be within the authority of the State, unless there is a positive conflict between that provision of this subchapter and that State law so that the two cannot consistently stand together."[74]

---

[73] See INFRA Chapter 13, "Adaptive Environmental Federalism."
[74] 21 U.S.C. § 903.

The Supreme Court rejected the preemption challenge in *Gonzales v. Oregon*.[75] It noted that, although Congress could, as a matter of constitutional power, establish national standards for the administration of prescription drugs for use in suicide, Congress had not done so. Rather, congressional objectives were relatively modest – barring doctors from using prescription-writing powers to engage in illicit drug trafficking. This narrow objective, coupled with the savings clause, convinced the Court that Congress intended states to continue exercising their historic police powers to protect the lives and health of their residents by regulating the practice of medicine.

HARMONIZING STATE REGULATIONS WITH FEDERAL LAW

Although the Court has not invariably found federal law fully preemptive of state law, during the past two decades the Supreme Court has often shielded industry from progressive state regulations in areas ranging from oil-spill prevention to workplace safety to automobile emissions. In cases involving constraints on economic interests, statutory savings clauses have been given short shrift or even blatantly ignored. If courts gave more careful attention to congressional choices reflected in statutory savings clauses, there would be fewer regulatory gaps. In some cases, savings clauses reflect congressional determinations of institutional competency, fairness, and efficiency, while in others savings clauses indicate congressional intent to allow regulatory overlap to ensure comprehensive coverage. In either case, the Court's pro-preemption trend is troubling, as it often relies on strained statutory interpretation and creates tension with congressional objectives. Federal law should not be construed to preempt state regulatory programs so long as the state regulation in question comports with congressional objectives and is a reasonable construction of the space left by the federal statute.

SAVING SAVINGS CLAUSES

Statutory savings clauses are intended to preserve the states' ability to provide increased protection over and above the federal regulatory floor, but Supreme Court precedent has left the courts free to interpret them in a fashion that actually diminishes overall protection of health, safety, and environmental quality. Ignoring explicit savings clauses or construing them unduly narrowly undermines congressional policy in the highly sensitive, politically charged area of federal-state relations. Conversely, giving savings clauses appropriate

---

[75]   546 U.S. 243 (2006).

weight would honor congressional choices, avoid regulatory gaps, and enhance institutional competency by empowering governments at all levels to protect the public.

Judicial narrowing of savings clauses is especially troubling when common law remedies for harmful activities are displaced. There are compelling reasons for courts to apply the presumption against preemption faithfully to preserve states' powers to protect human health and welfare through the common law. Leaving individuals without adequate means of redressing invasions of their privacy, health, and property causes a severe imbalance between government and corporate power and individual rights. Conversely, in most cases, federal regulatory requirements and state common law can be easily harmonized. Far from posing a conflict or undermining congressional objectives, state common law remedies give greater force to federal remedial purposes and in doing so give greater stability to the law as a whole.

Giving savings clauses proper weight is important in the regulatory arena, too. So long as the state regulation in question comports with Congress's remedial objectives and is a reasonable construction of the space preserved by the savings clause, state regulatory choices should be honored, particularly when those choices are made against a backdrop of the states' traditional police powers.

For its part, Congress can take positive steps with more precision in drafting. There is no magic formula, but in the event that Congress intends to save the broadest array of state and local remedies and requirements, it might craft a savings clause that reads as follows: "*Nothing in this act shall be construed to occupy the field on the topics subject to this act. Moreover, absent a direct conflict that makes compliance with both state and federal law impossible, nothing in this act shall be construed to affect state or local authorities, be they regulatory or judicial in nature, and nothing in this act shall in any way affect, or be construed to affect, statutory or common law rights or remedies.*" To ensure the broadest possible application, the savings clause should be placed within the statutory subchapter on "General Provisions" rather than tucked within a subchapter related to a discrete topic.

If, however, Congress chooses to include both savings and preemption clauses, either because it wishes to carve out an area for preemptive effect or because both clauses are necessary to achieve compromise and passage of the statute in question, it must be especially clear regarding the specific topic or activity to be preempted. It must also be clear regarding whether preemption extends only to positive enactments and regulations or to other types of requirements, such as common law remedies. This may be impossible if the two clauses were included not to carve out specific spheres of federal and state activity but instead to reach an ambiguous yet passage-enabling compromise. If this is the case, the presumption against preemption should still be given full force, but in the end judges, rather than Congress, will be left to resolve the preemption issue with little meaningful guidance from the Supreme Court.

8 Federal Preemption by Inaction

Robert L. Glicksman

Previous chapters show that courts sometimes find that the adoption and implementation of federal law preempts state law not only when Congress includes in a statute an explicit provision ousting state law but also when the courts discern the legislature's implicit intent to achieve that result. In a surprisingly large number of cases, the courts have declared state law to be preempted by federal legislative or regulatory action despite the presence in federal statutes of savings clauses whose objective is to preserve, rather than supersede, state law.[1] But the preemption doctrine has the potential to sweep even more broadly. On occasion, even the federal government's failure to act has been deemed sufficient to preclude state governments from pursuing regulatory initiatives and to bar common law tort actions seeking redress for harms caused by a defendant's activities.

This chapter analyzes when inaction by either Congress or a federal regulatory agency has been and should be deemed preemptive of state law. Like all preemption questions, determinations of whether federal inactivity bars state action has important implications for the values reflected in our federal system of government. The unique aspect of the preemption through inaction conundrum is the likelihood that if a court finds that federal legislative or administrative failure to act preempts state regulation, the problems that attracted the attention of state government in the first place will wind up being completely unregulated. That result may have significant adverse consequences for the states' traditional exercise of their police powers to protect public health, safety, welfare, or the environment.

This chapter introduces the issues raised by preemption through inaction by using a timely and important example as a reference point: the authority of the states to regulate activities that contribute to global climate change in light of

---

[1] The treatment of savings clauses is addressed by Professor Zellmer in Chapter 7.

the federal government's largely sluggish response to the environmental and health risks posed by climate change. It surveys the circumstances in which the federal government's failure to act should give rise to either express or implied preemption. It also analyzes the scope of authority of federal agencies that have declined to act to affect the preemption result. Finally, it inquires whether state law should ever be preempted in a situation in which the federal government lacks the authority to address the subject of state regulation.[2]

The chapter contains three basic recommendations, one for Congress and two for the courts. First, in deference to state prerogatives in areas of traditional state concern, Congress should not preempt state regulation in areas in which it has chosen not to regulate unless it determines that a state's effort to address market failure through regulation would inappropriately impose adverse impacts on other states, or that federal policies can best be achieved in the absence of targeted regulation at any level of government. Second, in the absence of federal regulatory action, the courts should never find implied preemption based on occupation of the regulatory field in which the state is engaged. Third, the courts should find implied preemption in the absence of federal regulatory action based on a conflict with federal objectives only if Congress has explicitly delegated to a federal agency the power to preempt state law to prevent it from subverting federal goals, and the agency has clearly and authoritatively exercised that authority.

GLOBAL CLIMATE CHANGE AND FEDERAL PREEMPTION BY INACTION

State efforts to regulate activities that contribute to global climate change provide a recent important example of the potential implications of allowing federal inactivity to preempt state regulation. Several states and regional entities have adopted restrictions on greenhouse gas (GHG) emissions from stationary sources, such as coal-fired electric utilities. Some observers have argued that these laws are at risk of preemption by the federal Clean Air Act (CAA), although no court has yet addressed the issue.[3]

---

[2] For more extensive treatment of the issues raised in this chapter, see Robert L. Glicksman, "Nothing Is Real: Protecting the Regulatory Void through Preemption by Inaction," VIRGINIA ENVIRONMENTAL LAW JOURNAL 26 (2008): 5.

[3] See, e.g., Joshua B. Fershee, "Levels of Green: State and Local Efforts, in Wyoming and Beyond, to Reduce Greenhouse Gas Emissions," WYOMING LAW REVIEW 7 (2007): 269, 279; Robert B. McKinstry Jr. and Thomas D. Peterson, "The Implications of the New 'Old' Federalism in Climate-Change Legislation: How to Function in a Global Marketplace When the State Takes the Lead," PACIFIC MCGEORGE GLOBAL BUSINESS AND DEVELOPMENT LAW JOURNAL 20 (2007): 61.

The preemption question also has arisen in the context of state vehicle-emission controls. In 2004, the California Air Resources Board adopted regulations restricting emissions of carbon dioxide (CO_2) from motor vehicles. A coalition of motor vehicle manufacturers and dealers, among others, sued the state to invalidate the regulations on the ground, among others, that they are preempted by section 209(a) of the CAA.[4] That provision declares generally that no state shall "adopt or attempt to enforce any standard relating to the control of emissions from new motor vehicles or new motor vehicle engines subject to" the provisions of the CAA that relate to motor vehicle emissions and fuel standards.[5]

Despite this prohibition, Congress has long allowed California to regulate motor vehicle emissions in light of the "compelling and extraordinary conditions" that make California "sufficiently different from the Nation as a whole to justify standards on automobile emissions which may, from time to time, need [to] be more stringent than national standards."[6] Accordingly, the CAA authorizes the federal Environmental Protection Agency (EPA) to waive the prohibition in section 209(a) for California if the state's standards are at least as protective of public health as any applicable federal standards and are necessary to meet compelling and extraordinary conditions. The act requires that EPA issue standards restricting motor vehicle emissions that, in the judgment of EPA's administrator, "cause or contribute to air pollution which may reasonably be anticipated to endanger public health or welfare."[7] In addition, the CAA authorizes any other state to adopt vehicle-emission standards that are identical to California's,[8] and at least fifteen states have

---

[4] CENTRAL VALLEY CHRYSLER-JEEP V. WITHERSPOON, 456 F. Supp. 2d 1160 (E.D. Cal. 2006).

[5] 42 U.S.C. § 7543(a). The plaintiffs also alleged that the California regulations are preempted by the Energy Policy and Conservation Act of 1975 (EPCA), 49 U.S.C. § 32919(a), the statute that authorizes the Department of Transportation to issue corporate average fuel economy standards. That argument involves preemption by federal regulatory action rather than inaction and is therefore not germane to the issues addressed in this chapter. In any event, the argument was weakened considerably when the U.S. Supreme Court concluded that regulations limiting CO_2 emissions from motor vehicles (in that case, by the federal EPA) would not be inconsistent with federal fuel economy standards. MASSACHUSETTS V. EPA, 127 S. Ct. 1438, 1461–2 (2007). The district court in the California litigation subsequently ruled that the EPCA does not preempt California's vehicle emissions controls for CO_2. CENTRAL VALLEY CHRYSLER-JEEP, INC. V. GOLDSTENE, 529 F. Supp. 2d 1151 (E.D. Cal. 2007). See also, GREEN MOUNTAIN CHRYSLER PLYMOUTH DODGE JEEP V. CROMBIE, 508 F. Supp. 2d 295 (D. Vt. 2007) (concluding that alleged conflict between the CAA and the EPCA does not give rise to preemption issues, but that, even if it does, the EPCA does not preempt state controls on CO_2 emissions from motor vehicles).

[6] H.R. Rep. No. 90-148 (1967), REPRINTED IN 1967 U.S.C.C.A.N. 1938, 1956.

[7] 42 U.S.C. § 7543(b).

[8] 42 U.S.C. § 7507.

done so. The court in the California climate-change litigation ruled that unless EPA issued the waiver California sought for its CO2 vehicle-emission control standards, the state's regulations would be preempted under the general preemption provision of section 209(a) of the CAA.[9] In late 2007, EPA denied the waiver,[10] prompting California to challenge the denial in court.

The preemption question raised by the adoption of state climate-change standards is relevant to this chapter because EPA has not regulated emissions of CO2 from either stationary or mobile sources under the CAA. For years, EPA took the position that it lacked the authority to regulate emissions of CO2 and other GHGs under the CAA because they do not qualify as air pollutants under the statute. In also stated that, even if it had such authority, it would refuse to adopt vehicle emission controls on GHGs on policy grounds because, for example, of the uncertainty regarding the causes, consequences, and means of redressing climate change, and because of the disincentives to reduce GHG production that unilateral U.S. regulation would create for nations, such as China, that are large producers of GHGs but that have not yet regulated responsible sources.

The Supreme Court in 2007 held that EPA does have the power to regulate GHG emissions under the CAA and that EPA's policy-based reasons for refusing to do so were arbitrary and insufficient to justify its refusal to regulate.[11] Despite that decision, EPA has still not regulated any source of GHG emissions under the CAA, and it is not clear whether or when it will do so. Pending such federal regulation, the rulings in the California climate-change litigation mean that, in the absence of statutory amendments authorizing state regulation or an administrative reversal of EPA's denial of California's waiver request, motor vehicle emissions of GHGs will remain completely unregulated. Given the consensus of mainstream scientific opinion that GHG emissions contribute to climate change – recognized by the Supreme Court in its 2007 decision – this

[9] CENTRAL VALLEY CHRYSLER-JEEP V. WITHERSPOON, 456 F. Supp. 2d 1160, 1174 (E.D. Cal. 2006). CF. GREEN MOUNTAIN CHRYSLER PLYMOUTH DODGE JEEP V. CROMBIE, 508 F. Supp. 2d 295, 302 (D. Vt. 2007) (assuming for purposes of analysis of EPCA preemption claim that EPA would grant a waiver to California but stating that if it denied the waiver, California's vehicle emissions controls and those of states adopting California's standards would be preempted).

[10] Letter of Stephen L. Johnson to The Honorable Arnold Schwarzenegger, December 19, 2007; U.S. EPA, "America Receives a National Solution for Vehicle Greenhouse Gas Emissions" (December 19, 2007), available at http://yosemite.epa.gov/opa/admpress.nsf/docf6618525a9efb85257359003fb69d/41b4663d8d3807c5852573b6008141e5!OpenDocument. EPA issued a formal version of its denial of the waiver petition in March 2008. "California State Motor Vehicle Pollution Control Standards; Notice of Decision Denying a Waiver of Clean Air Act Preemption for California's 2009 and Subsequent Model Year Greenhouse Gas Emission Standards for New Motor Vehicles," 73 FEDERAL REGISTER 12,156 (March 6, 2008).

[11] MASSACHUSETTS V. EPA, 127 S. Ct. 1438 (2007).

regulatory void is likely to pose threats to public health and the environment that at least some states deem worthy of immediate regulatory attention.

This particular statutory and policy puzzle will be resolved at some time in the coming years. It raises, however, a larger and more enduring question: When, if ever, is it appropriate for the federal government to preclude state regulatory initiatives to address a social challenge or risk, in this case state efforts to control GHG emissions, despite federal unwillingness to tackle the threat targeted by state regulation?

EXPRESS PREEMPTION

Congress may preempt state law in its entirety, assuming it is authorized under the enumerated powers set forth in Article I of the Constitution to intervene in the area that would otherwise be covered by state law. The exercise of that power to preempt should be exercised carefully, however, in circumstances in which the federal government has not established its own presence in the relevant field of regulation. The government regulates to protect the public health, safety, and the environment for various reasons. One basis for regulation is the conviction that the free market is incapable of providing the levels of protection that the government deems appropriate. The unconstrained free market's inability to supply adequate protection is often the result of the presence of one or more forms of market failure. In addition, democratically expressed preferences may result in laws seeking a cleaner environment or less risk than the market would produce on its own.

In the absence of regulation, for example, polluters have strong incentives not to control their polluting activities because the costs of pollution (such as adverse effects on the public health) are external to them (i.e., they are borne by other people). One function of government regulation of polluting activities is to internalize the costs of pollution by forcing polluters to bear them (such as through compliance with mandatory controls). If a polluter passes on to customers the increased costs of operation that result from regulation, those customers will receive more accurate market signals about the true costs of the polluter's activities and will be able to make informed decisions about whether the value provided by the polluter's goods or services is worth the costs. Other types of regulation seek to promote economic efficiency by addressing other kinds of market failure, such as the absence of competition, barriers to entry into a market, inadequate or inaccurate information for consumers, or inadequate provision of public goods. Still other regulatory regimes pursue noneconomic goals, such as redressing inequitable distribution of wealth or the pursuit of noneconomic collective values.

RATIONALES FOR PREEMPTION AND THE NEED
FOR CLEAR STATEMENT

The Framers of the Constitution sought to preserve state sovereignty at the same time that they created a new national government. The Supremacy Clause — the source of the preemption doctrine — undoubtedly allows appropriately adopted federal law to supplant state law. In light of the importance the Framers attributed to the preservation of state sovereignty, however, Congress should exercise that authority sparingly and only after careful consideration of the impact of the resulting infringements on state sovereignty. Notwithstanding the general desirability of leaving state regulatory authority intact, especially in areas of traditional state and local concern such as protection of the public health and safety,[12] two main rationales might justify federal preemption in the absence of federal regulation of a risk or harm. First, it is appropriate for Congress to preempt state A's regulation if it concludes that state A's approach to addressing a particular form of market failure will adversely affect the interests of other states who are not capable of protecting themselves against the externalities created by state A's regulatory regime. This justification for preemption mirrors the rationale the Supreme Court has developed in "dormant Commerce Clause" jurisprudence that interprets the Commerce Clause of the Constitution as imposing constraints on state activity that discriminates against interstate commerce or results in extraterritorial regulation.

Second, it is also appropriate for Congress to preempt state regulation, despite the absence of a federal regulatory program, if it concludes that federal interests are best served by confining legal constraints on the operation of the free market to those derived from traditional sources of law such as common law contract and property law rules. Congress might decide, for example, that the adoption of diverse state regulatory requirements threatens the development of a beneficial new technology and that, unless and until Congress decides to regulate the use of that technology, there should be no positive statutory or administrative regulation. It is quite another thing for Congress to displace a state's regulatory efforts simply because it concludes that the state's perception that market failure exists is mistaken, that the regulatory regime

---

[12] As the Supreme Court recently noted, "[p]ublic health does not define itself," and it is not always apparent whether a state regulatory scheme should be regarded as a "public health" or an economic regulatory program. ROWE v. NEW HAMPSHIRE MOTOR TRANSPORT ASS'N, 128 S. Ct. 989, 997 (2008). The state regulatory programs addressed in this chapter do not fall within that gray area. There is no question that a major goal of legislation addressing global climate change is to protect the public health.

the state has adopted to address market failure will be ineffective, or that democratically expressed preferences reflected in state laws seeking a cleaner environment or less risk than the market would produce on its own are ill-advised. The respect for state sovereignty reflected in our constitutional system of federalism supports allowing a state to regulate activities within the state's borders, even if its chosen method of regulation is ill-considered or unnecessary because of the state's mistaken diagnosis of market failure.

If Congress determines that one of the two circumstances that justify preemption despite the absence of federal regulation exists, it should include in the statutory preemption provisions an explicit justification for preemption. The statute should enunciate either that state regulation would impose unjustified externalities on states other than the adopting state, or that state regulation would interfere with federal objectives that can best be promoted by freezing the status quo, thereby blocking the adoption of constraints on the free market that are not reflected in existing sources of law such as rules of contract and property law. In the first case, the statute should identify the externalities the preemption provision is designed to prevent. In the second case, Congress should identify the federal interests it seeks to protect and the manner in which state regulation would frustrate those interests.

How would state regulation of climate change fare under this framework for assessing preemption of state regulation in the absence of federal regulatory activity? Because GHG impacts are felt worldwide due to their aggregate levels, one state's regulation of GHGs would not impose any environmental externalities on other states. If a regulated source, mobile or stationary, complies with the state's controls, adverse impacts on the environment will be reduced, not increased. Even if a stationary source subject to state A's constraints on GHG emissions decides to locate elsewhere to avoid state A's regulation, other states will not suffer any incremental adverse GHG-related environmental effects because the emission of GHGs will have the same adverse impacts on the environment regardless of where they take place. Thus, the degree to which a source subject to state A's regulation contributes to global climate change that adversely affects state B will be the same regardless of whether the source continues to operate in state A free of regulation, moves to state C to avoid regulation, or even locates in state B.[13]

---

[13] If the stationary source locates in state B, it might adversely affect state B's environment in other ways, such as by contributing to air pollution that is localized in nature or to water pollution. Those effects may justify preemption under federal regulatory programs that address those types of pollution, but preemption would not be justified on the basis of the impact in state B of state A's regulation of GHG emissions.

State regulation does, however, have the potential to impose economic externalities on other states. If, for example, state A restricts motor vehicle emissions of GHGs and the auto manufacturers decide to continue to market their products in those states, the economic interests of other states could be affected. Compliance with state A's regulation is likely to increase the auto manufacturers' production costs. Thus, a state like Michigan may suffer as a result of state A's regulation if the manufacturers experience reduced profits and therefore reduced state tax liability. If the manufacturers decide to market the same cars nationwide and to build them all to comply with state A's regulations, the costs of purchasing cars is likely to increase in all states. The creation of these adverse external economic consequences provides a stronger justification for preempting state A's regulation than the environmental externalities that flow from state A's regulation. As the next paragraph indicates, however, even this ground justifies only partial preemption of state regulation of motor vehicle emissions of GHGs.

The second ground for express preemption of state regulation in the face of federal inaction is the potential for state regulation to thwart federal goals such as uniformity and minimization of transaction costs. As indicated in the preceding text, section 209(a) of the CAA limits the degree to which the states may regulate motor vehicle emissions. The justification for preempting state regulation has always been that multifarious state regulatory regimes would create havoc for the auto manufacturers, whose production costs would increase significantly if they were forced to manufacture cars with different kinds of emission controls to meet the requirements of each state in which they do business. Exclusive federal regulation of tailpipe emissions ensures that the auto companies will have to deal with only one standard. This desire for uniformity and reduced transaction and production costs obviously bears on the wisdom of allowing state regulation of GHG emissions from motor vehicles.

As previously indicated, however, Congress has authorized EPA to waive the CAA's prohibition on state regulation for California. Further, the CAA allows other states to adopt standards identical to those adopted by California and approved by EPA. Allowing California to adopt GHG emission controls and allowing other states to piggyback onto the California standards would seem to pose no greater obstacles to the federal interest in uniformity and minimal transaction costs than the current CAA does for air pollutants already being regulated by EPA, even if Congress or EPA eventually adopts motor vehicle emission controls for GHGs. For this reason, EPA's assertion that denial of California's waiver request was necessary to prevent a "patchwork" of state regulation rings hollow.[14] The justification for preempting state

---

[14] U.S. EPA, "America Receives a National Solution for Vehicle Greenhouse Gas Emissions."

regulation of GHG emissions from factories and other stationary sources is even weaker because such sources tend to be constructed on a site-specific basis. The production cost economies of scale rationale on which federal preemption of motor vehicle emissions is based therefore exists only to a very limited degree, if at all, in the context of regulation of stationary sources.

NARROW JUDICIAL CONSTRUCTION OF EXPRESS PREEMPTION PROVISIONS

Respect for state sovereignty, especially in areas of traditional state concern, also supports narrow judicial construction of express statutory preemption provisions when the alleged preemption arises in the context of federal inaction. Congress is fully capable of expressing clearly its desire to preempt state regulation even though the federal government has chosen not to act. If an express preemption provision does not clearly cover situations in which the federal government has failed to act, the courts should presume that Congress did not intend to preempt through inaction.

The Supreme Court has adopted precisely that approach in cases in which federal statutes were alleged to preempt state law despite the federal government's failure to regulate the activities covered by the state regime. In *Puerto Rico Department of Consumer Affairs v. ISA Petroleum Corp.*,[15] for example, several oil companies sued Puerto Rico claiming that its regulations imposing excise taxes on oil refiners were preempted by federal law. In 1973, Congress adopted the Emergency Petroleum Allocation Act,[16] which authorized the president to issue regulations controlling the prices and allocation of crude oil and refined petroleum products. A subsequent statute extended the president's authority but subjected it to a sunset provision. The oil companies asserted that the 1973 act reflected Congress's decision to "enter the field of petroleum allocation and price regulation," and that, instead of countermanding that decision, the sunset provision "merely changed the nature of the federally imposed regime from one of federal hands-on regulation to one of federally mandated free-market control."

The Court disagreed and rejected the refiners' preemption challenge. It concluded that, although the Constitution allows Congress to create the kind of regime described by the refiners, the courts should not allow Congress to create one "subtly." It stated that "[w]ithout a text that can . . . plausibly be interpreted as *prescribing* federal pre-emption it is impossible to find that a

[15] 485 U.S. 495 (1988).
[16] Pub. L. No. 93-159, 87 Stat. 627 (1973).

free market was mandated by federal law." The Court distinguished a case decided in 1983, in which it had stated that "[a] federal decision to forego regulation in a given area may imply an authoritative determination that the area is best left *un*regulated, and in that event would have as much pre-emptive force as a decision *to* regulate."[17] According to the Court in the oil refiners' case, Congress enacted the statute at issue in the 1983 case "to fill a regulatory gap, not to perpetuate one." It therefore concluded that Congress's withdrawal from substantial involvement in regulation of the petroleum industry did not amount to an "extant action" sufficient to create an inference of preemption "in an unregulated segment of an otherwise regulated field[;] pre-emption, if it is intended, must be explicitly stated."[18]

The *Puerto Rico Department* case highlights the need for an explicit statement by Congress that it intends its inactivity to preempt state regulation. If anything, the inference that Congress intended to oust state regulatory authority is even weaker where the federal government has never regulated than where it has regulated and chosen to stop doing so. In the latter situation, it is at least plausible to infer that, after reviewing the effects of federal regulation, Congress decided that regulation was not having its intended beneficial effects, and that the absence of regulation was preferable. Thus, for example, in a case decided early in 2008, the Supreme Court interpreted broadly an explicit preemption clause in a federal statute relating to motor carrier service, holding that it preempted state statutes that regulated the delivery to tobacco customers within the state. The Court relied heavily on Congress's "over-arching goal" in repealing federal regulation of the trucking industry to assure that transportation services reflect "the maximum reliance on competitive market forces," which would stimulate efficiency, innovation, and low prices.[19] Citing the federal act's legislative history, the Court found that allowing state regulation of trucking services would conflict with "Congress's major

---

[17] Arkansas Elec. Cooperative Corp. v. Arkansas Pub. Serv. Comm'n, 461 U.S. 375, 384 (1983).

[18] Puerto Rico Dep't, 485 U.S. at 504.

[19] Rowe v. New Hampshire Motor Transport Ass'n, 128 S. Ct. 989, 995 (2008). The Court quoted a statute deregulating airline transportation, 49 U.S.C.A. § 40101(a)(12). In Morales v. Trans World Airlines, Inc., 504 U.S. 374 (1992), the Court had relied on that provision, an explicit statutory preemption provision, and the statute's legislative history to support its holding that state regulation of the airline industry was preempted. According to the Court, Congress decided when it deregulated the airline industry that allowing state regulation would conflict with Congress's determination that maximum reliance on competitive forces would best insure lower air fares and better service. In Rowe, the legislative history of the trucking deregulation statute indicated that Congress had similar goals and, accordingly, "copied the language of the air-carrier pre-emption provision" in the airline deregulation statute. Rowe, 128 S. Ct. at 994.

legislative efforts" to leave decisions concerning the range of services offered by truckers, "where federally unregulated, to the competitive marketplace."[20] In any event, whether the federal government has regulated and chosen to cease doing so or has never regulated at all in the field chosen for state intervention, the courts should not find preemption unless Congress has clearly stated in the statute that states may not regulate despite the absence of federal regulatory activity.

The Supreme Court has followed this approach in cases involving alleged preemption of common law remedies as well as positive regulatory enactments. In *Sprietsma v. Mercury Marine*,[21] for example, an outboard motor manufacturer asserted that a tort action following an accident in which a woman died when she fell out of a boat and was struck by the propeller was preempted by the Federal Boat Safety Act of 1971.[22] That statute authorizes the secretary of transportation, acting through the Coast Guard, to issue regulations establishing minimum safety standards for recreational vessels and associated equipment. Although the Coast Guard issued regulations that included boat performance and safety standards, those regulations did not include any propeller-guard requirement. The Court refused to interpret an express preemption provision to bar the pursuit of common law tort claims.

The CAA does not currently include provisions that specifically identify the degree to which state regulation of GHGs is allowed. The statute does have more general preemption provisions. One provision bars state regulation that is less stringent than standards adopted by EPA.[23] This provision has no bearing on state regulation of GHGs from either mobile or stationary sources because EPA has not adopted any standards restricting GHG emissions. Other provisions bar state regulation of motor vehicle emissions but allow EPA to exempt California from that prohibition and allow other states to adopt California's standards if EPA does so.[24] A narrow construction of those provisions might lead to the conclusion that the prohibition only applies when EPA has adopted motor vehicle emission controls for the particular air pollutant involved. Because it has not done so for GHGs, the states are free to regulate them.[25]

---

[20] ROWE, 128 S. Ct. at 996.
[21] 537 U.S. 51 (2002).
[22] 46 U.S.C. §§ 4301–11.
[23] 42 U.S.C. § 7416. This preemptive provision relates to the floor/ceiling preemption choice discussed by Professor Buzbee in Chapter 5.
[24] 42 U.S.C. § 7543(a)–(b).
[25] The district court in the California motor vehicle standards case did not take this position. CENTRAL VALLEY CHRYSLER-JEEP V. WITHERSPOON, 456 F. Supp. 2d 1160, 1174 (E.D. Cal. 2006) (concluding that California's regulations are preempted unless EPA issues a waiver under § 209(b)).

Even if the courts reject this interpretation, the CAA allows California to seek EPA's approval to regulate GHG emissions from motor vehicles. If a court or EPA were to reverse EPA's late 2007 denial of California's waiver request, other states could adopt controls identical to California's standards.

IMPLIED PREEMPTION

As previous chapters have demonstrated, it is well established that federal law may preempt state law implicitly even if it does not do so explicitly. Other chapters of this book suggest that the courts should be wary of finding implicit preemption, and even that the Supreme Court should abolish the implied preemption doctrine except in situations in which compliance with both federal and state law is impossible. The justification for the latter result would be that Congress is fully capable of including in a statute an explicit declaration of preemption and defining the scope of the preempted field. If the courts refuse to recognize implied preemption, Congress will have strong incentives to consider whether preemption is appropriate and, if so, state the rationale for and the scope of the preemption it desires on the face of the statute. This approach represents a significant departure from established Supreme Court preemption doctrine, but it is both consistent with the respect for state sovereignty on which the Constitution's federalism structure is based and desirable as a means of encouraging Congress to make the difficult policy choices associated with preemption instead of foisting them on the courts without providing guidance to assist the courts in making preemption determinations.

The argument in favor of abolishing implied preemption (except for situations involving physical impossibility) is perhaps at its strongest in circumstances in which the federal government has not intervened in the area affected by state regulation. The same considerations that support limited invocation of Congress's authority to preempt explicitly in the face of inaction are relevant when litigants assert that state regulation is implicitly preempted despite the absence of federal action. A court should not assume that Congress wanted to preempt to avoid the adverse spillover effects of state regulation, prevent interference with federal goals such as uniformity, or prohibit the states from seeking a cleaner environment or less risk than the market would produce on its own. Congress is fully capable of making such intent explicit. In addition, preemption in the face of federal inaction leaves the state whose law is preempted at the mercy of the market failure that prompted it to regulate in the first place because no substitute federal regulatory regime exists. Courts should therefore assume that Congress chose not to divest the states of their traditional authority to protect the health, safety, and welfare of their citizens unless Congress has provided some assurance that it has taken alternative steps to address the states' concerns.

Assuming the Supreme Court is not willing to jettison the implied preemption doctrine entirely, what approach is appropriate to the resolution of implied preemption challenges in situations in which the federal government has not acted? As the discussion later in this chapter indicates, implied preemption is never appropriate in a certain category of cases. In other cases, implied preemption is possible, but the courts should be reluctant to preempt in the face of inaction whether the basis for preempting state law is federal occupation of the field or an alleged conflict between federal and state law.

It is obvious that the complete absence of any federal activity can never provide a basis for preempting state law. The Supremacy Clause provides that the Constitution "and the Laws of the United States which shall be made in Pursuance thereof . . . shall be the supreme Law of the Land," anything in state law to the contrary notwithstanding. In the absence of any federal "Law," the Supremacy Clause simply does not apply, and there can be no preemption. As the Supreme Court recognized in the *Puerto Rico Department* case, "[t]here is no federal pre-emption *in vacuo*, without a constitutional text or a federal statute to assert it."[26] Thus, if Congress considers but decides not to adopt legislation that would authorize federal regulation of particular activities, the legislature's refusal to adopt the legislation has no preemptive effect. Federal law becomes effective only if it is passed by both houses of Congress and is signed by the president. The failure to enact regulatory legislation does not satisfy either the bicameralism or presentment requirements of Article I of the Constitution and therefore has no effect whatsoever, including preemptive effect on state law. The harder cases involve situations in which Congress has adopted legislation that does not cover the activities subject to state regulation, or Congress has authorized a federal agency to regulate the activities subject to state regulation, but the agency has chosen not to do so.

OCCUPATION OF THE FIELD PREEMPTION

Suppose that Congress has adopted legislation that addresses some aspects of a particular social or economic problem but not others. A state regulates in one of the areas not explicitly addressed by the federal statute. In such cases, courts should never find implied preemption based on occupation of the field subject to state regulation. If Congress wants to preempt an aspect of the field that

---

[26] Puerto Rico Dep't of Consumer Affairs v. ISA Petroleum Corp., 485 U.S. 495, 503 (1988).

it decides not to address in its larger regulatory program it is easy enough for it to say so in the statute. If it does not, respect for state sovereignty and preservation of the states' ability to protect their citizens from activities that threaten the public health, safety, or welfare dictate that the state regulatory regime survive. Even if Congress did not regulate the activities that the state has now chosen to address because it did not anticipate the problem when it initially adopted the statute, Congress has the authority to amend the statute to explicitly preempt state law on the basis of its capacity to foist problems on other states or interfere with federal goals such as uniformity. Unless and until Congress exercises that power, the state regulatory program should survive.

Although the Supreme Court has not enunciated an absolute prohibition on implied preemption based on occupation of the field in the context of federal inaction, it has been reluctant to preempt in that context. The *Sprietsma* case discussed in the preceding text is illustrative. After rejecting the boat manufacturer's claim that the Federal Boat Safety Act explicitly preempted state common law tort actions for damages arising from accidents involving propellers, the Court acknowledged that the plaintiff's tort claim might nonetheless be implicitly preempted. It held, however, that the statute clearly did not occupy the field of recreational boat safety so as to foreclose state common law remedies. The act neither required that the Coast Guard adopt "comprehensive regulations covering every aspect of recreational boat safety and design" nor reflected "a clear and manifest intent to sweep away state common law."[27] The manufacturer asserted that state common law damage awards would thwart the uniformity in regulation sought by Congress, but the Court found that the federal government's interest in uniformity was "not unyielding," as reflected in the Coast Guard's previous decisions to exempt some state regulations from the explicit statutory preemption provision.

Both federal and state courts have rejected a purported desire for uniform federal regulation as a basis for finding implied preemption based on occupation of the field in other cases of federal inaction. As one state court put it, a "generic concern for uniformity" should be regarded as insufficient to displace state law.[28] According to the Supreme Court, there must, instead, be evidence that "Congress intended to centralize all decision-making authority in one decision maker: the Federal Government."[29] Affirmative evidence of Congress's disavowal of a desire for national uniformity obviously should defeat an argument of field preemption by federal inaction.[30] Even in the

---

[27] SPRIETSMA V. MERCURY MARINE, 537 U.S. 51, 69 (2002).
[28] KOHN V. BURLINGTON N. AND SANTA FE R.R., 77 P.3d 809, 813 (Colo. App. 2003).
[29] FREIGHTLINER CORP. V. MYRICK, 514 U.S. 280, 286 (1995).
[30] See, e.g., TOY MFRS., INC. V. BLUMENTHAL, 986 F.2d 615, 624 (7th Cir. 1993).

absence of such evidence, *Sprietsma* indicates that the issuance of exemptions from any express statutory preemption provision by an agency explicitly authorized by statute to create such exemptions strengthens the argument that a regulatory field has not been exclusively occupied by the federal government to the exclusion of the states.

Nor should the apparently comprehensive nature of the regulations adopted by a federal agency under a regulatory statute provide the basis for the conclusion that the federal program occupies the field, thereby preempting state regulation of activities left unregulated by the agency. The Supreme Court has indicated that the "pervasive nature" of a federal regulatory statute may "make reasonable the inference that Congress left no room for the States to supplement it."[31] If the federal government has not regulated at all, it is impossible to characterize its regulatory presence as "pervasive." The Court has also cautioned, however, that courts should be wary of relying on the comprehensiveness of a federal regulatory program to find occupation of the field so as to preclude state regulation of activities falling within federal regulatory lacunae.

To infer preemption whenever an agency deals with a problem comprehensively is virtually tantamount to saying that whenever a federal agency decides to step into a field, its regulations will be exclusive. Such a rule would be inconsistent with the federal-state balance embodied in our Supremacy Clause jurisprudence.

> Thus, if an agency does not speak to the question of pre-emption, we will pause before saying that the mere volume and complexity of its regulations indicate that the agency did in fact intend to pre-empt. Given the presumption that state and local regulation related to matters of health and safety can normally coexist with federal regulations, we will seldom infer, solely from the comprehensiveness of federal regulations, an intent to pre-empt in its entirety a field related to health and safety.[32]

Whether one applies an approach that prohibits all types of implied preemption other than when compliance with both federal and state regulation is physically impossible or a more limited prohibition on implied occupation of the field, state regulation of GHG emissions by either stationary or mobile sources should not be preempted on the ground that the CAA has implicitly occupied the field of regulation of GHG emissions.[33]

---

[31] RICE V. SANTA FE ELEVATOR CORP., 331 U.S. 218, 230 (1947).

[32] HILLSBOROUGH COUNTY V. AUTOMATED MEDICAL LABS., INC., 471 U.S. 707, 717–18 (1985).

[33] The outcome of occupation of the field preemption cases often turns on how the court decides to define the scope of the allegedly occupied field. It is obvious that Congress did not intend for the CAA to occupy the broader field of regulation of air pollution.

CONFLICT AND OBSTACLE PREEMPTION

Even if Congress has not occupied a particular field of activity to the complete exclusion of state regulation, state law may be preempted based on a conflict between federal and state law, or if a court concludes that state law poses an obstacle to the pursuit of federal purposes. It is clearly not physically impossible for a car manufacturer subject to state controls on GHG emissions to comply with both federal and state law because there is no federal law with which to comply. If state regulation restricts GHG emissions, compliance with that constraint will not violate federal law; the absence of federal restrictions does not mean federal law mandates GHG emissions at a level that exceeds the state restrictions.

Assuming the doctrine of implied preemption remains good law, the next question is whether state law poses an obstacle to the accomplishment of federal goals. A decision by Congress or an administrative agency not to regulate particular activities cannot of itself be sufficient to demonstrate that state regulation of those activities would frustrate federal goals, as Supreme Court preemption decisions recognize. In *Sprietsma*, the outboard motor manufacturer claimed that the plaintiff's tort claims were implicitly preempted by the Coast Guard's decision not to regulate propeller guards. The Court held to the contrary, insisting that "[i]t is quite wrong to view that decision as the functional equivalent of a regulation prohibiting all States and their political subdivisions from adopting such a regulation." Instead, the agency's decision not to regulate only maintained the status quo of no federal regulation. According to the Court, "history teaches us that a Coast Guard decision not to regulate a particular aspect of boating safety is fully consistent with an intent to preserve state regulatory authority pending the adoption of specific federal standards."[34]

Sprietsma reflects the recognition that the absence of federal regulation is not necessarily indicative of a federal judgment that federal policies are best promoted by exempting the activities the state seeks to regulate from positive regulation by all levels of government. There are other possible explanations for the absence of federal regulation. Congress or a federal agency may not yet feel comfortable regulating based on the available information, or the problem may not be common enough or important enough to warrant federal regulatory resources. These reasons are not tantamount to a conclusion that federal purposes would be thwarted if state regulation proceeded in the

---

[34] Sprietsma v. Mercury Marine, 537 U.S. 51, 65 (2002).

absence of federal regulation. If a state takes a more precautionary approach to a health and environmental risk than the federal government, and is willing to regulate despite uncertainties, federal purposes are not thwarted. If a problem is concentrated in a state that therefore desires to regulate its causes, the decision by the affected state to regulate activities that are not federally regulated will not frustrate federal purposes. Such state experimentation may help all levels of government, as well as targets of regulation and those seeking its protections, by allowing more informed assessment of regulatory options. If the only reason that a state reaches a different decision on the desirability of regulation is that the two levels of government assess comparative risks differently — because, for example, the state places a higher priority than the federal government does in addressing a particular form of market failure, as compared to alternative uses of government resources — conflict or obstacle preemption is not justified on the ground that state regulation would interfere with the achievement of federal objectives.

THE RELEVANCE OF THE AGENCY'S JUDGMENT

The preceding discussion supports the premise that purpose-based conflict preemption should rest on more than just the absence of federal regulation of the activities that the state has decided to regulate. By definition, if the form of preemption at issue is implied preemption based on a conflict between state regulation and federal policies, Congress has failed to enunciate whether it wants the federal government's unwillingness or inability to act to preclude a particular state regulation. Assuming again that implied preemption based on conflict of purposes continues to be recognized as an appropriate doctrine for ousting state law, preemption may be appropriate if the relevant federal agency determines that state regulation would interfere with the achievement of federal statutory goals. Even then, the courts should declare state law to be preempted only in limited situations.

A court should not uphold a federal agency's assertion of preemptive power due to claimed frustration of federal statutory objectives unless Congress has explicitly delegated to that federal agency the authority to preempt state law.[35] A broad, general delegation of authority to an agency to implement the federal law should not suffice. After all, the preemption doctrine has the potential to alter radically the balance of state and federal power. Moreover, a federal agency may have an incentive to declare state law preempted because doing so vests in it exclusive authority to regulate in the affected area, thereby enhancing its own

---

[35] This issue is explored further by Professor Funk in Chapter 10.

power. In the absence of an explicit statutory delegation to an agency to determine the preemptive scope of the statute, the courts should refuse to interpret a general delegation of authority to implement the federal law as encompassing the power to declare state law ousted on the basis of the agency's perception of the presence of a conflict between state law and federal objectives.

Such a judicial approach to ascertaining the impact of an agency's declaration that state law must be preempted to prevent interference with federal policies is consistent with the Supreme Court's resolution of a closely related federalism issue that also involves an agency's ability to affect the balance of federal and state regulatory authority. In *Solid Waste Agency of Northern Cook County v. United States Army Corps of Engineers*,[36] the issue before the Supreme Court was how much weight to accord to a federal agency's interpretation of its own authority under the federal Clean Water Act (CWA) to require permits for the development of isolated intrastate waters. The Court refused to defer to the expansive interpretation of the scope of the CWA's dredge-and-fill permit program adopted by the U.S. Environmental Protection Agency and the Army Corps of Engineers because of the adverse implications such an interpretation would have on the maintenance of a proper balance between federal and state power. The Court stated:

> Where an administrative interpretation of a statute invokes the outer limits of Congress's power, we expect a clear indication that Congress intended that result. This requirement stems from our prudential desire not to needlessly reach constitutional issues and our assumption that Congress does not casually authorize administrative agencies to interpret a statute to push the limit of congressional authority. This concern is heightened where the administrative interpretation alters the federal-state framework by permitting federal encroachment upon a traditional state power.

Quoting an earlier decision, the Court declared that, "unless Congress conveys its purpose clearly, it will not be deemed to have significantly changed the federal-state balance."[37] Finding that the agencies' interpretation would result in "a significant impingement of the States' traditional and primary power over land and water use," the Court concluded that it was obliged to "read the statute as written to avoid the significant constitutional and federalism questions raised by [the agencies'] interpretation" and therefore to reject the agency's request that it defer to its broad reading of its statutory permitting authority.[38] Similarly, in a later case involving the same statutory provision, a

[36] 531 U.S. 159 (2001).
[37] Id. at 172–3.
[38] Id. at 174.

plurality of the Court refused to defer to the same agencies' interpretation of the scope of the permit program in another context because it did not qualify as a "'clear and manifest' statement from Congress to authorize an unprecedented intrusion into traditional state authority."[39]

Whether the courts should defer to an agency's statutory interpretation that stretches the limits of the federal government's exercise of an enumerated power is a somewhat different question than the question of whether Congress intended, in an area within the scope of an enumerated power, to allow federal agencies to oust state regulatory power. Both questions, however, have the potential to adversely affect the exercise of state regulatory authority. Particularly if the affected activities are within the scope of the traditional state police power, the courts ought to be just as reluctant to defer to a federal agency's interpretation that federal inaction ousts state power as the Supreme Court indicated they should be in defining the limits of an enumerated federal power such as the Commerce Clause. Both kinds of interpretation can impinge on state power. The Court has acknowledged that "conflict pre-emption analysis must be applied sensitively . . . , so as to prevent the diminution of the role Congress reserved to the States while at the same time preserving the federal role."[40]

Of the two kinds of intrusion, the exercise of preemptive authority may be the more devastating to the integrity of state sovereignty. The exercise of an enumerated federal regulatory power such as the Commerce Clause to adopt affirmative legislation does not necessarily result in exclusion of the state from the regulatory field. Concurrent exercise of federal and state environmental regulation, for example, is the norm, unless state regulation actually conflicts with federal law. At the very least, federalism concerns ought to impel the courts to consistently apply a presumption against the conclusion that Congress delegated to a federal agency the power to preempt state law. Thus, as the Supreme Court has put it in one case involving alleged preemption by federal inaction, "[t]he relevant inquiry is not whether Congress authorized or expected [state] regulation, but whether it indicated by its own actions to *forbid* it."[41] To prove that Congress intended that agency inaction have preclusive impact, some lower courts have required Congress or the agency to

---

[39] RAPANOS V. UNITED STATES, 126 S. Ct. 2208, 2224 (2006) (quoting BFP V. RESOLUTION TRUST CORP., 511 U.S. 531, 544 [1994]).
[40] NORTHWEST CENTRAL PIPELINE CORP. V. STATE CORP. COMM'N, 489 U.S. 493, 517 (1989).
[41] ARKANSAS ELEC. COOPERATIVE CORP. V. ARKANSAS PUB. SERV. COMM'N, 461 U.S. 375, 387 n. 11 (1983). See also BALTIMORE AND OHIO R.R. CO. V. OBERLY, 837 F.2d 108, 115 (3d Cir. 1988) (quoting HILLSBOROUGH COUNTY V. AUTOMATED MED. LAB., INC., 471 U.S. 707, 718 [1985]) (applying principle that federal agencies "will make their intentions clear if they intend for their regulations to be exclusive" in the context of an agency's failure to regulate).

declare "at a high level of specificity, its intention that its *in*action preempts state law."[42] A requirement that Congress explicitly delegate to the agency the power to preempt is consistent with that mechanism for avoiding preemption in the absence of clear congressional intent, as well as with the desirability of avoiding unwarranted infringements on state sovereignty and the protective exercise of traditional regulatory authority.

Even if Congress has explicitly delegated to an agency the power to preempt state law in order to avoid frustration of federal purposes, however, the courts should not find preemption unless the agency has clearly exercised that power. As one court put it, preemption by inaction "requires *an actual, concrete assertion of regulatory authority* as opposed to mere possession of authority."[43] Many courts have appropriately recognized a distinction between an agency's "mere failure" to act and its affirmative decision that regulation at any level of government would be inappropriate. As one court described it, the difference is between an agency saying that it has not yet looked at a problem and an agency saying that it has decided not to regulate because "it is appropriate to do nothing."[44] Inaction alone thus represents only "the *absence* of a real regulatory decision," which should be afforded no preemptive effect.[45] According to the Supreme Court, an agency's failure to regulate has preemptive effect only where that failure "takes on the character of a ruling that no such regulation [by any level of government] is appropriate or approved pursuant to the policy of the statute."[46]

An agency, just like Congress, may fail to regulate for myriad reasons, only one of which is a conclusion that leaving activities unregulated best promotes federal statutory policies. An agency may decide not to regulate, for example, because it is awaiting more information before doing so. Unless the agency explicitly declares that its own decision not to regulate also bars states from doing so, the courts should not find conflict preemption based on interference with federal purposes.[47] Under presidential administrations more protective of state regulatory authority than the George W. Bush administration, the

---

[42] BALTIMORE AND OHIO R.R. CO. V. OBERLY, 837 F.2d 108, 115 (3d Cir. 1988); ELSTON V. UNION PAC. R.R. CO., 74 P.3d 478, 488 (Colo. App. 2003) (requiring a "clear congressional directive").

[43] MANES V. METRO-NORTH COMMUTER R.R., 801 F. Supp. 954, 964 (D. Conn. 1992), AFF'D, 990 F.2d 622 (2d Cir. 1993) (Table).

[44] MISSOURI PAC. R. CO. V. RAILROAD COMM'N OF TEXAS, 833 F.2d 570 (5th Cir. 1987), REHEARING DENIED, 845 F.2d 1022 (5th Cir. 1988).

[45] BALTIMORE AND OHIO R.R. CO. V. OBERLY, 837 F.2d 108, 116 (3d Cir. 1988) (holding that EPA's decision not to regulate noise from railroad refrigerator cars did not preempt state noise control standards).

[46] RAY V. ATLANTIC RICHFIELD CO., 435 U.S. 151, 178 (1978).

[47] See, e.g., NORFOLK S. RY. CO. V. BOX, 2007 WL 1030320, at *9 (N.D. Ill. March 30, 2007).

agencies have recognized the propriety of that approach. The National Highway Traffic Safety Administration, for example, declared in 1995 that an agency's decision not to regulate a particular activity will not "negatively" preempt state law unless the agency has "affirmatively manifested an intention to shut out State action."[48]

Finally, the agency's exercise of its authority to preempt state law based on its own refusal to regulate is subject to judicial review. Although the agency's determination that preemption is needed to prevent frustration of federal objectives may in some settings be entitled to deference, the degree of deference depends on the manner in which the agency has exercised its authority. The Supreme Court in *Sprietsma* stated that a federal agency's enunciation of its position on the preemptive effect of federal inaction must be "authoritative" before inaction may be given preemptive effect.[49] In a related context, the Court indicated that agency determinations of the meaning or effect of the federal statutes they administer are entitled to considerable deference from the courts if Congress has delegated to the agency the authority "to make rules carrying the force of law" and the agency's determination represents the exercise of that authority.[50] If either of those conditions is not met, a more muted form of deference will apply.[51] Accordingly, the courts should lend greater credence to an agency's determination that its inaction preempts state law if that determination is made in the course of a rulemaking proceeding in which the agency invited and considered public comments than if it first asserts that its inaction preempts state law in the course of litigation or in issuing an internal policy statement.

This approach to resolving claims of conflict preemption based on agency inaction leaves relatively little room for EPA to preempt state regulation of GHG emissions. The CAA does not generally delegate to EPA the power to preempt state law.[52] As a result, EPA should not be able to declare any decision it makes not to regulate GHG emissions from stationary sources to be preemptive of state regulation. The statute does not exactly delegate to EPA the authority to preempt state regulation of motor vehicles either. The statute preempts state law of specified types and in particular circumstances.

---

[48] Department of Transportation, National Highway Traffic Safety Administration, Consumer Information Regulations; Vehicle Stopping Distance, 60 FEDERAL REGISTER 32,918 (June 26, 1995). See also Department of Transportation, National Highway Traffic Safety Administration, Low-Speed Vehicles, 65 FEDERAL REGISTER 53,219 (September 1, 2000).

[49] SPRIETSMA V. MERCURY MARINE, 537 U.S. 51, 66 (2002).

[50] UNITED STATES V. MEAD CORP., 535 U.S. 218, 226–7 (2001).

[51] Id. at 228.

[52] Nor does the EPCA, 49 U.S.C. § 32919, the statute that authorizes the Department of Transportation to issue corporate fuel-economy standards, delegate to that agency the power to preempt state law.

The provision authorizing EPA to waive the prohibition on state regulation for California might reasonably be interpreted, however, as a delegation to EPA of the power to determine the preemptive scope of the CAA's motor vehicle emission-control provisions. If so, EPA has the authority to determine that California (and other states seeking to adopt California's controls) may not regulate GHG emissions from motor vehicles, even though EPA has chosen not to do so. That was the position EPA took in denying California's waiver request in late 2007. The EPA claimed that its decision avoided a patchwork of federal and state regulations, the situation differed from previous approvals of California's waiver requests because of the global nature of climate change, and the congressional adoption of higher corporate average fuel economy standards in energy legislation[53] adopted the same day EPA denied the waiver precluded the need for additional state regulation. California has challenged the validity of that decision in federal court, and federal legislators have promised to introduce legislation to overturn it.[54]

THE IMPACT OF THE LACK OF FEDERAL REGULATORY AUTHORITY

This chapter takes the position that, aside from direct conflicts in which compliance with both federal and state law is impossible, the courts should never invalidate state laws or regulations based on implied preemption. Even if the courts continue to endorse implied preemption doctrine as a general proposition, however, they should refuse to apply it in cases in which the federal agency lacks jurisdiction over the activities being regulated by a state. The Supreme Court has repeatedly recognized the inappropriateness of implicit preemption based on the inaction of federal agencies that lack the power to regulate in areas subject to state regulation. It has done so both in contexts in which Congress has never authorized federal regulation in the first place and in instances in which existing federal regulatory authority has been repealed.

In a case decided in the 1940s, the Court reasoned that if Congress enacts a statute that deals only partially with a particular subject, and leaves outside the scope of its delegation to a federal agency closely related matters, "it implies

---

[53] The Energy Independence and Security Act of 2007, Pub. L. No. 110–40, § 102(a), 121 Stat. 1492 (to be codified at 49 U.S.C. § 32902(b)(2)).

[54] A report by the Congressional Research Service finds numerous flaws in the legal reasoning on which EPA rested the denial. Congressional Research Service, "California's Waiver Request to Control Greenhouse Gases under the Clean Air Act" (James E. McCarthy and Robert Meltz eds., December 27, 2007).

that in such matters federal policy is indifferent and . . . we can only assume it to be equally indifferent" to whether the state decides to regulate the activity excluded from federal regulation.[55] Similarly, in the 1983 *Arkansas Electric Cooperative* case involving federal and state regulation of rural electric rates, the Court refused to find preemption based on the Federal Power Commission's (FPC) decision that it lacked jurisdiction to regulate the wholesale rates charged by rural cooperatives. The federal agency's refusal to assert jurisdiction did not support preemption of state law because the FPC's refusal to regulate merely reflected its view that, "purely as a jurisdictional matter, the relevant statutes gave [the Rural Electrification Administration] exclusive authority among federal agencies to regulate rural power cooperatives. It did not determine that, as a matter of policy, rural power cooperatives that are engaged in sales for resale should be left unregulated."[56] Absent such a finding by Congress or the federal agency, a court should not find preemption by inaction. Finally, in the *Puerto Rico Department* case discussed in the preceding text, the Court refused to attribute to Congress an intention to preempt state regulation of the petroleum industry when it terminated its earlier delegation of authority to the federal government to regulate the industry. In the absence of textual evidence of Congress's desire to preclude state regulation, the Court deemed it "impossible to find that a free market was mandated by federal law."[57]

Even if the courts refuse to adopt an approach that precludes implied preemption in the absence of federal regulatory authority, judicial deference to the preemption views of an agency lacking jurisdiction over the regulated state activities is inappropriate. The courts should refuse to defer whether the federal agency claims power to occupy exclusively a regulatory field or the agency claims state regulation frustrates federal ends. In such settings, the well-established *Chevron* case rationales for deference are absent. Such an agency could not claim that Congress (implicitly) delegated to the agency responsibility to interpret gaps or ambiguities in the text. Nor could an agency lacking regulatory jurisdiction claim it has greater expertise than the reviewing court is likely to have and is therefore better able to understand the policy implications of the adoption of competing interpretations of the statute.[58]

[55] Bethlehem Steel Co. v. New York State Labor Relations Bd., 330 U.S. 767, 773 (1947).
[56] Arkansas Elec. Cooperative Corp. v. Arkansas Pub. Serv. Comm'n, 461 U.S. 375, 384 (1983).
[57] Puerto Rico Dep't of Consumer Affairs v. ISA Petroleum Corp., 485 U.S. 495, 501 (1988).
[58] Chevron U.S.A., Inc. v. Natural Res. Def. Council, Inc., 467 U.S. 837 (1984).

CONCLUSION

This chapter argues that preemption of state regulation based on federal inaction is rarely appropriate. Drawing primarily on decades of federalism decisions by the courts, it provides recommendations for scholars, Congress, agencies, and the courts in addressing whether federal inaction should or does result in preemption of state regulation. All should be sensitive and deferential to state prerogatives in areas of traditional state concern. Congress should not preempt state regulation in areas in which it has chosen not to regulate unless it determines that a state's effort to regulate would inappropriately impose adverse impacts on other states or that federal policies can best be achieved in the absence of targeted regulation at any level of government. If Congress fails to enunciate in statutory text its desire to preempt state regulation in the absence of federal regulatory action, neither agencies nor the courts should ever find implied preemption, unless it is physically impossible to comply with both federal and state law. That situation will occur rarely because, by definition, the federal government has not prescribed or proscribed any conduct.

If the courts continue to be willing to find implied preemption despite Congress's failure to make an explicit pronouncement of its preemptive intent, they should confine the implied preemption doctrine in cases involving alleged preemption by inaction to the conflict/purpose branch of implied preemption. Implicit occupation of the field should never occur as a result of inaction. The courts should be willing to find implied conflict preemption in the absence of federal regulatory action (other than a conflict based on physical impossibility) only if Congress has explicitly delegated to a federal agency the power to preempt state law to prevent it from subverting federal goals and the agency has clearly, authoritatively, and persuasively exercised that authority. Finally, the courts should never find implied preemption of state regulation of activities if the relevant federal agency lacks the authority to regulate those activities. Even if the courts refuse to impose an absolute prohibition on implied preemption based on inaction by an agency with no authority to regulate, they should afford no deference to such an agency's view that Congress intended to preempt state law, especially if the participatory process that often underpins deference rationales is lacking.

These rules strike an appropriate balance between the interests of the federal government in pursuing policy objectives within the competence of federal power and the need to respect state sovereignty, especially in areas of traditional state regulation, to achieve the benefits of the dual system of government that the Framers built into the Constitution. They also increase the chances that one level of government's failure to take action to protect the public health and safety or the environment will not preclude another from doing so, while preserving the authority of the federal government to supersede the judgments of state policy makers in appropriate instances.

9   Process-Based Preemption

Bradford R. Clark*

INTRODUCTION

The question of preemption arises because the Constitution establishes a federal system with two governments (one federal and one state) that have overlapping power to regulate the same matters involving the same parties in the same territory. To succeed, such a system requires a means of deciding when federal law displaces state law. The Founders chose the Supremacy Clause (reinforced by Article III) to perform this function. Although seemingly one-sided, the Clause actually incorporates several important political and procedural safeguards designed to preserve the proper balance between the governance prerogatives of the federal government and the states. It does this by recognizing only three sources of law as "the supreme Law of the Land": the "Constitution," "Laws," and "Treaties" of the United States.[1] Elsewhere, the Constitution prescribes precise and cumbersome procedures to govern the adoption of each source of supreme federal law. These procedures establish the exclusive means of adopting "the supreme Law of the Land." By requiring the participation and assent of multiple actors subject to the political safeguards of federalism, these procedures make supreme federal law relatively difficult to adopt. More importantly, these procedures suggest exclusivity because the Constitution guarantees states (regardless of size or population) equal suffrage in the Senate and gives the Senate (or the states) an absolute veto over the adoption of each and every source of law recognized by the Supremacy Clause. This means that courts must identify an applicable provision of the "Constitution," "Laws," and "Treaties" of the

*   For insightful comments and suggestions, I thank David Barron, Bill Buzbee, John Manning, Trevor Morrison, Amanda Tyler, and participants at the Conference on Federalism in the Overlapping Territory held at Duke Law School on November 10, 2006.
[1]   U.S. Const., art. VI, cl. 2.

United States adopted pursuant to specified procedures before they may pre-empt state law. By operation of the Supremacy Clause, these three sources override contrary state law. The negative implication of the Clause, however, is that state law continues to govern in the absence of "the supreme Law of the Land."

This process-based understanding of preemption has potential implications for two related federalism doctrines: the presumption against preemption and the more controversial clear statement requirement. The traditional presumption against preemption maintains "that the historic police powers of the States [are] not to be superseded by [a] Federal Act unless that was the clear and manifest purpose of Congress."[2] A clear statement rule is similar in function but requires that Congress make its intent to preempt state law clear on the face of the statute. In addition, some formulations go farther by suggesting that "if Congress intends to alter the usual constitutional balance between the States and the Federal Government, it must make its intention to do so *unmistakably* clear in the language of the statute."[3] Critics of these doctrines argue that the presumption against preemption contradicts the Supremacy Clause,[4] and that clear statement rules "amount to a 'backdoor' version of the constitutional activism."[5] Although certainly subject to abuse, both doctrines – if properly limited – may play a useful role in implementing the Constitution's political and procedural safeguards of federalism.

One recent example suggests how these doctrines may operate to ensure that preemption decisions are made in accordance with federal lawmaking procedures. In *Gonzales v. Oregon*, the Supreme Court arguably employed a clear statement rule of sorts by refusing to interpret an "obscure grant" in the Controlled Substances Act to "authorize the Attorney General to bar dispensing controlled substances for assisted suicide in the face of a state medical regime permitting such conduct."[6] Although the confines of this chapter do not permit a complete examination of the problem, several features of the

---

[2] RICE V. SANTA FE ELEVATOR CORP., 331 U.S. 218, 230 (1947). Nontextualist judges might find the requisite purpose by looking outside the enacted text of the statute.
[3] GREGORY V. ASHCROFT, 501 U.S. 452, 460 (1991) (emphasis added).
[4] Caleb Nelson, "Preemption," VIRGINIA LAW REVIEW 86, no. 2 (2000): 225, 290.
[5] William N. Eskridge Jr. and Philip P. Frickey, "Quasi-Constitutional Law: Clear Statement Rules as Constitutional Lawmaking," VANDERBILT LAW REVIEW 45, no. 3 (1992): 593, 598. More recently, Professor Eskridge has explored the implications of legislative vetogates and concluded that the Supreme Court should permit Congress to delegate preemptive authority to an agency only by enacting a clear statement to that effect. See William N. Eskridge Jr., "Vetogates, CHEVRON, Preemption," NOTRE DAME LAW REVIEW 83, no. 4 (2008): 1441, 1467–72.
[6] GONZALES V. OREGON, 546 U.S. 243, 274–5 (2006).

constitutional structure suggest that the Court's use of either a presumption against preemption or a modest clear statement rule in cases like *Gonzales v. Oregon* may guard against excessive federal preemption of state law at a time when states are increasingly adopting innovative measures to protect public health, safety, and the environment.

THE DUAL FUNCTION OF THE SUPREMACY CLAUSE

The Founders made the fundamental decision at the outset of the Constitutional Convention to preserve "the states as separate sources of authority and organs of administration" rather than attempt to abolish them in favor of a consolidated central government.[7] At the same time, the Founders decided to abandon the constraints of the Articles of Confederation and create a federal government capable of acting, within its assigned powers, "directly on the population rather than mediately through the states."[8] As a consequence of these decisions, there are two governments – one state and one federal – frequently operating at the same time, within the same territory, on the same people. Such a system inevitably gives rise to conflicts between state and federal law. Thus, establishing a mechanism for resolving such conflicts was essential to the success of the Convention.

As I have explained elsewhere in greater detail,[9] the Founders considered three potential mechanisms: (1) military force to coerce state adherence to federal law; (2) congressional power to negative state law; and (3) judicial enforcement of "supreme" federal law over contrary state law.[10] The Founders quickly dismissed coercive force. As James Madison put it, "[a] Union of the States containing such an ingredient seemed to provide for its own destruction."[11] The Founders initially embraced, but ultimately rejected, the congressional negative.[12] Delegates from the smaller states objected strongly and repeatedly to this mechanism. For example, Elbridge Gerry of Massachusetts

---

[7] Herbert Wechsler, "The Political Safeguards of Federalism: The Role of the States in the Composition and Selection of the National Government," Columbia Law Review 54, no. 4 (1954): 543.

[8] Jack N. Rakove, Original Meanings: Politics and Ideas in the Making of the Constitution (New York: A. A. Knopf, 1996), 169.

[9] See Bradford R. Clark, "Separation of Powers as a Safeguard of Federalism," Texas Law Review 79, no. 6 (2001): 1321, 1346–67.

[10] See ibid., 1348–55; see also Bradford R. Clark, "The Supremacy Clause as a Constraint on Federal Power," George Washington Law Review 71, no. 1 (2003): 91, 105–11.

[11] James Madison, "The Records of the Federal Convention (May 31, 1787)," in The Records of the Federal Convention of 1787, vol. 1, ed. Max Farrand (New Haven, CT: Yale University Press, 1911), 45, 54 (hereinafter Farrand's Records).

[12] See Clark, "Separation of Powers," 1349–53.

remarked that "[t]he Natl. Legislature with such a power may enslave the States" and predicted that "[s]uch an idea as this will never be acceded to."[13]

The Founders initially considered and rejected the third option – a Supremacy Clause – as part of the New Jersey Plan.[14] After the small states secured equal suffrage in the Senate,[15] however, the Convention embraced the Supremacy Clause.[16] The Clause performs the familiar function of instructing courts to prefer "the supreme Law of the Land" to contrary state law. The Clause, however, is something of a double-edged sword. The Clause recognizes only three sources of law as "the supreme Law of the Land": "This *Constitution*, and the *Laws* of the United States which shall be made in Pursuance thereof; and all *Treaties* made, or which shall be made, under the Authority of the United States."[17] The negative implication of the Clause is that, in the absence of these sources, state law continues to govern. Thus, the Clause both secures the supremacy of those sources of federal law it recognizes and preserves the states' prerogative to govern in their absence.

In order to apply the Supremacy Clause, it is necessary to identify "the supreme Law of the Land" with precision. The Constitution prescribes precise procedures to govern the adoption of each source of such law – that is, the "Constitution," "Laws," and "Treaties" of the United States.[18] Although different in important respects, these procedures all assign responsibility for adopting "the supreme Law of the Land" solely to actors subject to the "political safeguards of federalism."[19] These actors include the president, the House of Representatives, and the Senate. As Madison explained, the constitutionally assigned role of the states in the selection and composition of these entities would ensure that "each of the principal branches of the federal government will owe its existence to the favor of the State governments."[20] In this way, the Constitution was structured to retard "new intrusions by the center on the domain of the states."[21]

---

[13] James Madison, "The Records of the Federal Convention (June 8, 1787)," in 1 FARRAND'S RECORDS, 162, 165.

[14] See Clark, "Separation of Powers," 1351–2.

[15] James Madison, "The Records of the Federal Convention (July 16, 1787)," in FARRAND'S RECORDS, vol. 2, 13, 15–16.

[16] James Madison, "Notes on the Constitutional Convention (July 17, 1787)," in ibid., 22.

[17] U.S. Const., art. VI, cl. 2 (emphasis added).

[18] Ibid.

[19] Professor Wechsler used the phrase "political safeguards of federalism" to refer to "the role of the states in the composition and selection of the central government." Wechsler, "Political Safeguards of Federalism," 543.

[20] Clinton Rossiter, ed., THE FEDERALIST, no. 45 (James Madison) (New York: New American Library, 1961), 291.

[21] Wechsler, "Political Safeguards of Federalism," 558.

The Constitution magnified the effect of the political safeguards by singling out the Senate to participate in adopting all forms of supreme federal law. As discussed in the following text, the Senate was designed to represent the states and to give smaller states disproportionate power in the lawmaking process. By including the Senate in all types of federal lawmaking, the Constitution gives the Senate an absolute veto over every attempt to adopt "the supreme Law of the Land." For example, the Constitution provides that constitutional amendments ordinarily receive the approval of two-thirds of the House and the Senate and three-fourths of the states.[22] Similarly, the Constitution requires federal statutes to be approved by the House, the Senate, and the president or by two-thirds of both houses in the case of a presidential veto.[23] Finally, the Constitution specifies that treaties be submitted by the president and approved by two-thirds of the senators present.[24] The Founders understood that these internal constraints would make "the supreme Law of the Land" more difficult to adopt but thought that "[t]he injury which may possibly be done by defeating a few good laws will be amply compensated by the advantage of preventing a number of bad ones."[25]

Although the effectiveness of the political safeguards of federalism has waned over the years,[26] federal lawmaking procedures continue to constrain federal lawmaking simply by establishing multiple "veto gates,"[27] which effectively impose a supermajority requirement[28] and thus raise the cost of

---

[22] See U.S. Const., art. V. Alternatively, art. V requires Congress to call a convention for proposing amendments on the application of two-thirds of the state legislatures. Ibid.

[23] See ibid., art. I, § 7.

[24] See ibid., art. II, § 2, cl. 2.

[25] THE FEDERALIST, no. 73 (Alexander Hamilton), 444; see William N. Eskridge Jr. and John Ferejohn, "The Article I, Section 7 Game," GEORGETOWN LAW JOURNAL 80, no. 3 (1992): 523, 528 (explaining that the bicameralism and presentment model of legislation "reflects a carefully considered judgment by the Framers about how lawmaking should be structured").

[26] The Seventeenth Amendment has reduced the states' influence in the Senate by replacing appointment of senators by state legislatures with popular elections. See U.S. Const., amend. XVII. Changes in constitutional law have also limited the states' ability to influence the House of Representatives through control over voter qualifications and districting. See ibid., amend. XV (race); ibid., amend. XIX (sex); ibid., amend. XXIV (poll tax); ibid., amend. XXVI (age). Finally, the states' modern practice of appointing presidential electors on the basis of winner-take-all popular elections has reduced the role of state legislatures in selecting the president and all but eliminated the possibility that the president will be selected by the House of Representatives voting by states.

[27] See McNollgast, "Positive Canons: The Role of Legislative Bargains in Statutory Interpretation," GEORGETOWN LAW JOURNAL 80, no. 3 (1992): 705, 707 n. 5.

[28] See John F. Manning, "Textualism and the Equity of the Statute," COLUMBIA LAW REVIEW 101, no. 1 (2001): 1, 74–5; William T. Mayton, "The Possibilities of Collective Choice: Arrow's Theorem, Article I, and the Delegation of Legislative Power to Administrative Agencies," DUKE LAW JOURNAL 1986, no. 6 (1986): 948, 956; Michael B. Rappaport, "Amending the Constitution to Establish Fiscal Supermajority Rules," JOURNAL OF LAW AND POLITICS 13, no. 3 (1997): 705, 712.

lawmaking. If any of the specified veto players withholds its consent, then no new supreme law is created, and state law remains in force.[29] Thus, the Constitution is carefully structured to restrict both who may exercise lawmaking power on behalf of the United States (actors subject to the political safeguards of federalism) and how they may exercise it (only in accordance with precise procedures that require the participation and assent of the states or their representatives in the Senate).

The constitutional structure suggests, moreover, that the lawmaking procedures established by the Constitution are the exclusive means of adopting "the supreme Law of the Land."[30] The Senate is the only federal institution specified by these procedures to participate in adopting all forms of supreme federal law. In response to the demands of small states, the Constitutional Convention designed the Senate to represent the states in the new federal government. Under the original Constitution, states were guaranteed equal suffrage in the Senate and senators were appointed by state legislatures. By requiring the participation and assent of the Senate to adopt all three sources of "the supreme Law of the Land," the Founders agreed to the supremacy of federal law only on the condition that the states (through their representatives in the Senate) have the opportunity to veto each and every federal proposal capable of overriding state law under the Supremacy Clause. This arrangement gave the small states disproportionate power in the lawmaking process. As George Mason explained at the Constitutional Convention:

> The State Legislatures ... ought to have some means of defending themselves against encroachments of the Natl. Govt. In every other department we have studiously endeavored to provide for its self-defense. Shall we leave the States alone unprovided with the means for this purpose? And what better means can we provide than the giving them some share in, or rather to make them a constituent part of, the Natl. Establishment.[31]

---

[29] See Ernest A. Young, "Making Federalism Doctrine: Fidelity, Institutional Competence, and Compensating Adjustments," WILLIAM AND MARY LAW REVIEW 46, no. 5 (2005): 1733, 1792 ("A national government that can act only with difficulty, after all, will tend to leave considerable scope for state autonomy."). Today the status quo contains a substantial body of federal law built up over two centuries. Just as federal lawmaking procedures make it difficult for Congress and the president to add to this body of law, these procedures make it difficult to subtract from such law as well. See Clark, "Separation of Powers," 1340 n. 90.

[30] See INS v. CHADHA, 462 U.S. 919, 951 (1983). ("It emerges clearly that the prescription for legislative action in Art. I, §§ 1, 7, represents the Framers' decision that the legislative power of the Federal Government be exercised in accord with a single, finely wrought and exhaustively considered, procedure.")

[31] James Madison, "Notes on the Constitutional Convention (June 7, 1787)," in 1 FARRAND'S RECORDS, 155–6 (statement of George Mason).

If the federal government were free to adopt "the supreme Law of the Land" outside the constitutionally prescribed lawmaking procedures, then it could effectively deprive the states' representatives in the Senate of their essential gate-keeping role and deprive the small states of the primary benefit of equal suffrage in the Senate.[32]

The composition and role of the Senate were central issues at the Constitutional Convention of 1787.[33] Although the Convention agreed that state legislatures would appoint senators,[34] it initially deadlocked over the proper basis for representation in the Senate. The large states favored proportional representation[35] while the small states insisted on equal representation.[36] The debate was protracted, and disagreement over the issue brought the Convention to the brink of collapse.[37] The delegates ultimately broke the impasse only by reaching a compromise that granted the states equal suffrage in the Senate.[38] In addition, the proponents of equal suffrage even succeeded in exempting this feature of the constitutional structure from future amendment by ordinary means.[39] As Jack Rakove has observed, following these developments, "no one could deny that the Senate was intended to embody the equal sovereignty of the states and to protect their rights of government against national encroachment."[40]

The day after approving the states' equal suffrage in the Senate, the Convention adopted the Supremacy Clause.[41] The Clause was originally suggested by supporters of equal suffrage in the Senate as an alternative to the congressional negative[42] and reflects an important, if overlooked, compromise embedded in the constitutional structure. By conferring supremacy only on sources of law that require the approval of either the states or the Senate (i.e.,

---

[32] The Founders understood that the Senate's essential role in the lawmaking process would not only preserve the governance prerogatives of the states, see THE FEDERALIST, no. 62 (James Madison), 378 (noting "that the equal vote allowed to each State is at once a constitutional recognition of the portion of sovereignty remaining in the individual States and an instrument for preserving that residuary sovereignty"), but also provide an "additional impediment . . . against improper acts of legislation," ibid.

[33] See Clark, "Separation of Powers," 1360–3.

[34] Ibid., 1359.

[35] Ibid., 1360.

[36] Ibid.

[37] Ibid., 1362–3.

[38] Ibid., 1363–4. In exchange for equal suffrage, the Convention decided that bills for raising revenue must originate in the House.

[39] Ibid., 1366. See U.S. Const., art. V (providing that "no State, without its Consent, shall be deprived of its equal Suffrage in the Senate").

[40] Rakove, "Original Meanings," 170.

[41] See "Journal of the Constitutional Convention (July 17, 1787)," in 2 FARRAND'S RECORDS, 22.

[42] See Clark, "Separation of Powers," 1348–55.

the "Constitution," "Laws," and "Treaties" of the United States), the Supremacy Clause restricts federal supremacy to measures approved by the states or their representatives in the Senate. Those who drafted and ratified the Constitution agreed to the supremacy of federal law (and the corresponding displacement of state law) only on the condition that the Senate (structured to represent the states equally) would have the opportunity to veto all forms of supreme federal law as part of the lawmaking process.[43] Treating federal law adopted outside that process as "supreme" would deprive the small states of the fruits of their hard-won bargain and undermine an important feature of the constitutional structure. To be sure, direct election of senators under the Seventeenth Amendment reduced the states' influence in the Senate, but this shift neither altered the small states' disproportionate influence in the Senate nor disturbed the Senate's right to veto all forms of "the supreme Law of the Land" in accordance with federal lawmaking procedures. Recognizing the relationship between these procedures and preemption has potential implications for how courts should conceptualize and use the traditional presumption against preemption and the related clear statement requirement.

OBJECTIONS TO PRESUMPTIONS AND CLEAR STATEMENT RULES

The Supreme Court has long endorsed, if not always followed, a presumption against preemption. In *Rice v. Santa Fe Elevator Corp.*, the Court declared that when Congress legislates in a "field which the States have traditionally occupied," courts "start with the assumption that the historic police powers of the States were not to be superseded by the Federal Act unless that was the clear and manifest purpose of Congress."[44] Although inconsistent in applying the presumption,[45] the Court invokes it frequently.[46] For example, the Court recently explained that the presumption against preemption applies in all preemption cases, both "to the question whether Congress intended any

---

[43] See ibid., 1339; see also Bradford R. Clark, "Constitutional Compromise and the Supremacy Clause," NOTRE DAME LAW REVIEW 83, no. 4 (2008): 1421.

[44] 331 U.S. at 230.

[45] See, e.g., BUCKMAN CO. v. PLAINTIFFS' LEGAL COMMITTEE, 531 U.S. 341, 348 (2001) (declining to apply the presumption against preemption to a matter outside the historic primacy of state regulation).

[46] See, e.g., BATES v. DOW AGROSCIENCES LLC, 544 U.S. 431, 449 (2005) ("In areas of traditional state regulation, we assume that a federal statute has not supplanted state law unless Congress has made such an intention clear and manifest." [internal quotation marks omitted]); MEDTRONIC, INC. v. LOHR, 518 U.S. 470, 485 (1996) (stating that the Court starts with the presumption against preemption in "all pre-emption cases").

pre-emption at all" and "to questions concerning the *scope* of its intended invalidation of state law."[47]

At least in some cases, the Supreme Court has used a clear statement rule in lieu of the presumption against preemption. At a minimum, the former requires a clear statement on the face of a federal statute, and the Court sometimes suggests that even more is required. For example, in *Gregory v. Ashcroft*, the Court confronted the question whether the Age Discrimination in Employment Act ("ADEA") preempted a Missouri constitutional requirement that state judges retire at age seventy.[48] The ADEA prohibits employers from discharging any employee who is at least forty years of age "because of such individual's age."[49] The act defines employers to include states but defines *employee* to exclude "an appointee on the policymaking level."[50] The question before the Court was whether appointed state judges fall within this exception. The Court discussed various arguments as to whether state judges make policy within the meaning of the exception but found it unnecessary to resolve the question. Because the exception arguably applied, the Court found it "at least ambiguous whether Congress intended that appointed judges . . . be included" within the protection of the ADEA.[51] The Court refused to preempt state law on the basis of such statutory ambiguity. To the contrary, the Court said that it would "read the ADEA to cover state judges" only if "Congress had made it clear that judges are included."[52] Because it was not "plain to anyone reading the Act that it covers judges,"[53] the Court concluded that the plaintiffs' claims fell outside the scope of the statute.[54] Given

---

[47] MEDTRONIC, 518 U.S. at 485; but see CIPOLLONE V. LIGGETT GROUP, INC., 505 U.S. 504, 545 (1992) (Scalia, J., concurring in the judgment in part, and dissenting in part) (arguing that the presumption dissolves "once there is conclusive evidence of intent to pre-empt in the express words of the statute," and that the scope of preemption should be determined using "ordinary principles of statutory construction").

[48] 501 U.S. 452.

[49] 29 U.S.C. §§ 623(a), 631(a).

[50] 29 U.S.C. § 630(f).

[51] 501 U.S. at 470.

[52] Ibid., 467 (emphasis omitted). Although there is language in GREGORY suggesting that a clear statement requirement was necessary to avoid the question as to whether Congress has constitutional power to regulate state judges in this way, the Court had arguably already resolved this question in favor of broad congressional power to regulate "states as states" in GARCIA V. SAN ANTONIO METROPOLITAN TRANSIT AUTHORITY, 469 U.S. 528 (1985). Thus, the question in GREGORY was really just one of preemption turning on statutory interpretation: Does the ADEA cover state judges?

[53] GREGORY, 501 U.S. at 467.

[54] See also BFP V. RESOLUTION TRUST CORP., 511 U.S. 531, 539–40, 544 (1994) (invoking clear statement requirement).

its language, *Gregory* has been taken to impose not merely a clear statement requirement but also a more controversial *super*-clear statement requirement.

Commentators have questioned the presumption against preemption but have objected most strenuously to the Supreme Court's use of a heightened clear statement requirement in preemption cases. Leading commentators raise essentially three objections to the Court's "creation of a series of new 'super strong clear statement rules' protecting constitutional structures, especially structures associated with federalism."[55] First, they argue that such rules are incoherent because they frequently protect underenforced constitutional norms that the Court does not enforce directly because of a lack of judicially manageable standards. For example, they find *Gregory v. Ashcroft* problematic in light of the Court's previously "stated reasons for *un*enforcement of structural constitutional norms."[56] They stress that in *Garcia*, the Court announced that federalism-based limits on national power are unenforceable against Congress because the Court has been unable to develop "principled constitutional limitations" from the Tenth Amendment and the Commerce Clause and because "the principal means chosen by the Framers to ensure the role of the States in the federal system lies in the structure of the Federal Government itself."[57] In their view, these "reasons for unenforcement of federalism norms through judicial review are equally valid arguments for the unenforcement of federalism norms through statutory interpretation."[58] They suggest that once the Court decided to leave enforcement of federalism to Congress and the president, "the Court's creation of super-strong clear statement rules [is] a backdoor way for the Court to take these issues back from the political process."[59]

Second, commentators argue that clear statement rules represent "under-the-table constitutional lawmaking" and thus constitute a particularly questionable form of countermajoritarian judicial activism.[60] They maintain that "if the Court overruled *Garcia* and sought once again to enforce the Tenth Amendment, it would face a lot of political heat."[61] Because the Court may have "more freedom to interpret statutes to thwart legislative expectations

---

[55] Eskridge and Frickey, "Quasi-Constitutional Law," 597.
[56] Ibid., 633.
[57] Ibid. (quoting GARCIA V. SAN ANTONIO METROPOLITAN TRANSIT AUTHORITY, 469 U.S. 528, 550 [1985]).
[58] Ibid.
[59] Ibid., 635.
[60] Ibid., 636; see also ibid., 598 (stating that "the Court's new canons amount to a 'backdoor' version of the constitutional activism that most Justices on the current Court have publicly denounced").
[61] Ibid., 637.

than it does to strike them down,"[62] the Court's use of a clear statement rule in
Gregory may amount to greater activism than direct enforcement of a constitutional rule. These concerns are amplified, they point out, because clear statement rules cannot "be rebutted through reference to the circumstances of the
legislation, including legislative history."[63] Rather, such rules "require rebut-
tal on the face of, or by implication from, the statute itself."[64] For this reason,
they believe that "the Court's new super-strong clear statement rules are
extraordinarily countermajoritarian."[65]

Third, commentators argue that the modern clear statement rules cannot
be "defended as justifiable activism"[66] because they "reflect an overall constitutional vision that is strikingly old-fashioned."[67] As relevant to this discussion, they argue that under modern clear statement rules, "[o]rdering by
private elites is preferred over governmental intrusion," and "state power is
preferred over national power."[68] On the first point, they believe that clear
statement rules favoring private ordering reflect "*Lochner*-era baselines, in
which governmental regulation was the exception rather than the rule."[69]
On the second point, they maintain that "the Court has not grappled with
the truly difficult issue of why federalism . . . should not be sacrificed when
individual rights and public policies are at stake."[70] For these reasons, they
regard the values protected by modern clear statement rules as "constitutionally unworthy."[71]

Other scholars have raised distinct concerns based on originalism and
textualism. For example, one scholar has marshaled impressive historical
evidence that the Supremacy Clause was designed to be a "*non obstante*
clause*," signaling judges to give a federal "statute its natural meaning and
let it displace whatever law it contradicted."[72] This understanding, he maintains, "undermines the artificial presumption against preemption."[73] A leading textualist has also questioned the propriety of clear statement rules on

---

[62] Ibid.
[63] Ibid., 637–8.
[64] Ibid., 638.
[65] Ibid.
[66] Ibid., 640.
[67] Ibid.
[68] Ibid.
[69] Ibid., 642.
[70] Ibid., 643–4.
[71] Ibid., 598. Professors Eskridge and Frickey do not foreclose the use of clear statement rules
altogether. Rather, they suggest that they should be used only to protect "particularly important constitutional values." Ibid., 597.
[72] Nelson, "Preemption," 232.
[73] Ibid.

grounds of legislative supremacy. The argument is that "clear statement rules sometimes require judges to reject the most natural reading of a statute in favor of a plausible but less conventional interpretation."[74] Such an approach is arguably inconsistent with a central premise of textualism that judges should accept the semantic meaning of the enacted text as written if it is sufficiently clear in context, without regard to extratextual considerations such as the statute's underlying purpose or legislative history.[75] "If textualists believe . . . that statutes mean what a reasonable person would conventionally understand them to mean, then applying a less natural (though still plausible) interpretation is arguably unfaithful to the legislative instructions contained in the statute."[76] Arguably, textualist judges have not adequately addressed these concerns, and "there is room to demand further justification for the textualists' selection and application of particular clear statement rules."[77]

A PROCESS-BASED APPROACH

At least some of the objections to the presumption against preemption and a limited clear statement requirement can be alleviated by tying these doctrines more closely to the Supremacy Clause and the procedural safeguards of federalism that it incorporates. Critics charge that presumptions and clear statement rules further a set of substantive values that cannot be readily defended on their merits. Although these devices certainly may be (mis)used in this way, the constitutional structure appears to support a narrower, yet important, conception of these devices as a means of ensuring compliance with the exclusive federal lawmaking procedures established by the Constitution for adopting "the supreme Law of the Land." Using constitutionally prescribed lawmaking procedures to understand – and limit – these doctrines avoids many of the most serious objections associated with their more ambitious counterparts. At the same time, the constitutional structure suggests that courts should take care not to use process-based presumptions or clear statement rules in ways that distort the legislative process or undermine legislative supremacy.

---

[74] Manning, "Textualism," 123.

[75] See John F. Manning, "What Divides Textualists from Purposivists?" COLUMBIA LAW REVIEW 106, no. 1 (2006): 70, 91.

[76] Manning, "Textualism," 124. Similarly, some scholars have suggested that clear statement rules undermine legislative supremacy by encouraging willful misconstructions of federal statutes. See Jerry L. Mashaw, GREED, CHAOS, AND GOVERNANCE: USING PUBLIC CHOICE TO IMPROVE PUBLIC LAW (New Haven, CT: Yale University Press, 1997), 105.

[77] Manning, "Textualism," 126.

The first objection raised is that clear statement rules lack coherence because they protect underenforced or even unenforced constitutional norms. Commentators cite *Gregory v. Ashcroft* as an example because that case contains language suggesting that the Court used a clear statement rule to "avoid a potential constitutional problem" arising from federal regulation of state judges under the Commerce Clause.[78] As others have pointed out, this suggestion makes little sense in light of *Garcia*'s suggestion that there are few, if any, judicially enforceable limits on Congress's exercise of the Commerce power to regulate states. *Gregory*, however, also offered a second, more persuasive rationale for applying a limited, process-based clear statement rule.

The Court suggested that, in the face of statutory ambiguity, a clear statement requirement is necessary in order to ensure compliance with federal lawmaking procedures and to protect the residual authority of the states under the Supremacy Clause. As the Court explained, "inasmuch as this Court in *Garcia* has left primarily to the political process the protection of the States against intrusive exercises of Congress' Commerce Clause powers, we must be absolutely certain that Congress intended such an exercise."[79] Quoting Professor Laurence Tribe, the Court explained that "to give the state-displacing weight of federal law to mere congressional *ambiguity* would evade the very procedure for lawmaking on which *Garcia* relied to protect states' interests."[80] Thus, as Tribe subsequently observed, *Gregory*'s clear statement rule "ensures the efficacy of the procedural political safeguards that were *Garcia*'s focus."[81] As discussed in the following text, however, *Gregory* arguably went too far by suggesting that Congress must speak with absolute clarity.

Understood – and limited – in this way, *Gregory*'s clear statement rule is not only coherent, but also arguably necessary to implement the operation of the procedural and political safeguards of federalism built into the Supremacy Clause. The Court found that the text of the ADEA was ambiguous as to whether it applied to state judges. The question for the Court, therefore, was whether to allow an ambiguous federal statute to preempt state law or to conclude that mere ambiguity is not enough to trigger the operation of the Supremacy Clause. A clear statement rule ensures that courts will reach the latter conclusion. If judges permit an ambiguous provision of a federal statute to preempt state law, they risk circumventing federal lawmaking procedures and the political safeguards they

---

[78] 501 U.S. at 464.

[79] Ibid.

[80] Ibid. (quoting Laurence H. Tribe, AMERICAN CONSTITUTIONAL LAW § 6-25 [Mineola, NY: Foundation Press, 2nd ed., 1988]).

[81] Laurence H. Tribe, 1 AMERICAN CONSTITUTIONAL LAW § 5-11 (New York: Foundation Press, 3rd. ed., 2000).

incorporate. As one commentator put it, process rules of this kind reinforce "institutional checks by requiring Congress to make the decision, with all the procedural hurdles and roadblocks that process entails."[82]

This understanding of *Gregory*'s clear statement rule requires courts to undertake the difficult task of deciding when a statute is sufficiently clear to trigger preemption and when it is so ambiguous as to leave state law undisturbed. As applied to novel or unanticipated circumstances, all laws are more or less indeterminate.[83] Thus, in the course of applying statutes, courts necessarily engage in some degree of interstitial norm elaboration. The need for such elaboration, however, does not give courts free reign to engage in open-ended federal lawmaking.[84] Unlike Congress and the president, federal courts are structured to be independent of the political safeguards of federalism and are given no express role in federal lawmaking by the Constitution. For these reasons, courts should arguably be "confined from molar to molecular motions"[85] in expanding the scope of potentially applicable, but ambiguous, federal statutes. Although deciding where legitimate interpretation ends and improper lawmaking begins may be a difficult task, drawing some distinction of this kind is required by the constitutional structure and does not appear to be beyond judicial competence. Courts already perform an analogous task in deciding whether to give agency interpretations of federal statutes *Chevron* deference[86] and could borrow the analysis from *Chevron* step one for these purposes.

---

[82] Ernest A. Young, "Two Cheers for Process Federalism," VILLANOVA LAW REVIEW 46, no. 5 (2001): 1349, 1385.

[83] See H. L. A. Hart, THE CONCEPT OF LAW (Oxford, UK: Clarendon Press, 2nd ed., 1994), 127–8; see also THE FEDERALIST, no. 37 (James Madison), 229. ("All new laws, though penned with the greatest technical skill and passed on the fullest and most mature deliberation, are considered as more or less obscure and equivocal, until their meaning be liquidated and ascertained by a series of particular discussions and adjudications.")

[84] Professor Meltzer has recently questioned the Supreme Court's "selective judicial passivity," involving contemporaneous efforts to reduce the role of judicial lawmaking in some areas while expanding it in others. He observes that in decisions involving statutory preemption, "the Supreme Court has been willing to recognize in the federal courts a broad lawmaking power, based upon policy judgments about how best to further the purposes of federal enactments." Daniel J. Meltzer, "The Supreme Court's Judicial Passivity," SUPREME COURT REVIEW (2002): 343–4.

[85] SOUTHERN PACIFIC CO. V. JENSEN, 244 U.S. 205, 221 (1917) (Holmes, J., dissenting). ("I recognize without hesitation that judges do and must legislate, but they can do so only interstitially; they are confined from molar to molecular motions.")

[86] See CHEVRON U.S.A., INC. V. NATURAL RESOURCES DEFENSE COUNCIL, INC., 467 U.S. 837 (1984). Federal courts also routinely decide whether state law is so unclear as to warrant certification to the state's highest court. See Bradford R. Clark, "Ascertaining the Laws of the Several States: Positivism and Judicial Federalism after ERIE," UNIVERSITY OF PENNSYLVANIA LAW REVIEW 145, no. 6 (1997): 1459, 1544–9.

A second objection to clear statement rules is that they represent a form of countermajoritarian judicial activism. It may be useful to break this objection down into its constituent parts. The charge of judicial activism holds when the Court uses clear statement rules to import extraconstitutional values into their decisions. *Gregory* is open to this charge to the extent that the Court imposed a clear statement requirement simply as a means of circumventing *Garcia*. To the extent that *Gregory* used a clear statement rule to ensure the operation of the procedural and political safeguards of federalism, however, such use is harder to characterize as judicial activism. After all, the Constitution prescribes these safeguards, and the *Garcia* Court premised its decision on the assumption that they continue to perform their intended function.[87] From this perspective, a narrowly tailored, process-based clear statement rule does not further extraconstitutional values but merely fosters compliance with constitutionally prescribed lawmaking procedures.

Critics also object that clear statement rules are countermajoritarian. Inherent in this objection is the notion that such rules make it harder for Congress and the president to change the status quo. Clear statement rules encourage legislative commands to appear with clarity on the face of a duly-enacted statute. The constitutionally prescribed process of bicameralism and presentment creates multiple "veto gates" that make it difficult for clear statements to become law. Accordingly, commentators point out that "the legislative process offers numerous opportunities for determined minorities to thwart" legislative efforts to enact clear statements that would satisfy the Supreme Court.[88] In addition, they stress that when the president and the Court are aligned on issues "against the preferences of Congress, an override of a Supreme Court statutory decision requires the same supermajorities in Congress that a constitutional amendment requires."[89] Thus, commentators stress that "even ordinary clear statement rules are particularly countermajoritarian, because they permit the Court to override probable congressional preferences in statutory interpretation in favor of norms and values favored by the Court."[90]

To be sure, super-clear statement requirements are open to this charge because they make it harder for Congress and the president to legislate. It is useful to keep in mind, however, that even the ordinary procedures established by the Constitution for enacting "Laws" are countermajoritarian by

---

[87] See Tribe, 1 AMERICAN CONSTITUTIONAL LAW, § 5-11 (stating that "GREGORY set out the constitutional principles assumed by GARCIA and used them to justify its clear statement rule").

[88] Eskridge and Frickey, "Quasi-Constitutional Law," 640.

[89] Ibid., 639.

[90] Ibid., 638.

design. The House of Representatives is the most representative participant in the lawmaking process, but the Constitution does not permit it to enact laws on its own. It must obtain the assent of the Senate (the least-representative participant in the process) and ordinarily the president as well. The Senate was designed to represent the states, not the people. Each state has equal suffrage in the Senate regardless of population,[91] and this feature of the Constitution cannot be amended by ordinary means.[92] Thus, any process that requires the Senate's approval will necessarily be countermajoritarian because it gives disproportionate power to senators from small states.

This countermajoritarian effect is only enhanced by the constitutional requirement of bicameralism and presentment. Giving three actors a role – and therefore a veto – in the lawmaking process creates the effect of a powerful supermajority requirement that frequently operates to thwart the will of the majority. As the Supreme Court explained in affirming the exclusivity of these procedures, however, the Founders adopted these procedures precisely because they are countermajoritarian: "The choices we discern as having been made in the Constitutional Convention impose burdens on governmental processes that often seem clumsy, inefficient, even unworkable, but those hard choices were consciously made by men who had lived under a form of government that permitted arbitrary governmental acts to go unchecked."[93] In addition, the Founders assumed that states would continue to play their traditional and complementary role of providing background rules to govern society in the absence of applicable federal law. Under these circumstances, courts cannot be accused of improperly thwarting the will of the majority by using clear statement rules solely to ensure compliance with federal lawmaking procedures.

A third objection to at least some clear statement rules is that they reflect old-fashioned constitutional values unworthy of protection: "Ordering by private elites is preferred over governmental intrusion[, and] state power is preferred over national power."[94] To be sure, a super-clear statement requirement may overprotect these values. To some extent, however, the constitutional design protects these values. The interaction of the Supremacy Clause and federal lawmaking procedures creates a significant burden of inertia and makes it difficult for the federal government to adopt "the supreme Law of the Land." These procedures necessarily favor the status quo by frequently rendering the federal government incapable of adopting federal law.

[91] U.S. Const., art. I, § 3, cl.1.
[92] Ibid., art. V.
[93] CHADHA, 462 U.S. at 959.
[94] Eskridge and Frickey, "Quasi-Constitutional Law," 640.

Historically, the status quo tended to consist of state law and private order-ing.[95] Today, the status quo increasingly includes preexisting federal law. Thus, to the extent that a clear statement rule ensures compliance with federal lawmaking procedures, it necessarily favors the status quo, which still reflects private ordering and state law in many areas. But this phenomenon is attributable not to the operation of a process-based clear statement rule but to the underlying constitutional procedures upheld by the rule. The Founders put these procedures in place specifically to guard against excessive federal regulation. In this sense, the status quo may be old-fashioned, but it is not necessarily illegitimate.

Using a process-based approach to define – and limit – clear statement rules also helps to alleviate the concerns raised by originalists and textualists. There is a strong argument that the Supremacy Clause precludes application of an "artificial presumption against preemption" – that is, application of the presump-tion "even to federal statutory provisions that plainly *do* manifest an 'inten[t] to supplant state law.' "[96] Such (mis)use of the presumption against preemption is not required – or even permitted – by federal lawmaking procedures. Rather, such procedures favor applying state law only when a federal statute is ambig-uous as to whether Congress and the president meant to override state law. "[W]hen it is clear that Congress *is* entering a field traditionally occupied by the states, there is no automatic reason to adopt a 'narrow reading' of the words that Congress enacts."[97] In such cases, the Supremacy Clause requires state law to yield, and presumptions and clear statement rules are inapposite.

For similar reasons, a heightened clear statement requirement "is arguably unfaithful to the legislative instructions contained in the statute."[98] As dis-cussed, process-based clear statement rules should be used only to the extent necessary to ensure compliance with constitutionally prescribed lawmaking procedures. If the statute is clear in context, then courts should apply the statute faithfully and disregard contrary state law under the Supremacy Clause. A *super*-clear statement (of the kind *Gregory* suggests) is not required by federal lawmaking procedures and seems to contradict them by imposing unwarranted decision costs. The goal of interpretation is to determine whether the enacted text reveals that the participants in the lawmaking process faced the relevant question and resolved it in an intelligible way. Imposing "a

---

[95] See Frank H. Easterbrook, "Statutes' Domains," University of Chicago Law Review 50, no. 2 (1983): 533, 549. ("Those who wrote and approved the Constitution thought that most social relations would be governed by private agreements, customs, and understandings, not resolved in the halls of government.")

[96] Nelson, "Preemption," 291.

[97] Ibid., 301.

[98] Manning, "Textualism," 124.

super clear statement, 'magic words' requirement" is neither required by nor consistent with federal lawmaking procedures.[99]

By contrast, when a federal statute is not sufficiently clear to conclude that lawmakers have faced and resolved the relevant issue through the legislative process, a court might reasonably conclude that the statute does not supply an applicable rule of decision and thus does not preempt state law.[100] It is now widely acknowledged that certain types of ambiguity can only be resolved through a form of subsidiary lawmaking. This is the central premise of *Chevron*. One can argue about where ambiguity ends and clarity begins, but some judgments necessarily require interpreters to exercise a significant degree of policy-making discretion – that is, to fill in large gaps left by the statute. In such cases, courts should ask themselves whether attempts to answer such questions risk circumventing the political and procedural safeguards built into the Supremacy Clause. This is not the occasion to resolve all facets of this problem, but the question goes to the heart of the interpretive enterprise in a federal system.

Several cases suggest how courts might employ a process-based presumption against preemption or similarly limited clear statement rule. As discussed, in *Gregory v. Ashcroft*, the Supreme Court confronted the question whether the ADEA preempted a state constitutional requirement that state judges retire at age seventy.[101] The case turned on whether state judges were exempt as appointees "on the policymaking level" – a question susceptible of more than one reasonable answer. Historically, state judges were not thought of in these terms, but modern conceptions – informed by the rise of positivism and legal realism – recognize that state judges exercise substantial policy-making discretion. Had the *Gregory* Court allowed this ambiguous federal statute to override the state's retirement age for judges, it would have risked circumventing the political and procedural safeguards of federalism built into the Supremacy Clause. There simply appeared to be insufficient evidence on the face of the ADEA to conclude that the House, the Senate, and the president had decided to cover state judges. In *Gregory*, application of the traditional presumption against preemption arguably would have sufficed to ensure that actors subject to the political safeguards of federalism – rather than judges – make the crucial decision to override state

---

[99] IMMIGRATION AND NATURALIZATION SERVICE V. ST. CYR, 533 U.S. 289, 327 (2001) (Scalia, J., dissenting). The Court sometimes uses heightened clear statement rules to avoid difficult constitutional questions or to further particular substantive constitutional values. These practices are controversial and whatever their merits, they cannot be justified simply as a means of implementing federal lawmaking procedures.

[100] Cf. Easterbrook, "Statutes' Domains," 544. ("Unless the party relying on the statute could establish either express resolution or creation of the common law power of revision, the court would hold the matter in question outside the statute's domain.")

[101] 501 U.S. 452.

law. The Court's language, however, went considerably farther by suggesting that the ADEA need not be merely clear, but "unmistakably" clear "to anyone reading the Act." Such a super-strong clear statement rule not only is unnecessary to implement federal lawmaking procedures but also threatens legislative supremacy by unduly curtailing the ordinary effect of clear federal statutes.

The use of process-based presumptions and clear statement rules to evaluate administrative interpretations of federal statutes is somewhat more complex. In *Chevron*, the Supreme Court announced its familiar two-step analysis. "If the intent of Congress is clear," then "the court, as well as the agency, must give effect to the unambiguously expressed intent of Congress."[102] However, "if the statute is silent or ambiguous with respect to the specific issue," then courts must defer to the agency's reasonable interpretation of the statute.[103] Such *Chevron* deference is arguably inconsistent with a process-based presumption against preemption or limited clear statement rule because, as originally conceived, *Chevron* treats statutory ambiguity as an implied delegation to the agency to fill in the gap.[104] Although the Court has yet to resolve many issues relating to regulatory preemption,[105] it may be moving away from the implied delegation model and toward what Cass Sunstein sees as a constitutionally inspired nondelegation cannon – "the idea that administrative agencies will not be allowed to interpret ambiguous provisions so as to preempt state law."[106]

---

[102] CHEVRON, 467 U.S. at 842–3.

[103] Ibid., 843.

[104] See ibid., 844. One might conclude, as Judge Easterbrook has, that courts should declare "legislation inapplicable unless it either expressly addresses the matter or commits the matter to the common law (or administrative) process." Easterbrook, "Statutes' Domains," 552. Such express delegations might raise questions under the nondelegation doctrine but would at least ensure that Congress and the president made a conscious decision to delegate the matter. Alternatively, Nina Mendelson has suggested retaining the presumption against preemption in the administrative context by replacing CHEVRON deference with SKIDMORE deference. See Nina A. Mendelson, "CHEVRON and Preemption," MICHIGAN LAW REVIEW 102, no. 5 (2004): 737. Professors Verchick and Mendelson, in Chapter 1, and Professor Funk, in Chapter 10, offer further reflections on the question of judicial deference to agency assertions of preemptive power.

[105] See Catherine M. Sharkey, "Preemption by Preamble: Federal Agencies and the Federalization of Tort Law," DEPAUL LAW REVIEW 56, no. 2 (2007): 227, 243–5. Many observers thought that the Supreme Court would address some of these questions in WATTERS V. WACHOVIA BANK, N.A., 127 S. Ct. 1559 (2007), but the Court declined to consider "the dangers of vesting preemptive authority in administrative agencies" because it concluded that the underlying statute preempted state law, ibid., 1572 n. 13.

[106] Cass R. Sunstein, "Nondelegation Canons," UNIVERSITY OF CHICAGO LAW REVIEW 67, no. 2 (2000): 315, 331; see also Eskridge, "Vetogates" (exploring the relationship between legislative vetogates and CHEVRON deference). Cf. MEDTRONIC, 518 U.S. at 512 (O'Connor, J., concurring in part and dissenting in part). ("Apparently recognizing that CHEVRON deference is unwarranted here, the Court does not admit to deferring to these regulations, but merely permits them to 'infor[m]' the Court's interpretation.")

For example, in *United States v. Mead Corp.*,[107] the Supreme Court refused to give *Chevron* deference to a tariff classification ruling by the U.S. Customs Service because there was "no indication that Congress intended such a ruling to carry the force of law."[108] The Court subsequently relied on *Mead* in *Gonzales v. Oregon*[109] to reject federal regulatory preemption of state law. There, the Court considered "whether the Controlled Substances Act ['CSA'] allows the U.S. Attorney General to prohibit doctors from prescribing regulated drugs for use in physician-assisted suicide, notwithstanding a state law permitting the procedure."[110] Under the act, physicians must obtain a "registration" from the attorney general in order to issue lawful prescriptions of Schedule II drugs.[111] The act authorizes the attorney general to deny, suspend, or revoke this registration if such registration would be "inconsistent with the public interest."[112] Attorney General Ashcroft issued an Interpretive Rule stating that assisting suicide is not a legitimate medical purpose, and that "[s]uch conduct by a physician . . . may 'render his registration . . . inconsistent with the public interest' and therefore subject to possible suspension or revocation."[113] The state of Oregon, joined by medical professionals, challenged this Interpretive Rule.

Notwithstanding the broad language of the act, the Supreme Court refused to give the Interpretive Rule *Chevron* deference on the ground that the CSA "does not authorize the Attorney General to bar dispensing controlled substances for assisted suicide in the face of a state medical regime permitting such conduct."[114] In reaching "this commonsense conclusion," the Court stated that it was unnecessary "to consider the application of clear statement requirements or presumptions against pre-emption."[115] Elsewhere in its

---

[107] UNITED STATES V. MEAD CORP., 533 U.S. 218 (2001).
[108] Ibid., 221. The Court held that the agency's ruling was entitled only to so-called SKIDMORE deference, under which "the ruling is eligible to claim respect according to its persuasiveness." Ibid. (citing SKIDMORE V. SWIFT AND CO., 323 U.S. 134 [1944]).
[109] 546 U.S. 243.
[110] Ibid., 248–9.
[111] 21 U.S.C. § 822(a)(2).
[112] 21 U.S.C. § 824(a)(4); § 822(a)(2). In making this determination, the act provides that the attorney general "shall" consider five statutory factors. See ibid. § 823(f).
[113] 66 FEDERAL REGISTER 56,608 (2001).
[114] 546 U.S. at 274–5; see also ibid., 268 (stating that "the CSA does not give the Attorney General authority to issue the Interpretive Rule as a statement with the force of law"). For this reason, the Court thought that the Interpretive Rule was entitled only to SKIDMORE deference, and ultimately found the attorney general's opinion to be unpersuasive.
[115] Ibid., 274 (internal citations omitted).

opinion, however, the Court seemed to be influenced by considerations of just this kind.[116] For example, according to the Court, the attorney general's interpretation would have read the CSA to delegate "to a single Executive officer the power to affect a radical shift of authority from the States to the Federal Government."[117] The Court required a delegation of this magnitude to be explicit – rather than implicit – in the text of the statute.[118] The Court invoked the "importance of the issue" to suggest that Congress did not have the requisite intent to delegate the authority in question.[119] Similarly, near the end of its opinion the Court noted that "the background principles of our federal system also belie the notion that Congress would use such an obscure grant of authority to regulate areas traditionally supervised by the States' police power."[120] The absence of clearer statutory language authorizing the attorney general to issue an Interpretive Rule with the force of federal law led the Court to reject *Chevron* deference in this context.[121]

Although the Court offered a variety of reasons as to why the CSA should not be interpreted to authorize the attorney general's action, one suspects that the Court ultimately concluded that the decision by the federal government to outlaw assisted suicide in the states should be made by the House, the Senate, and the president pursuant to federal lawmaking procedures rather than by the attorney general acting alone. In this sense, *Gonzales v. Oregon* illustrates process-based preemption and appears to be defensible on that very basis. Because a duly-enacted statute did not clearly authorize the attorney general to preempt state assisted-suicide laws, the Court refused to interpret –

---

[116] See ibid., 270 (stating that the act's failure to manifest any intent to regulate the practice of medicine generally "is understandable given the structure and limitations of federalism, which allow the States great latitude under their police powers to legislate as to the protection of the lives, limbs, health, comfort, and quiet of all persons") (internal quotations omitted).

[117] Ibid., 275.

[118] Ibid., 267. ("The idea that Congress gave the Attorney General such broad and unusual authority through an implicit delegation in the CSA's registration provision is not sustainable.")

[119] Ibid. ("The importance of the issue of physician-assisted suicide, which has been the subject of an 'earnest and profound debate' across the country, . . . makes the oblique form of the claimed delegation all the more suspect." [quoting WASHINGTON V. GLUCKSBERG, 521 U.S. 702, 735 (1997)]).

[120] Ibid., 274.

[121] The Court seemed to acknowledge that the attorney general's "understanding of medicine's boundaries is at least reasonable," ibid., 272, but thought that Congress must legislate more specifically in order to extend the CSA's regulation, ibid., 273–5. In dissent, Justice Scalia argued that "the Attorney General's independent interpretation of the statutory phrase 'public interest'" is entitled to CHEVRON deference. Ibid., 276 (Scalia, J., dissenting).

or allow the attorney general to interpret – the statute to do so.[122] From this perspective, *Gonzales v. Oregon* is consistent with *Gregory v. Ashcroft* – Attorney General Ashcroft lost for the same reason that Governor Ashcroft won in the earlier case. As Professor Sunstein observes, the federal government has power to preempt state law in areas like these, but "the preemption decision must be made legislatively, not bureaucratically."[123] In his view, "[t]he constitutional source of this principle is the evident constitutional commitment to a federal structure, a commitment that may not be compromised without a congressional decision to do so – an important requirement in light of the various safeguards against cavalier disregard of state interests created by the system of state representation in Congress."[124]

CONCLUSION

The presumption against preemption and the related clear statement requirement have been criticized on the grounds that they constitute judicial activism, and that they undermine legislative supremacy. Properly limited, however, such interpretive devices may be used to implement constitutionally prescribed lawmaking procedures by ensuring that Congress and the president – rather than judges – make the crucial decision to override state law. The Constitution prescribes cumbersome and exclusive procedures to govern the adoption of all forms of supreme federal law. By design, these procedures rely solely on actors – the House, the Senate, and the president – subject to the political safeguards of federalism. A presumption against preemption and a limited, process-based clear statement requirement arguably prevent judges from circumventing these safeguards by limiting the ability of ambiguous federal statutes to displace state law.

---

[122] See Eskridge, "Vetogates," 1469–72 (discussing and defending the outcome in GONZALES V. OREGON); see also Clark, "Separation of Powers," 1438. ("Applying CHEVRON deference in this context . . . risks circumventing the very lawmaking procedures that the Constitution prescribes to adopt 'the supreme Law of the Land' and safeguard federalism.")

[123] Sunstein, "Nondelegation Canons," 331.

[124] Ibid.

10 Preemption by Federal Agency Action

William Funk

Although preemption questions often occur in contexts unrelated to federal agency action, preemption has also occurred as a result of federal agency action since at least *Gibbons v. Ogden*.[1] In *Gibbons*, the first Supreme Court case to assess the extent of the Commerce Clause of the Constitution, the Court held that a license to engage in the coastal trade given to Ogden by a federal agency preempted the New York law granting a monopoly to Gibbons for the use of steamboats in New York.

Today, as a result of the growth of the administrative state, most preemption questions involve federal agencies in some way. Most recently, the failure of the Republican Congress to enact meaningful tort reform at the national level led the Bush administration to attempt to achieve similar ends by preempting state tort law through administrative actions.[2] Increasingly, federal agencies in regulations, preambles to regulations, or amicus briefs are purporting to decide whether their regulations (or their failure to regulate) preempt state common law tort actions. The Food and Drug Administration (FDA) has received the most press on this issue, having filed amicus briefs in several tort cases supporting industry claims of preemption as well as asserting in a preamble to a regulation that the regulation preempted certain state tort law.[3] Other agencies have

---

[1]   22 U.S. 1 (1824).

[2]   See, e.g., Margaret Clune, Center for Progressive Reform, STEALTH TORT REFORM: HOW THE BUSH ADMINISTRATION'S AGGRESSIVE USE OF THE PREEMPTION DOCTRINE HURTS CONSUMERS (October 2004), available at http://www.progressiveregulation.org/articles/preemption.pdf; Nina A. Mendelson, "Chevron and Preemption," MICHIGAN LAW REVIEW 102 (2004): 737; Catherine M. Sharkey, "Preemption by Preamble: Federal Agencies and the Federalization of Tort Law," DEPAUL LAW REVIEW 56 (2007): 227; Catherine M. Sharkey, "Federalism in Action: FDA Regulatory Preemption in Pharmaceutical Cases in State Versus Federal Court," JOURNAL OF LAW AND SOCIAL POLICY 15 (2007): 1013.

[3]   Requirements on Content and Format of Labeling for Human Prescription Drug and Biological Products, 71 FEDERAL REGISTER 3922 (January 24, 2006).

taken similar actions. For example, in 2005 the National Highway Traffic Safety Administration (NHTSA) stated in the preamble to its proposed regulation setting roof crush-resistance requirements for automobiles that it would preempt state common law;[4] in 2006 the Consumer Product Safety Commission (CPSC) included a statement in the preamble to its new mattress-flammability standards that they would preempt state common law;[5] and in 2005 the Federal Railroad Administration adopted a regulation regarding requirements for reflectors on railroad cars that included a boilerplate provision preempting any state "law, rule, regulation, or order" covering the same matter but included in the preamble an explication of why the agency interpreted that provision likewise to preempt state common law actions.[6] The possibility of significant restrictions on traditional state common law remedies by agency action without express congressional authorization raises serious federalism concerns.

This chapter addresses the legal doctrines applicable to when and how federal agencies may preempt state law and the major questions that remain unanswered by existing Supreme Court precedent. In particular, one unanswered question is when and to what extent courts should give deference to agency statements regarding preemption. This chapter suggests that deference should only be given when Congress has explicitly delegated preemptive authority to the agency. Another unanswered question is whether a grant of substantive rulemaking authority should be construed as a grant of authority to an agency to make preemption determinations. This chapter argues that it should not and also includes a discussion of the presidential executive order relating to federal agency action that preempts state law. The chapter then turns to recent agency attempts to preempt state tort law and explains to what extent those attempts should be honored.

PREEMPTION AND AGENCY ACTION

Agency action may preempt state law in either of two ways. First, and most typically, an agency may adopt a regulation (or issue an order after an adjudication) that simply has the effect of preempting state law due to a direct conflict that arises between federal law and state law. An example would be the situation in *United States v. Locke*.[7] There the secretary of transportation,

---

[4]   Proposed Rules, Federal Motor Vehicle Safety Standards; Roof Crush Resistance, 70 FEDERAL REGISTER 49223 (August 23, 2005).

[5]   Final Rule: Standard for the Flammability (Open Flame) of Mattress Sets, 71 FEDERAL REGISTER 200671 (March 15, 2006).

[6]   Reflectorization of Rail Freight Rolling Stock, 70 FEDERAL REGISTER 144, 152 (Jan. 3, 2005).

[7]   529 U.S. 89 (2000).

pursuant to the federal Ports and Waterways Safety Act, adopted regulations governing the "design, construction, alteration, repair, maintenance, operation, equipping, personnel qualification, and manning of vessels."[8] Subsequently, the state of Washington adopted regulations requiring, among other things, that the crews of tankers entering Puget Sound have received a specified amount of training that was not the same as required by federal regulations. The Supreme Court held that the federal regulations preempted the state regulations. In this case, neither the agency nor its regulations said anything regarding preemption, and in reaching its decision, the Supreme Court did not consider the views of the agency, if it had any.

The second way an agency may preempt state law is to adopt a regulation or order that by its terms preempts state law. This is relatively unusual, but it does happen. For example, pursuant to the Hazardous Material Transportation Act,[9] the secretary of transportation decided that certain Nevada regulations requiring an annual permit of railroads before they might load or unload hazardous materials in the state were preempted by the secretary's regulations governing the transportation of such materials.[10]

The difference between these two types of preemption is that the former involves the agency taking some substantive regulatory action pursuant to a statute, and the preemptive effect of that action is governed by the statute – either through an express preemption provision in the statute or through application of the Court's doctrine of implied preemption. The latter type of preemption, however, involves the agency determining the preemptive effect of its regulations or a statute it administers. In either case, Congress must grant authority to the agency to take the action it did. In the usual case, a statute's grant of authority to an agency to take certain actions can implicitly or explicitly include the preemption of state law.[11] For example, the Medical Device Amendments of 1976 (MDAs) expressly preempt any state and local requirement that is different from or additional to any requirement relating to medical devices adopted by the FDA under the act. Thus, a requirement adopted by the FDA automatically preempts different or additional state or local requirements. Even in the absence of an applicable express preemption provision, courts may find that the statutory authority to adopt substantive regulations implicitly authorizes preemption of conflicting state and local regulations pursuant to judicial preemption doctrine.[12]

---

[8]   46 U.S.C. § 3703(a) as construed in RAY v. ATLANTIC RICHFIELD CO., 435 U.S. 151 (1978).
[9]   49 U.S.C. 5125(d).
[10] See SOUTHERN PACIFIC TRANSP. CO. v. PUBLIC SERVICE COM'N OF NEVADA, 909 F.2d 352 (9th Cir. 1990).
[11] See, e.g., FIDELITY FED. SAV. AND LOAN ASS'N v. DE LA CUESTA, 458 U.S. 141, 153–4 (1982).
[12] See, e.g., UNITED STATES v. SHIMER, 367 U.S. 374, 381–2 (1961).

In both of these situations, however, although Congress delegates the authority to the agency to determine what substantive policies are appropriate to carry out the statutory mandate, the appropriate preemptive effect of the agency actions remains a matter of judicial determination, either by interpretation of the statute or by application of judicial preemption doctrine.

Occasionally, Congress expressly delegates to an agency the authority to make preemption determinations. For example, the Federal Communications Act provides that the Federal Communications Commission (FCC), after notice and an opportunity for public comment, shall preempt any state law that the commission finds has the effect of prohibiting the ability of any entity to provide any interstate or intrastate telecommunications service.[13] Similarly, in the case noted in the preceding text in which the secretary of transportation ruled that certain Nevada regulations were preempted by the Hazardous Materials Transportation Act, that act specifically granted authority to the secretary to make preemption determinations.[14] In this type of situation, where Congress has delegated to the agency the authority to make the preemption determination, the preemption question is not one simply of statutory interpretation or application of preemption doctrine. Rather it is a typical administrative law question – whether the agency has acted arbitrarily or capriciously within its delegated power.[15]

In the most common type of judicial case involving agency action and preemption, the issue is whether the agency's substantive regulation does have the effect of preempting a particular state law. This may be due to a lack of clarity in an express preemption provision, such as in *Wisconsin v. Mortier*,[16] where it was not clear if the statutory preemption provision in the Federal Insecticide, Fungicide, and Rodenticide Act (FIFRA) relating to "states" also applied to units of local governments. Another recurring example of a lack of clarity in an express preemption provision is a prohibition against state "requirements or prohibitions" different from federal requirements, and the issue is whether state tort law constitutes a state "requirement" or "prohibition." This was an issue in *Cipollone v. Liggett Group, Inc.*,[17] involving a tort action against a cigarette manufacturer that had complied with federal labeling requirements. In these cases, courts must interpret the meaning and extent of the statutory preemption provision. In the former case, the

---

[13] See, e.g., 47 U.S.C. § 253(d) (authorizing FCC to determine that a state or local law is preempted).
[14] See 49 U.S.C. App. 1811(b)(1988), repealed and replaced by 49 U.S.C. 5125(d).
[15] See 5 U.S.C. § 706(2)(A).
[16] 501 U.S. 597 (1991).
[17] 505 U.S. 504 (1992).

Court held that the term "state" did not include local governments, so that local government regulation of pesticides was not preempted. In the latter case, the Court held that the term "requirements and prohibitions" in that statute did include the duties imposed by state tort law, resulting in the preemption of certain state tort law claims against cigarette manufacturers for a failure to warn of the dangers of smoking.

Where there is no express preemption provision, whether an agency's regulation preempts state law turns on an application of the Supreme Court's implied preemption doctrine. Where there is a direct, unavoidable conflict between the agency's regulation and state law, almost invariably courts will find preemption, presuming that Congress would intend federal law to govern over conflicting state law. It is a more difficult decision when there is no direct conflict, but the allegation is that the "state law stands as an obstacle to the accomplishment and execution of the full purposes and objectives of Congress."[18] For example, in *Geier v. American Honda Motor Co.*,[19] the Court found that a state tort action holding a manufacturer liable for not having provided an air bag was preempted, because such an action would interfere with the full accomplishment of the federal automobile safety program. Here, the Department of Transportation (DOT) had considered requiring air bags but instead decided on a phased-in approach to passive restraints. That is, DOT decided that the best means of furthering the statute's purpose was not to require air bags at that time. The Court held that to allow a state to maintain a tort claim for a failure to provide air bags would thwart that regulatory decision. This is an example of a court finding that an agency made a substantive policy decision pursuant to a federal statute, in this case the specific decision not to require air bags, and that decision then had the effect of preempting state law under implied preemption doctrine.

Whether there is an unclear express preemption provision, or whether the issue is one of implied preemption, the agency may have an opinion concerning the preemptive effect of its substantive regulation. The question arises as to what sort of consideration courts should give to such an opinion. A substantial body of case law relates to judicial deference to agency opinions, not all of which is consistent. The *Chevron* doctrine, from *Chevron, U.S.A., Inc. v. N.R.D.C.*,[20] establishes that, at least when an agency adopts a regulation interpreting an unclear statutory provision that it is responsible for administering, courts should defer to the agency's reasonable interpretation of that statutory provision. In addition, the Court has said that this

[18] Rice v. Santa Fe Elevator Corp., 331 U.S. 218, 230 (1947).
[19] 529 U.S. 861 (2000).
[20] 467 U.S. 837 (1984).

strong, *Chevron* deference should also be given to other agency interpretations of unclear statutory provisions that the agency administers, if the agency interpretation has "the force of law."[21] However, the Court has not provided any bright-line test for when an interpretation has "the force of law" other than when the interpretation is contained within a regulation or an order following formal agency adjudication.[22] When *Chevron* deference is not in order, courts should still give respectful consideration to the agency's views, but this is characterized as a weak or *Skidmore* deference, after the case in which the Court stated that the weight given to the agency interpretation will depend on the thoroughness evident in its consideration, the validity of its reasoning, its consistency with earlier and later pronouncements, and all those factors that give it the power to persuade, if lacking power to control.[23]

When a court upholds an agency interpretation of a statute under the *Chevron* doctrine, the court is not deciding what the statute means or what its best interpretation is. Rather, it is deciding that the agency's interpretation is acceptable, within the bounds of reasonableness, even if the court might not have reached that interpretation.[24] However, when a court reviews an agency interpretation under the *Skidmore* doctrine, the court is deciding what it believes is the best interpretation of the law. The court is interpreting the statute, aided by the views of the agency, not merely reviewing the reasonableness of what the agency has decided. This much is commonly accepted.[25]

When an agency interprets not a statute, but its own regulation, a different rule of deference applies. First articulated in *Bowles v. Seminole Rock and Sand Co.*,[26] the rule is that "the administrative interpretation [of the agency's regulation] . . . becomes of controlling weight unless it is plainly erroneous or inconsistent with the regulation."[27] Today, this is viewed as strong deference, on a par with *Chevron* deference.

---

[21] UNITED STATES V. MEAD, CORP., 533 U.S. 218, 229 (2001).

[22] "Formal" agency adjudication is adjudication conducted pursuant to the adjudication provisions of the Administrative Procedure Act, 5 U.S.C. §§ 554, 556–7.

[23] SKIDMORE V. SWIFT AND CO., 323 U.S. 134, 140 (1944).

[24] See, e.g., GENERAL ELECTRIC CO. V. U.S. E.P.A., 53 F.3d 1324 (D.C. Cir. 1995).

[25] Unfortunately, for clarity and predictability, it is not universally understood by all the members of the Supreme Court. Justice Scalia famously has stated that SKIDMORE was replaced by CHEVRON, and all deference is now strong deference. See MEAD, SUPRA, 533 U.S. at 239 (Scalia, J., dissenting). Justice Breyer has stated that he believes SKIDMORE and CHEVRON are essentially interchangeable, CHRISTENSEN V. HARRIS COUNTY, 529 U.S. 576, 596 (2000) (Breyer, J., dissenting), an opinion that may be shared by Justice Ginsburg who joined his opinion in CHRISTENSEN.

[26] 325 U.S. 410 (1945).

[27] SEMINOLE ROCK, 325 U.S. at 414.

Finally, the Supreme Court and the lower courts regularly take into consideration the views of agencies in a variety of contexts without attempting to fit that consideration into any particular doctrinal category. Preemption issues may arise in settings involving any of these different types of judicial consideration of or deference to agency views. Normally, courts acknowledge that standard *Chevron* deference applies when an agency adopts substantive rules interpreting ambiguous statutory provisions the agency administers, even if the effect of that rule is to preempt state law.[28] There are, however, exceptions. For example, in *Gonzales v. Oregon*,[29] the attorney general interpreted the Controlled Substances Act's term "legitimate medical purpose," an admittedly ambiguous term, not to include physician-assisted suicide. This interpretation, if valid, would have had the effect of preempting Oregon law, which explicitly provided that physician-assisted suicide, under the rules and requirements of the state, was an approved medical practice in the state. The Supreme Court held that Congress could not have intended the Controlled Substances Act, which was aimed at curbing substance abuse, to allow the attorney general to determine in a state what was approved medical practice contrary to what that state had determined.[30] Consequently, the Court did not give *Chevron* deference to the attorney general's interpretation of his authority under the act. In essence, the Court decided that in the Controlled Substances Act Congress had not delegated the authority to the attorney general to override a state determination of what was approved medical practice in the state. This may be seen as giving effect to the underlying principles of federalism by creating an implicit limit on the presumed delegation of authority to make substantive rules overriding state rules, when the federal rules interfere too greatly with a traditional state function. Here, an express delegation of such authority would be required.

A different situation is where an agency expresses an opinion – in a rule or elsewhere – as to the meaning of an ambiguous express statutory preemption provision applicable to a program administered by the agency. For example, the FDA has taken the position in several amicus briefs that the express preemption provision of the MDAs, which preempts any state or local "requirement," preempts state tort law. Should such an opinion receive strong deference from courts? In the application of the *Chevron* doctrine, courts have

---

[28] See, e.g., Bank of America v. City and County of San Francisco, 309 F.3d 551 (9th Cir. 2002) (upholding Office of Comptroller of the Currency's regulation authorizing banks to charge ATM fees and thereby preempting city ordinance prohibiting such fees).

[29] 546 U.S. 243 (2006).

[30] See also FDA v. Brown and Williamson Tobacco Co., 529 U.S. 120 (2000) (the Food and Drug Act did authorize FDA to regulate cigarettes notwithstanding that they might be drug delivery devices under the act).

often recognized that an agency may generally administer a particular statutory program; nevertheless, certain aspects of the statutory program are not administered by the agency but instead are subject to judicial administration.[31] Because *Chevron* deference only extends to an agency's interpretation of those statutory provisions actually administered by the agency, if some aspect of the statute is not subject to agency administration, courts should not defer to the agency's interpretation of that aspect of the statute. For example, in *Kelley v. EPA*,[32] the Environmental Protection Agency (EPA) had adopted a rule regarding lenders' liability under the Comprehensive Environmental Response, Compensation, and Liability Act (CERCLA).[33] Although EPA clearly administered CERCLA in many respects, the provision of CERCLA dealing with liability for cleanups did not provide any role for EPA in determining liability. Rather CERCLA simply stated who was liable. In *Kelley*, the D.C. Circuit Court set aside an EPA rule that purported to determine liability issues under CERCLA, saying "Congress, by providing for private rights of action under section 107, has designated the courts and not EPA as the adjudicator of the scope of CERCLA liability."[34]

In the preemption context, the fact that Congress has authorized an agency to administer a statute by adopting substantive regulations would not necessarily mean that Congress intended the agency also to be responsible for preemption determinations. That is, a statute may authorize an agency to determine what its substantive rules are without delegating authority to the agency to assess what are the preemptive effects of those rules. These are two distinct and separate issues, each requiring its own delegation, as is exemplified by those statutes that do expressly delegate both.[35] Because Congress does on occasion grant such explicit authority to agencies to make preemption determinations, an implicit authority to make such determinations arising out of the authority to make the substantive regulations probably should not be inferred, at least when the effect of the preemption determination would overrule a state's considered decision regarding a matter of the health or safety of its citizens. This conclusion is supported by the general presumption against preemption of state laws and its special application with respect to state laws protecting health and safety.[36]

---

[31] See, e.g., ADAMS FRUIT CO. V. BARRETT, 494 U.S. 638 (1990).

[32] 15 F.3d 1100 (D.C. Cir. 1994).

[33] 42 U.S.C. § 9607.

[34] KELLEY V. EPA, 15 F.3d at 1106.

[35] The MDAs, for example, which generally makes the FDA responsible for its implementation, contains a provision that explicitly empowers the FDA to assess whether state and local regulations should be preempted under the statute. See 21 U.S.C. § 360k(b).

[36] See HILLSBOROUGH COUNTY V. AUTOMATED MEDICAL LABORATORIES, INC., 471 U.S. 707, 715–18 (1985); RICE V. SANTA FE ELEVATOR CORP., 331 U.S. 218 (1947).

In *Bates v. Dow Agrosciences, LLC*,[37] for example, EPA submitted an amicus brief presenting its interpretation of the preemption provision of FIFRA. The Supreme Court in the past has given strong deference to agency interpretations contained in amicus briefs,[38] and EPA generally administers FIFRA, but FIFRA does not expressly grant EPA any authority to make preemption determinations. In *Bates* the Court did not find deference appropriate, stating that in areas of traditional state regulation the presumption against preemption could be overcome only by clear evidence of congressional intent. This case can be compared to *Medtronic, Inc. v. Lohr*.[39] In *Medtronic*, the Court deferred to the FDA's interpretation of the express preemption provision of the MDAs, but that act also contains an express provision delegating the power to FDA to make preemption determinations.

The facts and resolution of a recent case, *Watters v. Wachovia Bank, N.A.*,[40] might help to further distinguish between substantive rules that have the effect of preempting state law and rules in which the agency purports to make a preemption determination. The National Bank Act grants to national banks "all such incidental powers as shall be necessary to carry on the business of banking."[41] The ambiguous nature of this grant implicitly delegates to the comptroller, as the officer charged with administration of the National Bank Act, the authority to interpret or further define what those "incidental powers" are.[42] In the exercise of that authority, the comptroller has adopted a substantive regulation providing that national banks may create "operating subsidiaries" to conduct any activity the national bank can engage in.[43] The National Bank Act also contains the equivalent of an express preemption provision, stating that national banks, which are subject to oversight by the comptroller, are not subject to state regulation.[44] The question then becomes whether an "operating subsidiary," conducting an activity the bank could engage in and subject to the oversight of the comptroller, can also be subject to state regulation.

The comptroller had adopted a regulation specifically stating that "operating subsidiaries" are not subject to state regulation, explicitly preempting state law. The lower courts upheld the regulation, applying *Chevron* deference to this preemptive regulation, but in doing so they cited cases in which agencies

---

[37] 544 U.S. 431 (2005).
[38] See AUER V. ROBBINS, 519 U.S. 452, 461 (1997).
[39] 518 U.S. 470 (1996).
[40] 127 S.Ct. 1559 (2007).
[41] 12 U.S.C. § 24 (Seventh).
[42] See NATIONS BANK OF N.C. V. VARIABLE ANNUITY LIFE INS. CO., 513 U.S. 251, 256–7 (1995).
[43] See 12 C.F.R. § 5.34(e)(1).
[44] See 12 U.S.C. § 484(a).

had adopted substantive regulations that had the effect of preempting state law, not cases in which the agency had adopted a regulation that purported to preempt state law.[45] Nor did the courts recognize the distinction.

When the Supreme Court granted *certiorari*, many believed that the Court would address this issue. This did not come to pass. Instead, the majority's opinion explicitly ignored the comptroller's regulation, thereby mooting any question of deference to it,[46] finding instead that the National Bank Act preempted state regulation of the operating subsidiaries. The dissent, however, disagreed. Justice Stevens, in an opinion joined by Chief Justice Roberts and Justice Scalia, did not interpret the National Bank Act to preempt state regulation, and so he considered the validity of the comptroller's express preemption regulation, noting the distinction between an agency's authority to adopt substantive regulations and its authority to adopt regulations to preempt state laws.[47] His analysis concluded that "when an agency purports to decide the scope of federal preemption, a healthy respect for state sovereignty calls for something less than *Chevron* deference."[48] He concluded, "Never before have we endorsed administrative action whose sole purpose was to preempt state law rather than to implement a statutory command."[49]

As this decision demonstrates, these issues are yet to be definitively decided. The dissent clearly distinguished between substantive regulations with a preemptive effect and regulations that purport themselves to preempt. The latter, the dissent says, should not be subject to *Chevron* deference, at least absent an express statutory delegation to the agency to make preemptive determinations. Although this is only a dissent, the majority's intentional avoidance of the issue does not suggest rejection of the dissent's position on this issue. It would have been easy for the majority to take the same route as the lower courts, finding *Chevron* deference to the comptroller's regulation, if such deference had been deemed appropriate. Consequently, the avoidance of the issue by the majority may reflect some reluctance to apply *Chevron* deference to such preemptive regulations.

When an agency adopts a regulation limiting or denying preemptive effect or expresses an opinion that a regulation does not have preemptive effect, a different rule comes into play – courts always defer to this interpretation.

---

[45] See, e.g., WACHOVIA BANK V. WATTERS, 431 F.3d 556, 560–1 (6th Cir. 2005), aff'd sub nom. WATTERS V. WACHOVIA BANK, N.A., 127 S.Ct. 1559 (2007).

[46] See WATTERS V. WACHOVIA BANK, N.A., 127 S.Ct. 1559, 1572n13.

[47] See WATTERS V. WACHOVIA BANK, N.A., 127 S.Ct. 1559, 1573 (2007) (Stevens, J., dissenting). The majority of five justices did not reach the issue discussed here, finding that the statute preempted state law, see 127 S.Ct. at 1572 n. 13.

[48] Ibid., 1584.

[49] Ibid., 1586.

For example, in *Hillsborough County v. Automated Medical Laboratories, Inc.*,[50] although Congress had not explicitly provided the FDA with any authority to make preemption determinations regarding the federal regulation of biological products, the Court deferred to the agency's statement in the preamble to its regulation that the regulation would not preempt state law. Thus, there is an asymmetry between judicial consideration of an agency's interpretation that a statute or regulation does preempt state law and an agency's interpretation that a statute or regulation does not preempt state law. There are two possible reasons for this asymmetry. First, in the absence of an express preemption provision, agencies always have the authority not to preempt state law. Congress need not delegate the authority not to preempt any more than it need not delegate the authority not to regulate at all. Consequently, an agency's intentional failure to preempt does not raise any question of a lack of authority. Second, this asymmetric result may reflect the underlying federalism issues involved. That is, where the federal agency's interests and the state interests are coincident in having no preemption, there is less need for courts to play an active role than when the federal agency's interest in preemption is contrary to the state's interest. In the latter case, policing the boundaries of federalism becomes the judicial duty.

THE FEDERALISM EXECUTIVE ORDER

In 1999, President Clinton promulgated an executive order on federalism intended to provide guidance to agencies with respect to their actions that have effects on states.[51] It announced a general policy that agencies should not take actions limiting the policy-making discretion of states unless the national activity was appropriate in light of the presence of a problem of national significance. If a federal agency nevertheless limited such discretion, federal agencies were still to grant states the maximum administrative discretion possible. In addition, it imposed special requirements on agencies with respect to preemption of state laws. It calls on agencies not to construe statutes or authorizations in statutes to preempt state law in the absence of "clear evidence that the Congress intended preemption" or a direct conflict between federal and state exercises of authority.[52] If preemption is necessary, it is to be restricted to the minimum level necessary to achieve the purposes of the statute. Finally, the order prohibits agencies from issuing regulations that have

[50] 471 U.S. 707 (1985).
[51] See Executive Order 13,132, 64 FEDERAL REGISTER 43255 (1999).
[52] See ibid. § 4, 64 FEDERAL REGISTER at 43257.

the effect of preempting state law unless, to the extent practicable, the agency consults with state and local officials early in the process and in the preamble describes the consultation that took place, the concerns raised by the state and local officials, and the agency's response.[53] This executive order remains in force today.

It is perhaps ironic that, although the previous Democratic administration instituted restrictions on agency preemption of state law, the current Republican administration has been unusually aggressive and active in extending federal agency preemption of state law despite the executive order. This is ironic because traditionally the Republican Party was more protective of states' interests vis-à-vis the federal government, and the Democratic Party was more avowedly nationalistic in terms of government regulation. This irony is probably explained, however, by the stronger Republican policy of limiting government regulation and state tort law generally, and that the current Republican administration's use of federal regulation is generally light-handed, so that the effect of its claimed preemption of state law – both regulatory and tort law – is to preclude stricter state government regulation of industry.

As a result, agency attempts at preemption fall well short of the requirements of the executive order. For example, in the NHTSA proposed rule regarding roof crush-resistance standards, the agency announced its tentative determination that its rule would preempt all state and local laws, including state tort law, but it dismissed its obligations under the executive order by saying that the proposed rule did not have sufficient federalism impacts to justify consultation or consideration.[54] The FDA, in its adoption of the prescription drug labeling rule with its statement that the rule preempted certain state tort law, addressed the executive order but still did not comply with it. It noted that its proposed rule had not proposed preemption. Consequently, the agency did not comply with the order's requirements to consult with state and local officials about preemption, hear their concerns, and then respond to them in adopting a final rule.

This executive order, like all modern executive orders directed to agencies, contains a provision declaring that its mandates are not subject to judicial review.[55] Consequently, the only enforcement derives from the President or the Office of Management and Budget, which is given supervisory authority over implementation of the order. However, when an administration is not committed to the policy contained in extant orders, such enforcement is

---

[53] See ibid. § 6(c), 64 FEDERAL REGISTER at 43258.
[54] See 70 FEDERAL REGISTER at 49245.
[55] See ibid § 11, 64 FEDERAL REGISTER at 43259.

unlikely to occur. During the latter years of the Bush administration, the status of the order can only be termed benign neglect.

THE BUSH ADMINISTRATION'S ATTACK ON STATE TORT LAW

Following tort reform advocates' failures in the legislative arena, the Bush administration undertook a concerted attack on state tort law through agency preemption determinations in rule makings, as well as in amicus briefs in various courts. A good example of this is the FDA's notorious preamble to its regulation regarding prescription drug labeling. Historically, the FDA generally did not believe that its labeling regulations under the Food, Drug and Cosmetic Act (FDCA) preempted state tort law. As numerous cases reflected, the FDA generally considered the FDCA to set a minimum safety standard, not a ceiling. Tort law in particular was considered to supplement, not conflict with, the federal standards. The prescription drug labeling rule was proposed during the Clinton administration, and its preamble stated that the rule would not preempt state law.

The final rule, however, was adopted by the FDA in the Bush administration, and there this view had changed. In the preamble to the final rule the FDA concluded that the exercise of state tort law authority conflicted with the exercise of federal regulatory authority under the FDCA, because, if judges and juries could "reach conclusions about the safety and effectiveness information disseminated with respect to drugs for which the FDA ha[d] already made a series of regulatory determinations . . . , the federal system for regulation of drugs would be disrupted."[56] To explain this position, the FDA set forth in detail the position it had already been taking in amicus briefs before various courts, stating that it interprets the FDCA to establish both a "floor" and a "ceiling" for labeling standards. Thus, if the FDA does not require a particular warning, then, according to the FDA, manufacturers are forbidden from including such a warning, whether on their own or as a result of state requirements or incentives resulting from common law. Because manufacturers are forbidden from including such a warning, imposition of state tort liability on a manufacturer for failing to include such a warning would conflict with the federal regulatory scheme, even though a court (judge or jury) found that the failure to include such a warning caused an injury and was negligent.

Similarly, in proposing its new roof crush-resistance standard, the NHTSA asserted that its proposed standard would preempt state tort law because in its

---

[56] See 71 FEDERAL REGISTER at 3966, 3969.

view its standard provided the optimal balancing of safety and cost.[57] If a verdict in a state tort case could find a manufacturer liable for not providing greater roof crush resistance, despite a finding that it reasonably could have so provided, that verdict could induce manufacturers to divert resources from developing advanced vehicle technologies to increasing roof crush resistance. Likewise, the CPSC stated that its mattress-flammability standard would pre-empt state tort law because in its view its standard established the optimum relationship between safety and expense.[58] To allow verdicts in state courts to hold a manufacturer liable for not providing greater fire resistance would "upset the carefully tailored balance of costs and benefits this standard achieves."[59]

Each of these statements has in common two underlying interpretations of the statute in question. First, each agency interprets its statute as authorizing the agency to create a requirement that establishes not just a minimum requirement but also – in the FDA's words – both a floor and a ceiling. That is, each agency is interpreting its statute to provide the exclusive regulation of the matter. In addition, each agency is interpreting its statute to mean that exclusive regulation excludes not only state and local positive law in the form of statutes and regulations but also case law in terms of verdicts in tort cases.

The FDCA contains no express preemption provision, and, as noted in the preceding text, historically the agency had generally taken the position that its drug labeling rules were only minimum standards, and in particular that tort actions supplemented rather than interfered with the agency's regulations. Although the *Chevron* doctrine does not preclude deference to an agency simply because the agency has changed its mind, courts often consider the consistency of an agency's interpretation in deciding whether deference is appropriate. Moreover, for the same reasons that an agency's interpretation of an express preemption provision probably should not receive deference in the absence of an express delegation to the agency to make preemption determinations, the FDA's interpretation regarding the general preemptive effect of its labeling regulations probably should not receive deference.

The CPSC stands in a different situation. The Flammable Fabrics Act (FFA) does contain an express preemption provision.[60] Thus, it is clear that the CPSC's regulation is intended to be exclusive. However, whether this exclusiveness precludes state tort law, in addition to state positive law, is unclear. The preemption provision refers to a state "standard or regulation."

---

[57] See 70 FEDERAL REGISTER at 49245–6.
[58] See 71 FEDERAL REGISTER at 13496.
[59] Ibid.
[60] See 15 U.S.C. § 1203(a).

Two of the three commissioners adopting the mattress-flammability standard interpreted that language to apply to state tort law; one did not. Prior to the 2005 adoption of the mattress-flammability standard, courts had uniformly interpreted that language not to preempt state tort law.[61] However, the FFA also grants express authority to the CPSC to grant exemptions from preemption to a state "standard or regulation" under certain circumstances. Thus, the CPSC has been delegated the authority to make certain preemption determinations, but it remains unclear whether either the basic preemption provision or the exemption provision relates to state tort law.

The NHTSA situation is still different. The Motor Vehicle Safety Act, under which NHTSA proposed the new roof crush-resistance standard, also contains an express preemption provision, preempting any nonidentical state or local "standard."[62] However, it also contains a savings provision directly addressed to common law actions, stating that "compliance with a motor vehicle safety standard prescribed under this chapter does not exempt a person from liability at common law."[63] Although this savings provision might seem to preclude preemption of state tort law, the Supreme Court in *Geier* held that the savings provision only exempted tort claims from the express preemption provision; it did not preclude a finding of preemption when state tort law actually conflicted with a federal safety standard by standing as an obstacle to the accomplishment of the full purposes of the statute.[64] In *Geier*, as described earlier, the tort claim was that the manufacturer should have included an air bag in the car, even though NHTSA's regulation only required any form of passive restraint, not necessarily an air bag. However, in adopting that regulation, NHTSA had specifically considered requiring air bags but decided that to require air bags at once would interfere with their orderly and gradual phase-in. Consequently, the Court held that allowing tort liability against a manufacturer for not providing an air bag would directly contravene the decision that NHTSA had made. Clearly, NHTSA, in announcing the preemptive effect of its proposed roof crush-resistance standard, is attempting to bring itself within the rationale of *Geier*. One could say the same for the FDA and CPSC. The question is whether they have.

Each of the preceding described claims of preemption is generic. That is, the agency maintains that whatever standard or regulation it adopts is necessarily the optimal and exclusive standard, because that is its claimed statutory mandate.

---

[61] See, e.g., WILSON V. BRADLEES OF NEW ENGLAND, INC., 96 F.3d 552 (1st Cir. 1996); O'DON-NELL V. BIG YANK, INC., 696 A.2d 846 (Pa. Super. 1997).

[62] 49 U.S.C. § 30103(b).

[63] 49 U.S.C. § 30103(e).

[64] GEIER, 529 U.S. at 871.

That was not the case in *Geier*. There the Court's decision relied on the specific determinations made by the agency with regard to an air-bag requirement, and it was critical that the tort liability would be precisely for what the agency had specifically rejected and found would be detrimental to automobile safety. This suggests that the preceding described generic claims of preemption would not fall within the *Geier* conflict analysis. *Geier* did not find that nonuniformity alone would cause a conflict; rather the conflict must be between a particular tort claim and a particular determination made by the agency.

However, neither the FDA nor the NHTSA relied solely on its generic claim of preemptive effect. The FDA made an additional argument that, if, in approving a specific prescription drug, it considered a particular claimed adverse effect and determined that there was no scientific basis for believing that the drug caused that adverse effect, such that a warning of such an effect would be false or misleading, then a tort claim alleging a failure to warn of that particular claimed adverse effect would be preempted. Here, it could be argued, the situation would be the same as in *Geier*: the agency has specifically considered a particular issue; it has made a determination in the exercise of its administrative expertise with regard to that issue; and a determination of tort liability for action specifically rejected by the agency would conflict with the agency's determination. Since the FDA's adoption of its prescription drug labeling rule, several district courts have considered its preemptive effect. Uniformly, they have found preemption when the claim sought to hold a manufacturer liable for failing to give a warning that the FDA had specifically found to be unwarranted,[65] but they have not found preemption in the absence of such a finding.[66]

Similarly, the NHTSA also claimed in its proposed rule that it had specifically determined not to increase the roof crush-resistance because to do so would negatively affect the rollover propensity of the vehicle, and, if there were more rollovers, even with a tougher roof crush-resistance there might be more traffic deaths or serious injuries. Its proposed standard, the NHTSA said, "sought to strike a careful balance between improving roof crush resistance and potentially negative effects of too large an increase upon the vehicle's rollover propensity."[67] Thus, if a tort claim was brought alleging a failure of a

---

[65] See SYKES V. GLAXO-SMITHKLINE, 484 F.Supp.2d 289 (E.D. Pa. 2007); IN RE Bextra and Celebrex Marketing Sales Practices and Product Liability Litigation, 2006 WL 2374742 (N.D. Cal. 2006); COLAICCO V. APOTEX, 432 F.Supp.2d 513 (E.D.Pa. 2006).

[66] See SARLI V. MYLAN BERTEK PHARMACEUTICALS, INC., 2007 WL 2111577 (M.D.N.C., 2007); IN RE Vioxx Products Liability Litigation, 2007 WL 1952964 (E.D. La. 2007); WEISS V. FUJISAWA PHARMACEUTICAL CO., 464 F.Supp.2d 666 (E.D. Ky. 2006); PERRY V. NOVARTIS PHARMA. CORP., 456 F.Supp. 2d 678 (E.D. Pa. 2006).

[67] 70 FEDERAL REGISTER at 49245.

manufacturer to have provided greater roof crush-resistance, where the suggested method would increase the rollover propensity, that claim would
directly conflict with a specific determination made by the agency.

At the time of this writing, neither the Supreme Court nor any court of
appeals has rendered an opinion regarding the preemptive effect of either the
FDA's prescription drug labeling rule or the CPSC mattress-flammability
rule, and the NHTSA has not adopted a final rule in its roof crush-resistance
rule making.

CONCLUSION

This chapter has attempted to describe the current law regarding agency
actions that preempt state law, pointing out where the law is unclear – in
particular with regard to agency interpretations of the preemptive effect of
ambiguous express preemption provisions or of the agency's own regulations. In addition, this chapter has demonstrated that under the current
Bush administration, agencies are not following the requirements of the
executive order on federalism and its specific requirements regarding agency
actions preempting state laws. However, these requirements are not judicially enforceable, and in an administration intent on preempting state tort
laws, there is no interest in administratively enforcing the order's requirements. Finally, this chapter has provided examples of how the administration uses agencies to attempt to extend preemption of state tort laws as a
substitute for a failure to obtain legislation on tort reform. The chapter
suggests that the most expansive claims by these agencies should be rejected
as inconsistent with existing case law and principles of federalism, but that
their narrowest claims of agency preemption probably are and will be supported by the courts.

Congress, acting within its constitutional powers, clearly can preempt
state law – even state tort law relating to public health and safety. However,
because such action does such violence to states' interests, the respect for
those interests inherent in our concept of federalism demands that Congress
knowingly takes such action. This is the origin of the judicially created
presumption against preemption. When agencies act pursuant to congressional direction, the same principles of federalism should apply. If Congress
intends for agencies to be able to preempt state law, especially state tort law,
it should make that intent manifest, as it often has. Similarly, unless Congress makes clear that an agency has the power to make preemption decisions, an agency's opinion as to the preemptive effect of a statute or its
regulation should not command deference from the courts but only

respectful consideration. In the absence of a clear statement by Congress, only when a state law, including state tort law, directly and necessarily conflicts with an otherwise lawful agency action should that state law be preempted. For the most part, courts have followed this path, but the Supreme Court has been neither clear nor consistent on the subject, so it is no surprise that the path is not clear.

PART FOUR

PREEMPTION
TALES FROM THE
FIELD

11 The Regulation–Common Law Feedback Loop in Nonpreemptive Regimes

Thomas O. McGarity

Federal regulatory agencies and state common law courts play different but complementary roles in protecting citizens from the undesirable consequences of unregulated private markets. Congress created the regulatory agencies to provide *ex ante* protection by promulgating standards and establishing permit requirements applicable to private sector actors. Both permit requirements and regulatory standards often give targets of regulation a good deal of discretion in determining exactly how to comply. Nevertheless, agencies attempt to articulate the outer boundaries of legally permissible activities with some precision, because the government will ultimately bear the burden of proof in any subsequent enforcement action. State common law courts also craft rules for determining liability after a product or activity has caused harm, and in many cases those common law standards are designed to discourage socially undesirable behavior by forcing those who engage in it to compensate the victims. The broad standards that common law courts prescribe, such as the "reasonable person" test for negligence, are not stated with a great deal of precision, and their breadth and vagueness can leave prospective plaintiffs and potential defendants with little guidance as to whether a court will permit a jury to find that any particular product or activity violates the relevant standard.

Federal regulation and state common law litigation are both information-intensive exercises, imposing diverse burdens on regulators, litigants, and courts. Federal regulatory schemes typically impose threshold informational burdens but are far less comprehensive or consistent in tracking postaction developments. Federal licensing regimes, such as those under which agencies approve pharmaceuticals and register pesticides, ordinarily place the burden on the entity seeking the federal license to provide information demonstrating that the product or activity at issue meets the relevant statutory requirements. Standard-setting regimes, such as those under which agencies promulgate occupational health and motor vehicle safety standards, typically place the burden on the agency to ensure that there is sufficient information in the rulemaking record to demonstrate that the proposed standard is appropriate to implement the agency's statutory responsibilities. In the case of "risk-based" standards, this requires the agency to come up with information demonstrating that the standard will provide adequate protection to the relevant beneficiaries. In the case of "technology-based" standards, the information must demonstrate that the proposed standards are feasible and will not be unduly expensive to implement.

The plaintiff in common law litigation typically acts after a risk has caused injury. The plaintiff has the burden of proving that the defendant's product or activity violated the relevant legal standard, and that it was both a cause-in-fact and a proximate cause of a legally cognizable harm. This also requires a great deal of information that the plaintiff presents to the jury through the direct testimony of eyewitnesses, documents gathered from the defendant's files and elsewhere, and the testimony of expert witnesses who have assembled and analyzed various technical studies. Despite these formidable common law burdens, the desire of plaintiffs and their attorneys for redress and compensation motivates them to ferret out information to make their case.

In establishing the applicable legal requirements and applying those requirements to particular products and activities, each institution develops expertise and information that can be quite useful to the other. Thus, it should come as no surprise that informal "feedback loops" have developed between the courts and agencies in which each institution draws on information, experience, and different incentives of the other. These feedback loops have unquestionably improved the quality of decision making in both institutions.

One important, but often-overlooked consequence of allowing federal regulatory law to preempt state common law is the destruction of this feedback loop. In addition to depriving federal agencies of useful expertise and information, preemption reduces the overall protection that government provides to its citizens through both institutions. Drawing primarily on the regulatory and litigative history of the ubiquitous and highly persistent chemical perfluorooctanoic acid (PFOA), which is used in making the highly successful commercial product Teflon, this chapter will show how the feedback loops work, explain why they have an important role to play in protecting consumers and the environment, and argue that courts and agencies should therefore be very cautious about invoking federal agency preemption of state common law claims.

FEEDBACK FROM AGENCIES TO COURTS

The half of the feedback loop that flows from federal regulatory agencies to state common law courts contains at least two very useful items: detailed standards for distinguishing lawful conduct from unlawful conduct and information on the risks and benefits of the products and activities that they regulate. Common law courts are not obliged to incorporate standards and permit requirements that federal agencies have promulgated as the standard of care in negligence and products liability actions, but evidence of compliance with and violations of such standards is generally admissible in civil trials, and it can be quite persuasive to juries. We will examine in the following text how many courts have employed the negligence per se doctrine to afford a highly desirable procedural advantage to plaintiffs who can provide evidence of violations of statutes and regulations.

Likewise, common law courts are not required to take at face value agency assessments of scientific and engineering information, but the information that agencies rely on in such assessments may be quite useful in resolving difficult issues of causation that arise in civil trials and may not otherwise be available to litigants. This is especially true of scientific information that agencies require regulatees to generate as part of a licensing proceeding or through their independent authority to order health and safety testing on regulated products. Courts and common law litigants have little institutional capacity to engage in comprehensive review of a product's or production process's features and risks, so such regulatory information and standards can provide critical assistance in common law settings.

As the scope of federal regulation expanded during the latter quarter of the twentieth century, the courts in common law negligence actions began to rely on violations of those standards as evidence of negligence and compliance as evidence of nonnegligence. In the case of noncompliance, the courts gradually afforded federal regulatory agency requirements the status they have traditionally given to state statutes under the doctrine of "negligence *per se*." In the typical negligence case, the plaintiff has the burden of proving that the defendant did not behave as a reasonable person in the same or similar circumstances.[1] In most states, the plaintiff may gain a procedural advantage by showing that the defendant violated a statute or regulation that is intended

---

[1] Restatement (Second) of Torts (St. Paul, MN: American Law Institute, 2000), § 283.

to protect a class of people that includes that plaintiff from the type of harm that the plaintiff suffered. Variously characterized as raising a "rebuttable presumption" of negligence or as excusable negligence per se, such a showing will ordinarily be sufficient to meet the plaintiff's burden of proof on the question of the defendant's violation of the negligence standard of care, unless the defendant can demonstrate that the violation was excused.[2]

The common law courts have not, however, afforded the same status to evidence introduced by a defendant of its compliance with a state statute or a federal standard. The defendant's lawyers are free to introduce evidence of compliance, and they may rely heavily on the fact that the defendant's conduct complied with state or federal law in arguing their case to the jury, but that compliance does not give rise to any presumption of nonnegligence.[3] This asymmetry is based on the common law courts' traditional assumption that federal regulations establish minimum standards that companies are free to exceed when necessary to avoid damage to others.[4]

Products liability law came into its own with the American Law Institute's publication of the Restatement (Second) of Torts, under which the manufacturer of a product was liable if the plaintiff could prove that the product caused a legally cognizable injury and was in "a defective condition unreasonably dangerous to the user or consumer."[5] The more recent, but less well-accepted, Restatement (Third) of Products Liability requires the plaintiff to prove that the product was "defective." It then defines that term to include (1) a "manufacturing defect" that occurs when the product "departs from its intended design"; (2) a "design defect" that results "when the foreseeable risks of harm posed by the product could have been reduced or avoided by the adoption of a reasonable alternative design . . . and the omission of the alternative design renders the product not reasonably safe"; or (3) a "warning defect" that occurs "because of inadequate instructions or warnings when the foreseeable risks of harm posed by the product could have been reduced or avoided by the provision of reasonable instructions or warnings . . . and the omission of the instructions or warnings renders the product not reasonably safe."[6] Noncompliance with an applicable safety standard automatically "renders the product defective with respect to the risks sought to be reduced by the

---

[2]   Restatement (Second) of Torts, §§ 286, 288A, 288B; Dan B. Dobbs, The Law of Torts (St. Paul, MN: West, 2000), 311–28.

[3]   Restatement (Second) of Torts, § 288C.

[4]   David G. Owen, Products Liability Law (St. Paul, MN: West, 2005), 93; Robert L. Rabin, "Reassessing Regulatory Compliance," Georgetown Law Journal, 88, no. 6 (2000): 2051.

[5]   Restatement (Second) of Torts, § 402A.

[6]   Restatement (Third) of Torts – Products Liability (St. Paul, MN: American Law Institute, 2000), §§ 1, 2.

statute or regulation." By contrast, compliance "is properly considered" in determining whether the product is defective, but "such compliance does not preclude as a matter of law a finding of product defect."[7]

In both negligence and products liability cases, then, juries can benefit from the often-enormous effort that federal regulatory agencies put into crafting the protective standards and requirements that apply *ex ante* to the products and activities that later cause harm. They are not, however, required to defer to those standards in negligence actions. Compliance with federal standards is merely evidence of compliance with the common law standard of care that the jury may accept or reject at will. The jury may also disregard noncompliance in negligence cases if it is persuaded that the defendant had a legitimate excuse, and one excuse that is always available is that the defendant behaved reasonably in the particular circumstances of the case.[8] In the case of products, the Restatement (Third) approach, however, appears to limit jury discretion to disregard proof of noncompliance. In either case, the federal regulatory process provides useful feedback to common law decision makers on the standard of care.

Federal regulatory agencies can also make useful information available to common law litigants. Agencies employ scientists, engineers, economists, and social scientists who are familiar with the literature in their respective disciplines. They often assemble reports, compendia, and public notices that contain technical information that in understandable ways can help educate jurors.[9] Agencies can contract with the National Research Council of the National Academy of Sciences or appoint their own scientific advisory panels to provide input into scientific questions that arise during the regulatory process.[10] Courts can rely on these reports in determining "adjudicative facts" through the procedure of "judicial notice."[11] Although most regulatory agencies lack sufficient resources to support much empirical research, the information that is produced in federal agency laboratories and with agency funding is usually available to the public as well.

In addition, the standard-setting process ordinarily involves a public rule-making exercise in which interested parties are invited to submit additional

[7] Restatement (Third) of Torts – Products Liability, § 4(a), (b).

[8] Restatement (Second) of Torts, § 288A(2)(c).

[9] See Lars Noah, "Rewarding Regulatory Compliance: The Pursuit of Symmetry in Products Liability," GEORGETOWN LAW JOURNAL, 88, no.7 (2000): 2147, 2150–1 (unsophisticated jurors); W. Kip Viscusi, Steven R. Rowland, Howard L. Dorfman and Charles J. Walsh, "Deterring Inefficient Pharmaceutical Litigation: An Economic Rationale for the FDA Regulatory Compliance Defense," SETON HALL LAW REVIEW 24, no. 3 (1994): 1437.

[10] See Steven P. Croley and William F. Funk, "The Federal Advisory Committee Act and Good Government," YALE JOURNAL ON REGULATION 14, no. 2 (1997): 451.

[11] Federal Rules of Evidence, Rule 201 (2006).

information for the agency's consideration. As discussed in the preceding text, agency licensing procedures typically demand information from the entities seeking approval of their products or activities. For example, the Food Drug and Cosmetics Act (FDCA) requires the manufacturer of a new prescription drug to produce animal studies, pharmacology studies, and human clinical studies sufficient to demonstrate to the Food and Drug Administration (FDA) that the drug is "safe and effective." Information that might not otherwise become available to litigants can easily be located in agency files where it is usually subject to standard Freedom of Information Act (FOIA) requests.[12]

Several health and environmental statutes require regulatees to report to the relevant regulatory agency any information that they acquire indicating that their products or activities may have a significant adverse effect on human health or the environment. In addition, section 8(e) of the Toxic Substances Control Act (TSCA) requires any manufacturer, processor, or distributor of any chemical substance who receives "information which reasonably supports the conclusion that such substance . . . presents a substantial risk or injury to health or the environment" to "immediately inform" the Environmental Protection Agency (EPA) of such information, unless the agency has already been adequately informed of the information.[13]

Finally, some agencies have the authority to promulgate rules requiring regulatees to conduct specific scientific tests on products and byproducts that are not subject to federal licensure requirements. Under section 4 of the TSCA, for example, EPA may order scientific testing of chemical substances that "may present an unreasonable risk of injury to health or the environment" or that will be produced in substantial quantities and may give rise to significant human exposure or otherwise enter the environment in substantial quantities if "there are insufficient data and experience upon which the effects of the chemical on health or the environment can reasonably be determined or predicted" and "testing with respect to such effects is necessary to develop such data."[14] A special statutory Interagency Testing Committee (ITC), composed of representatives of several federal agencies, nominates chemicals for testing.[15] Once a chemical appears on the ITC "priority list" of fifty chemicals, EPA must in theory decide within one year whether to issue a rule ordering further testing.[16]

---

[12]   5 U.S.C. § 552.
[13]   15 U.S.C. § 2607(e). See 40 C.F.R. §§ 158.290, 158.490, 158.590.
[14]   15 U.S.C. § 2603(a)(1)(A), (B).
[15]   15 U.S.C. § 2603(e).
[16]   15 U.S.C. § 2603(e)(1)(B).

All of this information is in theory available to litigants for use in civil trials. In practice, however, private entities submitting information to federal agencies frequently claim that it is protected from disclosure by the "trade secrecy" or "confidential business information" exceptions to the FOIA.[17] Some statutes, such as the TSCA and the Federal Insecticide, Fungicide and Rodenticide Act (FIFRA), specifically provide that "health and safety" studies do not come within those exemptions.[18] The TSCA defines "health and safety study" very broadly to include "any study of any effect of a chemical substance or mixture on health or the environment or on both, including underlying data and epidemiological studies, studies of occupational exposure to a chemical substance or mixture, toxicological, clinical, and ecological studies of a chemical substance or mixture."[19] Despite this clear exclusion, however, EPA presumes that all information submitted under a TSCA confidentiality claim is a trade secret and demands that anyone desiring such information make a special request for it. When a request for such information comes in, the agency first notifies the company that submitted the information and gives it an opportunity to object. The companies usually do object, and the burden as a practical matter shifts to the person requesting the data to demonstrate that it does come within the health and safety testing data exception.

FEEDBACK FROM COURTS TO AGENCIES

The feedback loop has also worked in the other direction as agencies cite common law rules in writing regulations. For example, the Consumer Product Safety Commission (CPSC) relied on the Restatement (Second) of Torts in advising regulatees how to comply with the Consumer Product Safety Act's requirement that manufacturers of products notify the agency when they discover "defects" in products that could contain a "substantial product hazard."[20] Similarly, the Securities and Exchange Commission (SEC) relied on the Restatement (Second) of Torts in amending its rules of practice to allow the commission to censure, suspend, or bar persons for engaging in "improper professional conduct."[21] The Federal Trade Commission (FTC) relied on the

---

[17] 5 U.S.C. § 552(b)(4).
[18] 15 U.S.C. § 2613(b).
[19] 15 U.S.C. § 2602(6).
[20] Consumer Product Safety Commission, "Substantial Product Hazard Reports," FEDERAL REGISTER 71 (2006): 42028. See Robert L. Rabin, FEDERALISM AND THE TORT SYSTEM, 50 Rutgers L. Rev. 1, 8–9 (1997) (referring to the 'feedback dimension' of the common law).
[21] Securities and Exchange Commission, "Proposed Amendment to Rule 102(e) of the Commission's Rules of Practice," FEDERAL REGISTER 63 (1998): 33305.

Restatement (Second) of Torts in promulgating its Telemarketing Sales Rules under the Consumer Fraud and Abuse Prevention Act.[22]

Although agencies sometimes rely on common law standards, they much more frequently rely on information generated in common law litigation in writing rules and deciding whether to amend or revoke licenses for existing products and activities. Like the expert staffs of federal agencies, experts hired by plaintiffs' attorneys in toxic tort and products liability actions collect and analyze published studies and reports in the scientific literature to support their scientific conclusions about the cause-effect relationship between the plaintiff's exposure to the defendant's products or activities and the disease or damage that the plaintiff has suffered. These reports and supporting documentation are likewise available to agencies, typically through submissions by the participants in rule making and licensing proceedings, to use in deciding similar issues that arise in the regulatory context.

Unlike most federal agencies, plaintiffs' attorneys have the power to subpoena witnesses and compel defendants and others to produce documents. Such civil discovery can reveal information relevant both to the causation issues and to the degree to which the defendant's products or activities deviated from the relevant standard of care. As Professor Wendy Wagner observes, "the courts provide litigants with direct access to industry files and personnel, which allows them to pry 'stubborn information' on the adverse effects of their products and activities out of the hands of companies that have no incentive at all to make it available to regulatory agencies or the general public."[23] These resource-intensive investigations can yield treasure troves of information that is typically unavailable to agencies, including the occasional "smoking gun" document demonstrating not only that the defendant's product or activity was capable of causing harm, but also that the defendant was well aware of that characteristic and did nothing to protect potential victims. Quite often, the information that agencies obtain on underlying malfeasance by regulatees comes to them indirectly through tort litigation.[24]

Documents produced in common law litigation over Eli Lilly's schizophrenia drug Zyprexa, for example, showed that the company for more than a

---

[22] Federal Trade Commission, "Telemarketing Sales Rule," FEDERAL REGISTER 60 (1995): 43842.

[23] Wendy Wagner, "Stubborn Information Problems and the Regulatory Benefits of Gun Litigation," in SUING THE GUN INDUSTRY, ed. Timothy D. Lytton (Ann Arbor: University of Michigan Press, 2005), 271, 280. See also Daniel J. Gilveber and Anthony Robbins, "Public Health Versus Court-Sponsored Secrecy," LAW AND CONTEMPORARY PROBLEMS 69, no. 3 (2006): 132; David C. Vladeck, "Defending Courts: A Brief Rejoinder to Professors Fried and Rosenberg," SETON HALL LAW REVIEW 31, no. 3 (2001): 631–2; Wendy Wagner, "When All Else Fails: Regulating Risky Products through Tort Litigation," GEORGETOWN LAW JOURNAL 95, no. 3 (2007): 693.

[24] Carl T. Bogus, "War on the Common Law: The Struggle at the Center of Products Liability," MISSOURI LAW REVIEW 60, no. 1 (1995): 1, 4; Teresa M. Schwartz, "Prescription Products and the Proposed Restatement (Third)," TENNESSEE LAW REVIEW 61, no. 4 (1994): 1357, 1386; Vladeck, "Defending Courts," 633–4.

decade downplayed two serious side effects (rapid weight gain and diabetes) in its promotional materials and presentations to doctors. Other documents indicated that Lilly had circulated one set of data from a clinical trial internally but provided another set of data, much more favorable to Zyprexa, to doctors. It was unclear from the documents whether Lilly initially shared the internal data with FDA.[25] Although the company was prepared to share the clinical studies, adverse event reports, and literature reviews with doctors who specifically asked for the information, it instructed its sales representatives not to "introduce the issue."[26] The documents also indicated that the company promoted the $4.4 billion blockbuster drug for unapproved uses such as dementia in the elderly. If true, this would have been a clear violation of federal law.[27] The FDA was entirely unaware of this information. The company settled the civil litigation for approximately $1.25 billion with about 28,500 patients who alleged that the drug had caused diabetes and other health problems.[28] The information did not, however, inspire the agency to take immediate action, and Zyprexa remains on the market in spite of a growing body of information that it causes unnecessary weight gain.[29]

The ways information is handled, concealed, and sometimes revealed during common law litigation can lead to legislative and regulatory policy changes. In addition, the information can, at times, serve as a major bargaining lever in civil litigation settings. These diverse uses of information reveal the promise and limitations of civil litigation. For example, although the Eli Lilly documents came to light prior to the settlement, companies typically take precautions against such revelations during the litigation process by demanding protective orders from courts prior to producing documents and arranging depositions. The orders typically prevent parties receiving documents denoted "confidential" from sharing them with anyone other than experts and other parties to the litigation.[30]

[25] Alex Berenson, "Disparity Emerges in Lilly Data on Schizophrenia Drug," NEW YORK TIMES, December 21, 2006, C1.

[26] Alex Berenson, "Eli Lilly Said to Play Down Risk of Top Pill," NEW YORK TIMES, December 17, 2006, A1.

[27] Alex Berenson, "Drug Files Show Maker Promoted Unapproved Use," NEW YORK TIMES, December 18, 2006, A1; Alex Berenson, "Blockbuster Drugs Are So Last Century," NEW YORK TIMES, July 3, 2005, C1.

[28] Alex Berenson, "Lilly Settles with 18,000 over Zyprexa," NEW YORK TIMES, January 5, 2007, A1.

[29] Gautam Naik, "Antipsychotic Drugs' Link to Weight Gain Found," WALL STREET JOURNAL, February 13, 2007, B1.

[30] See, e.g., ESTATE OF FRANKL v. GOODYEAR TIRE AND RUBBER CO., 853 A.2d 880, 886–7 (N.J. 2004); Andrew D. Goldstein, "Sealing and Revealing: Rethinking the Rules Governing Public Access to Information Generated through Litigation," CHICAGO-KENT LAW REVIEW 81, no. 2 (2006): 375.

Protective orders reduce the incentive of defendants to resist discovery by providing some assurance that documents and testimony that they produce will not show up the next morning's *New York Times*.[31] This, in turn, reduces the amount of time wasted in discovery disputes.[32] The orders also protect legitimate privacy interests of litigants and nonlitigants as well as proprietary information that might give a litigant's competitors an undue advantage in the marketplace.[33] If the information is introduced in testimony in actual trials, it will be available to the public and the relevant federal regulatory agencies. Most litigation, however, ends short of an actual trial when the parties settle the case through settlement agreements that typically require the parties to keep confidential documents and testimony confidential.[34] The likelihood that damaging documents and testimony will become publicly available can be a powerful inducement to defendants to come to the settlement table.

In recent years, some courts have been unwilling to allow parties to use protective orders to cover up information that is relevant to public health and safety.[35] The Texas Supreme Court, for example, requires the party seeking to seal litigation documents to file a public motion with the court along with a public notice alerting the public to that fact.[36] A federal district court in South Carolina in 2002 promulgated a local rule discouraging secret settlements and limiting other aspects of judicially sanctioned confidentiality agreements.[37]

Reacting to the public outrage over internal documents showing that Bridgestone/Firestone knew that its tires were catastrophically failing on Ford Explorer sport utility vehicles, which became public only after a Texas district court agreed to grant an exception to a protective order, Congress enacted the Transportation Recall Enhancement, Accountability, and Documentation (TREAD) Act of 2000.[38] One section of that statute requires manufacturers

---

[31] Nancy S. Marder, "Introduction to Secrecy in Litigation," CHICAGO-KENT LAW REVIEW 81, no. 2 (2006): 305, 313.

[32] Goldstein, "Sealing and Revealing," 388–9, 406.

[33] Goldstein, "Sealing and Revealing," 378; Richard L. Marcus, "A Modest Proposal: Recognizing (At Last) that the Federal Rules Do Not Declare that Discovery Is Presumptively Public," CHICAGO-KENT LAW REVIEW 81, no. 2 (2006): 331, 339–41.

[34] Laurie Kratky Dore, "Public Courts Versus Private Justice: It's Time to Let Some Sun Shine in on Alternative Dispute Resolution," CHICAGO-KENT LAW REVIEW 81, no. 2 (2006): 463; Goldstein, "Sealing and Revealing," 378.

[35] Goldstein, "Sealing and Revealing," 383–4.

[36] Texas Rules of Civil Procedure 76(a); Texas Government Code Annotated § 22.010. See also Goldstein, "Sealing and Revealing," 422–3 (arguing that the Texas Supreme Court has interpreted the rule narrowly to limit outsider access to unproduced documents, thereby allowing the parties an opportunity to "contract around" the rule at the outset of litigation).

[37] Howard M. Erichson, "Court-Ordered Confidentiality in Discovery," CHICAGO-KENT LAW REVIEW 81, no. 2 (2006): 357–8.

[38] Public Law No. 106-414, 114 Stat. 1800 (2000).

of automobiles and tires to notify the National Highway Traffic Safety Administration (NHTSA) of repeated common law claims brought against their products. Similarly, the Florida legislature enacted a statute providing that "no court shall enter an order or judgment" that has the effect of concealing a "public hazard."[39] The CPSC promulgated a rule requiring manufacturers to report to the agency alleged product defects that were the subject of three judicial judgments or private settlements in any two-year period.[40] Civil litigation revelation of hidden-risk information thus prompted statutory and regulatory changes forcing greater hazard disclosures by industry.

FEEDBACK IN THE REAL WORLD: THE CASE OF PFOA

For almost half a century, E. I. duPont de Nemours and Company has manufactured a highly successful coating called Teflon from the little-known chemical PFOA at its Parkersburg, West Virginia plant. Teflon and related compounds are widely used throughout the world as coatings for products, including cooking utensils, glasses lenses, and even medical devices, that need to be waterproof.[41] PFOA belongs to a chemical family of "perfluorinated" organic compounds in which fluorine atoms are connected to every available niche in a carbon chain. Scientists working for the 3M Corporation discovered the antistick properties of the perflourinated compounds by accident in the 1950s and soon put one of them to use in a similar successful water repellant called Scotchgard.[42] DuPont purchased PFOA from 3M's Cottage Grove, Minnesota plant until the early 2000s when 3M decided to quit manufacturing perfluorinated compounds, at which point DuPont manufactured PFOA at its own plant in Fayetteville, North Carolina.[43]

Because PFOA is not a naturally occurring chemical, all PFOA found in the environment is the result of human activity.[44] During the 1970s and 1980s,

[39] Florida Statutes § 69.081(3).
[40] 16 C.F.R. pt. 1116. See 15 U.S.C. § 2084.
[41] Environmental Protection Agency, "Perfluorooctanoic Acid (PFOA), Fluorinated Telomers; Request for Comment, Solicitation of Interested Parties for Enforceable Consent Agreement Development, and Notice of Public Meeting," 68 FEDERAL REGISTER (2003): 18626, 18628. This document contains a summary of available toxicological information on PFOA and related compounds. Much of the information reported therein became available long after the events described in this chapter highlighted the risks posed by that chemical.
[42] David Shaffer, "Former 3M Chemical is Widespread," MINNEAPOLIS STAR TRIBUNE, August 15, 2004, A1; Minnesota Public Radio, "Toxic Traces: Part 1: The Science" (2005) (available at http://news.minnesota.publicradio.org/projects/2005/02/toxictraces/).
[43] Minnesota Public Radio, "Toxic Traces"; Michael Hawthorne, "Internal Warnings," COLUMBUS DISPATCH, February 15, 2003, A1.
[44] Environmental Protection Agency, "Perfluorooctanoic Acid (PFOA)," 18628.

both 3M and DuPont conducted numerous tests related to the toxicity and persistence of perfluorinated compounds, and they shared the results of such tests with each other.[45] By 1978, studies conducted by 3M scientists had demonstrated that the compounds were, in the words of one of those scientists, "completely resistant to biodegradation."[46] A great deal of subsequent testing has reinforced EPA's less-dramatic conclusion that PFOA is "persistent in the environment."[47] Like their cousins, the chlorinated hydrocarbon pesticides, perfluorinated compounds also bioaccumulate and bioconcentrate in the environment.[48] Unlike the chlorinated hydrocarbons, however, perfluorinated compounds do not accumulate in fatty tissues. Instead, they remain in the bloodstream, circulating through the body over and over again for three to five years.[49]

Despite the common misimpression that legislation and regulation comprehensively regulates risks posed by chemicals and associated production processes, PFOA, like many other chemicals, has never been regulated by any governmental entity in the United States. Therefore, little information on the toxicity of PFOA to human beings has been available until recently after the chemical achieved a degree of notoriety as a result of the events related in the following text. We know that it is carcinogenic in laboratory animals at high dose levels.[50] It also causes birth defects in laboratory animals at dose levels that are not much higher than some human exposures.[51] In a preliminary "rangefinder" screening study conducted by 3M in 1981, which it duly reported to EPA as required by section 8(e) of the TSCA,[52] all sixteen fetuses taken from rats exposed to a perfluorinated compound at high doses suffered from eye defects.[53] A 1982 follow-up study concluded that the incidence of skeletal abnormalities in rabbit fetuses was significantly higher in the exposed animals than in the control animals.[54] Beyond that, EPA and the public knew very little about the increasingly ubiquitous chemicals.

---

[45] Robert A. Bilott, "Request for Immediate Governmental Action/Regulation Relating to DuPont's C-8 Releases in Wood County, West Virginia and Notice of Intent to Sue under the Federal Clean Water Act, Toxic Substances Control Act, and Resources Conservation and Recovery Act" (March 6, 2001): 5. PFOA and C8 are the same compound. To avoid confusion, this chapter refers exclusively to PFOA.

[46] 3M Corporation, "Biodegradation Studies of Fluorocarbons – III" (July 19, 1978): 2.

[47] Environmental Protection Agency, "Perfluorooctanoic Acid (PFOA)," 18628.

[48] Environmental Working Group, "PFCs: Global Contaminants: Part 3: PFCs Last Forever" (undated) (available at http://ewg.org/reports/pfcworld/part3.php).

[49] Minnesota Public Radio, "Toxic Traces."

[50] Environmental Protection Agency, "Perfluorooctanoic Acid (PFOA)," 18629.

[51] Ibid.

[52] 15 U.S.C. § 2607(e).

[53] George L. Hegg, "Letter to Document Control Officer" (March 20, 1981).

[54] Environmental Working Group, "PFCs: Global Contaminants: Part 4: PFC Health Concerns" (undated) (available at http://ewg.org/reports/pfcworld/part4.php).

This all began to change in the late 1990s, when a Cincinnati plaintiffs' lawyer named Rob Billott agreed to represent Wilbur and Sandra Tennant in a case against DuPont. They alleged that releases of PFOA from DuPont's Dry Run Landfill and other nearby DuPont facilities into groundwater and streams in the vicinity of their farm had killed almost three hundred head of their cattle and caused them numerous health problems.[55] Billot's discovery requests and his independent investigative efforts had turned up information indicating that PFOA was contaminating the groundwater flowing under DuPont's facilities and onto neighboring properties.

These civil litigation plaintiffs and their counsel sought directly to provoke EPA to action. On March 6, 2001, Billott sent a letter to EPA demanding that the federal government prevent further releases and force DuPont to clean up existing contamination. In addition, Billot asked EPA to use its power under the TSCA to order DuPont to cease all production activities related to PFOA at its Parkersburg, West Virginia, plant until it had conducted scientific studies demonstrating that PFOA and related compounds did not present an "unreasonable risk of injury to health or the environment."[56] Billot attached to the letter relevant information he had secured through civil discovery from DuPont's files.[57] DuPont had asked the judge to issue a "gag" order preventing Billot from sending the information to EPA,[58] but the judge declined. The EPA, however, failed to take any action in response to Billot's petition.

Meanwhile, discovery against DuPont continued as other landowners filed their own lawsuits, and other attorneys entered the fray. As the discovery proceeded, they learned that at about the same time that 3M was discovering the adverse reproductive effects of the perfluorinated compounds in the early 1980s, DuPont had become aware of other information indicating that PFOA caused birth defects in humans that it had declined to share with EPA.[59] Both companies had taken action to limit exposures of their female workers, and DuPont had been engaged in a screening program to determine the levels of PFOA in the blood of female workers since 1978 when 3M had detected perfluorooctanesulfonates (PFOS) in the blood of its workers.[60]

---

[55] Bilott, "Request for Immediate Governmental Action," 3.

[56] Ibid., 3.

[57] Ibid., 5.

[58] Ken Ward, Jr., "Both Sides Hope for Answers on C8," CHARLESTON GAZETTE, March 6, 2005, B1.

[59] Environmental Protection Agency, "Perfluorooctyl Sulfonates; Proposed Significant New Use Rule," FEDERAL REGISTER 65 (2000): 62319, 62326.

[60] R. J. Burger, "Memorandum to Supervision through Division Superintendents re C-8 Compounds" (March 31, 1981). See Jim Morris, "Coming Clean," MOTHER JONES (September/October, 2001): 17.

After finding PFOA in umbilical cord blood from one baby and in the blood of another baby born to female workers at its Parkersburg, West Virginia plant, DuPont discovered that one out of seven monitored offspring was born with a severe nostril and eye defect and another was born with an unconfirmed eye and tear duct defect.[61] DuPont did not inform EPA of this discovery, but it did warn its workers that "a female who has an organic fluorine blood level above background level should consult with her personal physician prior to contemplating pregnancy."[62] The company's medical office urged its management to undertake a formal epidemiological study of the offspring of pregnant workers at the plant.[63] After a meeting between DuPont's medical division and the products production division on July 22, 1981, however, the management decided to put the epidemiological study " 'on hold' until further notice."[64] The study was never undertaken.[65] Both companies eventually reversed their protective policies on completing four full-scale animal teratology studies and concluded that the compounds did not pose reproductive risks at the levels of exposure typically encountered in the workplace.[66]

The discovery of PFOA in the blood of its workers inspired DuPont in 1984 to test the groundwater in surrounding communities. It quickly discovered PFOA in a nearby drinking water well used to supply the small town of Lubeck, West Virginia.[67] Instead of addressing the problem directly by cleaning up the unlined anaerobic digestion ponds at its facility, however, the company simply purchased the public well, and the wells were relocated two miles downgradient.[68] DuPont also found traces of PFOA in tap water in Little Hocking, Ohio, a town located immediately across the Ohio River from the DuPont plant.[69] DuPont made no

---

[61] E. I. DuPont de Nemours, Co., "C-8 Blood Sampling Results" (undated ca: August 1981); see "Environmental Working Group, PFCs: Part 2: PFOA Is a Pervasive Pollutant in Human Blood, as are other PFCs" (undated) (available at http://www.ewg.org/reports/pfcworld/part2.php).

[62] E. I. DuPont de Nemours, Co., "Washington Works Proposed Communication to Females Who Had Worked in Fluoropolymers Area" (April 9, 1981).

[63] Bruce W. Karrh, "Memorandum to Carl DeMartino re Epidemiology Study – C-8 (FC-143)" (April 6, 1981); Bruce W. Karrh, "Memorandum to Carl DeMartino from re Epidemiology Study – C-8 (FC-143)" (April 2, 1981).

[64] E. I. DuPont de Nemours, Co., "Project Control # 57," (undated ca: August 1981); see Kenneth A. Cook, "Letter to Richard H. Hefner" (August 15, 2003) (available at http://www.ewg.org/issues/PFCs/20030813/index.php).

[65] Ken Ward Jr., "DuPont Proposed, Dropped '81 Study of C8, Birth Defects," CHARLESTON SUNDAY GAZETTE-MAIL, July 3, 2005, A1.

[66] Andrea V. Malinowski, Letter to Richard H. Hefter (June 20, 2003).

[67] Bilott, "Request for Immediate Governmental Action," 7.

[68] Ibid.

[69] Environmental Working Group, "DuPont Hid Teflon Pollution for Decades" (December 13, 2002) (available at http://www.ewg.org/issues/PFCs/20021113/20021213.php).

effort to communicate this fact to government officials, and Little Hocking citizens continued to drink the potentially contaminated water until January 2002, when city officials learned of the groundwater contamination in West Virginia and asked the West Virginia Department of Environmental Protection to test its water for PFOA as well.[70] Those tests revealed PFOA at levels of up to 2 parts per billion (ppb) (twice DuPont's own "community exposure guideline" of 1 ppb) in the wells of the Little Hocking Water Association.[71]

Many years after DuPont's disturbing discoveries, 3M in the late 1990s received the results of scientific studies indicating that perfluorinated compounds were more ubiquitous in the environment and more toxic than scientists had previously supposed, and it duly reported them to EPA. In particular, a rat reproduction study commissioned by 3M indicated that PFOS (a closely related compound that 3M used in manufacturing Scotchgard fabric-protection products) caused postnatal deaths and other adverse developmental effects in offspring.[72] This alarming information inspired EPA toxicologists to undertake a preliminary review that concluded that the perflourinated compounds were "of significant concern." A preliminary EPA risk assessment indicated potentially unacceptable margins of safety for workers and possibly the general population.[73] On May 16, 2000, 3M announced that it would be "phasing out of the perfluorooctanyl chemistry used to produce" most Scotchgard products.[74] By the end of the year, many of the affected products were back on the market with formulations that did not contain PFOS.[75] DuPont, however, did not follow suit, and it continued to use PFOA purchased from 3M to manufacture Teflon until it built its own PFOA production facility in North Carolina.

In September 2002, EPA initiated a "priority review" of PFOA in light of data that it had received on developmental toxicity, carcinogenicity, and blood monitoring in response to a request for information.[76] By the end of March 2003, EPA scientists had concluded that PFOA was ubiquitous in the environment and that the human exposure levels were close enough to the

[70] Ibid.

[71] Hawthorne, "Internal Warnings."

[72] David Brown and Caroline E. Mayer, "3M to Pare Scotchgard Products," WASHINGTON POST, May 17, 2000, A1; Terry Fiedler, "3M to Drop Scotchgard Lines," MINNEAPOLIS STAR-TRIBUNE, May 17, 2000, A1.

[73] Environmental Protection Agency, "Perfluorooctyl Sulfonates; Proposed Significant New Use Rule," 62326.

[74] 3M Corporation, "Press Release: 3M Phasing Out Some of its Specialty Materials," May 16, 2000, 1.

[75] "Minnesota Mining Bringing Scotchgard back to Market," NEW YORK TIMES, September 23, 2000, C3.

[76] Environmental Protection Agency, "Perfluorooctanoic Acid (PFOA)," 18628.

levels at which PFOA caused birth defects in laboratory animals that, like
PFOS, the margin of safety was unacceptably small.[77] The agency recognized,
however, that "considerable uncertainty regarding potential risks remained,"
and DuPont took the position that there was "no evidence or data that demonstrates PFOA causes adverse health effects."[78]

For a time it appeared that EPA might take action under the federal TSCA
to ban or limit production of PFOA pending the development of additional
toxicity and exposure data, but EPA Assistant Administrator Steve Johnson put
DuPont officials' minds at ease when he told them on a conference call that
EPA would not be assigning a high priority to PFOA. Instead, the agency
would entertain "letters of intent" from companies to conduct further
research.[79] According to Johnson, "[w]e need to get the science sorted out
first, [and] "then undertake regulatory action if necessary."[80]

On April 11, 2003, the Environmental Working Group (EWG), an environmental group that attempts to draw public attention to the risks posed by
chemical substances, wrote to EPA Administrator Christine Todd Whitman
to provide evidence that the group had obtained from attorneys engaged in
litigation with DuPont. That evidence indicated that DuPont had failed to
report the information it collected in 1981 on the presence of PFOA in umbilical cord and baby blood, the information it received soon thereafter on the
two birth defects in babies born to mothers who worked in the DuPont plant,[81]
and the drinking water monitoring studies that it had undertaken between
March and June of 1984 on the Little Hocking, Ohio, tap water.[82] The EWG
maintained that DuPont's failure to report all of this information within the
required sixty-day reporting period violated TSCA's requirement that companies inform EPA of all information in its possession that "reasonably supports
the conclusion that" a chemical substance "presents a substantial risk of
injury to health."[83]

---

[77] "EPA Weighs Rare TSCA Regulation for Widely Used Industrial Chemical," Inside E.P.A.
Weekly Report, March 28, 2003, 1; See Environmental Protection Agency, "Perfluorooctanoic Acid (PFOA)."

[78] Ken Ward Jr., "DuPont's C8 Risks above Acceptable Limits, Feds Find," Charleston
Gazette, March 28, 2003, D3.

[79] "EPA Suspends Plan for Expedited Regulation of Controversial Chemical," Inside EPA
Weekly Report, April 11, 2003, 5.

[80] Michael Hawthorne, "DuPont Chemical under Scrutiny," Columbus Dispatch, April 15,
2003, A1.

[81] Kenneth A. Cook, Letter to Christine Todd Whitman (April 11, 2003) (available at http://
www.ewg.org/issues/PFCs/20030411/letter.php).

[82] Id.

[83] 15 U.S.C. § 2607(e).

The EPA responded to the EWG petition somewhat belatedly on July 8, 2004 with a formal complaint against DuPont alleging that it had violated the TSCA "substantial risk" reporting requirement just as the EWG had alleged.[84] The EPA also claimed that DuPont had violated its hazardous-waste disposal permit by failing to submit the same information.[85] The head of EPA's enforcement office told the press that the complaint was "intended to send a message to DuPont and everyone else this type of information must be provided to EPA."[86] The EPA action apparently inspired the Justice Department to launch a criminal investigation into DuPont's TSCA violations as well. In May 2005, a District of Columbia grand jury issued a subpoena to DuPont for relevant documents.[87] In its formal response to EPA's complaint, DuPont argued that "[t]he small amounts of PFOA" that it "discovered in a blood sample and in drinking water did not suggest that there was any risk to human health, let alone the sort of 'substantial risk' that is necessary to trigger reporting requirements."[88]

In early September 2004, DuPont announced that it had agreed to pay up to $340 million to settle a class action lawsuit brought on behalf of the citizens of Parkersburg, West Virginia, and Marietta, Ohio.[89] Under the settlement, DuPont agreed to pay $50 million to the sixty thousand or so members of the class, $22.6 million to the lawyers for their fees and expenses, $20 million to fund local health projects, $10 million to build new water treatment facilities, and $5 million for a two-year health study conducted by independent scientists from the London School of Hygiene, the University of North Carolina School of Public Health, and Emory University.[90] If the study demonstrated that PFOA was harming the health of the residents, DuPont agreed to pay up to $235 million for continuing doctor visits to monitor their health.[91] A judge approved the settlement on March 6, 2005.[92]

---

[84] In re E. I. duPont de Nemours and Company, Docket Nos. TSCA-HQ-2004-0016, RCRA-HQ-2004-0016, Complaint and Notice of Opportunity for Hearing (July 8, 2004).

[85] Id., 20.

[86] Juliet Eilperin, "EPA to Fine DuPont for Silence on Teflon Chemical," Washington Post, July 9, 2004, A3.

[87] "Perfluorooctanoic Acid Materials Subpoenaed by Federal Grand Jury in D.C., DuPont Says," BNA Product Safety and Liability Reporter 33 (2005): 555.

[88] In re E. I. duPont de Nemours and Company, Docket Nos. TSCA-HQ-2004-0016, RCRA-HQ-2004-0016, Answer and Request for Hearing (August 11, 12004): 1.

[89] Mike Lafferty, "DuPont Settles Lawsuit," Columbus Dispatch, September 10, 2004, A1.

[90] Ward, "Both Sides Hope for Answers on C8"; Lafferty, "DuPont Settles Lawsuit."

[91] Mike Lafferty, "Few in Village Seem Angry about Proposal in DuPont Suit," Columbus Dispatch, September 11, 2004, B1.

[92] Ward, "Both Sides Hope for Answers on C8."

Matters went from bad to worse for DuPont in November 2004 when the
EWG petitioned EPA to take additional action under the TSCA to punish the
company for failing to report the results of a July 29, 2004 study in which
"DuPont learned of high levels of the Teflon chemical PFOA in serum from
12 people living" near the West Virginia plant.[93] The EPA quickly responded
to the EWG petition with another administrative action alleging that DuPont
had violated the TSCA reporting requirement by failing to report the community serum sampling results.[94] In December 2005, DuPont and EPA settled
the entire administrative action with an agreement in which DuPont did not
admit guilt but did agree to pay $16.5 million in total penalties for its viola-
tions, an amount that far exceeded any previous penalty that EPA had
imposed under the TSCA.[95] A month later, DuPont and seven other companies announced that they entered into a voluntary agreement with EPA under
which they would reduce environmental releases of PFOA by 95 percent by
2010 and eliminate them altogether by 2015.[96]

PRESERVING THE VALUE OF FEEDBACK

Although regulatory agencies can provide common law courts with both a
standard to apply and such scientific information as is available under the
Freedom of Information Act, common law litigants can return the favor by
providing regulatory agencies with information produced as a result of or in
response to litigation. Litigation can yield settlements in which the defendant
agrees to conduct additional scientific tests that can be very useful to regulatory agencies. In providing for a two-year health study by independent
scientists, for example, the PFOA agreement between DuPont and the class
action plaintiffs ensured that a great deal of new scientific information on the
health risks posed by PFOA would become available to regulatory agencies
and the public. One of the plaintiffs' attorneys hoped that the study would
"provide a real scientific answer to the question . . . based on real facts and real
data."[97] Although this may have been an overly optimistic assessment of the

---

[93] Kenneth A. Cook, Letter to Michael Leavitt.
[94] IN RE E. I. duPont de Nemours and Company, Docket No. TSCA-HQ-2005-5001, Complaint
   and Notice of Opportunity for Hearing, December 6, 2004.
[95] Pat Phibbs, "DuPont to Pay $16.5 Million to Settle Alleged Violations of EPA Reporting
   Rules," BNA ENVIRONMENT REPORTER 36 (2005): 2581; Julie Eilperin, "DuPont, EPA Settle
   Chemical Complaint," WASHINGTON POST, December 15, 2005, D3.
[96] Juliet Eilperin, "Harmful Teflon Chemical to be Eliminated by 2015," WASHINGTON POST,
   January 26, 2006, A1.
[97] Bebe Raupe, "Court Approves Class Action Settlement with Possible $340 Million DuPont
   Payout," BNA ENVIRONMENT REPORTER 38 (2005): 424–5.

capabilities of a single scientific study, the agreement provides a good example of the capacity of common law to generate fresh scientific research.

Far more frequently, common law litigants provide information gleaned from company files like the PFOA studies that provided the basis for EPA's TSCA enforcement action against DuPont. Agencies typically assume that the information that they receive from regulated entities is free from bias and manipulation, and they rarely probe into company files or require employees of regulatees to testify under oath regarding the bona fides of the information that companies supply to the agencies. Most agencies lack subpoena power to give them access to such information and testimony.[98] In addition to studies that the company did not bother to provide to the relevant agency, common law discovery frequently turns up evidence of manipulation of scientific information and even fraud on the public and the agencies that is of obvious interest to agencies interested in dealing with consumer fraud and agency manipulation.

Because EPA had taken no action with respect to PFOA prior to receiving that information from the plaintiffs' attorneys, DuPont could not argue that the TSCA's regulatory regime preempted the plaintiffs' common law claims. If EPA had taken some action under the TSCA, DuPont could have argued that it was preempted by the TSCA's express preemption clause, which employs the magic word *requirement* and preempts any state requirement that is not identical to EPA-promulgated federal requirement.[99] Had the PFOA plaintiffs' claims been preempted, the information in the company files that was critical to EPA's TSCA enforcement action would never have seen the light of day.

PREEMPTION AS A THREAT TO THE FEEDBACK LOOP

As other chapters in this book have highlighted in some detail, federal regulatory statutes can preempt state common law claims. Such preemption can be expressly required in legislation, but it can also be claimed by agencies or found by courts based on language that is less than explicit. Ever since the Supreme Court in *Cipollone v. Liggett Group, Inc.*[100] held that the word *requirement* in an express statutory preemption clause that did not explicitly mention state common law could nevertheless be read to include the incentive that a successful common law action for damages sends to potential defendants to modify their products or activities, courts have seized on that

---

[98] Vladeck, "Defending Courts," 633–4.
[99] 17 U.S.C. § 2617.
[100] Cipollone v. Liggett Group, Inc., 505 U.S. 504 (1992).

word and similar words in express preemption clauses to find that Congress has preempted state common law tort claims.

The Court in *Geier v. American Honda Motor Co.*[101] greatly extended the reach of federal preemption when it held that a federal statute could impliedly preempt a state common law claim that stands as an "obstacle" to achieving one or more of the broad statutory purposes underlying a federal regulatory program, despite a savings clause expressly preserving state common law actions. The Court retreated somewhat from its expansive reading of the word *requirements* in the more recent case of *Bates v. Dow Agrosciences, LLC*,[102] where it rejected an "effects-based" test for determining whether a common law claim constitutes a "requirement." The Supreme Court's decision in *Riegel v. Medtronic*,[103] revealed a Court majority broadly construing the term *requirements* to preempt not just regulatory requirements but also potential common law liabilities for injuries from approved medical devices. It remains to be seen whether in the future the Court will back away from the expansive application of implied preemption that it adopted in *Geier* and *Riegel* or further develop the less preemptive logic evident in *Bates*.

According to Professor Peter Schuck, "[a] legal system's ability to mobilize high-quality policy-relevant facts . . . at a relatively low cost is perhaps the most important precondition for the effectiveness of its policies – and ultimately their legitimacy."[104] The superior expertise and access to resources of federal regulatory agencies is perhaps the most frequently cited reason for allowing federal administrative standards to preempt state common law claims.[105] Yet to the extent that regulatory agencies lack the resources or the authority to generate or require someone else to generate the information they need for accurate decisions, the advantage in technical expertise that they have over common law courts is lost.[106] Professor Wendy Wagner

[101] GEIER V. AMERICAN HONDA MOTOR CO., 529 U.S. 861 (2000).
[102] BATES V. DOW AGROSCIENCES, LLC, 544 U.S. 431 (2005). But see RIEGEL V. MEDTRONICS, INC. 128 S. Ct. 999. (The Court holds that the word "requirement" includes common law claims in a forceful opinion by Justice Scalia.)
[103] 128 S. Ct. 999 (2008).
[104] Peter H. Schuck, "Why Regulating Guns through Litigation Won't Work," in SUING THE GUN INDUSTRY, ed. Timothy D. Lytton (Ann Arbor: University of Michigan Press, 2005), 225, 231.
[105] See, e.g., Richard A. Epstein, OVERDOSE (New Haven, CT, Yale University Press: 2006), 201; Peter W. Huber, LIABILITY: THE LEGAL REVOLUTION AND ITS CONSEQUENCES (New York: Basic Books, 1988), 214; Peter Huber, "Safety and the Second Best: The Hazards of Public Risk Management in the Courts," COLUMBIA LAW REVIEW 85, no. 2 (1985): 277–337; "Regulation, Deregulation, Federalism, and Administrative Law: Agency Power to Preempt State Regulation," UNIVERSITY OF PITTSBURGH LAW REVIEW 46, no. 3 (1985), 607, 654–5; W. Kip Viscusi, "Overview," in REGULATION THROUGH LITIGATION, ed. W. Kip Viscusi (Washington, D.C.: AEI Press, 2002), 2.
[106] Wagner, "Stubborn Information," 231, 271, 273–4.

notes that "the courts are able to penetrate the rising information costs that can fog in the regulatory system by transforming low-stakes issues regarding general public safety into high-stakes damages claims, at least for a subset of issues."[107] Similarly, Professor Robert Rabin observes that insofar as lawsuits "provide the educational function of revealing massive cover-ups of health information by industries like asbestos, or occasional efforts to conceal risk information from regulatory agencies . . . , then it is undeniably the case that tort law is serving a positive function of some consequence."[108] Common law litigants will perform this "positive function," however, only to the extent that they are able to pursue the lawsuits that yield such information.

Federal preemption thus poses a serious threat to the feedback loop by cutting off the information that flows from the common law courts to the regulatory agencies. If federal regulatory standards preempt state common law claims on the matters addressed by those standards, then attorneys like Rob Billot will not bring cases on behalf of clients like Mr. and Mrs. Tennant, and they will not uncover the kind of documents that proved critical to EPA's TSCA enforcement action. The net result will be that both the protective goals of the regulatory programs and the common law's potential to administer corrective justice will suffer. Preemption eliminates the need for the half of the feedback loop that flows from the agencies to the courts because the state courts are no longer available to award damages to common law litigants. Preemption thus presupposes that the agencies are doing such an effective job of protecting the public *ex ante* that the added incentives provided by the common law are unnecessary and the amount of residual damage caused by the regulated products or activities is acceptably low.

Because neither of these propositions is warranted in most cases, the courts should not lightly presume that Congress reached that conclusion when it employs words such as *requirement* in express preemption clauses, and they should conclude that federal regulatory statutes containing no express preemption clause at all "impliedly" preempt state common law claims only when presented with the strongest evidence that Congress intended that result, and when Congress explicitly provides a savings clause preserving state common law actions that should be the end of the matter for purposes of both express and implied preemption. If the "presumption against preemption" has

---

[107] Wagner, "When All Else Fails."

[108] Robert L. Rabin, "Reassessing Regulatory Compliance," GEORGETOWN LAW JOURNAL 88, no. 7 (2000): 2049, 2069. See also Timothy D. Lytton, introduction to SUING THE GUN INDUSTRY, ed. Timothy D. Lytton (Ann Arbor: University of Michigan Press, 2005), 1, 31; Bogus, "War on the Common Law," 85.

any vitality left at all,[109] it should carry sufficient weight to protect state common law claims from preemption by federal regulatory statutes that do not expressly preempt such claims.

CONCLUSION

The feedback loop of information that flows from federal regulatory agencies to state common law courts and back again has functioned very well in many regulatory and litigative contexts over the years, but it has recently been placed in jeopardy by judicial opinions that honor the so-called presumption against preemption largely in the breach and by aggressive agency attempts to engage in "stealth tort reform" by preempting state common law claims.[110] The FDA, in particular, has benefited from the feedback loop because documents produced during common law litigation, like the Zyprexa lawsuits discussed in the preceding text, uncovered information of which the agency was unaware, which showed that pharmaceutical companies have frequently misled the agency.[111] It is therefore quite ironic that the FDA has been especially aggressive in its efforts to preempt common law failure to warn litigation.[112] If these courts and agencies persist in their preemptive ways, they will disrupt the functioning of a rare real-world manifestation of the often-elusive ideal of "cooperative federalism."

[109] See Bates v. Dow Agrosciences, LLC, 544 U.S. 431, 449 (2005); CSX Transportation, Inc. v. Easterwood, 507 U.S. 658, 664 (1993); English v. General Electric Co., 496 U.S. 72, 87–90 (1990); Silkwood v. Kerr-McGee Corp., 464 U.S. 238, 251 (1984); Rice v. Santa Fe Elevator Corp., 331 U.S. 218, 230 (1947). But see Mary J. Davis, "Unmasking the Presumption in Favor of Preemption," South Carolina Law Review 53, no. 4 (2002): 967, 968 (arguing that there is now a de facto presumption in favor of preemption).

[110] Margaret H. Clune, Stealth Tort Reform: How the Bush Administration's Aggressive Use of the Preemption Doctrine Hurts Consumers (Washington, D.C.: Center for Progressive Regulation, 2004), 2–3.

[111] See Marcia Angell, The Truth about the Drug Companies (New York: Random House, 2005), 106–9; Thomas O. McGarity and Wendy E. Wagner, Bending Science (Boston, MA: Harvard University Press, 2008), ch. 4.

[112] Food and Drug Administration, "Requirements on Content and Format of Labeling for Human Prescription Drugs and Biological Products," Federal Register, 71 (2006): 3922, 3934–6. See Allison M. Zieve and Brian Wolfman, "The FDA's Argument for Eradicating State Tort Law: Why It Is Wrong and Warrants No Deference," BNA Product Safety and Liability Report 34 (2006): 308.

12 Delegated Federalism Versus Devolution: Some Insights from the History of Water Pollution Control

William L. Andreen

This chapter examines the claim that state and local governments were beginning, prior to the enactment of the Clean Water Act in 1972, to make significant progress in the fight against water pollution. Based on this premise, some have argued that there is good reason to be skeptical about the necessity for continued federal involvement in water pollution control. At their broadest, such scholars use this revisionist history to question other federal environmental statutes' structures as well. The implication of this argument is that the devolution of regulatory authority to the states would not produce lower levels of environmental protection. Thus our present approach to water pollution control – delegated program federalism, a form of cooperative federalism with federal regulatory floors preempting any more lax state regulation, and federal oversight of state delegated programs – is really not necessary from a practical point of view and can be discarded without producing substantial environmental harm.

After setting forth the Clean Water Act's approach to delegated federalism, the chapter discusses the flawed nature of the data on which this claim is made. The experience of the 1960s simply does not support the argument in favor of devolution. This does not mean that every state was retrograde in its protection of water quality. The chapter, therefore, will also look at the progressive approach taken by some states, while also focusing on the action of the federal government during the 1960s to improve water quality. Nevertheless, the best evidence we have indicates that water quality was not improving nationwide before the enactment of the Clean Water Act. In contrast to that level of performance, the Clean Water Act has produced considerable progress; progress, however, that would surely be jeopardized should the nation revert to the regulatory paradigm of the 1960s. The true story reveals substantial benefits from federal regulation within a structure that preserves room for state participation, creativity, and even greater stringency.

THE CLEAN WATER ACT'S APPROACH TO DELEGATED FEDERALISM

In the fall of 1972, Congress enacted one of the most revolutionary statutes in history – the Clean Water Act. The act cast aside an earlier program that had relied almost exclusively on state agencies to adopt and implement water-quality standards. In Congress's view, that program had failed due to the reluctance of many states to adopt acceptable standards and appropriate implementation plans. Congress was also exercised by what some characterized as the near absence of enforcement. So in place of nearly exclusive reliance on state water standards, Congress adopted a radically new concept and applied it to tens of thousands of water polluters. The new strategy was predicated on the federal establishment of uniform, technology-based performance limitations.[1] These limitations, in turn, were to be applied to point-source dischargers[2] through a new permit system that would specifically define the legal obligations of municipal and industrial dischargers.[3] The state water-quality standard program was retained, however, to supplement the technology-based limitations in cases where such a uniform approach was not adequate to meet specific water-quality objectives.[4] Although the newly established U.S. Environmental Protection Agency (EPA) issued many of the initial permits, state agencies could obtain, and the vast majority of them have obtained, authority to administer the permit program within their borders.[5] Hence, the Clean Water Act's structure is not just federal but also involves overlapping and intertwined federal and state roles. All fifty states, moreover, enjoy the freedom to establish and enforce regulations that are more protective of the environment than EPA would require.

Although this kind of delegated program federalism is commonly referred to as "cooperative federalism," the fact remains that EPA is the senior partner

---

[1] 33 U.S.C. §§ 1311(b)(1)(A), (b)(1)(B), (b)(2), 1316(b)(1)(B).

[2] The act defines point sources as "any discernible, confined and discrete conveyance" such as pipes, conduits, ditches, and the like "from which pollutants are or may be discharged." 33 U.S.C. § 1362(14).

[3] 33 U.S.C. § 1362 (creating the National Pollutant Discharge Elimination System [NPDES] permit system).

[4] 33 U.S.C. § 1313, 1311(b)(1)(C). The application of water-quality–driven permit conditions depends on the existence and subsequent administrative recognition of monitoring data indicating that a particular water is water-quality impaired. See generally, Oliver A. Houck, THE CLEAN WATER ACT TMDL PROGRAM: LAW, POLICY, AND IMPLEMENTATION 5 (Washington, D.C.: Environmental Law Institute, 2nd ed., 2002) (recounting the paucity of both data and political will).

[5] 33 U.S.C. § 1362(b). Currently, forty-five states possess the authority to issue NPDES permits.

in most aspects of the relationship. In addition to setting uniform effluent standards, EPA is given veto power over state-issued permits,[6] the power in extreme instances to withdraw state permitting authority,[7] the power to review and disapprove state water-quality standards,[8] concurrent enforcement authority,[9] and the power to shape state programs through the provision of federal financial assistance[10] and the promulgation of EPA's program regulations.[11] Congress thus placed primary authority for policy creation and standard setting in the hands of EPA, making the federal government the dominant authority in an area in which state agencies had long held sway. Congress, however, did reserve a significant role for the states and many local governments to play.

In addition to permitting, states establish their own water-quality standards,[12] are responsible for implementing those standards through the establishment of waste load allocations,[13] are responsible for establishing programs to combat nonpoint-source pollution,[14] and take the majority of enforcement actions.[15] Many local governments, furthermore, have a vital role to play in the implementation and enforcement of the pretreatment program, which is designed to regulate industrial discharges to municipally owned wastewater treatment facilities.[16] State and local governments may also adopt additional measures that directly or through incentives provide additional protection of their waters. This reservation of authority is found in the act's approach to federal preemption.

The Clean Water Act only expressly preempts less stringent state and local requirements, not more stringent ones.[17] Through this kind of floor preemption, Congress expressly gave states and their political subdivisions the latitude to adopt limitations and other requirements that are more stringent than federal limitations and requirements. They can thus be more protective if they wish to be. The act's floor preemption is endowed with additional punch by virtue of a certification provision that gives states with water-quality concerns the power to veto or impose conditions on a wide variety of federal

---

[6] 33 U.S.C. § 1362(d).

[7] 33 U.S.C. § 1362(c).

[8] 33 U.S.C. § 1313(c)(3), (4).

[9] 33 U.S.C § 1319.

[10] 33 U.S.C. § 1256.

[11] 40 Code of Federal Regulations Part 123 (2006) (setting forth the requirements of state permitting programs under the Clean Water Act).

[12] 33 U.S.C. § 1313(c).

[13] 33 U.S.C. § 1313(d).

[14] 33 U.S.C. § 1329.

[15] William L. Andreen, "Motivating Enforcement: Institutional Culture and the Clean Water Act," PACE ENVIRONMENTAL LAW REVIEW 24, no. 1 (2007): 67, 74–5.

[16] 40 Code of Federal Regulations Part 403 (2006).

[17] 33 U.S.C § 1370.

licensing activities.[18] Another considerable reservation of state prerogative is found in the act's savings clause. This provision preserves "any right which any person (or class of persons) may have under any statute or common law to seek enforcement of any effluent standard or limitation or to seek any other relief."[19] By virtue of the savings clause, citizens can use state common law tort actions to obtain damages for their own injuries while also encouraging, sometimes requiring, dischargers to reduce the kind or amount of pollution they discharge.[20]

THE STATES AS LABORATORIES OF DEMOCRACY

The states, however, infrequently adopt more stringent regulatory standards for water pollution.[21] At least twelve states have enacted legislation either forbidding their programs from promulgating standards that are tougher than federal minimum requirements or imposing additional procedures that must be satisfied before such requirements become effective.[22] Many states have also often been slow to utilize the authority that Congress reserved to them. Most, for example, have been reluctant to establish waste load allocations that are necessary for the implementation of water-quality standards.[23] In addition, many states have chosen nonregulatory and often-ineffective approaches for the control of nonpoint-source pollution.[24] Even state enforcement efforts have been declining for more than a decade.[25] Instances where

---

[18] 33 U.S.C. § 1341.

[19] 33 U.S.C § 1365(e).

[20] Alexandra B. Klass, "Common Law and Federalism in the Age of the Regulatory State," IOWA LAW REVIEW 92, no. 2 (2007): 545. Although the Clean Water Act has been held to preempt the federal common law of nuisance (MILWAUKEE V. ILLINOIS, 451 U.S. 304, 313–15 [1981]), litigants may seek relief under the common law of the state where the polluter is located. INTERNATIONAL PAPER CO. V. OUELETTE, 479 U.S. 481, 497 (1987).

[21] Daniel P. Selmi and Kenneth A. Manaster, 1 STATE ENVIRONMENTAL LAW § 11:12 (Eagan, MN: Thomson/West, 2006).

[22] Jerome M. Organ, "Limitations on State Agency Authority to Adopt Environmental Standards More Stringent than Federal Standards: Policy Considerations and Interpretive Problems," MARYLAND LAW REVIEW 54, no. 4 (1995): 1373, 1376–86.

[23] Houck, THE CLEAN WATER ACT TMDL PROGRAM, 63; Linda A. Malone, "The Myths and Truths that Ended the 2000 TMDL Program," PACE ENVIRONMENTAL LAW REVIEW 20, no. 1 (2002): 63, 78–81.

[24] William L. Andreen, "Water Quality Today – Has the Clean Water Act Been a Success?" ALABAMA LAW REVIEW 55, no. 3 (2004): 537, 545 n. 42.

[25] Andreen, "Motivating Enforcement," 75. In contrast to the Clean Water Act, which empowers private citizens to enforce its requirements, less than half of the state programs do, and of those that do, only one-third allow costs to be shifted in favor of a successful, injured plaintiff. James R. May, "The Availability of State Environmental Citizen Suits," NATURAL RESOURCES AND ENVIRONMENT 18, no. 4 (2004): 53, 55–6.

states have vetoed or conditioned a federal license on water-quality grounds are relatively rare.

One might well conclude that many of these states are engaging, at least in part, in a race to the bottom in order to attract and retain industry through weaker environmental standards, lax implementation, and lethargic enforcement.[26] Such economic development concerns resonate deeply in many, if not most, state capitals because state politicians generally lack access to any other macroeconomic instruments that can deliver such material benefits to their constituents.[27] Another significant governor on the vigor of state environmental management efforts may be simple ideological hostility to regulation or the existence of a strong preference for voluntary, private efforts to control water pollution. State environmental agencies, however, may just be reluctant to do battle with entrenched economic interests, interests that in many, if not most, instances wield far more power in state capitals than relatively weak state bureaucracies.[28]

A number of states have taken advantage, at least occasionally, of the power that floor preemption gives them and have forged ahead with innovative approaches to some environmental problems. The most notable recent example of this type of state action involves climate change. Due to the reluctance of the federal government to regulate greenhouse gases (GHGs) such as carbon dioxide, about one-third of the states have enacted new legislation or implemented executive orders designed to reduce the generation of GHGs within their borders.[29] With regard to water pollution, perhaps the most obvious examples of more protective state action are found in a number in water-quality certification cases. In *PUD No. 1 of Jefferson County v. Washington Department of Ecology*, the Supreme Court upheld the state of Washington's imposition of a minimum stream-flow requirement as a condition precedent to the issuance of a federal license for the construction of a new hydroelectric dam.[30] More recently, the Supreme Court upheld a state

---

[26] Kirsten Engel, "State Environmental Standard-Setting: Is There a Race and Is It "To the Bottom"? HASTINGS LAW JOURNAL 48, no. 2 (1997): 271.

[27] Timothy Doyle and Aynsley Kellow, ENVIRONMENTAL POLITICS AND POLICY-MAKING IN AUSTRALIA 129 (Melbourne, Australia: Macmillon, 1995).

[28] Peter Grobosky and John Braithwaite, OF MANNERS GENTLE: ENFORCEMENT STRATEGIES OF AUSTRALIAN BUSINESS REGULATORY AGENCIES 207 (Melbourne, Australia: Oxford University Press, 1986) (finding a more cooperative regulatory approach among agencies that deal with smaller numbers of regulated entities).

[29] Kirsten H. Engel and Scott R. Saleska, "Subglobal Regulation of the Global Commons: The Case of Climate Change," ECOLOGY LAW QUARTERLY 32, no. 2 (2005): 183, 185; Barry G. Rabe et al., "State Competition as a Source Driving Climate Change Mitigation, NEW YORK UNIVERSITY ENVIRONMENTAL LAW JOURNAL 14, no. 1 (2005): 1, 8–11.

[30] 511 U.S. 700, 709–10 (1994).

certification for the federal relicensing of five hydroelectric dams on Maine's Presumpscot River that not only stipulated minimum stream flows but also required passage around or through the dam for migratory fish and eels,.[31] In the aftermath of another Supreme Court case, this one reducing the jurisdictional scope of the Clean Water Act,[32] a number of states took some action to ameliorate the resulting jurisdictional void.[33]

So the states can serve and many have served, from time to time, as "laboratories of democracy."[34] In doing so, these states have filled various regulatory gaps left by the federal government. They have also, through their trial-and-error experimentation with new approaches, created models worthy of emulation by other jurisdictions. Congress based the citizen suit provision found in the 1970 Clean Air Act on an earlier Michigan statute, and the concept of using water pollution permits in the Clean Water Act had its origin in the systems created by a number of states. State establishment of more stringent requirements, however, often provokes a backlash among the economic and industrial powers whose interests have been adversely affected. Thus, the victory that the state of Washington enjoyed in setting minimum flow conditions in *PUD No.* 1 led the Republican-dominated House of Representatives in 1995 to pass a bill that would have deprived states of this authority.[35] Many of the chapters in this book discuss recent legislative and regulatory actions that similarly attempt to impose federal limits or ceilings on state action.

DEVOLUTION?

The debate about the appropriate approach to federalism in water pollution control does not only involve the question of precluding more protective action by state government and state courts. The most common debate about the appropriate distribution of power between the states and the federal government in this policy arena has focused on whether the federal government should have a primary role to play, aside perhaps from the provision of financial and technical assistance to the states and dealing with the spillover effects of interstate pollution. Richard Revesz, for instance, has argued that federal environmental statutes that set regulatory floors hobble state efforts to craft

---

[31]   S.D. WARREN CO. v. MAINE BOARD OF ENVIRONMENTAL PROTECTION, 126 S.Ct. 1843, 1847 (2006).

[32]   SOLID WASTE AGENCY OF NORTHERN COOK COUNTY v. ARMY CORPS OF ENGINEERS, 531 U.S. 159, 171 (2001).

[33]   Michael J. Gerhardt, "The Curious Flight of the Migratory Bird Rule," ENVIRONMENTAL LAW REPORTER 31, no. 9 (2001): 11,079, 11,085.

[34]   NEW STATE ICE CO. v. LIEBMANN, 285 U.S. 262, 311 (1932) (Brandeis, J., dissenting).

[35]   "State Authority to Ensure Water Quality under Attack," AMERICAN RIVERS 23, no. 2 (1995): 5.

regulatory regimes that meet their own conceptions of the public good.[36] Thus, if they are constrained from competing over environmental regulation because it has been nationalized in part, they will be forced to compete in other ways such as by offering lax standards in other regulatory areas or by providing various financial incentives to industry.[37] In a different vein, Jonathan Adler has contended that a reduced federal presence could enhance the effectiveness of environmental regulation by increasing the need for innovative state reforms.[38] More specifically, Adler has suggested that federal regulatory floors can actually discourage more stringent or wiser state action by either signaling that state action is unnecessary or by "crowding out" the need for state action.[39]

Those who favor a more decentralized approach to environmental regulation – a devolution of authority from the federal to the state level – often point to commentators who claim that the states were actually making significant environmental progress prior to the 1970s and the enactment of the modern federal pollution-control statutes. Although most of these commentators focus on our nation's experience with two air pollutants, particulate matter and sulfur dioxide,[40] one of these commentators looked at water pollution. After examining reports discussing EPA's first national water-quality inventory, which was issued in 1974, A. Myrick Freeman concluded that "there had been significant improvements in most major waterways" during the 1960s "at least in regard to organic wastes and bacteria."[41] Adler, in turn, based on Freeman's work, has argued that this evidence "suggests that states began addressing those water quality problems that were clearly identified and understood well before the federal government."[42] History, therefore, demonstrates the

---

[36] Richard L. Revesz, "Rehabilitating Interstate Competition: Rethinking the 'Race to the Bottom' Rationale for Federal Environmental Regulation," NEW YORK UNIVERSITY LAW REVIEW, 67, no. 6 (1992): 1210.

[37] Richard L. Revesz, "The Race to the Bottom and Federal Environmental Regulation: A Response to Critics," MINNESOTA LAW REVIEW 82, no. 2 (1997): 535, 541.

[38] Jonathan H. Adler, "Judicial Federalism and the Future of Federal Environmental Regulation," IOWA LAW REVIEW 90, no. 2 (2005): 377, 464.

[39] Jonathan H. Adler, "When Is Two a Crowd? The Impact of Federal Action on State Environmental Regulation," HARVARD ENVIRONMENTAL LAW REVIEW 31, no. 1 (2007): 67, 94–9.

[40] Indur Goklany, CLEARING THE AIR: THE REAL STORY OF THE WAR ON AIR POLLUTION (Washington, D.C.: Cato Institute, 1999), 49–56; Paul R. Portnoy, "Air Pollution Policy," in PUBLIC POLICIES FOR ENVIRONMENTAL PROTECTION, ed. Paul R. Portnoy and Robert N. Stavins (Washington, D.C.: Resources for the Future, 2000), 77; Robert W. Crandall, CONTROLLING INDUSTRIAL POLLUTION: THE ECONOMICS AND POLITICS OF CLEAN AIR (Washington, D.C.: Brookings Institution, 1983), 19.

[41] A. Myrick Freeman, "Water Pollution Policy," in PUBLIC POLICIES FOR ENVIRONMENTAL PROTECTION, ed. Paul R. Portnoy and Robert N. Stavins (Washington, D.C.: Resources for the Future, 2000), 187.

[42] Adler, "Judicial Federalism," 465.

"environmental benefits of decentralization" and provides "ample reason to question the assumption that lessening federal environmental regulatory authority necessarily results in lessened environmental protection."[43] Hence, our present reliance on delegated federalism is unnecessary and federal power can be curtailed without producing negative environmental ramifications.

Such claims must be closely scrutinized against the historical record for any substantial change in our current regulatory paradigm could seriously undermine the effectiveness of our national effort to obtain and maintain clean and healthy waters. The question is not whether or not we are going to permit state experimentation. State experimentation is clearly available under the current approach to preemption, an approach that permits states to innovate and institute new policies as long as they do not fall below minimum environmental standards. The question, rather, is whether we are willing to remove that floor, that safety net, and permit states to pursue policy initiatives that fall below those minimum requirements.

A careful examination of the 1974 EPA report,[44] reveals no historical support for the broad contentions that have been based on it. Although it does conclude that some improvement had occurred with respect to a few water pollutants, the report cannot be considered a comprehensive assessment of progress in the fight against water pollution. The report is flawed in many ways, reflecting, no doubt, the complexity of attempting to detect trends in water quality. The EPA, for example, did not attempt to control for variations in stream flow, a factor that strongly affects concentrations of organic pollutants due to the impact of dilution. The monitoring stations, from which the data was drawn, moreover, were not held uniformly constant – thereby injecting a degree of ambiguity into many of the report's conclusions. In short, EPA's report is not good evidence that water pollution was improving nationwide during the ten years prior to the enactment of the Clean Water Act, and it lends no support to the claim that federal authority can be reduced today without incurring adverse environmental impact.

Water quality, however, was improving in some locations in the years leading up to 1972. This progress was largely the result of the construction and upgrading of a number of municipal wastewater treatment facilities. These local improvements, however, were not exclusively the product of state and local action because the federal government was also active in some water-pollution control activities in the 1960s and early 1970s. During those years, the federal program was providing funding, albeit at inadequate levels, for the

---

[43] Ibid., 464–5.
[44] U.S. Environmental Protection Agency, "National Water Quality Inventory" (1974).

construction of municipal sewage treatment plants; pushing state agencies to adopt water-quality standards, antidegradation policies, and adequate implementation plans; and involved in a number of enforcement actions.[45]

Nevertheless, the best data we have indicates that the overall quality of the nation's waters was not improving at this time; to the contrary, the situation appears to have been growing worse. Not only had the earlier federal program been inadequate to the task, but state efforts had been also. It was time, therefore, to institute a wholly new approach, an approach that has produced remarkable progress over the past thirty-five years.

A CLOSER LOOK AT THE 1974 EPA REPORT

The Clean Water Act requires each state to prepare a biennial report on the condition of its water quality and its progress toward achieving the act's goal of fishable and swimmable waters. The EPA, in turn, must transmit these reports to Congress along with the agency's analysis of the state results.[46] The EPA's 1974 section 305(b) report, however, could not rely on state submitted data because the states had not had time in the short period following the passage of the act to collect the stream quality and effluent data on which their reports would depend. The EPA, therefore, prepared the 1974 report using its STORET (storage and retrieval) database to try to analyze national trends in water quality during the previous decade.[47] In doing so, EPA relied on data from 1,300 monitoring stations located along twenty-two waterways in an effort to discern what if any changes in water quality had occurred between the period of 1963–7 and that of 1968–72.[48] Because many of these stations did not collect data throughout the duration of the study period, EPA often substituted data from stations located elsewhere along that particular waterway,[49] adding a variability that substantially lessens the confidence that one might otherwise have in the trends the report claims to have detected.[50]

---

[45] William L. Andreen, "The Evolution of Water Pollution Control in the United States – State, Local, and Federal Efforts, 1789–1972: Part II," STANFORD ENVIRONMENTAL LAW JOURNAL 22, no. 2 (2003): 215, 239–42; 249, 252–5.

[46] 33 U.S.C. § 1315(b).

[47] U.S. Environmental Protection Agency, "National Water Quality Inventory" (1974), 1, 9. EPA's STORET database, first developed in 1964, is one of the most venerable environmental database systems still in use. Maintained by the agency's Office of Wetlands, Oceans, and Watersheds, STORET contains data from ambient water-quality monitoring stations, effluent monitoring, and intensive surveys. U.S. Environmental Protection Agency, "National Water Quality Inventory 1996," 381.

[48] U.S. Environmental Protection Agency, "National Water Quality Inventory" (1974), 13.

[49] Ibid., 13, 72, 110, 133.

[50] Ibid., 110.

According to the report, there had been "general improvements" in organic pollution, bacteria, ammonia, and suspended solids.[51] Organic pollution, commonly measured as biological oxygen demand (BOD), had apparently improved in 74 percent of the river segments that were analyzed, producing improved dissolved oxygen (DO) levels on 61 percent; bacteria levels had improved on 58 to 78 percent; ammonia on 76 percent; and suspended solids on 82 percent. Nevertheless, EPA noted that bacteria levels and suspended solids remained at persistently high levels. In addition, EPA reported significantly worsening trends for two nutrients – nitrogen and phosphorus. Concentrations of total phosphorus had apparently increased in 82 percent of the river segments and nitrates in 74 to 76 percent.[52] Overall, EPA concluded that more stream segments had become moderately polluted during the decade, although fewer were heavily polluted. But the vast majority of the thirty-six river segments that were assessed appear to have been in violation of EPA water-quality guidelines for at least one pollution parameter in the period of 1968–72 and more than 60 percent were in violation of eight or more parameters.[53]

The limitations of the report were recognized at the time. The Council on Environmental Quality (CEQ) urged that the report "should be interpreted with caution" because, among other things, DO concentrations fluctuate with stream flow and temperature.[54] The concerns expressed by CEQ were well founded. The Northeast, Mid-Atlantic, Midwest, and Central states had all experienced widespread drought conditions from 1963 to 1966,[55] thus overlapping with three of the four years in EPA's initial snapshot of the nation's water quality. Low precipitation produces lower flow conditions, and lower flows produce the highest concentration of organic pollution and thus the lowest levels of DO.[56] By contrast, the years between 1968 and 1972 were not

---

[51] Ibid., 22.

[52] Ibid.

[53] Ibid., 24–5. It would be impossible to accurately compare the waters violating EPA guidelines in 1974 with those that are classified as violating the guidelines in later years because many of the reference points have been strengthened to better protect human health and the environment. In 1974, for example, EPA used a reference point of 4.0 mg/l for DO (for fish and wildlife) and 2,000 fecal coliforms per 100 ml (for recreation). U.S. Environmental Protection Agency, "National Water Quality Inventory" (1974), 24–5. In 1976, those criteria were strengthened to 5.0 mg/l and 200 fecal coliforms per 100 ml, respectively. U.S. Environmental Protection Agency, "Quality Criteria for Water" (1976), 42, 123. Subsequent revisions are found in U.S. Environmental Protection Agency, "Quality Criteria for Water" (1986), 42–50, 209–19.

[54] Council on Environmental Quality, "Fifth Annual Report" (1974), 287.

[55] Andrew Stoddard et al., MUNICIPAL WASTEWATER TREATMENT: EVALUATING IMPROVEMENTS IN NATIONAL WATER QUALITY (New York: John Wiley and Sons, 2002), 111; U.S. Environmental Protection Agency, "National Water Quality Inventory" (1974), 104 (acknowledging that the period 1968–72 was much wetter than 1963–7 in the Ohio River watershed).

[56] Stoddard, MUNICIPAL WASTEWATER TREATMENT, 108–11.

years characterized by widespread drought,[57] and hence one would expect lower concentrations of organic pollution and higher levels of DO.

Because a major variable was not held constant, it would stretch credibility to conclude that levels of organic pollution in the nation had actually improved over the course of the 1960s. A recent EPA study indicates that the effluent loading of organic pollutants from municipal wastewater treatment facilities had actually increased 8 percent between 1962 and 1972.[58] Therefore, what EPA may have been comparing, at least to some extent, was the impact of dilution on discharges of municipal waste, which typically contains organic material, bacteria, and ammonia.[59] That would explain much of the observed "improvement" in those parameters. The impact of increased dilution would also have minimized the contribution of organic discharges from industry, which, as the next section explains, were nearly equal to the contribution from the municipal sector.

The improvement in suspended solids, however, cannot be attributed to higher stream flows because one would expect suspended solids to rise with higher flows due to greater runoff and the scouring of sediment and silt from stream bottoms. Rivers are simply more turbid, as a general matter, during high flows than during low flows. Thus EPA's report suggests a striking improvement in concentrations of suspended solids. The EPA attributed the improvement to many factors. In its detailed discussion of the Ohio River, for instance, EPA stated that the downward trend along the river may have been due to the fact that the same monitoring stations were not being relied on during both periods of time. At stations that were measured during both time periods, levels of suspended solids were actually increasing.[60] The introduction of new high-head dams may also account for part of the observed improvement,[61] and higher flows and increased velocity may actually improve turbidity levels in some rivers.[62] At any rate, the overwhelming majority of suspended solids in our nation's waters result from nonpoint-source discharges – erosion from agricultural fields, construction sites, mining operations, logging activities, and urban runoff; discharges that went virtually unregulated during those years. If there was any improvement

---

[57] Ibid., 554–8.
[58] Ibid., 477.
[59] One would expect runoff related pollutants, such as bacteria from animal feeding operations, to increase during periods of high precipitation. Such increases in rural areas, however, may not have offset the broad-scale dilutional impact that increased flows had on bacteria discharged by urban sewerage systems.
[60] U.S. Environmental Protection Agency, "National Water Quality Inventory" (1974), 110.
[61] Ibid. (referring to new dams along the Ohio).
[62] Ibid., 72 (referring to the lower Mississippi River).

with regard to suspended solids, it is unlikely that much of it was the result of state regulatory action.

The more widespread use of wastewater treatment technology (especially primary treatment where solids are removed from raw sewage) by the nation's cities and towns did produce lower discharges of suspended solids from that point-source category. The EPA has recently concluded that discharges of suspended solids from publicly owned sewage treatment plants decreased 9 percent between 1962 and 1972.[63] This decrease, however, was likely undetectable because it would have been dwarfed by the combined level of suspended solids from industry[64] and nonpoint sources.

AN EVALUATION OF PROGRESS IN THE DECADE PRIOR TO ENACTMENT OF THE CLEAN WATER ACT

Although EPA's 1974 report does not appear to be a reliable barometer of an improving trend in national water quality, there is no doubt that some progress was being made in the years before the Clean Water Act was passed. That progress – generally limited to specific streams in particular states or regions – was primarily, but not exclusively, the result of state and local action.

The state of Oregon, for instance, made great strides in cleaning up the Willamette River, a river that had been known as the filthiest stream in the Northwest. As the result of state action, all of the municipalities discharging to the river implemented primary treatment, which removes about 30 percent of organic waste, between 1949 and 1957. In 1960, the state increased the requirement for these municipal facilities to secondary treatment, which removes approximately 85 percent of organic waste, and, in 1967, it extended the secondary treatment requirement to industrial dischargers. As a result, by 1972 BOD discharges by point sources to the river had dropped 75 percent from 1957 levels.[65] Nevertheless, bacteria counts still violated standards more often than not, and toxic discharges from the paper and pulp industry remained high in the lower eighty miles of the river.[66]

---

[63] Stoddard, NATIONAL WATER QUALITY, 481.

[64] Discharges of suspended solids from industry in 1973 amounted to approximately 898,010 metric tons per day compared to 7,531 metric tons per day from municipal wastewater treatment plants. Ibid., 589.

[65] Ibid., 405–6. In response to the federal Water Quality Act of 1965, Oregon established intrastate and interstate water-quality standards in 1967, standards that were among the first of the new state standards to be approved by the federal government. Ibid., 405. The federal government also provided millions of dollars for the construction and upgrading of municipal wastewater facilities along the Willamette between 1956 and 1972.

[66] U.S. Environmental Protection Agency, "National Water Quality Inventory" (1974), 235.

Although the Twin Cities of Minneapolis and St. Paul constructed a primary treatment facility in 1938, increased discharges associated with population growth had overwhelmed the assimilative capacity of the Mississippi River by the 1960s. According to the Federal Water Pollution Control Administration, which studied this section of the Mississippi in 1964, the river bottom for twenty miles was "thick with sewage sludge" and devoid of the organisms associated with a healthy stream.[67] Not surprisingly, the water was low in DO and high in bacteria. The bleak situation prompted local officials to upgrade the Twin Cities facilities to secondary treatment in 1966, an action that immediately improved water quality below the plant. However, 88 percent of the suburban sewage treatment plants in the Twin Cities metropolitan area persisted in discharging inadequately treated waste to the Mississippi River,[68] bacteria counts remained high, and DO occasionally fell to extremely low levels.[69]

Along the Delaware River, most municipal sewage plants above Philadelphia had installed secondary treatment by 1960. Below Philadelphia, however, DO levels remained abysmally low.[70] In Chattanooga, improvements to the sewage treatment plant rendered the Tennessee River suitable for recreation downriver, except for areas immediately downstream of the plant and along the city's waterfront.[71] Many other waterways, such as the James River, the Potomac River, the Connecticut River, and large stretches of the Chattahoochee River, remained grossly polluted.[72] The progress that had been made was, unfortunately, neither national in scale nor comprehensive in nature.

Much of the progress that was made, moreover, was due to federal efforts. Of the nearly $5.3 billion that was spent on the construction of sewage treatment facilities during the 1960s, $1.1 billion came from the federal government.[73] Although the federal contribution may have amounted to only a fifth of the total amount spent, the existence of this federal grant program

---

[67] Stoddard, NATIONAL WATER QUALITY, 369.

[68] Ibid., 368–9.

[69] U.S. Environmental Protection Agency, "National Water Quality Inventory" (1974), 73, 76.

[70] Stoddard, NATIONAL WATER QUALITY, 262.

[71] U.S. Environmental Protection Agency, "National Water Quality Inventory" (1974), 140. The Tennessee River had been the focus of some federal enforcement attention during the 1960s and had been listed as the subject of a potential enforcement conference as early as 1963. Stoddard, MUNICIPAL WASTEWATER TREATMENT, 419.

[72] Stoddard, MUNICIPAL WASTEWATER TREATMENT, 204–5, 285, 316, 334.

[73] U.S. Environmental Protection Agency, "The Cost of Clean Water, Volume II: Cost Effectiveness and Clean Water" (1971), 19. Federal expenditures on the construction grants program would have been nearly twice as large in the 1960s, but the program's funding fell victim to the cost of fighting the Vietnam War. Andreen, "Evolution of Water Pollution Control: Part II," 252 (relating that $750 million of the sums authorized for expenditure in 1968 and 1969 were never appropriated).

created an incentive that often prompted state and local governments to invest in their infrastructure.[74] As a result of these state, local, and federal efforts, the number of municipal treatment facilities providing secondary treatment rose from 6,719 in 1962 to 13,893 in 1972.[75] Unfortunately, the number of sewer systems providing no treatment remained stationary – rising marginally from 2,262 to 2,265 – while the number of systems providing only primary treatment fell slightly from 2,717 to 2,530.[76] Despite the expansion of efforts during the 1960s to build modern treatment facilities for municipal waste, the amount of sewage discharged with inadequate treatment (less than secondary) remained essentially unchanged at 9,375 million gallons a day (MGD) in 1972 compared with 9,372 MGD in 1962 – although the amount discharged without any treatment did fall by 1,594 MGD. In terms of organic material discharged from these facilities, the nation was losing ground. The discharge of organic pollutants from the nation's sewer systems grew from 11,765 metric tons per day in 1962 to 12,558 metric tons per day in 1972.[77] That rise might account, at least in part, for the results of a CEQ-contracted study that found that oxygen-demanding water pollution had grown, primarily in urban areas, between 1965 and 1970.[78]

Much responsibility for that apparent growth, however, must be borne by industry as well. In 1973, industry was responsible for approximately 43 percent of the sewered oxygen demand in U.S. waters.[79] Industry's overall contribution to the pollution of the nation's waterways, moreover, was staggering – representing roughly 63 percent of all wastewater discharged by point sources

---

[74] According to the Associate Director of the U.S. Conference of Mayors, approximately half of the money that state and local government contributed to this effort was stimulated by the availability of federal grant money. Water Pollution Control: Hearings before a Special Subcommittee of the Senate Committee on Public Works, 88th Cong. 93 (1963) (testimony of Hugh Mield Jr.). In addition, some state and local actions were no doubt spurred by the publicity generated and recommendations issued by some fifty-one federal-enforcement conferences that were convened between 1957 and 1970. Water Pollution Control Legislation, 1971: Hearings before the House Committee on Public Works, 92d Cong. 179 (1971) (statement of John Quarles, General Counsel of EPA, recounting the spotlight which the conferences shone on persistent water-pollution problems).

[75] Stoddard, NATIONAL WATER QUALITY, 458.

[76] Ibid.

[77] Ibid., 469. Because the influent of organic material had grown during the decade, the overall removal efficiency, however, had improved from 38.3 percent to 45 percent. Ibid., 470.

[78] Council on Environmental Quality, "Third Annual Report" (1972), 13. The study, performed by Enviro Control, Inc., made some corrections to account for flow variations. However, due to a limited number of monitoring locations from which the data was drawn, the study did "not represent a complete and properly weighted cross section of all U.S. waters." Ibid.

[79] Stoddard, MUNICIPAL WASTEWATER TREATMENT, 588. A much earlier EPA study, however, estimated that industry was responsible for nearly 80 percent of sewered oxygen demand in 1968. U.S. Environmental Protection Agency, "The Cost of Clean Water, Volume II," 64.

into waters of the United States.[80] As late as 1968, some 70 percent of the annual industrial discharge of more than 14 trillion gallons of wastewater received absolutely no treatment whatsoever,[81] and much of the rest enjoyed only rudimentary treatment.[82] The amount of untreated industrial effluent, moreover, increased at an annual rate of 1.6 percent between 1964 and 1968,[83] while the overall percentage of industrial waste treated to one extent or another improved only modestly from 29.2 percent to 30.4 percent.[84]

The nation, in short, appears to have been losing ground in its struggle with water pollution. The amount of industrial waste that received treatment remained ridiculously low, and the amount of untreated industrial effluent was growing. Meanwhile, the amount of organic waste being discharged from municipal facilities was still rising. In 1969, 41 million fish were killed by water pollution, the highest number of fish deaths reported since an annual census had begun in 1960,[85] but a record broken in 1971 when nearly 74 million fish were killed in U.S. waters.[86] Other examples of foul-smelling, repulsive water conditions appeared year after year.[87] It was no surprise in 1971, therefore, when the federal government announced that a substantial portion of U.S. waters were "persistently polluted"[88] – waters that consistently violated established water-quality criteria.[89]

---

[80] In 1968, municipal sewer systems discharged 23,116 million gallons of wastewater per day (Stoddard, MUNICIPAL WASTEWATER TREATMENT, 460) or 8,437 billion gallons per year. By contrast, a total of 14,276 billion gallons of wastewater were discharged in 1968 by large manufacturing facilities – defined as those facilities using more than 20 million gallons of water per day. U.S. Environmental Protection Agency, "The Economics of Clean Water, Volume I" (1972), 20. This comparison, therefore, is a rough one, not only because small, medium, and fairly large manufacturing plants were not included in the industrial discharge statistic but also because approximately 7 percent of the waste that was disposed of by the surveyed "large" industrial facilities was discharged to municipal sewer systems. Ibid., 17.

[81] Ibid., 25, 28.

[82] William H. Rodgers Jr., "Industrial Water Pollution and the Refuse Act: A Second Chance for Water Quality," UNIVERSITY OF PENNSYLVANIA LAW REVIEW 119, no. 5 (1971): 761, 764. According to EPA, the absence of data at this time made it impossible to estimate "the degree of treatment received by final industrial waste discharge." U.S. Environmental Protection Agency, "The Economics of Clean Water, Volume I," 28.

[83] Ibid., 28.

[84] Ibid., 26.

[85] Federal Water Quality Administration, "1969 Fish Kills" (1969), 1.

[86] U.S. Environmental Protection Agency, "Fish Kills Caused by Pollution: Fifteen-Year Summary 1961–1975" (1975), 5.

[87] William L. Andreen, "The Evolution of Water Pollution Control in the United States – State, Local, and Federal Efforts, 1989–1972: Part I," STANFORD ENVIRONMENTAL LAW JOURNAL 22, no. 1 (2003): 145, 197–8.

[88] U.S. Environmental Protection Agency, "The Cost of Clean Water, Volume II: Cost Effectiveness and Clean Water" (1971), 52.

[89] Ibid., 55.

THE IMPACT OF THE CLEAN WATER ACT ON WATER QUALITY

In contrast to the stubbornly degraded conditions that dominated water quality in the 1960s, the Clean Water Act has produced real, substantial progress. An EPA-funded study that was conducted in the late 1990s found that municipal wastewater treatment plants discharged 23 percent less organic waste in 1996 than in 1968, despite the fact that loadings of BOD (influent) had increased by 35 percent over the same period.[90] Over a shorter period of time (1973 to 1995), the amount of BOD discharged by industry fell by 40 percent.[91] Even though a substantial portion of the decline in industrial BOD discharges can be linked to the fact that many industrial facilities shifted their discharges to municipal systems, the overall decline in BOD discharges is significant and can be attributed to the construction and renovation of thousands of municipal treatment facilities,[92] as well as to the imposition and enforcement of technology-based effluent limitations.[93]

The most innovative aspect of this particular study, however, was its approach to assessing nationwide trends in ambient DO concentrations brought about by regulating point-source discharges of BOD. The study examined DO levels before and after the passage of the Clean Water Act and evaluated changes in DO only for monitoring stations that were impacted by point sources; stations influenced solely by nonpoint sources were excluded.[94] In an effort to isolate low-flow conditions (thus screening out the noise produced by seasonal variations in precipitation, flow, and temperature and minimizing the impact of nonpoint-source loadings),[95] the monitoring data was limited to the months of July through September, and to represent comparable worst-case, low-flow conditions, two especially dry periods were chosen: 1961–5 (before passage) and 1986–1990 (after passage).[96] The study was also intended to go beyond prior inquiries and determine whether

---

[90] Stoddard, MUNICIPAL WASTEWATER TREATMENT, 61 (measuring ultimate BOD of the carbonaceous and nitrogenous components of oxygen consumption).

[91] In 1973, industrial discharges of BOD amounted to 5,406 metric tons per day compared to 3,243 in 1995. Ibid., 588, 590.

[92] Between 1970 and 1999, the federal government provided $77.2 billion for the construction of publicly owned treatment works, a sum that was combined with state and local expenditures of roughly the same magnitude. Andreen, "Evolution of Water Pollution Control, Part II," 552.

[93] Stoddard, NATIONAL WATER QUALITY, 5–6.

[94] Ibid., 122.

[95] Ibid., 120.

[96] Ibid., 107–21.

point-source controls had only produced localized effects, as some previous reports had noted,[97] or had actually produced broader stream improvement.[98] The study, therefore, evaluated changes at three different scales: river reaches (small scale); catalog units (medium scale); and major river basins (large scale).[99]

Perhaps surprisingly, the investigators documented "significant improvements" in summer DO conditions at all three spatial scales.[100] They found progress in more than two-thirds of the reaches, catalog units, and major river basins that they surveyed. Sixty-nine percent of the river reaches that were assessed (representing largely urbanized, industrial areas) experienced improved levels of DO. The reaches with the greatest increases saw improvements ranging from 4.1 to 7.2 mg/L, and the percentage of reaches having worst-case, low-flow DO levels above the benchmark of 5.0 mg/L[101] rose from 46 percent to 69 percent. In addition, 68 percent of the larger catalog units (again dominated by urban/industrial areas) enjoyed higher levels of DO. As with the smaller scale reaches, the percentage of catalog units with worst-case DO levels meeting or exceeding 5.0 mg/L also rose, this time from 53 percent to 74 percent.[102] Finally, eight of the eleven major river basins that were examined enjoyed "statistically significant improvement," while the other three basins did not suffer significant degradation.[103] According to the investigators, "Given the very large spatial scale of the major river basins, it is remarkable to observe statistically significant before and after DO improvements as detected using the systematic methodology [which we employed]."[104]

Many water-quality problems remain, especially those linked to nonpoint-source discharges, contaminated sediments, sewer overflows, hydrologic modifications, and habitat degradation.[105] The evidence, however, is unambiguous; the initial regulatory strategy contained in the Clean Water Act has been successful. The application of technology-based limitations through the National Pollutant Discharge Elimination System (NPDES) permit system,

[97] Debra S. Knopman and Richard A. Smith, "20 Years of the Clean Water Act," ENVIRONMENT 35, no. 1 (1993): 16, 34–5.
[98] Stoddard, MUNICIPAL WASTEWATER TREATMENT, 105.
[99] Ibid., 7–10.
[100] Ibid., xvi.
[101] Five mg/l is considered to be the dividing line between healthy and unhealthy levels of DO. Ibid., 6. However, the actual water-quality standards in a number of southern states permit DO excursions down to 4.0 mg/l during specifically defined low-flow conditions.
[102] Ibid., 175.
[103] Ibid., 176.
[104] Ibid.
[105] Andreen, "Water Quality Today," 542–6, 564, 578–91.

which allows for state participation, enforcement, and amplification, although not perfect, has largely lived up to its preenactment billing. Together with the expenditure of some $150 billion on municipal wastewater treatment facilities, this classic form of command-and-control regulation within the structure of delegated federalism has produced astonishing improvements in water quality. The continuation of this success, however, is by no means assured. One of the oldest approaches to pollution control, state water-quality standards, still awaits full implementation. It is ironic that so many states, having expressed a strong preference for water-quality standards over technology-based limitations when the Clean Water Act was written, have proven so reluctant to impose water-quality derived restrictions on point sources and nonpoint sources.[106] Another great challenge, albeit one that receives much less attention, is the future federal funding of municipal wastewater treatment facilities. Our growing population and aging infrastructure will likely reverse much of the progress we have made since the early 1970s unless many existing plants are upgraded and new, more sophisticated facilities constructed.[107] A new and significantly enhanced federal commitment must be made and sustained, or many of our gains will be lost.[108]

CONCLUSION

Despite the efforts of state and local government, the fight against water pollution at the end of the 1960s was foundering. Insufficient resources had been committed to the construction of municipal wastewater treatment facilities, while the regulation of industry was in most cases nonexistent. Seventy percent of all industrial wastewater still received no treatment. State water-quality standards were often weak, and so were state enforcement programs.[109] Even if the will to enforce were present, the general lack of monitoring data made proving or even learning of a water-quality violation difficult, and the nearly uniform lack of discharge-specific limitations made linking a violation to a specific polluter nearly impossible in many cases.[110] The result was pervasive pollution and hundreds of impaired waters. One should, therefore, be wary of broad claims that state and local water pollution programs "were

---

[106] Houck, The Clean Water Act TMDL Program, 5, 63; Linda A. Malone, "The Myths and Truths that Ended the 2000 TMDL Program," Pace Environmental Law Review 20, no. 1 (2002): 63, 78–81.

[107] Stoddard, National Water Quality, 99.

[108] U.S. Environmental Protection Agency, "The Clean Water and Drinking Water Infrastructure Gap Analysis (2002), 6, 14–15.

[109] Andreen, "Evolution of Water Pollution Control, Part II," 252–5.

[110] Houck, The Clean Water Act TMDL Program, 313.

making environmental progress" in the 1960s.[111] Although some programs were producing progress, the overall picture was dismal. "In the face of a growing population and rapidly expanding manufacturing activity, state regulatory efforts were proving too little, too late."[112]

That lack of general success cannot be ascribed entirely to state and local government. The federal government had been active in some aspects of water pollution control for decades, and the pace of its involvement was accelerating during the 1960s with an expanded construction-grant program, a new water-quality standards program, and the use of section 13 of the Rivers and Harbors Act as a device in the struggle against water pollution.[113] This expanded federal program, however, was clearly not equal to the task. Despite some increasing effort at the state, local, and federal levels and some success stories, the overall trend at the advent of the 1970s was not encouraging. Relying on more of the same in the hope that state efforts "would pick up steam in the years to come"[114] was a course that Congress, clearly annoyed with the growing degradation of our waters, rejected in 1972.

Congress, therefore, charted a completely new regulatory course with the enactment of the Clean Water Act. The navigation of that new course has not been easy, and there have been and continue to be numerous pitfalls. However, the application of federal technology-based effluent limitations through the NPDES permit system has proven to have been a wise, initial course of action. Together with an expanded construction-grant program, the technology-based approach has produced tremendous reductions in the level of both industrial and municipal point-source pollution. More, much more remains to be done. But, we should recognize success, even partial success, when it occurs; and the credit for this success must be shared broadly.

It, nevertheless, must be recognized that the effort prior to 1972 was primarily a state effort, as it had been for decades. The overall failure of that approach stands in stark contrast to the success that we have witnessed under the Clean Water Act. Those results ought not to be forgotten whenever there are calls to deconstruct the Clean Water Act by stripping EPA of the authority to set and oversee the achievement of basic regulatory requirements. Such calls, which run counter to the lessons of history, need to be carefully and critically evaluated.

[111] Jonathan H. Adler, "Fables of the Cuyahoga: Reconstructing a History of Environmental Protection," FORDHAM ENVIRONMENTAL LAW JOURNAL 14, no. 1 (2002): 89, 138.
[112] Andreen, "Evolution of Water Pollution Control, Part I," 196–7.
[113] Rodgers, "Industrial Water Pollution and the Refuse Act," 761.
[114] Adler, "Fables of the Cuyahoga," 138.

Part of the genius of the Clean Water Act, however, lies in its grant of authority to the states and state common law litigants to go further and seek protections that lie beyond the minimum requirements of federal law. Thus, the Clean Water Act permits states and state courts to pitch in and fill regulatory voids wherever the act fails to address modern environmental concerns or whenever EPA fails to adequately implement or enforce existing law. Such gap-filling actions, unfortunately, are not common enough. It seems as if many states would prefer not to vigorously enforce or implement even the basic requirements of the Clean Water Act. It is fortunate, therefore, that the basic federal floor requirements remain as part of a regulatory structure that has, despite its flaws and occasional poor leadership, served the nation well since 1972.

13   Adaptive Environmental Federalism[*]

David E. Adelman and Kirsten H. Engel

INTRODUCTION

Environmental law is not neatly divided between the federal government and the states. The federal government continues to involve itself in highly localized issues with little clear connection to interstate environmental issues or a manifest need for federal uniformity. At the same time, states and local governments, especially recently, are not content to confine their attention to issues of local concern but are developing policies on environmental issues of national and even international importance. Nor do environmental issues "stay" in the control of any particular level of government but rather tend to pass back and forth, much like the proverbial football, between different levels of government.

The current system of environmental federalism is therefore a dynamic one of overlapping federal and state jurisdiction. However, it is threatened by federal legislation and Supreme Court rulings. A wave of preemptive legislation has emerged from Congress in recent years. Numerous bills pending in Congress, for example, would preempt state actions to reduce greenhouse gas emissions (GHGs) that contribute to climate change.[1] Similarly, following a long line of cases in which the Supreme Court has preempted a variety of state actions designed to protect the public, the Court recently (2004) preempted state auto-pollution regulations, despite, at best, ambiguous statutory language.[2]

---

[*]   This chapter draws on and condenses arguments made in a longer article that will be published in volume 92, issue 6, of the MINNESOTA LAW REVIEW.

[1]   H. Joseph Hebert, "Bill Would Block States on Auto Rules," WASHINGTON POST, June 4, 2007, C1.

[2]   ENGINE MANUFACTURERS' ASSOCIATION V. SOUTH COAST AIR QUALITY MANAGEMENT DISTRICT, 541 U.S. 246 (2004); Paul Teske, REGULATION IN THE STATES (Washington, D.C.: Brookings Institute Press, 2004), 11–12.

Legal academics are similarly hostile to the dynamism of environmental federalism because it runs contrary to the prevailing view that an optimal level of government exists from which to set environmental policy. The orthodox variant of this view, which we refer to as the "matching principle," is premised on the elementary economic theory that efficient regulation is possible only when the regulating entity fully internalizes the costs and benefits of its policies.[3] A corollary of this principle is that exclusive regulatory authority should reside at the level of government that roughly "matches" the geographic scope of the subject environmental problem. Hence regulation of intrastate groundwater ought to be regulated by state and local governments, whereas climate change should be addressed at the international level.

Our approach rejects the static matching principle for an adaptive model. We start with the unremarkable observation that environmental problems are multi-faceted. Sources of environmental harm may be the manifestation of numerous failures, market as well as regulatory, that arise along numerous dimensions and at different scales. The political initiative to address environmental problems will also originate from more than one level of government based on a variety of political, economic, and environmental factors, each differing from the other in the mix of these variables. Moreover, whereas an idealized optimization problem is akin to locating the peak of a single, isolated mountain, say Kilimanjaro, environmental policies are set in a domain analogous to the Himalayas.[4] As we will show, rigid adherence to optimization premised on attempting to internalize all costs and benefits is counterproductive in such an environment, as it increases risks of freezing policies in local maxima (dead ends) and is less responsive to changing environmental and socioeconomic conditions.

Ecosystems, one of the best-known adaptive systems, are the exemplar for this chapter. Successful ecosystems balance two seemingly incompatible processes: (1) weeding out less-fit organisms, which in essence is a process of biological optimization; and (2) maintenance of biological diversity, which, though running in the opposite direction, is essential to long-term resilience to unpredictable environmental change.[5] The essence of an adaptive system is

---

[3] Jonathan H. Adler, "Jurisdictional Mismatch in Environmental Federalism," NEW YORK UNIVERSITY ENVIRONMENTAL LAW JOURNAL 14, no. 1 (2005): 157; Henry Butler and Jonathan R. Macey, "Externalities and the Matching Principle: The Case for Reallocating Environmental Regulatory Authority," YALE LAW AND POLICY REVIEW 14, no. 1 (1996): 23, 25; Daniel C. Esty, "Revitalizing Environmental Federalism," MICHIGAN LAW REVIEW 95, no. 2 (1996): 587; Richard O. Zerbe, "Optimal Environmental Jurisdictions," ECOLOGY LAW QUARTERLY 4, no. 1 (1974): 245.

[4] Simon A. Levin, "Complex Adaptive Systems: Exploring the Known, the Unknown, and the Unknowable," BULLETIN OF THE AMERICAN MATHEMATICS SOCIETY 40, no. 1 (2002): 11.

[5] Ibid., 5–6.

its operation on multiple geographical and temporal scales, such that environmental conditions are aggregated at different levels and along different dimensions. Species' exposure to putatively the same environment is thus highly variable, such that while some are buffered from disruptions, others are extremely vulnerable to them, while still others benefit.[6] This diversity of experience exposes species to different selective influences and allows pockets of them that might otherwise succumb to global competitive pressures to survive, thereby maintaining biological diversity and safeguarding the long-term adaptability of the ecosystem.

To avert any misperceptions, we want to renounce two of the more extreme implications of our adaptive model. We do not believe that a single model can account for all aspects of the federal system or, for that matter, the many legal doctrines that it implicates. We do not intend for our use of adaptive systems generally, and ecosystems in particular, to imply a normative messge.[7] We will argue instead that an adaptive model of federalism is well suited to the complexity of the problems native to environmental policies. Nor do we believe that an adaptive model captures everything worth saying about environmental federalism. To the contrary, we accept that the matching principle has its merits, particularly its generality and simplicity (although its accuracy is often seriously wanting). Instead, we intend to show that an adaptive model is superior to the matching principle as an organizing framework for environmental federalism.

The question we seek to address in this chapter is whether the strategy embodied in adaptive systems adds additional support to arguments for overlapping federal and state jurisdiction and against static attempts to carve out separate state and federal regulatory roles. We are particularly interested in what theories about complex adaptive systems have to say about the benefits of a more dynamic federalism, as well as the appropriateness of an adaptive approach to federalism in managing a highly complex and changing system such as the natural environment and the human impacts upon it. We

---

[6] Simon A. Levin, "The Problem of Pattern and Scale in Ecology," ECOLOGY 73, no. 6 (1992): 1945.

[7] The multilevel structure of an adaptive model also mirrors the current system of environmental federalism. But one must be careful not to take the analogy too far. Clearly, many features of the federal system have no analogue in the natural world. Ecosystems, e.g., have nothing akin to a national government that has hierarchical authority over its subdivisions, and natural systems are not "designed" to achieve societal ideals, such as justice or economic efficiency. As we will show, these differences do not diminish the value of an adaptive model – its basic structure is uniquely suited to sustaining both a diverse range of environmental policy options and processes for winnowing and refining them that a federal system would do well to duplicate.

conclude by applying the lessons of complex adaptive systems to the regulation of emissions of GHGs that contribute to global climate change.

THE ENVIRONMENTAL FEDERALISM DEBATE

Environmental federalism scholarship is currently very much in flux. Two primary schools of thought, which we will refer to as "classical" and "dynamic" federalism, dominate the current debate. The classical school is largely defined by its commitment to the matching principle as a means of selecting the level of government that should regulate an environmental problem. The dynamic school prizes governmental regulatory autonomy, the virtues of multiple regulatory approaches, and the benefits of a dynamic give-and-take between regulatory officials across different jurisdictions. Both conceptions are used as theoretical bases for revisions to the cooperative federalism structure that currently characterizes much of U.S. environmental laws. This section of the chapter provides an overview of each.

STATIC MODELS OF ENVIRONMENTAL FEDERALISM

Much of the modern scholarly debate over environmental federalism has focused on seeking the proper allocation of regulatory authority between the states and the federal government. Commentators have assumed implicitly that an optimal regulatory jurisdiction for each environmental problem exists. Support for this assumption is typically drawn from static economic models that scholars use as the foundation for their arguments. Within the scholarly literature, a general consensus exists that environmental problems that transcend state boundaries should be addressed by the federal government, as this raises a classic instance of an unaccounted-for externality in state decision making. Where scholars part company, however, is on the question of the optimal jurisdiction for the regulation of purely intrastate environmental harms, such as localized groundwater contamination, isolated contamination from solid waste sites, and any of the myriad environmental harms that are unlikely to have measurable interstate effects.

Beginning with Professor Richard Stewart, many scholars have argued that federal regulation is appropriate for certain intrastate environmental problems when state standards are likely to be suboptimally lax due either to the influence of powerful interest groups, so-called public choice problems, or competition between states for mobile industries that precipitates a "race-to-the-bottom" in state standard setting.[8] Although initially accepted as

---

[8]   Richard B. Stewart, "Pyramids of Sacrifice? Problems of Federalism in Mandating State Implementations of National Environmental Policy," YALE LAW JOURNAL 86, no. 6 (1977): 1210.

dogma, both theories have come under close scrutiny, and some scholars now claim that neither interstate competition nor public-choice dynamics support a reversal of the traditional preference for state-level regulation.[9]

Other environmental federalism scholars take different tacks, but they too are wedded to the view that an optimal regulatory jurisdiction exists for each environmental problem. Professor Daniel Esty, for instance, argues that no single jurisdiction should be presumed to be optimal for particular classes of environmental problems. Instead, he claims that a careful case-by-case analysis must be applied to each environmental problem, taking into account its particular ecological or public health harms, its technical complexity, time lags, threshold effects, and influence of specials interest groups on policy development.[10] Esty further recognizes that a seemingly simple environmental problem may have multiple dimensions, some of which are best addressed at the national level and others that favor local control. He argues that in such circumstances this will call for dividing regulatory responsibility between different levels of government. Esty's ultimate goal, however, is to identify an "optimal fit" between the regulatory jurisdiction and these elements of environmental problems.

The classical school of environmental federalism provides a simple framework that draws on standard economic metrics to determine the level of government at which regulation should take place. This simplicity has proved to be superficial. Scholars have unearthed a number of complicating theoretical and empirical pitfalls, such as the importance of regulatory "races to the bottom" between states that are hotly contested even among its adherents. Deeper problems lurk beyond the debate within the classical framework. Most importantly, the classical school ignores the benefits of concurrent jurisdiction by state and federal authorities, as well as the characteristics of environmental problems that belie efforts to identify the single "efficient" level of government from which to regulate.

DYNAMIC, INTERACTIVE, AND "POLYPHONIC" FEDERALISM

Against this backdrop, a new trend in federalism scholarship is emerging that is alternatively named "empowerment federalism,"[11] "polyphonic

---

[9] Adler, "Jurisdictional Mismatch," 157; Butler and Macey, "Externalities and the Matching Principle," 25; Richard Revesz, "Rehabilitating Interstate Competition: Rethinking the 'Race to the Bottom' Rationale for Federal Environmental Regulation," NEW YORK UNIVERSITY LAW REVIEW 67, no. 6 (1992): 1238–42.

[10] Esty, "Revitalizing Environmental Federalism," 652. See also Daniel Esty, "Toward Optimal Environmental Governance," NEW YORK UNIVERSITY LAW REVIEW 74, no. 6 (1999): 1495, 1554–6.

[11] Erwin Chemerinsky, "Empowering States When It Matters: A Different Approach to Preemption," BROOKLYN LAW REVIEW 69, no. 4 (2004): 1313; Erwin Chemerinsky, "Empowering States: The Need to Limit Federal Preemption," PEPPERDINE LAW REVIEW 33, no. 1 (2005): 69.

federalism,"[12] "interactive federalism,"[13] "dynamic federalism,"[14] "contextual federalism,"[15] and even "vertical regulatory competition.[16] This school of thought rejects the matching principle, that is, efforts to identify areas of authority in which states are sovereign and safe from federal interference, and it instead embraces the existing overlap between state and federal jurisdiction.[17] One of our goals in this essay is to integrate the insights of this new scholarship into the environmental federalism debate, albeit with the further support provided by insights from research on adaptive systems.

These scholars argue that important values are advanced through the dynamic interaction between courts and policy makers at the state and the federal levels. Robert Schapiro, for example, argues that dynamic federalism supports the values of plurality, dialogue, and redundancy over the dualist values of choice, self-governance, and the prevention of tyranny.[18] To this list, other scholars have added the benefits that flow from greater regulatory competition, policy innovation, and resistance to monopolization and interest group capture.[19] Scholars of dynamic federalism argue against any sort of presumption in favor of the exclusive or primary regulatory jurisdiction of any particular level of government with respect to particular issues. Some scholars argue that any matter should be presumptively within the authority of both the federal and state governments.[20]

Scholars arguing for a dynamic conception of federalism typically do not focus on specific fields of law, and no central framework currently exists that links the various theories and approaches together. A few scholars, however, have used a dynamic model of federalism as a framework for examining and reassessing current modes of environmental regulation. For instance, Professor William Buzbee has long argued that a dynamic interplay exists between

---

[12] Robert A. Schapiro, "Polyphonic Federalism: State Constitutions in the Federal Courts," CALIFORNIA LAW REVIEW 87, no. 6 (1999): 1411–13; Robert A. Schapiro, "Toward a Theory of Interactive Federalism," IOWA LAW REVIEW 91, no. 2 (2005): 250 (hereinafter "Interactive Federalism").

[13] Robert A. Schapiro, "Justice Stevens' Theory of Interactive Federalism," FORDHAM LAW REVIEW 74, no. 4 (2006): 2133.

[14] Renee M. Jones, "Dynamic Federalism: Competition, Cooperation and Securities Enforcement," CONNECTICUT INSURANCE LAW JOURNAL 11, no. 1 (2004): 107.

[15] William Buzbee, "Contextual Environmental Federalism," NEW YORK UNIVERSITY ENVIRONMENTAL LAW JOURNAL 14, no. 1 (2005): 120–1.

[16] Ibid., 122.

[17] Schapiro, "Interactive Federalism," 246.

[18] Ibid., 288.

[19] Chemerinsky, "Empowering States," 74.

[20] Schapiro, "Interactive Federalism," 296.

state and federal regulatory efforts, and that these interactions have been crucial to innovations in environmental regulation throughout the country.[21]

One of the important dynamics that Buzbee highlights is the opportunities for state government officials to make a name for themselves by promoting and implementing aggressive environmental regulatory initiatives when the federal government fails to act. He provides an elegant illustration of this by drawing on regulatory developments with so-called brownfield sites, which are contaminated industrial sites abandoned in urban areas. Through this example, Buzbee exposes the shifts between federal and state innovations and the important synergies that emerge from this back-and-forth dynamic. Buzbee touts the virtues of overlapping jurisdiction in facilitating knowledge transfer and learning, counteracting pressures to succumb to the race-to-the-bottom, and enhancing citizen enforcement through multiple fora.[22]

Complementing Buzbee's work, Kirsten Engel, one of the co-authors of this chapter, and Scott Saleska emphasize the power of regulation at one level of government to prompt regulation at another.[23] The benefit of this "domino effect," they argue, is that regulation stalled at one level of government, may be ripe for action at a different level of government where the political environment is more favorable.[24] Others scholars have advocated a more radical departure from the classic model. They focus on the institutional impediments, at both the state and federal levels, to effective environmental regulation, arguing that current institutional models delimited by traditional jurisdictional boundaries are ineffective. Jody Freeman and Daniel Farber, in particular, contend that efficient, more responsive environmental regulation is dependent on overcoming cross-agency coordination problems at all levels of government.[25] They argue that the complexity and uniqueness of many environmental problems demands flexible institutional frameworks that can be tailored to a specific problem.[26]

The rising influence of dynamic federalism suggests that federalism theory as a whole is moving away from the presumptions of the classical matching principle that have dominated much of the debate over environmental federalism. Rather than searching for the optimal level of government, scholars

---

[21] Buzbee, "Contextual Environmental Federalism," 115–16.

[22] Ibid., 122–6; William Buzbee, "Recognizing the Regulatory Commons: A Theory of Regulatory Gaps," Iowa Law Review 89, no. 1 (2003): 1.

[23] Kirsten H. Engel and Scott R. Saleska, "Subglobal Regulation of the Global Commons: The Case of Climate Change," Ecology Law Quarterly 32, no. 1 (2005): 183.

[24] Teske, Regulation in the States, 16–17.

[25] Jody Freeman and Daniel A. Farber, "Modular Environmental Regulation," Duke Law Journal 54, no. 2 (2005): 809.

[26] Ibid., 799.

are emphasizing the benefits of simultaneous federal and state jurisdiction over the same problem. Although the redundancy inherent in such an approach appears inefficient from the perspective of classical economic theory, dynamic federalism maintains that such apparent inefficiencies are more than offset by increased innovation, dialogue, and a "safety net" approach to regulation.[27]

DEVELOPING AN ADAPTIVE FRAMEWORK
FOR ENVIRONMENTAL FEDERALISM

We use the term *complex adaptive system* descriptively and normatively in this chapter. It is used descriptively as a model of complex environmental systems, particularly ecosystems, and it is used normatively as a framework for understanding environmental federalism. We argue further that it provides compelling support for a dynamic conception of federalism.

A complex adaptive system, in its simplest formulation, is one that evolves through a combination of optimizing processes and randomized trial and error. As such, it is shaped by exogenous factors, which provide the boundary conditions for optimization, and endogenous path-dependent processes. For example, whereas competition over limited legislative and administrative resources culls potential environmental policies, ecosystem optimization is driven by the competitive pressures of natural selection. However, because optimization is imperfect – global optima are lost in a vast range of peaks – optimization is local and relative, not absolute.[28] Processes of randomizing and trial and error provide mechanisms for a system to avoid becoming stuck on a local maxima and hence vulnerable to dramatic exogenous change.

Diversity, the counterpoint of strict optimization, is the end result of such trial-and-error processes. For ecosystems, genetic diversity within a species and maintenance of a diverse range of species ensure adaptability, as they provide a storehouse of genetic traits and species that may be well adapted to subsequent changes in environmental conditions.[29] In the face of the winnowing effects of natural selection, diversity is maintained by localized disturbances

---

[27] For an application of the emerging ideas of dynamic federalism to environmental law generally, see Kirsten H. Engel, "Who's Afraid of Overlapping State and Federal Jurisdiction? Harnessing the Benefits of Dynamic Federalism in Environmental Law," EMORY LAW JOURNAL 56, no. 1 (2006): 159.

[28] Simon Levin, FRAGILE DOMINION: COMPLEXITY AND THE COMMONS (Reading, MA: Perseus Books, 1999), 68.

[29] Stuart Kauffman and Simon Levin, "Towards a General Theory of Adaptive Walks on Rugged Landscapes," JOURNAL OF THEORETICAL BIOLOGY 128, no. 1 (1987): 15; Sewel Wright, "Evolution in Mendelian Populations," GENETICS 16, no. 1 (1931): 97–9.

(e.g., fires, storms) and the heterogeneity of ecosystems at small scales.[30] Functional redundancy is a byproduct of this diversity and a general characteristic of complex adaptive systems that buffers them from the inevitable losses of individual components.

The defining characteristics of adaptive systems – optimization, diversity, and redundancy – contrast those of standard optimization-focused economic analysis. An adaptive model of environmental federalism is one that embraces optimization but acknowledges its limitations in a world that is far too complex and changeable for global optimization to be either attained or maintained. A corollary of these constraints is that optimization and resiliency are often in tension. To the extent that a system is optimized to a specific set of conditions, it may be less adaptable to changed circumstances, and the more dramatic the changes, the less adaptable it will be. The challenge is to maintain a process of optimization, which leads to specialization and efficiencies, while cultivating a diversity of backup options in the wings.

We believe that the dialectic between optimizing and diversifying forces embodied in complex adaptive systems is essential to effective environmental policy making, which is subject to similar complexity and natural variability. Using ecosystems as an exemplar, this section of the chapter explains how complex adaptive systems provide a powerful model for environmental federalism. The section begins by describing complex adaptive systems and then examines how their basic features are already reflected in environmental federalism and how they can be enhanced to strengthen U.S. environmental law.

PRIMER ON COMPLEX ADAPTIVE SYSTEMS

Complex adaptive systems are products of historical contingency and external constraints. They are partly driven by deterministic processes and partly by the product of contingent events. The hybrid nature of complex adaptive systems is a central reason that their behavior, particularly at small scales, is so unpredictable. The other feature that makes their behavior complex is that their dynamics span a very broad range of scales, whether spatial, temporal, or functional.[31] This multilevel structure of complex adaptive systems is essential to their ability to balance optimizing and diversifying processes.

A forest ecosystem, because it is so familiar, provides an accessible example from which to understand the basic elements of complex adaptive systems.

[30] John Holland, HIDDEN ORDER: HOW ADAPTATION BUILDS COMPLEXITY (Reading, MA: Addison-Wesley, 1995).
[31] Levin, "Complex Adaptive Systems," 1944.

Forests evolve at multiple spatial and temporal scales, ranging from tiny microbial communities to massive, long-lived trees. Food webs and interactions between species connect the different levels of an ecosystem. However, although species interactions are horizontal and vertical, any given species will interact strongly with only a few other species and therefore is not subject to global competition for resources; they reside instead in ecological niches. Species also exist in stable functional groups that provide a variety of services (e.g., nitrogen fixation), and this specialization and redundancy is essential to the modularity of ecosystems that enhances their resiliency.

Forest ecosystems also follow a successional process that is driven by natural selection.[32] If natural selection dictated ecosystem dynamics entirely, it would cause a steady loss of species diversity and ultimate domination by the most competitive species.[33] Two factors mitigate the denuding effects of natural selection: (1) the existence of ecological niches at small scales, such as microclimates or processes by which species avoid the extremes of a given environment (e.g., dormancy), and (2) regular periods of localized ecological disruption, such as fires, storms, and droughts, that effectively restart the successional process in discrete areas.

Disturbance and small-scale niches are essential to the maintenance of diversity. As one commentator has explained, far from being monolithic:

> [Forests are] a tapestry of patches in different stages of succession, and hence a tapestry of diversity. The small local disturbances not only maintain the character of the system by maintaining the species that are early colonists but poor competitors; they also maintain the *resiliency* of the system, preserving the opportunistic species that thrive under the conditions accompanying the unpredictable but inevitable environmental changes that occur at broader spatial scales, such as massive wind throws or fire.[34]

The variety of environmental conditions creates positive feedbacks that enhance diversity further, as species' interactions, whether antagonistic or cooperative, alter the environmental conditions experienced by other species. In this way, evolutionary changes within and among species feed back into

---

[32] "A forest is a complex of species, some adapted to the slow growth and eventual dominance of the canopy, others adapted to rapid exploitation of the temporary gaps that form. . . . As the forest develops, light availability in the understory diminishes, and these species are replaced in succession by those that make their living not by opportunism but by their ability to grow under low-light conditions and that hence will prosper in a highly competitive environment." Levin, FRAGILE DOMINION, 50.

[33] Ibid., 159.

[34] Ibid., 88.

evolutionary processes and act as a basis for further adaptive changes that enhance diversity.

Using these types of mechanisms, complex adaptive systems embody a strategy similar to that of a balanced investment portfolio. They sacrifice short-term growth potential that is pure optimization for the more stable dynamics and diminished risk of catastrophic loss provided by diversification. Human-dominated environments aside, the beauty of an ecosystem, and complex adaptive systems generally, is that this diversity emerges as a byproduct of their inherent heterogeneity and temporal variability. Paradoxically, it is the "certainty of local uncertainty" that maintains diversity and ensures adaptability.[35] In opposition, natural selection provides the directive component of adaptive change by culling the diversity of genetic resources through a process of "tight reward and punishment loops" operating at the individual-species level; as such, natural selection is essentially a grassroots enterprise.[36]

THE VIRTUES OF AN ADAPTIVE MODEL

Environmental policy making must contend with problems that are complex and unpredictable. To anyone remotely familiar with environmental law and policy, this is stating the obvious. It is nevertheless an important point for us to make up front, as the discussion that follows is premised on it. A central tenet of our argument is that an adaptive model, which is designed to manage unpredictable change, is better suited to the complexities of environmental policy making than the matching principle, which assumes many of them away.

Given the complexity and variability of environmental problems, the number of potential regulatory options inevitably will be overwhelming, and only limited grounds will exist for discriminating among them. Our rejection of the matching principle in favor of an adaptive model thus turns on two variants of this basic problem: (1) the difficulty of identifying the efficient (i.e., optimal) regulatory approach, and (2) the undefined scale of most environmental problems. We discuss both in turn as they apply to the matching principle and then examine how the structure of an adaptive model mitigates them and effectively manages unpredictable change.

One need only consider a sampling of environmental problems to appreciate their intricacies. Prairie potholes, which are depressional wetlands found in the Upper Midwest, function as critical watering holes for migratory birds

[35] Simon Levin and Robert T. Paine, "Disturbance, Patch Formation, and Community Structure," PROCEEDINGS OF THE NATIONAL ACADEMY OF SCIENCES 71, no. 7 (1974): 2744–5.
[36] Levin, FRAGILE DOMINION, 156, 203.

and protect against local flooding. Thus, although geographically localized, their biological importance is national if not international in scope.[37] Similarly, mercury emissions from coal-fired power plants have local and global impacts. Mercury is emitted in two reactive states.[38] One is of only local significance because it quickly precipitates from the atmosphere. The other persists in the atmosphere and is a major contributor to rising mercury levels in ocean mammals globally. In both of these examples, the problem does not exist on a single geographical or even temporal scale but on multiple scales simultaneously.

These technical challenges have both natural and human dimensions. The complexity of natural systems is by now well known, and the examples of misdirected federal and state programs abound. For instance, government officials for many years believed that a strict regime of fire suppression would protect forests.[39] It took decades for foresters to appreciate the important role that fire plays in maintaining the biological diversity and resilience of forest ecosystems and for them to alter their policies.[40] Analogous stories could be told about the environmental effects of intensive agriculture, the dynamics of groundwater and surface-water management, and the many challenges of assessing the risks of industrial pollutants. In all of these cases, the phenomena are complex, the data are scarce, and the understanding is thin.

Environmental problems, because of their complexity and variability, do not lend themselves to standard optimization methods. Whereas an idealized optimization problem is akin to locating the peak of a single isolated mountain, environmental policies are set in a domain analogous to the Himalayas, where the number of peaks (potential optima) is so large that it would be impossible to explore all of them to identify the highest one. The complexity of ecosystem management exemplifies this point, but many other environmental problems ranging from pollution control, to land use, to waste management raise issues of similar difficulty. It is therefore implausible that a single government entity, including the federal government, could identify the efficient regulatory solution, and although the probability of success improves with multiple, independent state regulators, success is far from guaranteed even then.

[37] U.S. Environmental Protection Agency, "Prairie Potholes," accessed October 12, 2007, http://www.epa.gov/owow/wetlands/types/pothole.html.
[38] Lisa Heinzerling and Rena I. Steinzor, "A Perfect Storm: Mercury and the Bush Administration," ENVIRONMENTAL LAW REPORTER 34, no. 6 (2004): 10303–5.
[39] George Busenberg, "Wildfire Management in the United States: The Evolution of a Policy Failure," REVIEW OF POLICY RESEARCH 21, no. 1 (2004): 146–8.
[40] Ibid.

Our second objection challenges the assumption implicit in the matching principle that eliminating all, or even most, externalities is possible. One of the basic features of ecosystems, for example, is that they operate on multiple spatial, organizational, and temporal scales. A single forest ecosystem will contain tiny microbial species with brief lives and small territories, large mammals with moderate life spans and large territories, and trees with very long lives and modest but sizable territories. Moreover, specific environments or species may have impacts that extend beyond state or national jurisdictions. As mentioned in the preceding text, prairie potholes appear to be purely local in their extent, but their importance transcends local, state, and national boundaries because of their importance to migratory birds.[41]

The matching principle fails because no systematic way exists to bound most environmental problems and thus to ensure that all of the costs and benefits are internalized by the regulating entity. Static economic models work because their predictions can be updated and refined according to a predetermined scale of the problem. Economists, for example, make useful predictions about U.S. market trends in part because they understand the different scales of the system. This knowledge bounds their use of the models – they would never put much faith in predictions about an individual stock over the next six months or about the U.S. market in ten years. In both cases, the time variance of the system nullifies the reliability of the model over the time scales of these predictions. Although such limits do not invalidate economic models – no model is accurate under all conditions – they do significantly circumscribe when and how they can be used.

ADAPTIVE FEDERALISM AND THE DEBATE OVER ENVIRONMENTAL FEDERALISM

The adaptive model of federalism we advocate is a variant of dynamic federalism and, as such, rejects the pure optimizing principle of the classical school. It goes beyond current scholarship on dynamic federalism, though, insofar as it provides a robust theoretical framework for dynamic federalism. Adaptive federalism differs further in its structural focus on managing complex, time-variant problems that are characteristic of environmental policy.

---

[41] This position should not be read as the stale platitude that everything is linked together in nature. That view is an overstatement, if not a mischaracterization, of how natural systems are interconnected. Our point is that individual components of natural systems are linked across a very broad range of scales, although, as one would expect, the larger the spatial scale the fewer and weaker the connections.

This subpart sketches these distinctions to clarify the unique virtues of adaptive federalism.

Like its dynamic counterparts, adaptive federalism rejects the exclusive focus of the matching principle on optimization. It recognizes that static optimizing strategies, on their own, are a prescription for the turgid policy making that is prey to the complexities of environmental problems. Rather than engaging in the charade of identifying the one putatively "efficient" level of government for environmental policy making, an adaptive model is structurally designed to contend with unpredictable change and informational uncertainty. The philosophies of the two approaches could not be more different – one is premised on stable equilibrium conditions and rigid control; the other seeks to exploit disruptive change as a source of resilience and adaptability.

The basic elements of an adaptive model – fragmented operation on multiple scales – are clearly evident in the multilevel jurisdictional structure of the federal system. The overlapping federal-state regulatory authority of dynamic federalism follows naturally from this arrangement. Similarly, the existence of multiple jurisdictions at a variety of geographic scales mirrors the fragmented structure of adaptive systems that is essential to maintaining diversity. Adaptive federalism simultaneously sustains competitive legislative and administrative processes that promote the refinement of policies (including ones consistent with static, full-cost internalization) and processes that produce a diverse range of policy options.

Adaptive federalism, if accepted, would support and enhance the dynamic, multijurisdictional elements of the current system of environmental federalism. As we have seen, this approach is incompatible with the single-level framework dictated by the classical matching principle. For putatively local issues, such as those related to drinking-water standards or land use, an adaptive model would allow for a significant federal role. Conversely, for putatively national (or international) issues, such as biodiversity or climate change, it would encourage state and local policy innovation.

The multilevel approach of adaptive (and dynamic) federalism is not cost-less. Uniformity, accountability, and finality are all sacrificed to some degree by allowing multiple jurisdictions to address environmental problems simultaneously. However, in many, if not most, areas of environmental regulation, uniformity is as much a problem as it is a virtue. One need only consider widespread calls from regulated industries for "flexible" standards, such as those found in market-based regulations, and the vehement opposition to command-and-control regimes.[42] Finality, which is often in opposition to

---

[42] Tom Arrandale, "The Pollution Puzzle: The Federal Government Isn't Solving It. States Are Giving It a Shot," GOVERNING (August 2002): 23.

adaptability, is also a double-edged sword in constantly changing natural, technological, and commercial environments that otherwise would create at least the possibility of new information and beneficial policy experimentation.

Public accountability (i.e., unambiguous and transparent decision-making authority and responsibility for government action) is possibly the most troublesome of these factors. Yet in practice there are important factors that mitigate against public confusion. Legislative action is challenging at any level of government, and there are always more legislative opportunities than time permits. Typically, when legislators make the effort to pass a law – particularly when it is public spirited, as opposed to narrow, interest-group driven – legislators want to get credit for it to establish or strengthen their reputations.[43] This motive is clearly evident in the recent spate of climate change initiatives at the state and local government levels, and it is certainly true of environmental legislation at the federal level.[44] Further, it is not as though the matching principle is a model of clarity for public accountability. Dan Esty's multifaceted, disaggregated approach, for instance, anticipates intricate intergovernmental arrangements that, at least in the abstract, raise precisely the same problems with accountability.

Adaptive federalism also differs in important respects from current conceptions of dynamic federalism set forth by Robert Schapiro, Erwin Chemerinsky, and others. Dynamic federalism is premised on empowering states, that is, treating them as coequal with the federal government and then letting them "battle it out" when the policy preferences of the two levels of government conflict. Thus, rather than avoiding conflict by preserving enclaves of exclusive state jurisdiction (the approach of the out-dated dualism approach), dynamic federalism embraces it. States gain autonomy but must win battles over policy on the merits. By contrast, adaptive federalism emphasizes the critical role that a multijurisdictional framework of government plays in allowing policy diversification and optimization to coexist.

IMPLICATIONS OF AN ADAPTIVE MODEL
FOR ENVIRONMENTAL FEDERALISM

This section draws on our adaptive framework to ground several policy recommendations for sustaining overlapping state and federal jurisdiction.

---

[43] Buzbee, "Contextual Federalism," 126; E. Donald Elliott et al., "Toward a Theory of Statutory Evolution: The Federalization of Environmental Law," JOURNAL OF LAW, ECONOMICS AND ORGANIZATIONS 1, no. 2 (1985): 327.

[44] Denise Scheberle, "The Evolving Matrix of Environmental Federalism and Intergovernmental Relationships," PUBLIUS (Winter 2005): 77.

We begin by describing and defending our policy proposals and then drawing on specific initiatives related to climate change. We examine the implications of our recommendations and, more generally, of a dynamic system of overlapping state and federal jurisdiction for environmental policy.

THE ASYMMETRY OF FEDERAL PREEMPTION

The authority of the federal government, particularly its supremacy power, introduces a critical asymmetry between federal and state governments, as well as a fundamental difference between the federal system and an adaptive model. Adaptive systems do not have anything equivalent to a hierarchy of institutional powers. Different aggregate levels of an ecosystem, for example, may be connected, but their interactions are not hierarchical in the sense that large-scale divisions can dictate the functions of smaller ones. Similarly, competition occurs between species, not at higher levels of organization, and fitness is solely a species' attribute.

Institutional hierarchy is unique to human systems of governance, but it has been embraced only reluctantly. Traditional theories of federalism are premised on limiting the role of the federal government and thus expect federal assertions of regulatory power to be justified.[45] In modern environmental law, federal regulation is premised on several standard grounds, including the need for uniform regulations for interstate commerce, the economies of scale that come with federal-level regulation, and the distorting effects of externalities on state laws.[46] Thus, unlike natural adaptive systems, which emerge from the ground up, humans have the temerity to assert control from the top down.

The implications of this distinctive federal authority are severalfold. First, the federal government can function as an agent of innovation, identifying new solutions derived at the state level and either mandating them or simply communicating them to other states. Second, the federal government enhances the complexity and dynamic qualities of government. Third, because the very power of the federal government renders it an attractive forum for interest groups, it poses a danger to the diversity of the federal system if wielding that power too aggressively. We believe that balancing these factors calls not for the devolution of policy making, nor its elevation, but rather for a more selective use of the federal government's power of regulatory preemption.

---

[45] Schapiro, "Interactive Federalism," 257–8.
[46] Stewart, "Pyramids of Sacrifice?" 1215.

THE DISTINCTIVE BENEFITS OF FEDERAL
REGULATORY AUTHORITY

An important virtue of the federal government is its capacity to facilitate the spread of regulatory innovations.[47] The value of innovation is one of the oldest justifications for a federalist system, encouraging, as it does, the role of states as "laboratories of democracy." However, even if most innovations originate at lower levels of government, the federal government is uniquely positioned to disseminate them. The capacity of the federal government to do so far outstrips that of the states by virtue of its unique relationship with each state, as well as the status of the national government as the top regulator. Although regulators in Maine may communicate only rarely with those in Oregon about water-quality issues, they will interact regularly with federal regulators. This hub-and-spokes network facilitates the transfer of innovations in Maine to Oregon, either on the strength of the federal Environmental Protection Agency's (EPA's) suggestion, or mandate, or simply through more effective knowledge transfer.

These points do not denigrate the traditional justifications for federal regulation that have animated debate over environmental federalism. The benefits of regulatory uniformity, the race-to-the-bottom rationale, and the possible disparity in public-choice dynamics between legislative processes at the state and federal levels are all important. The hierarchy inherent in the federal system thus clearly has its place. Yet, as the Framers understood from the outset, it poses many risks as well. From the standpoint of adaptive systems and traditional theories of federalism, the most obvious one is the dramatic loss in diversity that can result from preemptive federal regulation. This loss may be a direct result of a strict standard or may arise more subtly from the highly aggregated level at which federal regulators view environmental problems.

THE MERITS OF OVERLAPPING FEDERAL
AND STATE JURISDICTION

The structure of adaptive systems exposes the tradeoffs implicit in limiting policy development to a narrow range of government actors. Further, as

---

[47] Brian J. Gerber and Paul Teske, "Regulatory Policymaking in the American States: A Review of Theories and Evidence," POLICY RESEARCH QUARTERLY 53, no. 3 (2000): 870–1; Susan Welch and Kay Thompson, "The Impact of Federal Incentives on State Policy Innovation," SOCIAL SCIENCE QUARTERLY 61, no. 2 (1980): 715–16.

discussed in the preceding section, the federal government has a unique role in the federal system. We thus reject the opposing calls for devolution to the states as well as for enhanced federal regulatory authority.

If policy making is limited to lower levels of government, one not only risks policy-maker myopia, but also such lower-level policy makers may be overwhelmed by the greater inherent levels of uncertainty. Because variability decreases with scale, one of the great virtues of a broad regulatory perspective is the increased stability that follows from evaluating problems at an aggregate level.

Conversely, limiting regulation to the federal level washes out the diversity of local environmental, political, and economic conditions that produce unique sets of selective pressures for environmental regulation. It comes as no surprise to anyone that progressive environmental policies have repeatedly emerged from California, and that these initiatives are driven by a combination of environmental, political, and socioeconomic factors. Further, a defining characteristic of adaptive systems and ecosystems, in particular, is the variation in competition for resources that occurs over time and space. Without this variability, much of the diversity in an ecosystem would be lost to natural selection – the fittest species would win out in the absence of localized disturbances and ecological niches.

Limiting environmental policy making to the federal government through the doctrine of preemption undermines this essential dynamic. Moreover, public-choice theory predicts which interest groups are likely to prevail. Concentrated industry interest groups negatively impacted by environmental regulation will have a competitive advantage over the diffuse, poorly organized public threatened by regulatory inaction.[48]

The benefits of greater predictive stability and full cost internalization that come with elevating an issue to the federal level sacrifice other factors as well. One of the great strengths of natural selection is that by operating at a small scale, the feedbacks between the benefits and costs of individual variation are relatively strong and swift, in part because individual species are inherently more vulnerable than ecosystems collectively. These tight feedbacks are essential to adaptive change, as buffering mechanisms, by their very nature, diminish sensitivity to exogenous pressures.[49] Accordingly, although aggregation

---

[48] Disagreement exists over whether this imbalance in lobbying power is greater or lesser at the federal versus the state level. Revesz, "Rehabilitating Interstate Competition," 1238–42; William Buzbee, "Brownfields, Environmental Federalism, and Institutional Determinism," WILLIAM AND MARY ENVIRONMENTAL LAW AND POLICY REVIEW 21, no. 1 (1997): 44–6. We believe that these differences are typically overwhelmed by the broad variance that exists in political, socioeconomic, and environmental conditions across the states (e.g., California vs. Oklahoma) and between the state and federal levels of government.

[49] Levin, FRAGILE DOMINION, 203.

promotes stability and resiliency, it increases the inertia of a system and its ability to respond to changing environmental conditions. The slow progress of environmental regulation at the federal and international levels owes a great deal to the more abstract and diffuse nature of environmental problems that come with addressing them at a higher level of government.

THE UNIQUE THREAT OF FEDERAL PREEMPTION
TO ADAPTIVE FEDERALISM

Preemptive federal authority threatens the dynamism of a healthy system of overlapping jurisdiction. If policy making is allowed to gravitate to the federal level to the exclusion of the states, it risks triggering powerful feedback effects.[50] Such a shift would increase the attractiveness of the federal government for lobbying efforts, intensifying competition, and further marginalizing less-powerful interest groups. These effects would in turn encourage powerful interests to direct more resources to lobbying at the federal level and to elevating more issues. Moreover, as noted in the preceding text, because business interests are substantially fitter at playing this game, they will benefit disproportionately from such feedbacks.

These dynamics suggest that federal preemption ought to be disfavored by the courts and only selectively used in federal environmental statutes. However, because the overarching goal of an adaptive system is enabling optimizing and diversifying processes to coexist, this presumption cannot be applied woodenly. Clearly, where a proliferating polyglot of state-level regulations becomes enormously disruptive to the economy, federal preemption may be warranted.

By the same token, though, one must be careful not to presume that state-level regulation is immune to public-choice problems or that the federal government is incapable of acting in the interests of the general public. In particular, federal floors on environmental regulations are inconsistent with the standard public-choice scenario, while still affording states significant freedom to develop innovative policies and ensuring minimum levels of public protection. The same cannot be said of federal ceilings, which – although admittedly flexible – pose a much greater risk that concentrated interest groups will use their power at the federal level to stifle potentially innovative policy making at the state level.

---

[50] Roderick M. Hills Jr., "Against Preemption: How Federalism Can Improve the National Legislative Process," University of Michigan Law, Public law Working Paper No. 27 (2003), accessed October 12, 2007, http://papers.ssrn.com/sol3/papers.cfm?abstract_id=41200.

Judgments about the proper balance between federal and state regulation will clearly span a continuum, and difficult cases will exist on the margins. As a general matter, though, efforts to identify the optimal level of government for environmental regulation are misconceived. Our findings suggest further that federal preemption should be used sparingly, and that exclusive federal control of environmental regulation should be reserved for exceptional circumstances.

CLIMATE CHANGE CASE STUDY

Regulatory efforts to mitigate global climate change illustrate the virtues of adaptive federalism. Because climate change is caused, in part, by human-induced GHG emissions from around the globe, climate change is widely regarded as the textbook example of a global common problem that is best addressed at the national and international levels.[51] According to this view, unilateral regulation of GHGs is unlikely, as the jurisdiction risks losing large-scale GHG-emitting industries to other jurisdictions that do not regulate them, along with the jobs and other economic benefits that accompany these industries (the so-called leakage problem).[52]

The Bush administration's policies on global warming reflect this theory. The United States is neither a signatory of the Kyoto Protocol, the only international agreement that requires binding emissions reductions from sources of GHGs nor has it established national emissions standards for GHG sources.[53] Yet, despite federal intransigence, state and local governments have become quite active in this area. For example, California is leading the way by enacting a cap on the state's carbon dioxide emissions[54] and mandating vehicle GHG emission limits.[55] Other states, especially in the northeastern United States, have also been active on climate-change mitigation with perhaps the most significant action being the creation of the Regional Greenhouse Gas Initiative, which when fully implemented, will consist of a cap and

---

[51]   Roger W. Findley et al., CASES AND MATERIALS ON ENVIRONMENTAL LAW (St. Paul, MN: Thomson/West, 2006), 47.

[52]   Robert Stavins, "Policy Instruments for Climate Change: How Can National Governments Address a Global Problem?" UNIVERSITY OF CHICAGO LEGAL FORUM no. 1 (1997): 293; Daniel C. Esty, "Toward Optimal Environmental Governance," NEW YORK UNIVERSITY LAW REVIEW 74, no. 6 (1999): 1555.

[53]   Kyoto Protocol to the United Nations Framework Convention on Climate Change, Kyoto, Japan, December 11, 1997, accessed October 12, 2007, http://www.unfccc.int.

[54]   Global Warming Solutions Act of 2006, California Assembly Bill 32.

[55]   California Assembly Bill 1493, California Health and Safety Code § 43018.5.

trade program covering GHG emissions from the electric utilities located in eight states.[56]

These developments are difficult to square with standard economic reasoning. Of all the levels of government that might address global climate change, state and local governments ought to be the least likely to take the lead. The prospects of leakage for them are the greatest, as the smaller the jurisdiction the less political and market muscle it has and presumably the more alternative locations exist. Further, efforts by small jurisdictions to combat a global problem such as climate change are analogous to an ant battling an elephant – the potential benefits hardly seem worth the effort. This apparent anomaly makes global climate change an ideal case for exploring the benefits of a multi-jurisdictional, adaptive response to complex environmental problems.

The multilevel model exemplified by adaptive systems provides an alternative framework for explaining recent regulatory trends. In adaptive systems, competition occurs at multiple levels and, by virtue of this, under a broad range of conditions. As we have seen, it is the diversity of contexts that sustains diversity of kinds. In the realm of environmental law, the diverse range of socioeconomic, political, and environmental conditions found in different jurisdictions is a critical, and often undervalued, source of innovative policy development. For example, some jurisdictions are much more vulnerable to the potential impacts of climate change (e.g., coastal jurisdictions, the desert southwest) and may have far less to lose economically, either because they are a large enough players, such as is the case with California, or their industrial base would be only indirectly affected by regulation or might even benefit from it. Alternatively, the political leanings of a jurisdiction may place a high value on environmental protection and be less concerned about a strict cost-benefit rational for setting environmental policies.[57]

Even a cursory review of climate-change initiatives at the state and local levels bears out this basic insight. For example, twenty-eight states and the District of Columbia currently require energy suppliers' portfolios to contain a certain percentage of renewable power.[58] These policies have a simple economic rationale that defies the leakage problem raised by economists.

[56] Regional Greenhouse Gas Initiative, accessed October 12, 2007, http://www.rggi.org/index.htm.

[57] Kirsten Engel, "State and Local Climate Change Initiatives: What Is Motivating State and Local Governments to Address a Global Problem and What Does This Say about Federalism and Environmental Law?" URBAN LAWYER 38, no. 4 (2006): 1015; Kirsten H. Engel and Barak Y. Orbach, "Micro-Motives and State and Local Climate Change Initiatives," HARVARD LAW AND POLICY REVIEW 2 (2008): 119.

[58] Pew Center for Global Climate Change, accessed May 20, 2008, http://www.pewclimate.org/what_s_being_done/in_the_states/ (updated May 2, 2008).

Renewable energy is generally more job-intensive than conventional energy sources,[59] and, for states that import electricity from out-of-state suppliers, investment in renewable energy can pave the way for a stepped-up intrastate energy sector. The economic benefits of a renewable portfolio standard are often advanced as a rationale for maintaining or enhancing such mandates.[60]

Climate-change regulation also represents a political opportunity for local politicians. Increasingly, states are being led by elected officials whose political stance is enhanced by taking strong stands against what are perceived as entrenched industrial interests.[61] For many of these politicians, climate change provides an ideal issue for aligning themselves with a progressive energy agenda in opposition to big oil and gas interests. Similarly, climate change has also become such a sufficiently high-profile issue that it can be used to attract much-needed media attention. State initiatives and the politicians behind them have received significant media coverage, arguably in part because of the contrast between their proactive approach and the federal government's passive stance.[62]

This political support is further borne out by recent studies. Today 49 percent of Americans claim global warming is extremely or very important to them personally; up from 31 percent in 1998, and even more importantly, seven out of ten Americans say that government should do more to address global warming.[63] As our model of adaptive federalism predicts, this broad public consensus is manifesting itself first at the state and local levels, where the feedbacks are tighter (i.e., perceived risk or importance) and the process of passing legislative initiatives, due their smaller scale, less subject to the inertia or rigidity risks of federal legislative processes.

Global climate-change policy illustrates the power of the bottom-up dynamics that are characteristic of complex adaptive systems. Although the "wrong" jurisdictions from a static economic perspective, state and local initiatives can play an instrumental role in propelling change at higher levels

---

[59] U.S. Department of Energy, DOLLARS FROM SENSE: THE ECONOMIC BENEFITS OF RENEWABLE ENERGY, accessed October 12, 2007, http://www.nrel.gov/docs/legosti/fy97/20505.pdf.
[60] Barry G. Rabe and Philip A. Mundo, "Business Influence in State-Level Environmental Policymaking," in BUSINESS AND ENVIRONMENTAL POLICY, ed. Michael Kraft and Sheldon Kamieniecki (Cambridge, MA: MIT Press, 2007), 265–97.
[61] Ibid.
[62] Sarah Ferriter, WHILE ADMINISTRATION AND CONGRESS BALK ON KYOTO MANY U.S. STATES MOVE FORWARD ON GREENHOUSE EMISSION EFFORTS, accessed October 12, 2007, http://www.climate.org/topics/localaction/grnhs.shtml; Margaret Kriz, "Warm-Up Drills," NATIONAL JOURNAL (March 26, 2005): 906; Jennifer Lee, "The Warming Is Global but the Legislating, in the U.S., Is All Local," NEW YORK TIMES, October 29, 2003, A21.
[63] Gary Langer, POLL: PUBLIC CONCERN ON WARMING GAINS INTENSITY, accessed October 12, 2007, http://abcnews.go.com/Technology/GlobalWarming/story?id=1750492&page=1.

of government. First, state actions bring much-needed public and media attention to climate change and its local effects. Second, state and local governments prompt, albeit on a small scale, critical technological, social, and economic changes essential to mitigating climate change. Third, state and local governments, as the old saying goes, function as "laboratories of democracy" by allowing parallel testing of initiatives in a range of contexts, which then can serve as models for other jurisdictions. Finally, action at the state and local level can feed back to the national level, as the threat of fifty distinct state laws regulating a single industry has, as in the past, the potential to prompt Congress to act.

CONCLUSION

The study of complex adaptive systems provides a valuable theoretical framework for a dynamic conception of federalism that is premised on the value of parallel development of environmental policies at multiple levels of government. By revealing the deficiencies of a one-sided focus on optimization and the virtues of sustaining policy development in a diverse range of local conditions, our analysis has shown that a shift to a dynamic model of environmental federalism would enhance government responsiveness, policy innovation, and socioeconomic adaptability to unpredictable environmental change.

Conclusion: The Menu of Preemption Choice Variables

William W. Buzbee

This book's structure and chapters illuminate each actor and setting in which preemption choices must be made. Using theory, history, and legal doctrine, the book's diverse contributors also identify the menu of variables relevant to preemption choices. Rather than recount each chapter's contribution, this conclusion distills the chapters' strains and arguments to identify these variables and how they should influence preemption choice.

Preemption choice is first and foremost influenced by the Constitution's Supremacy Clause, its federalist design, and the procedures it requires for the creation of law. The Constitution undoubtedly anticipates that federal law can and will in some settings preempt contrary state law, whether it is a statute, a regulation, or common law. This capacity is inherent in federal legislative power and federal law's supremacy. But the mere possibility of federal assertion of preemptive power is distinct from the question of whether it has been asserted. As virtually all chapters explain, the dominant and most common political choice is not to preempt but to set a federal floor and "save" state and local laws that do not conflict, provided that they are at least as protective as federal law. As Professor William Andreen discusses in his analysis of the Clean Water Act's structures and history, many cooperative federalism regimes, especially in delegated program federalism schemes, explicitly retain concurrent, overlapping, and intertwined federal, state, and local roles, including preservation of common law. Far less frequently, federal legislation does in clear language preempt state and local law or at least indicate that a judicial or agency finding of preemption can be appropriate. In addition, all agree that where political actions create truly irreconcilable conflict between federal and state law, federal law prevails. So the federal legislative choice to preempt or not preempt is beyond dispute.

The next variable in the preemption choice menu is to establish and then apply standards by which one can assess whether or to what extent a law does manifest an intent to preempt. Several chapters address this question, drawing on different materials and arguments. One argument, articulated by Professor Bradford Clark, is that preemption assertions must conform to the procedures the Constitution erects before it can constitute "Supreme" law and thereby potentially preemptive law. He embraces both the Court's long-stated but inconsistently applied "presumption against preemption" and supports application of a clear statement requirement before a law will be held to preempt or authorize preemption by agencies. Similarly, Professors William Funk, Robert Glicksman, and Chris Schroeder embrace these two hurdles to assertion of preemption power, arguing that courts should more carefully scrutinize the precise ways laws grant or withhold power that federal agencies may later assert. Professor Sandi Zellmer's analysis of savings clauses' reception in the courts shows a judiciary that often gives little weight to the distinctive legislative choices of whether to preempt state law or preserve it. She too argues for courts to give closer attention to distinctions among legislative preemption choices.

But still there remain settings in which legislators, regulators, or courts must make tough choices whether to preempt. Apart from questions of constitutional power or interpretive frameworks, what variables should influence that choice? Preemptive regimes make best sense when federal requirements are literally design or behavioral mandates that simply leave no room for contrary action. Making such regulatory mandates preemptive is especially compelling when the requirements are not only uniform, but also where producers benefit from production economies of scale or substantial diseconomies of scale result if producers confront diverse legal requirements in different jurisdictions. A somewhat less compelling preemption setting arises when a federal action, for example, approval of a product for the market, is not just a clearance but tantamount to a determination that the product represents the optimal design, where any change would create risks and conflict. Although this latter setting of arguable optimal product design might seem a compelling setting for complete preemption of other possible liabilities, much depends on postapproval regimes and actions. A product that at the time of approval was optimal may quickly prove risky, or other products posing far fewer risks may enter the market. A claim of optimal design hence may have a short time horizon, and the law might unwisely immunize producers for a long-past regulatory approval.

As demonstrated in numerous chapters in discussing and critiquing common pro-preemption arguments, a desire for uniformity and legal stability are the two most common arguments for preemption. A lesser variable is concern with states making regulatory choices that, in effect, externalize regulatory burdens by foisting them off on other jurisdictions. This concern can justify uniform federal floors for pollution but also has been used to argue against imposition of tort liabilities for approved products where an underlying motive of plaintiffs and their lawyers, and perhaps judges and juries, may relate to making out-of-state manufacturers pay.

Even if one finds compelling these arguments for preemption and attendant uniformity, one must remember that in an economy the size of the United States, allowing some latitude for different design or product requirements in different jurisdictions can make sense. As Professor Robert Glicksman discusses at the close of his chapter, this is just the choice made in the Clean Air Act, which allows California to seek approval for motor vehicle emissions requirements different than the otherwise applicable federal standards.

But it is the other side of the preemption scale that has been most neglected in doctrine and scholarship. In what settings and for what reasons should legal actors embrace a nonpreemptive choice? Why might it make sense to embrace the ongoing existence and overlapping applicability of federal, state, and local statutes, regulations, and common law? Drawing on history, theory, close case analysis, and other disciplines' perspectives on analogous challenges, Professors Mendelson, Verchick, Schapiro, Vladeck, Morrison, Buzbee, McGarity, Adelman, and Engel identify numerous intertwined normative arguments against preemption. The scholars' chapters share a concern with leaving any regulatory challenge to one actor, freezing the law unless that actor decides to revisit some initial choice. Any regulatory scheme must take into account pervasive risks of regulatory inertia, capture, limited government resources, changing information, regulatory evasions, monetary self-interest, dislike of embarrassment, and risk avoidance. Stability is surely a legal value, but frozen or ossified law is seldom a desirable condition. By preserving several venues in which legal decisions can be challenged or revisited, law is less likely to become unduly rigid.

In addition, preserving a diversity of actors and different regulatory modalities further gives the law a valuable flexibility or adaptability. For this reason, Professor Trevor Morrison reviews the functional value and distinct position of state attorneys general and argues that their role should be given special protection from claims of preemption. Similarly, Professors David Vladeck and Thomas McGarity show how regulatory actions can leave major product and environmental risks unaddressed, thereby preserving a valuable role for common law and the incentives for improvement that liability can create. Professor McGarity further shows how both regulatory agencies and common law regimes benefit from each other in an informational "feedback loop." Tort and nuisance private plaintiffs and their lawyers have incentives to ferret out

neglected information, and the different discovery procedures of civil litigation can elicit information never considered in the regulatory process. As
discussed by Professor William Buzbee, aggressive assertions of federal regulation as a "ceiling" inherently destroy the possibility of a diversity of actors,
regulatory modes, and diverse stakeholder incentives, heightening the risk that
poor decisions will go unchanged. The more common federal "floors" limit
the regulatory menu but typically retain a diversity of actors and institutions.

In both opening and closing chapters, contributors identify more than just
risks of preemptive regimes. They also identify benefits of nonpreemptive
regimes that remain the prevailing political choice. With a diversity of legal
actors and venues for action, a plurality of voices can be heard. Diverse
incentives mean different information will be sought and revealed. Dialogue
and interaction, or what Professor Robert Schapiro calls "polyphony," will be
possible with numerous actors and institutions addressing related challenges.
Retaining latitude for decentralized actors and institutions to have different
priorities and make different choices will illuminate a broad realm of possible
answers to a problem. Regulatory challenges are more likely to be addressed in
a sequential, incremental manner, with pragmatic learning and attention to
other institutions' and jurisdictions' successes and failures. Especially in settings where information about a challenge is changing, or the problem is
dynamic in nature, legal regimes that allow for pragmatic adjustment provide
value. Professors David Adelman and Kirsten Engel illustrate these benefits in
their review of the evolution of environmental law and in their explanation of
analogies between regulatory schemes and ecosystems' adaptive systems.

This book thus acknowledges the possibility of preemptive regimes and the
values of preemption but emphasizes the far too neglected counterarguments
against preemption. The theory and arguments in support of the prevailing
political choice not to preempt have been underdeveloped. Long-standing
presumptions against preemption are justified by far more than just respect for
state sovereignty. Complex regulatory challenges will often best be addressed
by retaining space for different choices and reexamination by other jurisdictions, actors and institutions. By its nature, preemptive action undercuts the
latitude needed for pragmatic adjustment and learning. Few regulatory challenges can be addressed on a once-and-for-all basis.

Index

Lightning Source UK Ltd.
Milton Keynes UK
26 March 2011

169902UK00004B/13/P